Empire of the Soul

PAUL WILLIAM ROBERTS

EMPIRE

of the

SOUL

Some Journeys in India

RIVERHEAD BOOKS   NEW YORK   1996

RIVERHEAD BOOKS
a division of G. P. Putnam's Sons
Publishers Since 1838
200 Madison Avenue
New York, NY 10016

First American Edition 1996

Originally published in 1994 by
Stoddart Publishing Co. Limited, Canada.

Library of Congress Cataloging-in-Publication Data

Roberts, Paul William.
Empire of the soul : some journeys in India /
Paul William Roberts.—1st American ed.
p.   cm.
ISBN 1-57322-047-7
1. Roberts, Paul William—Journeys—India.
2. India—Description and travel.   I. Title.
DS414.R49 1996
915.404′52—dc20   96-17492   CIP

Printed in the United States of America
1   3   5   7   9   10   8   6   4   2

This book is printed on acid-free paper. ∞

BOOK DESIGN BY KATE NICHOLS

FOR MARC GABEL,

with love, respect, gratitude,

and in friendship

Acknowledgments

*T*his book could not have been written without the generous assistance of the Canada Council, the Ontario Arts Council, the Government of India Tourist Office, and the Taj Hotel group. Like my previous books, it also could not have been researched or written without the continued support, patronage, and encouragement of Lufthansa German Airlines, their delightful staff around the world, and their Canadian Director of Public Relations, the incomparable Chris Wendland. Thanks are due also to Roger Fielding of TourCan Vacations, California, for his expertise and his knowledge of a place we both regard as a second home. To my dear friend and agent, Mildred Marmur of New York, I owe fifteen percent of the money but eighty-five percent of the career. For opening up cyberspace and the delights of e-mail harassment, I thank my editor, Amy Hertz, to whom I also owe many hours, many words, much skill, more patience, along with Faith, Hope, Dharma, and a laughing voice. To her liaison back on Planet New York, Dolores McMullan, I am greatly indebted for translating concept to thought and thought into action. Thanks to Stella Connell for bringing country air to the city, music to the noise, and concrete realities to mere concrete. I owe much to Malcolm Kaswan, M.D., both for professional humanity and for lucid insights about the mysteries of the human heart that in demystifying much made much else all the more magnificent in a greater mystery.

Without Nelson Doucet, a Gulliver in Lilliput, this book would not exist at all. For inspiration and many kinds of assistance over many years, I need to thank: the late Bill Byrom, Simon Harling, the ever-present Paramahansa Yogananda, the Honorable Victoria Mills, David Davidar, Phyllis Krystal, Shudha Mazumdar, Lady Anjoo Sinha, V. S. Naipaul, Mark Tully, Mark Shand, Isaac Tigrett, George Harrison, Rahul Singh, Graham Hancock, Norman Snider, Arvind Singh Mewar, John Anthony West, the late J. Krishnamurti, R. K. Narayan, the late Christopher Isherwood, and all the countless strangers who showed me such kindness and generosity during my time in India over the last two decades. No words can afford to repay what I owe to Tiziana Buttignol Roberts, my best friend.

Author's Note

Consistency in the spelling of transliterations from Sanskrit and the many other Indian languages is a nightmarish problem for the writer (and editor). I have endeavored to maintain some semblance of it, but when quoting another writer have been obliged to use his or her preferences. There simply is no right or wrong when rendering into English sounds from a language with no written vowels. Similarly, I have tried to remain constant with the names of gods and goddesses, but have inevitably run into trouble not just with quotations but with the names of people. Ganesh, for example, is also called Ganesa, Ganapati, and so on. The god Siva often appears as Siv, Shiv, or Shiva; I did not feel justified in respelling Shiva Naipaul's name, for instance, or retitling a Hindu charity for the sake of consistency. The resulting confusion a reader may find is, however, a faithful reflection of the apparent chaos visitors to India often mistake for the rule of anarchy rather than the teeming profusion of too much sheer energy and life. At least, that's the way I choose to see it. Translations from the Sanskrit of the Vedic hymns are my own and aim more for a spiritual than a linguistic accuracy.

Contents

Part Two: The Nineties

Introduction

I lived in India for a few years during the seventies, and have returned for various reasons some twenty times since then. It is the only country that feels like home to me, and certainly the only country whose airport tarmac I have ever kissed upon landing.

Like many of my generation, I originally went searching for that vague and tantalizing thing, Truth. What I found, of course, was a different sort of truth, another kind of relationship. Like all relationships, it has its ups and downs, its love *and* its hate. To portray this in all its variety, its simplicity, and its complexity, I have divided the book into two sections: "The Seventies" and "The Nineties."

Thus, you have not just the sense of a changing country, but also the problem of a changed narrator. I have relied heavily on notebooks, diaries, and journals for "The Seventies," deciding to stay as close to my original perceptions as possible, with little revisionist hindsight beyond the addition of historical and philosophical information that, I hope, benefits the reader as much as it would have benefited me had I possessed it myself back then. Just out of university, I was naive and impressionable. Over a decade of further mundane and material concerns later, in "The Nineties," my impressions are mostly more objective. Mostly. In certain areas, however, India still makes me wide-eyed with wonder, as naive and impressionable as ever—though with, I hope, a deeper appreciation for people, the individuals who are engaged in forging a modern nation from eight hundred years of internal division and foreign domination. *Their* task is truly daunting, but their achievements in a mere fifty years are little short of miraculous.

✤ ✤ ✤

When I arrived in the first hotel room on my penultimate visit, in 1992, I switched on the television out of habit. Before, there had been only one risibly antiquated state channel to watch, Doordarshan. Now, to my utter amazement, I found the Star TV Network beaming in via satellite from Hong Kong such choices as CNN, the BBC World Service, and even a special Asian version of MTV. This last, with Madonna bouncing around in her underwear—the kind of sight you couldn't *pay* to see legally in pre-1992 India—caused plenty of heated controversy in the press. Until someone noticed that two or three Indian performers had videos playing regularly, too, and that they looked just like everyone else's. . . . It was an inspiring novelty for Indians to find that they could clearly compete on the common ground of international pop music. Yet, I soon learned, other novelties had been coming thick and fast for some time under the progressive, if troubled, government of Narasimha Rao.

With what may be the largest middle-class consumer market in the world, 375 millon strong, India was starting to interest foreign companies as never before. There really hadn't been much of a middle class when I first arrived. Now, however, in the midst of coping with a tragic resurfacing of communal violence worse than any since Partition in 1947, the government had managed to relax protectionist trade restrictions and was actively courting international investment. Indian industries were even beginning to make a considerable impact on world markets themselves. Although the old pessimism remained in many quarters—a legacy of colonialism—even the population problem was being viewed by some as a potential resource rather than a liability. It was indeed a brave new India, one that I believe is set to amaze the world in the next millennium.

I last visited the subcontinent in February 1996—after this book was written—and found myself already amazed. New Delhi was a boomtown, the big hotels filled to capacity with foreign business reps paying more for a room than they would in New York, but happy to do so, happy to have a foot in the door leading to 375 million potential customers. MTV had gone, replaced by Channel V, an all-Indian facsimile that is actually hipper and better than the original. New glossy magazines abounded, filled with suggestions for exotic vacations, objects, items, clothing for a new caste of super-rich international Indians, people as at home in Los Angeles or Paris as they are in Tokyo. Although a stupendous corruption scandal was about to topple Narasimha Rao's government and the Supreme Court had stepped in to assume unusual powers during an investigation that included the Prime Minister, Indian democracy seemed stronger than ever—because it was evident that close to a billion people cared enough about it to give it whatever help it needed to survive. As the election itself was to prove, Hindu fundamentalism is not an idea whose time has come or whose time will ever come.

The newspapers were full of stories about India's growing economic and military might, predicting the nation would soon be a superpower in the region that would rival the United States. These were the Pakistani newspapers, I should add, and were then preoccupied with the upcoming cricket match between Pakistan and India in the semifinals for the Wills World Cup. "A continuation of war through other means," more than one writer termed this confrontation, which even the Indian bookies predicted 2 : 1 that Pakistan would win. When India won, and won decisively too, Pakistan went into mourning. Many Muslims there now look with envy at the country they left. They didn't have to leave—and most in fact did not—but they cannot return easily anymore. With Hindu fundamentalism defanged by the elections of 1996, and the Islamic Republic threatened by its own fundamentalism, many Pakistanis wish they could join the big party in full swing south of the border. Most Indians would no longer care if they did. If Kashmir erupts into another war, it will be over swiftly and conclusively—in India's favor—and the walls may well come down. Gandhi was right in opposing the creation of an Islamic Indian state, and now that India is confident enough and big enough to concern itself with greater issues, the wrong may be put right. Peacefully, though, one hopes.

During the coming century, India's population will exceed that of China, the only nation capable of challenging her for economic and political domination of the East. While there is an odd cohesion among Indian states, and some, like Kerala, have worked social miracles in eradicating poverty and attaining literacy rates above 95 percent, China is falling dangerously far behind in everything. This is the stuff on which wars are made: "When you ain't got nothing, you got nothing to lose. . . ." India has much to lose; China little. And, we tend to forget, China counts an area of Kashmir among things she has lost and wants back. If the worst war in human history is to come, it will start in Kashmir, and it will be nuclear. Whoever emerges the victor will rule the Pacific rim; but whatever happens, the blame for creating the situation that caused it can be placed fairly and squarely in the laps of the British. If I am harsh on the British in this book, it is my privilege: I am British by birth, and I now live in another ex-colony that still bears the unmistakable scars of imperialism.

Whatever the political upheavals that rock the subcontinent, religion and India remain inseparable. My understanding of what spirituality means changes—*evolves,* I hope—over the following pages, along with my understanding of a land that like no other pullulates with every imaginable variety of it.

I have spent some of the happiest days of my life in India, as well as some of the most bizarre. No other country has ever made me laugh so much, or cry so much. I hope the humor will not be taken amiss any more than the tears.

It was also not my intention to offend anyone's religious sensibilities, but accounts like that of the Inquisition in Goa can hardly avoid passing judgment on those institutions and individuals concerned with the atrocities I catalogue. Similarly, my experiences with the late Bhagwan Rajneesh and with Mother Teresa of Calcutta merely record honestly what I personally heard, saw, and felt.

From enough material to fill three books this length, I have selected episodes and incidents, journeys inner and outer, anecdotes, and little histories and conversations that I trust will provide a mosaic image of a land that in its richness, complexity, and sheer *size* defies any definitive portrait. If what means much to me fails to please the reader, it is not India's fault. I take full responsibility.

The circle of history revolves. India has now turned outward, preoccupying itself more and more with the West's materialism. At the same time, much of the West has come to preoccupy itself not with India's material riches, but with those spiritual treasures that to seekers of Truth have always comprised the subcontinent's real wealth. Finally, then, I have also attempted to show that what Mahatma Gandhi termed an "empire of the soul" is not as easy to colonize as some of its new conquistadores would have us believe.

PWR
Toronto, June 1996

PART ONE

The Seventies

Whatever we do reacts upon us. If we do good, we shall have happiness and if evil, unhappiness. Within you is the real happiness, within you is the limitless ocean of divine nectar. Seek it within you, feel it. . . . It is here, the self: it is not the body, the mind, the intellect, the brain; it is not the desire or the desiring. It is not the object of desire. Above all these, *you are*. All these are simply manifestations. You appear as the smiling flower, as the twinkling stars. What is there in the world which can make you desire anything? It is the heart that reaches the goal. Follow the heart. A pure heart seeks beyond the intellect. It gets inspired.

—SATHYA SAI BABA

Prologue

It was the summer before I went up to Oxford. We were in Tintagel, Cornwall, by the ruins of what was supposed to be King Arthur's castle, high on a cliff over-looking the wild Atlantic Ocean. There were three of us—Andrew, Barbara, and me—and we'd been up all night on LSD. The stuff was still legal in England then, and what we'd taken was pure, straight from the laboratories of Hoffman-LaRoche. It was a magical night, infused with the presence of something divine, and as a rosy-fingered dawn broke, we floated down to the little cove behind which gaped what was known as Merlin's Cave. A light, peach-colored mist wafted over the sea while we sat on the stones, entranced by the beauty of this planet, of life itself, and our young lives.

Suddenly, on the far side of the cove, a naked figure with long black hair darted across the beach and plunged into the surf, swimming powerfully for several strokes, then lying back and bobbing on the heaving waves.

"Now, there's a good idea," said Andrew.

He tore off his clothes and ran into the ocean's foam.

Barbara and I soon followed, the three of us swimming out to where the long-haired stranger lay. He was East Indian, probably, and though somewhat chubby exuded an aura of immense strength.

"Thanks for the tip!" Andrew shouted to him.

The man nodded back, then asked us if we would like to share his breakfast with him. We eagerly accepted.

"Of course," the man said, "we've all really had our breakfast."

"Huh?"

He told us that the mineral salts in the water here were particularly nourishing and beneficial. He drove out as often as he could, to "revitalize" himself.

Back on the beach, we realized that towels were one item we'd overlooked. But it didn't matter.

In the back of his old station wagon the man had spare towels, fruit, yogurt, honey, and home-baked bread. No one in England thirty years ago ate such stuff for breakfast; yet, in my peeled condition, it tasted better than any food I'd ever eaten. There was something about this man, too: He seemed to glow with health, and with something else, something ineffable. When I realized he was staring back at me, I felt an odd jolt in my core.

"Have you read this?" he was asking, holding out a book.

It was the Bhagavad Gita, *and I'd never heard of it, let alone read it.*

"Keep it," he told me.

There was something profoundly haunting and beautiful in his eyes and his smile. Like da Vinci's St. John the Baptist *or* Mona Lisa. *The smile of wisdom, of the Truth that is Beauty.*

When he finally packed up to leave and we said our good-byes, his car was unable to grip the muddy track well enough to ascend the cliff road. I recall that there seemed to be something deeply symbolic about the three of us being obliged to push him until he gained firmer ground. It was as if we'd paid off a debt.

In the weeks that followed, I read the book he'd given me and found that it answered many of the questions that had been much on my mind after several consciousness-expanding encounters with LSD. But it was still the psychedelic pharmaceutical that I placed my faith in. Like many, I believed it could and would cause change . . . if enough of the world took it.

It was with this end in mind that Andrew and I approached George Harrison, the Beatle. He's still a very nice man, and he was no different then. I remember that his house was filled with plastic dipping birds bobbing up and down over bowls of water. He gave us tea, then listened to our story: We had a line on a huge quantity of bargain-priced LSD; if he provided the money, we could purchase enough to pour into the vast reservoirs in Wales that supply much of England with drinking water. Half the country could be "turned on" overnight. You have to laugh. George looked benignly amused, then told us to wait while he fetched something. He returned with a vinyl single record in its Apple sleeve, and a book.

"This is where it's at," he announced. "LSD can take you only so far."

I was about to object when I saw the face on the cover of the book he held. It was the man we'd seen in Tintagel. George seemed not at all surprised, recounting how he'd come across the book himself: It simply fell from the sky onto a balcony in New York where he was sitting. He assumed someone had dropped it, but no one appeared to be looking down.

The book was Autobiography of a Yogi *by Paramahansa Yogananda, a great Indian teacher who had been among the first to bring the spiritual science of India to the West. He'd died while conducting a public meditation in Santa Barbara the year I was born, and, as the Los Angeles County Morgue recorded, his body revealed no signs of decay for more than a week before he was buried.*

The record turned out to be the "Hare Krishna Mantra," set to be released by Apple Records later that month. Andrew was pissed off with George; he'd expected more.

"Can I keep the book, then?" I asked him.

I was never the greatest devotee—I'm not devotee material—but I remained, and still remain, devoted to Yogananda and his teachings. It was he who, in a dream, told me to visit India and see another teacher—a very different kind of teacher than any I'd ever wanted or expected. . . .

1

"Who's in Charge Here?"

BOMBAY, 1974

❧ ❧ ❧

*And though I have discarded much of past tradition and custom,
and am anxious that India should rid herself of all shackles that
bind and constrain her and divide her people, and suppress vast
numbers of them, and prevent free development of the body and the
spirit, though I seek all this, yet I do not wish to cut myself off
from the past completely. I am proud of that great inheritance that
has been, and is, ours, and I am conscious that I too, like all of us,
am a link in that unbroken chain which goes back to the dawn of
history in the immemorial past of India. That chain I would not
break, for I treasure it and seek inspiration from it. And as a
witness of this desire of mine and as my last homage to India's
cultural inheritance, I am making this request that a handful of my
ashes be thrown into the Ganga at Allahabad to be carried to the
great ocean that washes India's shore.*

—JAWAHARLAL NEHRU, LAST WILL AND TESTAMENT

*O*n September 5, 1974—my birthday, in fact—I first set foot on Indian soil. Indian dust, to be exact. Bombay's airport did not create a winning first impression on visitors to the subcontinent twenty years ago.

After the dryness of the Middle East, where I'd stopped over, the air that hung in Bombay's steaming predawn gloom felt and smelled like the enveloping breath of a monster gorged on overspiced sewage. The hot, sodden shroud hung oppressively on all sides, and within minutes I felt I was dissolving into it. You soon realize why Indians wear Indian clothes. . . .

Drenched in sweat, irritable from jet lag, brain lag, and all the other lags a modern traveler's flesh is heir to, I found myself in a lineup, waiting to reach a man who resembled a black Errol Flynn in soiled khaki—the ubiquitous uniform, it seemed, of all Indian officialdom. Above him, a battered sign read "Immigration Control" in English and Hindi. Although there were only twenty or so people ahead of me, it took nearly half an hour before he asked for my passport and handed me a form to fill out, indicating Dickensian writing equipment: a gnarled nib pen leaning in a blackened, ink-encrusted pot. I used a ballpoint that was destined to explode in my pocket a week later—as unhappy with the new climate as its owner—and felt the porous form disintegrate beneath my damp fist as I struggled to answer questions that seemed either irrelevant *(Grandfather's Surname?)* or impossible to satisfy in the centimeter of space allowed *(Purpose of Visit?)*. Several times I had to ask the man what certain questions really wanted to know. His teeth, I noticed, were the color of terracotta tiles. *Jew?,* for example, turned out not to be a worrying inquiry about religious affiliation, but an abbreviation asking if you were bringing jewelry into the country.

The man flipped through my passport upside down and encountered its photograph—taken in 1969, shoulder-length hair—and asked, "This is your sister?" I told him it was me. He shrugged and went on examining small print and blurred visas. He then hefted the largest rubber stamp I've ever seen and smashed it down on an empty page, producing something illegible, across which he scribbled something, also illegible, with a nib that scored the paper deeply, spattering ink in several directions. He waved me on. I thanked him and turned to see the hundred sweltering souls still waiting behind me.

You would have thought the luggage would have been unloaded by that time, piled up on conveyor belts. It was not—and there were no conveyor belts. The ceiling fans overhead turned only marginally faster than the second hand on my watch, perhaps *slicing* the sultry, turgid air, but not *moving* it. The airport's whole interior struck me as a scene from some discount *Inferno.* Hundreds of people shouted furiously at each other, roaming aimlessly; dozens of officials looked either whacked out on opium or more confused than the arriving visitors, who tried to interrogate them on tricky subjects: *Where's our luggage? . . . Where's the washroom? . . . Where do we get a cab? . . . Who's in charge here?*

"*This* is fucking *crazy!*" a lone and desperate voice yodeled from somewhere in the vast, seething hangar of a room.

Finally I swung my case onto a stand beneath a sign reading "Customs." Another official demanded that I open it and began sorting through its contents with obscene curiosity.

"You have any camera?"

"Yes."

He continued poring over letters and notebooks, unzipping toilet bags, feeling the quality of my shirts, while I dangled the camera that had been over my shoulder all this time in front of his face.

"Nikon?" he eventually said, holding the object with measurable awe.

"Yup."

"Best camera," he stated with absolute conviction.

"Not quite."

He then gave me another blanket-size sheet of paper to fill out, which had me peering for serial numbers and manufacturers' codes, struggling to recall places and dates of purchase. Eventually his own massive stamp came down on the form, which was then attached to a page in my passport with a tailor's pin. What was the purpose of this?

"You must hand in form when you exit country, also producing camera."

India had severe import restrictions—and has only just relaxed them—but this struck me as a rather fallible method of ensuring I would not sell my superlative Western camera while there. I *was* eventually obliged to sell it, as it happened, but the form had fallen from my passport several months before, and no one ever questioned me about its absence when I finally did exit the country.

With some flourish, this customs man chalked a symbol on my case and waved me on. On to where a plate-glass wall was filled with faces pressed against it from the outside, staring in, gesticulating, hollering mutely at us new arrivals on their planet. To leave the airport meant passing from relative security into this mad, babbling throng of wrecked humanity, much of it lacking limbs, noses, eyes, teeth, and certainly any sense of decorum.

Outside a thousand voices called out. Hands clutched at my soaking sleeves: *Woh, swami! You want taxi? . . . Paise, pa? Paise? Taxicab, taxicab . . . Best taxi, sahib, absolute best . . . Karma, pa . . . karma . . .* Little children gazed up with woeful kohled eyes, rubbing their tummies through shirts that looked as if they'd done a stint as mechanics' rags before getting promoted to garments. Mayhew's London was a welfare utopia compared to this. I allowed one man with pipe-cleaner legs and a face like a spray-painted skull to toss my bag on his head, and another man who resembled Albert Einstein's unwashed and unsuccessful twin to haul me by the elbow through the Babel and Bedlam of Bombay's professional greeters and over to a car no one in the West would have taken off his hands as a gift.

Painted black and yellow by hand, it appeared, with ordinary household exterior gloss some decades previously, the vehicle reminded me of a British car that was popular in the fifties. In fact, India in those days featured only two varieties of automobile: this contraption, the Ambassador, a hybrid Hindustan Motors edition of a four-door Austin now vanished; and the Premier Padmini, sleeker but tinnier, a mutation of some Fiat sedan that had disappeared from European streets by 1963.

Though plush and springy to look at, the Ambassador's backseat yields as little comfort as concrete. Combined with an apparent lack of any suspension system, it made riding in the car feel like driving across the moon. The floor consisted of blasted metal patched with planks from fruit crates, below which the pitted road was actually visible. Leaving the sinister sodium glare of the airport lights behind us, we turned onto a metaled surface whose camber was so drastic the whole track could well have been a partially buried oil pipeline; at times I was forced to lean at forty-five degrees to remain upright.

Then there was The Smell.

Initially, I assumed that the failed Einstein, clutching his steering wheel as if it might fly off unless sufficiently restrained, had produced a silent epic of a fart. But, cranking down the window, which failed to budge at first then fell like a guillotine from sight, I realized The Smell was in fact crowding in, was indeed worse outside than it was inside.

Off beyond the road now stretched miles of huts made from ramshackle wood, corrugated-tin-and-tar-paper dog kennels, or tents left over from the Crimean War, crammed together side by side. Fires burned brightly or faintly in front of them, smoke rising, vague forms scuttling in the half light. These were Bombay's slums, Bombay's famous shame—the bustees. A North American rat lives better than those who dwell around the perimeters of Bombay like lost souls waiting to be summoned back to real life. What struck me as most oppressive then, and still does, though I have since seen wars and famines from Ethiopia to Cambodia, was the sheer normality of the life going about its business under such conditions. These people did not complain about their miserable portion. Indeed, many were happy just to be near the land of Oz that Bombay represented. Very few of them were beggars. They were workers—either working or seeking work. The beggars were actually well-off by comparison, with steady jobs that kept roofs over their heads and wolves from their doors.

At the time, Bombay's beggars were a syndicate, handing their paise and rupees to a "king of beggars," who in return housed and fed them. He was reported to be a millionaire.

In a Westerner's eyes, the bustees represented the most shocking introduction to India. Yet I later decided that it was only fitting that they were precisely where and what they were. Horrifying, sobering, a cattle prod of culture shock, they were also the worst sights I encountered in all of India. After the bustees, everything else was an improvement, everything else was icing.

A dawn like bloodstained mercury poured up from the eastern horizon as we bumped down the winding labyrinth leading into downtown Bombay—Gateway to the East, the port that put an end to the great Silk Route. Like London, like Venice, like Cairo, like Shanghai, Bombay was once one of the most vital cities on earth, and it still shows it. And, like New York, it reminds you tirelessly that it's never over until it's over.

With a population density of 100,000 human beings per square mile—more than four times that of Manhattan—the city cannot help but pullulate with activity, with what Shiva Naipaul describes as "a hundred minute specializations of function, a hundred strategies for survival" on any stretch of sidewalk. If you can make it *here,* I thought, you can make it *any*where.

And this city doesn't sleep, either. At dawn the streets teemed with belching cars; bullock carts; weaving bicycles; and wandering cows with bells, paint, and gold foil decorating their elegant horns. At every turn an accident nearly happened somewhere, but never did, amazingly, as pedestrians sidestepped out of the paths of vehicles and animals with the skill and grace of matadors. Flower sellers hawked their garlands of fresh jasmine, strolling from shop front to doorway around wood-framed string beds, many still containing their occupants—stretching or shaving or smoking beedies or sipping chai from tiny glasses.

A tailor sat beneath a peepul tree, one foot pumping the pedal of a sewing machine, his hands guiding a length of orange fabric past the needle. Here a fat Brahmin with ritual bands freshly painted across his fore-head did *puja* before a tiny shrine to Ganesh—the elephant god, the Re-mover of Obstacles—lighting a fistful of joss sticks and hanging a *mala* of yellow flowers around the statue's neck. There an ancient toothless woman squatted on a burlap square, upon which, arranged in neat rows like soldiers, she offered perhaps a hundred small green chili peppers for sale. Here a man repaired sandals, his workbench a portable box placed on a low whitewashed wall. There another man, wearing only a bandage of soiled linen around his groin, cleaned out the ears of a prosperous-looking fellow with oiled hair who was reading the *Times of India* upside down. A skeletal figure with dessicated brown skin hanging in folds from his bones, as if it had melted, carried a wooden yoke on his bent shoulders, from which swung two aluminum pails. A formidable woman up-holstered in a tartan sari, her oiled hair tied in a bun as tight as a black lacquer skullcap, hacked at a giant breadfruit with an ancient machete, aggressively offering the shorn fleshy chunks to passersby.

We were swerving down toward the bay itself now, both sea and sky mottled with limpid metallic-gray clouds, the air mightily still, as if un-certain what to do next. A faded red double-decker London bus careered by, so crowded that its conductor was actually clambering along a ledge outside, collecting fares through the glassless windows. Then, suddenly, the Gateway of India loomed before us, the imposing triumphal arch through which countless viceroys and visiting dignitaries from the West had first disembarked onto the subcontinent, many heading, as we were, into the guarded compound of the stately Taj Mahal Hotel. The Gate-way then housed entire tribes of the sick, the hungry, and the homeless—the orphans of Empire.

To step into the Taj Mahal's lobby, with its white marble fountains and air-conditioned breeze, after the dust and humidity, was to enter a desert nomad's vision of paradise. Even its inhabitants moved and spoke and looked like the members of another species—clean, cool, starched, relaxed.

I stood for a while on my balcony. Finally I was alone in India, for the first time since my arrival. Two sights below impressed themselves into my memory: a man mowing a lawn which grew incongruously on a flat rooftop; and a Western hippie with blond dreadlocks sitting beneath a banyan tree, with a monkey squatting on his shoulders. The monkey was picking out fleas from matted tubes of hair and eating them with the delicacy of a gourmet. Symbiosis?

With these two images, I fell asleep, the heavy, rotting, spiced and salty, sultry air pushing its way in from my open balcony to do battle with the room's pristine air-conditioned blast. Two Titans, two Lords of the Air, fighting it out overhead. I had no idea then of the real battle that would take place *inside* my head. Like all good stories, this one is about a love affair and a war. Both began that dawn back in September 1974.

2

"Meditate More and Find Out"

BANGALORE, 1974

❧   ❧   ❧

*How can the mind take hold of such a country? Generations of
invaders have tried, but they remain in exile.*

—E. M. FORSTER, *A PASSAGE TO INDIA*

*C*aptain Singh piloted his Indian Airlines jet through air that felt and
looked like steaming broth with big lumps in it. Bombay from a few
thousand feet above looked overwhelmingly verdant—at least it did when
you could see anything of it. The predominant color of the city from street
level, however, struck me as faded ocher. Green it was not. Captain Singh
continued speaking to his passengers with an aeronautical bedside manner, giving much information on wind speeds, height, local geography
below the clouds, while his plane felt as if giants were playing catch with
it. Whenever we hit an especially savage air pocket, we plummeted about
three hundred feet, landing on what felt like boulders but were presumably clouds. During one of these abrupt descents, the man next to me
threw an entire cup of orange juice over his pristine white pajamas, as if
intentionally.

"There is some turbulence," he said, laughing inanely, and wiped
at the dripping yellow stains with a piece of tissue the size of a postage
stamp.

A man seated in front with what looked like a tuning fork sketched
in white paint on his forehead turned to peer between the headrests at
us. "Turbulence turbulence," he stated, in case we hadn't noticed.

Some rows down, an overhead locker had spilled its contents onto the
passengers below. Uncomplaining, people were handing briefcases, a bag
of mangoes, some shawls, a tattered cardboard box elaborately swathed

in string, back to a flight attendant wearing a sari of such opulence she could have been the subject of a wedding.

"Bombay mangoes," the man beside me said as the attendant tried to squash the sodden and ragged bag of fruit back in its locker. *"Best* mangoes."

I smiled at him and attempted conversation. He owned some sort of electronics factory in Bangalore and was returning from doing business in Bombay. Did he think India could one day compete with the Japanese in electronics? I wondered. He nodded his head confidently in the south Indian manner, from side to side rather than up and down. In my ignorance, I thought he was saying no. Having tried to start a conversation, or so I'd assumed, he was now doing his best to avoid one. My questions deteriorated to the level of asking him if he liked living in Bangalore, most receiving the same smug and circumspect rocking of the head. Since then I've come to believe the gesture doesn't mean either no or yes, but, in a quintessentially Indian way, both and/or neither.

Bangalore, from my porthole, lay spread out like a vast flat garden. On a plateau high above sea level, it *was* essentially that in 1974. Tall rain trees waved their ragged arms in a mild breeze. As I stepped out, I noticed the air had markedly cooled and dried compared to Bombay's Turkish bath. We walked over to the airport: a low building, a control tower, some basic radar equipment. The luggage was wheeled from the airplane on a huge cart to an area beyond two high chain-link gates. On the other side waited an orderly, well-dressed crowd. Everyone was meeting someone. Flower garlands were placed over heads; children reverently touched the feet of elders; small pujas were performed: hand-size trays of burning camphor waved around as friends and relatives clapped and chanted, praising the gods for a safe arrival. With us it's a hug, then hand over the bottle of duty-free. Indians do things with grace and style. They've had more practice at it.

Far from being harassed by competing cabdrivers, I noticed only one taxi waiting outside the airport, and someone was already commandeering it. A little distance off were several of the covered three-wheel motorcycles known as autorickshaws. I consider them a distinct improvement on the old rickshaw: Who feels good about having some emaciated octogenarian in a loincloth and turban hauling him barefoot around the city streets? There is a drawback: Most of these vehicles are piloted by maniacs. I was approached by a short man with a crazy smile, no shoes, and a filthy tea towel wrapped around hair that shot out like black palm fronds.

"Autoauto?" he said, as if it meant something.

I had the address of a cheap hotel, the Bombay Ananda Bhavan (literally the "Bombay Bliss House") on Grant Road. I asked him if he knew the place.

He nodded in that unreassuring south Indian manner and hefted my bag over to the buggylike rear of his machine. Then he proceeded to get into a nasty argument with one of his colleagues, a man who could have been his twin, that was clearly related to my custom and seemed to reach the verge of blows but went no further.

Cursing and spitting red gobs of betel-nut juice through rusty-looking teeth, the driver finally kick-started his sputtering engine, and we took off. I bounced from side to side like a bell clapper until I learned to brace myself with steel struts supporting the auto's canvas roof. Between the driver's handlebars and the murky windshield were attached several small framed portraits of gods and movie stars. In their midst, an incense holder held two burning joss sticks emitting a smell both sweet and charred.

We turned abruptly onto a broad boulevard teeming with every vehicle known to humankind, entering the vast honking caravan like a weaver's shuttle. I wondered if my driver had a personal problem with everything and everyone else on the road. When I dared to look, there were faded but elegant Raj-era bungalows—some, in their cuteness of detail, almost gingerbread houses—on either side. The bungalows of Bangalore attained enough fame to have once merited a picture book of that name, but were not famous enough to survive into the nineties. With its tolerable climate and strategic position in the center of the South, the city was a major army base during colonial times—indeed, was still a significant base in the third decade of independence. As the focal point of Karnataka state, Bangalore, which borders Communist-influenced Kerala to the west and the troublesome and occasionally separatist-minded states of Tamil Nadu and Andhra Pradesh to the east, is still valuable in military terms. India's bewildering variety of politics usually coexists in a kind of querulous harmony. *Usually*.

Relaxing his grip on the accelerator for the first time in fifteen minutes, the driver zigzagged through cows, donkeys, and people, coming to a jarring halt in the heart of a stupefyingly chaotic and noisy fruit and vegetable bazaar.

"Bombay Ananda Bhavan?" I asked, hoping it wasn't.

The driver raised a grimy palm. He clambered out and began a belligerent conversation with a skinny and toothless man who must have been at least ninety-five years old. Both lit up beedies, the tiny, lung-ripping cigarettes wrapped in leaf that in those days cost about a cent for fifty and still weren't worth the price. The old man pointed in several different compass directions over the course of this conversation, and I detected a look of desperation in my driver's eyes as he glanced my way.

"Grant Road," I reminded him.

I soon learned that, in India, even someone who lived on Grant Road might be unable to tell you how to get to Grant Road—not that this would prevent him from offering utterly wrong directions. There was a certain shame in admitting you didn't know, so people frequently and confidently offered me complex and entirely erroneous instructions. The driver evidently knew this and was not about to head off in the five different directions suggested by the old man. He waylaid a porter carrying about a ton of huge red bananas on his head, who uttered what sounded like one word a hundred syllables long. The driver pulled on his beedie, brows knotted. Then he jumped back and, sitting sidesaddle now, zipped off at maximum velocity, terrifying animals and any humans unfortunate enough to be in our path.

Twice more I endured similar stops, and presumably similar misinformation. Finally we hit Mahatma Gandhi Road—there is at least one of these in every town and city the length and breadth of the subcontinent. Then we turned onto St. Mark's Road, and off this onto a quiet, lushly tropical street of large, stately houses and bungalows . . . actually labeled Grant Road.

The whole history of Indian cities could be told through street names. The signs reading Grant Road and St. Mark's Road have now gone, replaced by Vithalpatai Road, by Indira Nagar, or some such—yet the old names survive unofficially. Grant Road is still somewhere a taxi or auto driver will take you, if you're patient.

The Bombay Ananda Bhavan proved to be one of the stately houses, its title on a weather-weary board looking at once out of place and a sign of the times. A semicircular drive drew you up to a robust, monsoon-proof porch over steps leading to double doors. After a screaming argument over the fare, my driver flew off, his machine sounding more and more like an angry bee trapped in a jar.

A reception desk with a bell greeted my entrance. There was no sign of human life. I rang the bell and heard an odd guttural gurgling, apparently from beneath the floor. I rang again, shouting out that I was here. Nothing. Just the subterranean sounds of a viscous drainage. A clock ticked. A pleasant breeze blew in, carrying perfumed greenhouse smells on its wings. A fly the size of a small bird—or possibly a small bird the size of a fly—zoomed straight for my nose, veering drastically away at the last moment. I looked in a room to my left—a bed draped in mosquito netting—and a room to my right—a bed draped in mosquito netting, and an armoire the size of a van. Then I peeked behind the narrow reception desk to discover a bearded man in a T-shirt and *lungi,* sound asleep on the floor.

The occasional gurgling was his snore, which aggravated a standard-sized fly that was busy gathering sebum from his glistening nose. It darted back and forth to the safety of a nearby shelf each time the man's mouth puckered with another imminent snore. He had toenails like a bear, this sleeper, and the soles of his feet looked like dessicated mud flats, riven with cracks half an inch deep in some places. They weren't *like* leather; they *were* leather.

He looked serene, with his hands behind his head. I called to him quietly. Getting no response, I finally shouted at him. Beyond an irritable gurgle, still no response. This was no ordinary nap. In the end I took him by the shoulders and shook, all but slapping his face as if he'd OD'd or passed out from booze, or both. Finally his droopy eyelids fluttered.

Standing up, he could have been Peter Lorre's son. Both eyes looked off to the side, adding to the impression that he wasn't certain that I was there, that he was there—that it wasn't all a dream. Pretending he hadn't just woken up, he spoke gibberish and performed menial and meaningless tasks—dusting the counter, checking his saucer-size wristwatch, and closing the heavy shutters about one-tenth of an inch. Then he indicated a ledger, handing me a ballpoint pen from the Sheraton Hotel, Kathmandu. The last entry in this huge tome read: "Maynard Billings, San Diego. A really beautiful stay." I wrote my name and address, assuming it was premature to comment.

"Mr. Billing," the man said, pointing at the previous entry with swaggering pride. "He like this place too much. Very good man, Mr. Billing. *Very* good. You know him?"

I confessed I did not.

"You want room, is it?"

On one wall hung a framed photograph of Sathya Sai Baba, the local holy man. A garland of flowers placed around it perhaps a week before gave the image a funereal appearance.

"You come for Bhagavan?" asked the concierge, noticing my interest in the picture. Bhagavan means God, basically, but in India, where all that lives, and much that is inanimate, is holy, it is a term liberally applied to *gurus, yogis, sadhus,* movie stars, musicians, teachers, and even politicians. I had indeed come to Bangalore ostensibly to see the famous "Man of Miracles," Bhagavan Sri Sathya Sai Baba.

"Currently out of station," the concierge informed me.

"Where?"

"Puttaparthi going."

Sai Baba, I knew, generally stayed near Bangalore but had his main *ashram* in the village of Puttaparthi, in Andhra Pradesh, where he was born. Puttaparthi was notoriously difficult to get to, I'd been told, at least a day's journey away.

I did not want to give this sleepy man the satisfaction of seeing I was disappointed. "Any other gurus in the area?"

He pondered the question seriously, as if I'd asked him to recommend a good local restaurant. I assumed this was a preamble to saying no, but I was wrong. He mentioned someone apparently named Siva Bala Yogi— or possibly Sivabalayogi.

"Where do I find him?"

Near the Bangalore Dairy was the closest I got to an answer.

✤　✤　✤

Saints explain that the soul is a drop of the Divine Ocean. Separated from her source, she has become caught in the net of illusion and has taken the mind as her companion. The mind, however, is in the grip of the senses and dances to their tune. Whatever it does under their influence, the soul has also to reap the consequences.
—MAHARAJ CHARAN SINGH, *SPIRITUAL DISCOURSES*

I don't think any foreigner had asked an auto driver for a ride to the Bangalore Dairy before. I'd discovered by now the mysterious value of saying key words twice. "Dairydairy," I told this particular three-wheeled road hazard. It appeared to work, although, since the Dairy was a long way outside Bangalore, I initially had my doubts. We were in open countryside now, which made some sense when I considered the nature of a dairy's business. Of course, once we'd reached the place—a large barnlike structure, recently erected, with a corrugated asbestos roof—I had to break the news that where I really wanted to go was actually supposed to be nearby. Obviously I'd just confirmed this driver's worst suspicions about Westerners. The first problem was that there were no other buildings nearby, or indeed even visible, nor were there any people to ask for bad directions. We sputtered up the monotonously straight flat road, spotting a five-year-old boy in some kind of school uniform, barefoot and carrying three books on his head as if practicing lessons in deportment.

"Sivabalayogi ashramashram?" I asked him hopefully.

He grinned impishly, saying, "Sheevbalashramum, ha?"

I nodded. He pointed to a clump of trees, saying something to the driver in Kannada, the language of Karnataka and about as closely related to Hindi as Japanese is to Russian. The driver nodded as if he'd known this all along. "America?" the boy asked me. I nodded, to save time. "Give me one pen," he demanded bluntly, his hand out. I reached in my shirt pocket and discovered the Sheraton Hotel Kathmandu ballpoint, which I must have boosted from the sleepy concierge. The boy's smile broadened until half his face was pure ivory.

We buzzed and bounced on toward the copse of palms. Gradually a low, drab, flat-roofed bungalow crept into view, squatting in the midst of a dusty compound bordered by more fields. "Sivabalashram," a humble wooden sign proclaimed. A couple of scruffy middle-aged men in lungis milled around outside the building's main door, holding coconuts and flowers, sucking the smoke from their cigarettes through clenched fists as if puffing on joints. I asked them if the yogi was home.

"Fiveo'clockfiveo'clock," one man said, pointing at the wristwatch he wasn't wearing. I looked at my own. It was ten past five already.

"The bhagavan coming five o'clock," my driver explained, adding that he would wait for me, as if this were a client relations thing. I joined the men, squatting on a concrete step decorated with handpainted swastikas, the same traditional Sanskrit symbols originally and popularly thought to signify eternity and good fortune that Hitler adapted for his own purposes, tilted and reversed.

A woman of startling antiquity, so bent that her back and head were horizontal to the ground, scuttled from behind the bungalow, holding a switch of stiff straw with which she commenced sweeping footprints and auto tread marks from the compound dust. Her neat but threadbare sari was tied up between her spindly legs as if it were a huge diaper, and her withered breasts hung down like a spaniel's ears. With not a tooth in her head, she looked over, displaying what could have been a smile or a scowl. After all, I was responsible for most of the footprints and tread marks.

Now, the story of Siva Bala Yogi (literally, Siva the Baby Yogi), as I heard it sometime later, was this: When still a boy of thirteen, and bearing another name, of course, he'd been playing one day with some friends under a mango tree. A fruit fell from the tree, and out of this fruit sprang the god Siva. Siva told the boy to sit in *padmasan,* the yogic lotus posture, but the boy was understandably reluctant to comply, so Siva had to force him down. He immediately went into a trance, and he stayed in it for ten years, eating and drinking nothing ("He live on air only"). Rats came and nibbled his fingers, severing the nerve ends and locking them into the clasped lotus *mudra;* his legs withered from lack of circulation, his whole body growing around the position he was in. Villagers came and built a hut around the holy phenomenon; then, as his frame spread, they built a bungalow around the hut. When he was twenty-three, he emerged from the trance with Wisdom, and with his present name, or title. He began to recount the tale of his divine encounter and teach his devotees meditation—a subject he clearly knew much about—and remained consistently frugal with food: Besides air, he consumed only fresh orange juice. He was then, in 1974, I was told, a mere thirty-five years old, yet he had collected a small but fervent crowd of believers around him, most, by the looks of them, very local villagers. Considering that I went on to meet a yogi in the Himalayas who claimed to be 963 years old, Siva Bala *was* just a baby in his line of business.

These villagers drifted in to sit beside me in a large antechamber or hallway just inside the door. A man sold me half a coconut and a small string of flowers, the requisite offering for Bhagavan. They were lean, wiry people, these devotees, all of them freshly washed and neatly dressed, with sandal-paste marks on their foreheads and the incessant mumbled buzz of sacred *mantra*s on their lips. The covertly gathering sunset had set this bare concrete hall on fire, a gilded pink blaze of pulsing light that blasted straight from the western horizon as if aimed just at us.

Soon a pair of double doors opened onto a dimly lit room. We rose as one and pushed in. Almost bare but for a gigantic Victorian four-poster bed, the room was sepulchral and choking with clouds of cheap incense, a tacky floral perfume reminiscent of Bangkok hookers. At the rear of this preposterously ornate bed, on three tiger skins, sat Siva Bala Yogi himself.

He had a broad, serenely unwrinkled and youthful face, and wiry hair matted with cow dung (a traditional and sacred bug deterrent, apparently) into a single tube, thick as a drainpipe and hanging down to his waist. His eyes were closed; a vague smile played through his spidery, gleaming black beard. In accordance with the story, the legend, his torso was impressively huge, like a barrel perched over pathetically spindly legs still locked, still crossed in padmasan, the smooth soles of their delicate brown feet facing upward on top of either thigh. His rat-gnawed fingers indeed looked gnarled and permanently bent, interlaced, resting on his lap. He was utterly naked except for a tiny loincloth all but invisible beneath an edifice of a gut that was not fat but solid and muscly in appearance. Through the haze of joss sticks and in the flickering light of oil lamps, he was—*whatever* he was—certainly not ordinary.

I sat down near the foot of the bed, aware of the spiced, earthy smell of those village men, now wedged in on either side of me, as it mingled with blowsy two-bit incense. When all present were seated on the hard stone floor, the doors of this solemn and resonant room were closed with a clanking finality of bolts, shutting us inside the yogi's permanent night. Thick wooden shutters on the far wall did not look as if they'd been opened much, if ever.

Nothing appeared to be happening. We sat. The yogi sat—possibly fast asleep. Before long, I was aware of a building sensation that felt like a cross between panic and a sinus headache. In retrospect, it was the experience of raw and rather aimless energy: unpleasant, unnerving . . . yet intriguing. This sitting business must have lasted for a good thirty minutes; then someone started ringing a large, shrill bell, and everyone stood, chanting unintelligible words. The yogi opened his eyes and raised his right hand as if in greeting, his clawed fingers making the gesture somewhat primitively hostile, too—although it was the traditional blessing of a guru or god. His eyes were moist and boyish, but curiously devoid of human content—the lights were on, but no one was home.

Next, people formed a line on the right-hand side of the bed, humbly touching the yogi's feet and placing their offerings of flowers, coconuts, and crumpled rupees upon the moth-eaten tiger skins. I thought of the parable about the woman and her mite. What did he *do* with all those coconuts . . . ?

An official-looking man in a lurid red shirt and drastically flared pink trousers tugged at my sleeve, saying, "You may ask Bhagavan some question—if you are wishing. . . ."

Although the yogi did not seem to notice my big, pale, clumsy, Western face, I felt as obvious as a Zulu in a synagogue among all these tiny Karnatakan villagers. What would I ask him, my first Indian holy man? I'd better make it good. . . .

"What is Truth?" I finally said. It was, after all, what Pilate had asked Christ.

The official-looking man bent over to mutter in the yogi's ear. The yogi blinked. I wondered if he *could* speak, if perhaps I was supposed to receive the vital answer telepathically. Then he emitted a low, husky growl of syllables, still staring straight ahead.

"His Holiness say," the man proudly told me, "for you to meditate more and find out." Then he took what looked like a lump of chalk from a small pile near the yogi's knee and presented it to me with a flourish. I thanked this translator for the chalk and for Baby Siva's wise words, returning to stand in the throng of adoring faces. It was a good all-purpose answer, and I assuaged my mounting disappointment by conceding that it could well be the *only* answer there was. After all, Jesus hadn't even *replied* to Pilate's question. . . .

Suddenly, however, quite loudly and clearly, the yogi said, *"Siva!"* in a big, hollow, booming voice. Was he reading my thoughts? And then what? The god's name thundered around that hushed and reverent space, plucking at the nerves of my spine like a mad harpist.

I was definitely glad to be outside again, beneath one of those sudden evenings that swoop westward across the south Indian sky, turning it gold, then purple, then into a quivering basalt dome studded with stars. Others were carrying lumps of chalk, too, I noticed. Pale gray, not white, the stuff turned out to be something called *vibhuti*—ash, basically. A symbolically pure substance, though—that which has passed through the fire . . . I collected a ton of vibhuti before I left India.

"What is Bhagavan replying to your question?" a man with smiling eyes and a huge, happy mouth stacked with opalescent teeth inquired.

"He told me to meditate more. . . ."

"Oh." This man nodded knowingly, hauling in his lips around that bursting smile for a moment. "You are too much blessed, isn't it?"

I readily admitted the possibility. Something about these simple people moved me, all of a sudden; I found myself sharing the man's explosive happiness.

3

"I Am Always with You"

PUTTAPARTHI, 1974-75

❧ ❧ ❧

A stick floats on the waves of the sea. So does a swimmer. It is the
swimmer that the sea loves to bear, for he has sensed its depths.

—SATHYA SAI BABA

*B*eyond Bangalore's sputtering, inchoate suburbs, you descend toward mountainous plains, a primeval landscape of stark, rocky outcrops, palm-cluttered desert, and outrageously fertile paddies that look as if some Titan had mischievously plugged them into the smoldering wasteland for the sheer hell of it. A ragged blue ribbon of road snaked through haphazard villages of thatch and palm that seemed to exist solely because of the trade this crumbling shred of asphalt brought their way. As predictable as small towns in the American Midwest, though with barely a fraction of the opulence, these outposts of humanity elicited first despair, then, finally, abject boredom. They were anonymous, miserably interchangeable.

I was traveling with a nineteen-year-old girl from Arizona who called herself Joy but had once been Betty. She had put me on to our driver, a shifty-looking character named Abdul. Joy wanted to "share" the cost of paying him for driving us in his cab to Puttaparthi. Her notion of sharing meant I'd share her company in return for paying the cab fare. She was a devotee of Sathya Sai Baba and had followed the holy man around for two years now, dumping her passport in the Ganges, at one point, and writing to inform her parents that she was no longer their daughter—she was the bride of God. *Gopi* was the term she used for herself, however—gopis, in this case, at least, being one of the horde of sixteen thousand nubile milkmaids who are often portrayed as the god Krishna's harem. She believed Sathya Sai would one day marry her.

"He provides for his own" was all she would say about how she financed herself without parents.

With little conversation to interrupt the silence between us, I studied the passing landscape. Recently crippled two- and three-wheeled vehicles stood propped up by piles of rocks. Rusty engines leaned against huge roots, wild and naked men smashing stones against crowbars and levering up blasted carburetors, pulverized gearboxes; mangled remains of entire burned-out vehicles were being cannibalized by hunter-gatherer mechanics for parts. Nothing is wasted in India, where recycling has long been essential common practice.

"Detroit in the Stone Age?" I commented to Joy at one point.

"It's all His will," she replied, her right leg bouncing through layers of sari cotton to some private inner beat.

"What?"

"Everything is His will."

A handpainted sign read "Now enting Anda Pradess." The disastrous road seemed to have given up, exhausted. We bumped and lurched over entire miles of bare dust, suddenly rediscovering briefly a blistered and forlorn metal track. The air buffeting my face now was as hot as that pouring from a bread-oven door. Andhra Pradesh knew no winter; besides the monsoon—if it came—there were only varying calibers of summer, usually with a heat that left you breathless and speechless. Maybe Joy had been here too long.

Twisting around one especially drastic corner, Abdul gnashed down through objecting gears to bring his cab to an unsteady halt beneath a spinney of huge, overarching trees. In the enormous shade below, there squatted one lonely, lurching thatch-roofed shack, with a telltale collection of handmade wooden benches and tables spewed out in the mottled dust from its dim and smoky maw. It was a commercial enterprise.

"*Chaichai?*" the pathologically untalkative driver inquired. He'd extracted the bald ignition key and opened his squeaking door.

Some relative or dear friend must have owned this excessively humble rustic joint, plunked down at the edge of burned mountains, stacked and verdant paddies, and flailing groves of tall palms.

"What a landscape!" I remarked to my companion, who slurped a stained glass of milky chai, absently pulling her *choli* down, putting it in its place.

"God keeps the best for Himself," she announced.

A blind beggar with empty eye sockets that were as dry and black as a dead dog's nose approached us, urgently wailing, "Sai Ram, Sai Ram, Sai Ram!" He held a kind of theater vendor's tray, with a garlanded portrait of Sai Baba propped on it against his chest. Some coins were scattered on the otherwise empty surface, to give you a hint. He smiled and intoned, sensing where we'd sat, and picked his way over. I placed a rupee under some coins.

"Sai Ram! Woh, Sai Ram!"

It was a phrase I'd come to be very familiar with, connecting Sai Baba's name with the god Rama, and used as a mantra, greeting, and all-purpose response to almost anything by those around him.

"Baba says you shouldn't give money to beggars. It teaches them that begging is a profession," Joy said loftily.

"The guy's blind, Joy. I think begging probably is one of his few career options."

"He's a millionaire. He's not even a devotee of Baba. . . ."

Joy was putting me off the spiritual life of Sathya Sai Baba before I had even met the man. I had no idea what a "spiritual life" was then, of course, or what it entailed.

✤   ✤   ✤

Returned to the unyielding rear seat of Abdul's cab, I watched our vehicle oscillate through what increasingly seemed a paradise untouched by everything but searing heat since time began. This heat was a third passenger. It slapped my cheeks, eventually embracing my whole damp body with fierce, hot, and powerful arms. Joy fanned her face with a slim paperback of Hermann Hesse.

"Sai Ram," she mumbled constantly, like the blind man. "Sai Ram . . ."

When the huddle of sparkling domes, stunted *gopura,* and scattered concrete and palm-thatch bungalows of Puttaparthi eventually came into view, "Sai Ram" was all she had to say.

It was indeed one of the most exquisite stretches of land I'd ever seen: the majestic, parched, and barren mountains; the profound and stubborn boulders that seemed their offspring; the fertile groves and paddies; the broad, mercurial river. And, in the midst of it, a small, relatively prosperous south Indian village where life had changed little in seven hundred years.

In those days Puttaparthi started as yet another unplanned, cluttered community, but rapidly became something more as you drove in through the dust, something you hadn't seen before. After eight hours of careering through rural eastern Karnataka and southwestern Andhra Pradesh, I felt I'd seen all there was to see, which had not amounted to much. But Puttaparthi, where this road literally ended, more than fulfilled my expectations for the home of a great holy man.

Cupped in the muscular brown palm of black-capped mountains—mountains whose peaks were burned, as legend had it, by the monkey god Hanuman's blazing tail as he flew down to Lanka to do battle with the demon king, Ravana—the village had an elegance about it that reminded me of some unspoiled spot in the Greek islands. Everywhere were whitewashed mud-brick houses, many boasting the novelty of terra-cotta-tiled roofs and neat, cool courtyards. The broad Chitravati River flowed past these dwellings, its waters swollen deep and heavy that September, a month or so after monsoon season; a tide of liquid turquoise beneath an enormous blue sky, a sky more exposing than sheltering.

In the center of it all, the ashram: an enclosure surrounded by thick twenty-foot-high walls that contained a domed temple made of sculptured concrete as ornate as a gigantic wedding cake. This extravaganza of Dravidian rococo was offset by banks of three-story buildings that would not have looked out of place in Warsaw. Yet the temple's riotous opulence somehow granted them respite from this blast of industrial ugliness, as did the fierce sunshine that flashed red from their whitewashed walls and made them at times seem like monoliths carved from solid light. There was more than enough beauty to go around here. Immaculately combed ocher sand filled the spaces between these structures and their temple hub, holding tall, majestic palms that stood like wild sentries, flailing their arms, turning their heads to see who came, who went.

Immediately without the ashram walls, lining the dust road we drove along, was a strip of ad hoc bamboo lean-tos of varying structural ingenuity. "Brahmin Meels Hotele," proclaimed a clumsily hand-painted board outside one; next to it was the Military Meals Hotell. The former catered to India's vegetarian priestly caste, while its neighbor sought business from the carnivorous Kshatriya, or warrior, caste—not that Brahmins are necessarily priests, or Kshatriya soldiers, these days. There were other, less specialized restaurants as well. Virtually all the other precarious structures appeared to deal exclusively in the Sai Baba souvenir trade: cheaply framed and frequently garish photographs of the curious figure, with his orange robe and black halo of incongruous Afro hair, peered out from stacks of Sai Ram Incense; coils of sandalwood or *rudraksha* bead rosaries held enamel lockets emblazoned with his image; heaps of shoddily bound tomes typeset by dyslexics dispensed his wisdom. There were Sai Baba calendars, Sai Baba pens, Sai Baba dashboard magnets, and thousands of Sai Baba bumper stickers—the kind that require glue to stick. Almost any object that could be retailed for less than ten rupees seemed to be available with the holy man's likeness stuck, stamped, or painted on it. Near the main gates of the ashram, however, this explosion of spiritual materialism was tempered by the more pragmatic appearance of a laundry that specialized in white garments, and a tailor who appeared to manufacture such white garments exclusively. These were, I soon found, the all-but-mandatory uniform of the male Baba devotee.

"No rooms available," snapped Mr. Nithyagiri Rao, supervisor of accommodations. Short, muscular, nervous, this supervisor was swathed in pristine white homespun, or *khadi*. Somehow just being near him made me tense.

"But I've come all the way from England," I told him, unable to believe there was no room at the inn.

He avoided my eyes, pretending to deal with papers piled on his desk. "No accommodations available," he muttered.

The ashram was named Prasanthi Nilayam—Abode of the Highest Peace. As was often and eagerly pointed out, Jerusalem has an almost identical meaning.

Joy had vanished the moment Abdul heaved on his hand brake. I tracked her down in a dingy café full of Westerners hunched over chai. Everyone wore hybrid Indian outfits: saris with straw hats and tennis shoes; *dhotis* with denim vests. Most looked as if they also had American Express cards tucked away somewhere, too: *Don't renounce the world without it.*

"Sai Ram," she said, hearing my plight.

A kindly old woman from New York, with white hair and a necklace made of large nuts, offered to show me where I could rent a room.

Beyond the ashram walls, at the foot of a steep hill, I found "Nagamma's Hotel": six ten-by-six-foot concrete rooms off a bare corridor, sharing a washroom without running water and without any fixtures or fittings except for a hole in the floor. The rent was five hundred rupees a year. I handed over the full amount. I planned to stay a year.

✢   ✢   ✢

Who is Sathya Sai? This name is not the name of a body. It is the name of the divine consciousness which is enthroned in the heart. This consciousness is universal: it is there for all human beings, not merely my devotees. Vishnu sleeps on Shesha, the great serpent, in the ocean. Similarly, Sathya Sai sleeps on Sathya or Truth. Truth, which is something universal, is the substance of his bed. It is this truth, this principle of life that animates this body. And this is how you must recognize the inner significance of all persons and personalities. —SATHYA SAI BABA

Sathya Sai Baba was born Sathya Narayana Raju on November 23, 1926, to a family of pious Hindu farmers. By our standards, they were comfortably middle-class. His brother and sister still, in 1974, lived in the same little house off a dusty lane in Puttaparthi village. They were their brother's devotees now, but apparently enjoyed no more privileges than anyone else in the ashram that had sprung up on the outskirts of the village. They occupied their days more with teaching, agriculture, and animal husbandry than with devotions.

As a small child, Baba had exhibited magical powers, his schoolfriends reporting that he materialized candies and other objects for them out of thin air. In a land soaked with superstition and supernatural yarns, these antics were a cause more for concern than for celebration. The family called in exorcists and pundits, often subjecting the strange little boy to painful ordeals in an attempt to make him normal. For days on end, according to a village elder who had witnessed it, Baba would sit in trance, chanting verses in Sanskrit—a language he had never studied, which was by then the sole preserve of Brahmin scholars.

On March 8, 1940, at around seven in the evening, so the story goes, Sathya Narayana was stung by a "big black scorpion." No one else ever saw a scorpion or snake. In any case, the boy then fell stiff and unconscious. A day or two later he revived and began to act in an even more bizarre manner.

His parents were completely exasperated by now. On May 23 that same year, his father demanded to know who or what he was. "I am Sai Baba," the boy calmly replied. "I shall not remain in your house any longer. I am no longer your Sathya. I am Sai. I don't belong to you. My devotees are calling me." With that, he left home, sitting in a nearby garden and ecstatically chanting spontaneous hymns to the small group of locals who even back then revered him.

Having named his son Sathya Narayana, his father was understandably perplexed to find the boy calling himself a name that then meant nothing to him. It turned out that Sai Baba had been the name of a holy man in Shirdi, a town weeks away from Puttaparthi and some days' journey north of Bombay. This Sai Baba had died at the beginning of the century and had been a low-key, enigmatic figure to whom miraculous powers were attributed by a small circle of devotees. No one even seemed too sure if he was a Muslim or a Hindu. His starkly unadorned message had been one of love and the unity of all faiths, his dress ambiguous, his home a ruined mosque. To his followers he had announced that he would be reincarnated in the South eight years after his death. He had died in 1918.

Someone once told me a story that appeared to confirm this. M. K. Raman was ninety-seven when I met him. He'd been an ardent devotee of Shirdi Sai Baba, one of those who'd personally heard the holy man announce his next incarnation. Nearly half a century elapsed before he learned of a south Indian guru who claimed to be the reincarnation of Sai Baba and thus felt "mildly obliged" to set out for Puttaparthi. He did not really believe he'd find there "any truth to the outlandish claim."

When they first met and before either had spoken a word, Sathya Sai Baba waved his hand and materialized two coins for M. K. Raman—four annas in the old and long-obsolete Raj-era currency. "I knew then that it was true," Raman recalled, his creaky old voice quavering with emotion. A lifetime earlier, he told me, just before his death, Shirdi Sai Baba had mysteriously demanded of Raman four annas. As this old Sai Baba, like the new model, never asked for anything, and rarely even accepted personal gifts, the incident had stuck in Raman's mind for fifty years. Such stories are common to the point of cliché around Sathya Sai Baba.

From 1940 on, Baba devoted himself exclusively to spreading a simple message of love and selfless work to a burgeoning horde of followers from all walks of life, from numerous religions, and from the four corners of the earth, as well as the humble villages of India. He also continued to display apparently miraculous powers: usually materializing sacred vibhuti ash, candies, and small objects, but occasionally performing far more extravagant acts. Incidents, some well documented, a few even on film, have him creating fairly large objects, substantial amounts of food, raising the dead, healing the sick, appearing in two places thousands of kilometers apart at the same time, and altering at will the laws of time, space, and basic physics.

Having announced that he was the reincarnation of a holy man almost no one in south India had even heard of, Baba gradually elaborated on the issue of his identity, claiming at various times to be an incarnation of the god Vishnu or the god Siva—the two poles of the Hindu trinity, which is completed by Brahma, the Creator, the Formless One.

Vishnu is the Sustainer of Life; Siva is the Destroyer of Worlds, the one who paves the way for new creation. According to Hindu lore, Vishnu has appeared on earth throughout history in various forms, including Rama, Krishna, and, some say, the Buddha. There is no account of Siva ever having assumed human form—although he has appeared as himself occasionally—yet it is an avatar of Siva that Baba has most frequently hinted himself to be.

At times, the claim has included more complicated details: Shirdi Sai Baba, says Sathya Sai, was a manifestation of the pure Siva force; he, however, is an incarnation of the Siva-Shakti force, a combination of the Destroyer of Worlds and his terrifying consort, also called Kali and frequently depicted wearing a necklace of human skulls while feasting on someone's head. There will be one more manifestation in this series of avatars, Baba has often declared, and that will be the incarnation of Shakti alone. After he dies—this to be at the age of ninety-six, in the year 2022—Prema Sai Baba will be born four years later somewhere also in south India.

A Californian named Jack Hislop showed me an enameled ring that Baba had materialized for him, bearing the image of a shaggy, vastly bearded man. This, he'd been informed, was Prema Sai Baba. The image was rather terrifying. Prema means love. Sathya Sai's version of the Hindu theory of avatars, which itself became very confused after the Buddha's appearance, would be heretical in any other religion. But since the incarnations of Vishnu range from a large fish to a turtle, a boar, a humanoid lion, and a dwarf—easily suggesting a parable of evolution—Baba's additional confusion is hardly noticed. All agree, however, that there is one *avatar* left to come: Kali, who will orchestrate the end of all creation.

Sathya Sai's message, though, is devoid of apocalyptic overtones. Indeed, his is a vision of the coming golden age, a heaven on earth brought about by man's return to the cardinal rules of Truth, Selfless Work, Peace, and Love. This is what he has emblazoned on his logo—a lotus with the sign of *Om,* the primal word, surrounded by the symbols of all the major world religions.

At least that's how the logo was explained to me. Jews who came to Baba were openly hurt or offended by the absence of any Magen David on this logo, which included the cross, the star and crescent moon of Islam, the Buddhist wheel of *dharma,* and the Om. There was also another symbol few Westerners recognized: a burning Olympic-style torch. This turned out to be the Zoroastrian fire. It was not, of course, all the major *world* religions that Baba had on his emblem, but rather all the major *Indian* religions. While India has never persecuted Jews, and it surprises many to learn there are still a few exceptionally beautiful synagogues functioning, the Jewish population, never large, has now dwindled to fewer than a hundred. Most Jews have left for Israel, which came into existence at the same time India achieved independence.

Besides preaching universal brotherhood and religious unity, Sathya Sai Baba and the huge organization that gradually evolved around him embarked on a program of building schools, colleges, and hospitals that spans the subcontinent today. His legion of critics, however, maintain that his real intention is to found a new religion with himself as God. I personally could never see this. In a book called *Lord of the Air,* an American ex-devotee claimed Baba was Satan incarnate and fed on the love of those he trapped with his lies. The Bible warns us of this, of course, of the devil disguised as the Messiah. With so many messiahs around these days, one is more inclined to wonder *which* is or was the devil. The tradition of saints and holy men in the East, however—and the lack of any devil—seems to make this a nonissue to Hindus.

I once heard someone ask Baba if he was Christ. "No," he replied. "I'm the One who sent him. . . ."

⚜   ⚜   ⚜

Inmates of the Ashram sat daily in the sand around the central temple, where Baba lived in a tiny room, waiting for *darshan,* the blessing they believed emanated from his presence—even the mere sight of him. As in all strict Hindu arrangements, the sexes were separated in the temple compound—something Westerners always had trouble with. It reminded me of elementary school.

The birds, the palm fronds, the high blue air: It was a tranquil, idyllic scene, yet the atmosphere always seemed to border on the hysterical, the anxious, the expectant, and even the desperate. It seems that peace and quiet and inner calm are the last things you find in an ashram with a living guru in residence. These are places where hard work is done, inner work. You don't go there for a vacation; you go there to confront yourself . . . and *change*. Transformation is the one true goal of spiritual work. I came to liken the process to smelting metals: When it's hot enough, the crap rises to the surface and can be scraped off.

Squatting on the warm, smooth sand, constantly shifting to ease aching bones and numb flesh, I recognized my own excitement, expectation, even awe. For the first time it dawned on me that everything said about Sathya Sai Baba might actually be true—and if it was, what would it mean to me?

When he finally appeared, without warning, a tiny figure with a huge, frizzy bonnet of hair and an unadorned orange robe that covered his feet, I experienced an extraordinary sensation. It was love, certainly, but more being *loved* than being *in* love. So unexpected and so strong was this feeling that tears streamed down my cheeks as I watched Baba's slow, graceful movements.

Baba stood, swaying slightly, gazing dreamily out over the semicircle of devotees, whose palms were now pressed together as if in prayer, all eyes on him. He raised one hand as if testing for rain, and appeared to stir the air with his middle finger. Then, with his other hand, he made a gesture that looked as if he were writing on something invisible with his forefinger. Someone told me later that this was how he rewrote destiny. His presence seemed suddenly vast and remote, not connected at all to anything around it. There was an aura of stillness combined with majesty that I have never since encountered in any other person, no matter how famous or powerful. He looked like someone in absolute control of all.

After some minutes, he moved slowly along the rows of adoring faces, pausing to take a note, bless a child or some religious object held up for his attention. Then, fifteen feet away from me, he stopped by an old man in a wheelchair and made a curious polishing motion with his right hand, palm down, from which suddenly poured a quantity of grayish powder into the waiting cupped hands of the man, who sobbed in gratitude. Baba pressed his thumb on the man's forehead, leaving a chalky mark there, and moved on.

As he drew still nearer, I trembled with almost painful emotions. My heart beat faster and faster. His dark, remote gaze swept over the people on all sides. Then he passed and was gone, without so much as a glance my way. I felt oddly humiliated, spurned, jilted.

✤   ✤   ✤

Remote as Puttaparthi was, there were times during those months I spent
there when it felt like the center of the world. Life in the ashram never
varied in its routine, while the people who came and went could not have
varied more. One day John Lennon and Yoko Ono were sitting in the
sand with the rest of us; next day it was the president of India, a producer
of the James Bond films, the photographer David Bailey, or some high-
ranking Italian politician. Yet there was only one star in that small world,
and he seemed unimpressed by those who walked tall in the world beyond, often paying more attention to some ragged group of peasants who
had walked miles for his blessing than to those who had arrived in air-
conditioned limousines. Ignored, John and Yoko left in a huff. Indira
Gandhi reportedly cried when Baba refused to meet her privately.

Sathya Sai continued to ignore me, so I settled into the ashram's routine, increasingly enjoying the tranquil, pastoral life of the village around
it and my walks in that elegant countryside. I also enjoyed observing the
devotees more than emulating them. Fast friendships were formed. Some
have continued half a lifetime, some turned inexplicably into bitter enmities.

I returned to my rented cell from a typically fruitless meditation ses-
sion one morning as the klieg-light sun rose above the hills yet again and
shadows slid like deadly serpents from rocks and scrub. Pacing down the
winding path toward me strode a fearful sight: a young blond man, close
to seven feet tall, with a vast, flowing beard and two yards of hair coiled
into a turret above his head. Powerfully muscular and certainly not fat,
he possessed a belly like a witch's cauldron, bulging over a faded orange
loincloth that barely contained a set of male equipment a stallion would
have envied. In one hand he grasped a massive trident, like Neptune's
but swathed in dangling colored ribbons that held little stones and carved
talismans; in the other was a *kamandalam,* a sadhu's begging bowl carved
from wood. Despite these features, what I first noticed was the string of
nine human skulls hanging from his neck. It was fairly noticeable. The
clacking noise he made as he strode forcefully through pebbles and dust
was caused not by crania knocking together, however, but by wooden
sandals, the kind held on only by a mushroom-shaped peg clasped between the toes. They are often made of sandalwood—hence the name.

"Bum-bum bolo!" he roared at me.

"Sai Ram!" seemed a better response than "Top o' the mornin' to you,
squire. . . ."

Bum-bum bolo, or something like it, was, I found out later, a phrase popular with hard-core devotees of Siva. That morning I was perfectly prepared to believe this apparition could well be Siva himself, come to personally bring creation to an end. But he swung on past, pale blue eyes flashing in the sun's first rays, bearing down on an unsuspecting bazaar.

Kali Das was his name, although you could apparently call him Klaus without getting a trident plunged through your heart. Never allowed through the ashram gates—not just because he looked the way he looked, but because he looked the way he looked *and he was a Westerner*—he seemed not to mind this affront at all, hanging around for many weeks and reportedly living in a cave up in the hills—when he wasn't living in Joy's little gopi's cell, that is.

Klaus, unsurprisingly, turned out to be German. He'd been in India since 1964, studying *tantric* yoga, apparently with a guru up in the Himalayas. He'd then married a Bengali girl, made himself a dugout canoe, and sailed down the Ganges. Somewhere along the way he'd managed to lose both the canoe and the Bengali girl, and proceeded on by foot. He must have walked more than two thousand miles already, I estimated, but since he was in no hurry and not going anywhere in particular, this meant nothing to him. Tantric yoga has a lot to do with arcane sexual practices—which probably explained why Joy was seen following Klaus Kali Das around the village from the moment he appeared. She was also soon announcing to anyone who'd listen that he was some kind of stand-in for Baba.

I knew Klaus, whatever else he was about, was definitely into some fairly arcane practices when I stumbled across him up in the hills one afternoon. He was standing on one leg with a large rock tied to his penis, which hung well below his knee and was a bright, mottled purple. His other foot was wedged into his groin, his palms were pressed together above his head, and he was repeating "Om Siva" over and over in a voice that rumbled up from the kettledrum of his belly like a military tattoo. I thought better of interrupting him.

There is a pervasive belief in Indian mystical schools that male semen and the life force itself are one and the same thing. Thus, "squandering sperm" is a concept that, in the Indian male, often develops into an obsession and even goes on to blossom into a full-blown mental illness. Throughout history, ascetics who "raise the seed upward" through celibacy and meditation have been deeply revered. But, as the distinguished psychoanalyst and scholar Sudhir Kakar points out in his fascinating study of Indian sexuality, *Intimate Relations* (New Delhi: Penguin, 1989, p. 122), there is an area where celibacy, in its "ultimate if ironic refinement," becomes tantric sex, "where the aspirant is trained and enjoined to perform the sexual act itself without desire and the 'spilling of the seed,' thus divorcing the sexual impulse from human physiology and any conscious or unconscious representation of it." Dr. Kakar terms such a ritual of sex "unbelievably passionless," explaining that it's thought to stir up the semen and evoke "energetic forces that can be rechanneled upwards." He also points out that the actions of Mahatma Gandhi, who was rumored to test his celibacy in old age by sleeping with one or even two young naked women, were just the tail end of a tradition that goes back many centuries. On one hand, Gandhi could resemble Chaitanya, the fifteenth-century founder of the Vaishnavite (Vishnu-worshiping) sect to which Gandhi belonged, and who once banished a devotee distracted by a woman, saying, "I can never again look upon the face of an ascetic who associates with women. The senses are hard to control, and seek to fix themselves on worldly things. Even the wooden image of a woman has the power to steal the mind of a sage. . . ." On the other hand, however, Gandhi could also resemble Ramananda, Chaitanya's devotee and constant companion, who "used to take two beautiful young temple prostitutes into a lonely garden, where he would oil their bodies, bathe, and dress them while himself remaining 'unaffected.' "

Not only is this sex-within-celibacy deeply embedded in the Indian psyche, but the concept of celibacy itself is, curiously, both lauded and derided. Even the *Kama Sutra,* that often graphically illustrated hard-core manual of seduction and copulation, portrays the truly skillful lover as anything but a hot-blooded ladies' man. Instead, his talents come from being above passion, his sensuousness from having mastered the senses through austerities and meditation. As in Eden, the woman and her devious ways challenge the man to overcome desire. No culture on earth ascribes such power to female sexuality as the Indian. Countless myths and fables revolve around men fighting over a woman; and that greatest of all Indian epics, the *Ramayana* itself, unfolds from and around this theme.

In many tales the gods find themselves threatened by a mortal who has seemingly mastered his desires and now progresses up toward their immortal realm by a kind of point system of selfless achievements. Usually, the gods' solution for this cosmic social climber is to beam down a

heavenly nymph he cannot resist. Like Olympic judges, the gods gleefully look on as some poor ascetic who's spent his life in a lonely cave
eating weeds and meditating suddenly has the equivalent of Uma Thur-
man in a gossamer sari draping herself over his bony old body. Even the
emission of a single drop of semen is deemed a catastrophic failure, ban-
ishing him back into the communal cesspit of carnal humanity.

More popular as subject matter than accounts of successful ascetics,
these tales of the noble male finally succumbing to lust include even the
Creator himself. In the *Brahmavaivarta Purana,* we read:

> The heavenly nymph Mohini fell in love with the Lord of creation,
> Brahma. After gaining the assistance of Kama, the god of love, she
> went to Brahma and danced before him, revealing her body to him
> in order to entice him, but Brahma remained without passion.
> Then Kama struck Brahma with an arrow. Brahma wavered and
> felt desire, but after a moment he gained control. Brahma said to
> Mohini, go away, Mother, your efforts are wasted here. I know
> your intention, and I am not suitable for your work. The scripture
> says, "Ascetics must avoid all women, especially prostitutes." I am
> incapable of doing anything that the Vedas consider despicable.
> Mohini laughed and said to him, "A man who refuses to make love
> to a woman who is tortured by desire—he is a eunuch. . . . Come
> now and make love to me in some private place," and as she said
> this she pulled at Brahma's garment. Then the sages bowed to
> Brahma, "How is it that Mohini, the best of all celestial prostitutes,
> is in your presence?" Brahma said, to conceal his scheme, "She
> danced and sang for a long time and then when she was tired she
> came here like a young girl to her father." But the sages laughed
> for they knew the whole secret, and Brahma laughed too.

Rumors of lengthy tantric rituals involving Klaus Kali Das and Joy
abounded among the gossip-prone Westerners of Puttaparthi. It was said
he wore a jade ring at the base of his penis to prevent any possible loss of
that vital fluid, and had trained himself to perform intercourse uninterrupted for twelve hours at a stretch. By the look of Joy during those weeks,
such rumors seemed entirely believable. There was, however, something
about the gigantic German that made it difficult to believe he derived a
purely spiritual satisfaction from this tantric jamboree. He swaggered

around Puttaparthi like a studhorse, terrifying the struggling celibates among the women and tantalizing those men who had often wondered if the tantric path might well be a more pleasurable shortcut to the nirvana they were seeking.

Clearly Joy was not the only eager disciple Klaus acquired during his stay. When a vicious catfight broke out in the village bazaar between her and a New Yorker renamed Bliss, Klaus must have decided it was time to move on. He'd often talked wistfully of hacking himself out another canoe and sailing off down the Chitravati; but the river had dwindled to a stream about a foot wide and an inch deep by now. He finally left on the dawn bus for Anantapur, still wearing his skulls, the begging bowl and trident his only luggage. A month later Bliss left for New York, carrying inside her what she firmly believed was the son of Siva. Two years later I heard she'd miscarried a girl in the fourth month and committed suicide two weeks later.

Joy herself, perhaps feeling her reputation as Baba's bride-to-be and chief gopi was a little tarnished by the whole Klaus episode, left for an extended vacation in Bombay. To those who would listen she explained that Klaus had been Baba in another form, come to elevate her consciousness in a way the guru could not, for obvious reasons, manage to achieve in his usual form. She never returned to Puttaparthi.

ᛣ   ᛣ   ᛣ

Words
Actions
Thoughts
Character
Heart
—SIGN IN PRASANTHI NILAYAM

"Many come for miracles, petty cures, worldly things," Baba once said. "But few of you come for the gift I am here to give you: bliss." This seemed true, and he wasn't referring to Klaus's unfortunate girlfriend. We Westerners were full of intellectual theories, eager for answers to issues of predetermination versus free will, and so on; the Indians sought blessings for businesses, marriages, babies. I once looked at the childlike quotations from Baba painted on tombstonelike slabs of granite planted all over the ashram grounds, and felt very sad that so few of us paid attention to his simple message. "Start the day with love; spend the day with love; end the day with love. This is the way to God," read one. And another: "Love is selflessness, self is lovelessness." It was the very simplicity of Baba's teaching that was so disconcerting.

Yet as the days and weeks and months passed, it was all too easy to sink into petty concerns, all too easy to accept Baba's presence as yet another mundane reality. Seeing him materialize vibhuti, rings, lockets, rosaries, with a wave of the hand—and often so close I could actually watch the moment when an object glittered out of thin air—I still found myself forgetting what it was I really saw: the mastery over laws of nature that made nonsense of contemporary physics. I'd come to think of Baba as the tiny form in an orange robe. It was all too easy to do, and it was a trap.

As the eminent Indian literary scholar Vinayak Krishna Gokak wrote in his book *Sri Sathya Sai Baba: The Man and the Avatar:*

> An avatar is always at work and always at rest. His vision is world-wide and it embraces all the dimensions of Time. He has an effortless command over metempsychosis, *parathahkarana pravesh* or entry into the innermost hearts of others, the power to open up new channels of thinking, the power to exercise the will for the benefaction of individuals or the race, and the power to restore life to the dead. An avatar is an integral manifestation of the Divine.

Without Dr. Gokak's patient encouragement and example, I doubt I would have had the fortitude to persevere with the enigma of Sathya Sai Baba. To see this venerable gray-haired figure, this man of immense erudition, author of some sixteen books, chancellor of a university, sit like a child at Baba's feet or openly weep with emotion when talking about him—this gave me pause whenever I was irritably about to write the whole thing off to experience. Gokak's encyclopedic knowledge of Indian philosophy also helped me free myself of the narrow Christian dogma that prevented my acceptance even of things I'd actually experienced myself.

✤　✤　✤

The Sivarathri Festival, the night of Siva, is held on a full moon sometime in late February or March. This had always been the most important holy day in the year for Baba's devotees, one connected exclusively to the Siva avatar, and one where what most considered Baba's most significant miracle was regularly performed before hundreds of people. As it turned out, I was among those who saw this public miracle for the last time. Baba had often said that the phase of miracles would pass. He also told the early devotees that Puttaparthi would one day be a great city. That seemed absurd for a place barely a village, not even on any map. He also said that there would come a time when the crowds around him would be so large that people would be happy to see a glimpse of him from miles away. On days when there were often no more than thirty or forty people in the ashram and he regularly talked and even sang to us like a friend, this too seemed farfetched.

A huge crowd gathered in the Poornachandra (literally Full Moon) hall as darkness fell. People had been arriving from all over India and beyond during the previous days. The atmosphere crackled with expectation. Brahmin pundits chanted the Vedas as drums thudded and discordant reed horns wailed. The drums and pipes reached a deafening pitch when Baba himself finally entered the packed hall, accompanied by a procession of priests. He looked different, somehow swollen and pained, the way an expectant mother can. Taking his seat behind a little desk on the stage, he seemed uncharacteristically withdrawn, preoccupied, as various students from his colleges and sundry devotees delivered very boring speeches. Finally, he rose and spoke in Telegu, pausing while what he was saying was translated into what was just about English.

As usual, the speech summed up the significance of the holy day, pointing out that the act of creation was the merging of the material with the divine and that we should all try to do the same, blending our lower natures into our higher ones. *Be good, do good, see good*—the message was so ridiculously simple I wondered how Baba found the patience to keep repeating it.

Just as his speeches always seemed to begin at no particular point, so did this one actually stop in the middle of a sentence, as Baba suddenly began singing a *bhajan*. The entire hall echoed his lead, repeating each phrase, the tempo growing toward restrained frenzy until the bhajan abruptly stopped. The chants had quite a rigid form when sung by devotees, but Baba, who had composed them all, prolonged or curtailed them at will. There was a plaintive and honeyed sweetness to his voice. That night the mood was more subdued than it usually was, as if all of us were less preoccupied with our egos and trying to outsing one another. After a mere three or four bhajans, Baba began one that consisted entirely of the phrase *Om Sivaiah, Om Sivaiah, Shambo Shankara Om Sivaiah*—a great booming hymn to Siva, Destroyer of Worlds, Cosmic Dancer. Unlike the previous bhajans, this one appeared to have no ending, and Baba sank into his chair and fell silent, letting the chorus continue without his lead.

A sense that something immensely important was happening descended. The crowd continued to repeat the one phrase in low restrained voices. Baba conducted with his finger, his body occasionally contracting as if in pain. *Om Sivaiah, Om Sivaiah*—the throbbing chant continued with solemn power, every eye in the room fixed on the tiny figure. After some fifteen minutes he suddenly clasped his throat and convulsed, rocking back and forth in his chair. Only fifteen feet away, I thought I saw a kind of dreamy agony in his eyes. There was something truly awesome, rather than frightening, about this spectacle. The bhajan was gradually increasing tempo now, the entire hall thumping with it like the great heart of some vast machine. Then Baba lurched forward, opening his mouth. I glimpsed an odd green glow inside it. He heaved violently, his eyes closing as if he were in pain. Then, with one hand, he began to pull from his mouth what looked like a large, crystalline egg. Indeed, so large was it that blood appeared at the corners of his lips as the object came through. Like a new baby, it was suddenly out. He caught it in a handkerchief, wiped it clean, then transferred it to his other hand as he dabbed at the blood around his mouth and smiled, every bit the proud new mother.

The crowd roared. It was such an extraordinary sight that I felt no one seemed quite sure how to respond. Baba stood, holding up this egg of greenish crystal, inside which a light pulsed like a heartbeat, like something alive. Then something burst inside my heart and I started sobbing uncontrollably. At that moment it was exceedingly hard to doubt that Baba was indeed who he said he was. Here was the symbolic reenactment of Creation itself: the Siva-Shakti force, the *yin* and *yang,* the mighty opposites, the bisecting circles giving birth between them to the *lingam* that represents life itself, life plucked from nothingness. Because of what I felt and saw, I have never for a moment thought that he had swallowed the object earlier and then regurgitated it.

Long after Baba left, leaving the glowing, pulsing lingam in a little stand on his table, everyone sat, as if held like spokes on a wheel to the hub of creation symbolized before us, chanting bhajans until dawn broke. It seemed the only conceivable response to what had happened.

❧   ❧   ❧

Seeing the rose, separating it from the thorn and the shrub, is Concentration. Plucking the rose, separating the heart from the mind and all else, is Contemplation. Offering the rose at the Lord's feet is Meditation.

—SATHYA SAI BABA

One day, several months after arriving in Puttaparthi, I suddenly felt it was time for me to leave, that I'd learned all I could in Sathya Sai Baba's ashram, and that the path of devotion was not to be my path. From all I now understood, God lay within, and *that* was where one ought to start looking for any truth. The holy man's presence seemed to stand in the way of this. Here *he* was God. I'd decided to travel around the country next, to study, to listen, to learn whatever there was to learn from whoever was willing to teach me. But I was also feeling the seductive pull of the material world, I must confess. My idyll was over. On the day I made up my mind to leave, Baba told me he would talk to me. I was shocked.

Finally I found myself walking over the compound to the door of Baba's living quarters. I had wondered for months what was behind it. I stood, looking into a concrete room scarcely larger than a pickup truck and virtually bare. It smelled nice, at least, smelled of the incense that burned in the temple. I've never encountered that fragrance anywhere else.

Several people sat beside me; no one spoke. Baba appeared after the darshan from the compound outside, as he must have done every day I'd been there. He stood, looking at us. He said something about seeing God in everyone, and then, rolling up a sleeve, waved his hand and slowly produced a huge rosary of pink stones. It seemed to emerge from a hole in space just below his palm, swinging in a circle until it was all there, all present in its new dimension. I was no more than a yard from his hand. He presented this sparkling *japamala* to an old Chinese woman, beckoning her and her husband to follow him through a door covered by a cloth flap.

Soon—or maybe not soon—the couple emerged in a daze, followed by Baba, who beckoned someone else inside that other room. Muffled grunts could be heard, and then this person would emerge as if stunned. What was he going to say to me? I didn't want to leave anymore.

Finally I was inside that room. I recall being amazed by how small and bare it was, too. My room at Nagamma's was bigger and more comfortable, and I had regarded my room as a penance. This was also the first time I had ever really stood beside Baba. Like the room, he was unbelievably small. As I looked down into his eyes, trying to think of something to say, I began to shake, gasping with emotion. Quite involuntarily, I said, "I love you, Baba," over and over and over again.

He hugged me, his hair soft as lamb's wool in my face. This surprised me. I'd imagined it would be wiry. *Ba-ba,* I thought absurdly, *the Lamb of God.* Looking down at him, though, I had the odd impression that I was really looking up at him.

"Baba love you, too," he said.

He meant it—I could *feel* it. To *be loved*: That was not the same as to *love.* I had never let myself *be loved* before, I realized.

And I was so grateful that I merely wept more. It was all I could do.

Baba then proceeded to basically deliver a summary of my life and a breakdown of my personality in machine-gun bursts that had me reeling, nodding humbly, speechless. With all my faults, there I was, "the thing itself." It seemed to be his way of reassuring me that there was nothing he did not know about me, and that none of it bothered him. The sum total was, as he usefully confided, "much confusion." I had to agree. He reassured me that he would sort things out. It was a workmanlike statement.

"Thanks," I managed.

He'd moved back by now, and was circling his hand in the space between us. Expecting some trinket, I was surprised to see a white, oily substance appear in his palm. Somehow, I knew what he wanted to do, so I lifted my shirt and let him rub this substance into my chest.

I kept thanking him profusely. Then he said, "Don't worry. I am always with you. Baba love you."

Next thing I knew, I was back in the antechamber.

The subsequent few days are a blur. I recall walking around in a daze, so happy that I couldn't speak. It once crossed my mind to start walking out across the great subcontinent and never stop, never question again what was undeniably true.

Perhaps I should have done that, but I didn't. When I eventually tried to tell people what had happened, I found I was not even sure what *had* happened. Words failed, simply did not adapt to the feelings I wished to express. A week later, I could no longer return my consciousness to wherever it had been at all. It was like waking from a beautiful dream and realizing that you could never ever explain *why* the dream was beautiful. I was certain of only one thing again: I should leave Puttaparthi. As soon as possible.

As my bus finally turned onto the Bangalore road, I felt an enormous sense of relief. As if I'd survived some dreadful test, as if I'd passed through the fire. I hardly knew that person who had arrived there the previous September. Something of him had been burned away, some part I didn't miss. Even the searing air now seemed kinder and cooler. As many have attested, before and since, Puttaparthi is a crucible. It would be twenty years before I physically saw the place again, although in dreams I returned often.

4

"Bhagavan Is Still with Us"

BANGALORE TO TIRUVANNAMALAI, 1975

🌱 🌱 🌱

*So long as the mind remains away from the philosopher's stone, it
remains lost and absorbed in family and friends, it is continually
tossed about by the waves of lust and anger; remains engulfed in
the lure of wealth and possessions, and misses the golden
opportunity of cleansing and transmuting itself. The instinct of love
which God granted us for devotion to Him, we dissipate in
sensuous pleasures. The mind keeps us away from the goal and
never uncovers the Reality which it keeps hidden. The mind is the
great slayer of the Real, and a true devotee must slay the slayer.*

—MARAHAJ CHARAN SINGH, *SPIRITUAL DISCOURSES*

After more than half a year in Puttaparthi, everything I did in Bangalore on returning there made me feel I was wallowing in dissipated,
sensuous pleasures. Indeed, I stayed at the West End Hotel this time, a
sprawling Raj-era establishment set in a giant but unruly garden opposite the racetrack. It desperately needed an overhaul. Everything from
management and staff to rooms and food was sadly decayed. Yet after
Nagamma's concrete box it still represented shameless luxury. I read a history of Tipu Sultan, ruler of Mysore and one of the noblest and most
heroic figures in Indian history. After my diet of spiritual tomes and es-
oterica, it seemed rakishly worldly. Having a drink felt virtually criminal;
I was deeply embarrassed once to be caught guzzling a beer by some Baba
devotees I knew. Even in my new surroundings, something still made me
restless, eager to resume my quest. I soon decided to head off for another
holy spot.

🌱 🌱 🌱

There always seem to be inexplicable problems with transport in India. Planes were overbooked, sometimes by twice the number of seats, or delayed for hours without explanation; trains halted in the middle of nowhere for no apparent reason, sometimes stationary for half a day; and buses had similar quirks, coupled with a hierarchical system far more mysterious than the straightforward three classes of train carriage. There were "luxury buses" of various kinds, and there were ordinary buses. The ordinary bus companies would sell you a ticket without guaranteeing you a seat. However, the unavailability of seats on buses did not prevent people from traveling. The ordinary buses had no glass in their windows and no suspension systems—which, with wooden benches for seats, left you feeling you'd been riding a jackhammer by the end of each journey.

Nor did there appear to be bus stops as such. Everyone who flagged down the vehicle got a ride, along with whatever menagerie accompanied them. Any number of passengers were accommodated in this manner. An hour into any trip and you often had your nose embedded in someone's butt, a chicken on your shoulder, ten people squashed onto your bench, and a herd of goats burping beneath your feet. Anyone wishing to enter or leave the bus by this stage of any trip had to use a window. The marvel of it all was that no one seemed to mind such arrangements.

The luxury buses were supposed to be different. They were supposed to boast upholstered seats, Sun–Dym windows, and even air-conditioning. Again, none of these luxuries was guaranteed, even though a ticket could cost fifty times more than you'd pay for the same journey on an ordinary bus. Before purchasing my ticket for a luxury bus to Tiruvannamalai at the Bangalore terminus, I tried to get the facts straight. Was it air-conditioned? Were there windows? Upholstered seats? And would only those possessing tickets for these seats be allowed to travel? Absolutely, I was assured on all counts.

"Best luxury bus, sahib. *Best!*"

I bought a ticket for a bus leaving early the next day, and set off to spend a solitary evening on the town.

✤ ✤ ✤

It is my belief that our basic task is to guarantee material welfare of our people—full employment and the satisfaction of their needs for food, clothing, housing, education of their children and adequate leisure. I cannot be-

lieve that principles of natural justice and human rights can be honoured
unless people are assured of economic wealth. —TIPU SULTAN, 1788

Bangalore is unusually dark at night, a consequence of all the unlit parks
and public gardens responsible for its title, "Garden City."

Off M.G. Road—Mahatama Gandhi Road—ran Brigade Road, a
mildly disreputable street of bars, restaurants, and many bookstalls selling
salacious movie magazines. Their covers flashed photographs of busty
Bombay starlets—hot items even back then. On sidewalk corners, vendors roasted corncobs over charcoal, basting them with salt, lime juice,
and spices.

An especially terrifying crew of beggars also worked this strip. A boy
whose spine had been tied in a reef knot at birth bounded along after me
in the dirt on all fours, nearly naked, his limbs gnarled and filthy and mottled by blackened sores. He gazed up hopefully, his face almost serenely
beautiful, with clear, bright eyes that seemed to hold no resentment or
pain. A belief in *karma* and reincarnation entirely changes Western notions of luck and egalitarianism. When I handed him a rupee and the bag
of milk candies I'd just bought, he smiled like a saint in paradise. A leper
who would never smile again, his face having melted, leaving only slits
for eyes, thrust out the bandaged stumps of what had been his fingers.
Another creature with no arms or legs wriggled through the cow shit,
dust, and garbage like a filthy sack of rice with a head. Somehow he kept
a cigarette always burning in his mouth, which had countless other functions to perform, not the least of which was picking up coins or gifts of
food and secreting them in a pocket positioned below his thick, muscular neck. An old blind man with frosted pearls for eyes had tied his right
hand by a length of rope to the neck of a young boy, who led him around.
It was an image of hideous symbiosis, the boy and the blind man forced
to share the charity their partnership earned, till death did them part.

Brigade Road, in 1975, often seemed like the City of Dreadful Night
itself. But after Prasanthi Nilayam, everywhere was Babylon at best. Here
a dollar would buy you a ten-year-old hooker for the night; a girl of eighteen was thirty cents; a boy was ten cents. You could still buy a teenage
girl to use in any way you wished forever—wife, slave, both—for less than
a hundred. Today she would cost at least four hundred. And it was rumored that even more refined pleasures were available to those less easily pleased: For ten dollars you could watch a beggar being slowly hacked

to death by two men with machetes . . . or do the job yourself, if *that* was what you needed.

I sat in a bar with no name next to the Band Box Cleaners and drank a furtive rum with fresh lime soda, the finest drink in India.

"You like to buy some silk, maybe?" the barman asked.

I said no.

"Then what you like, sir? Some ivory statue, yes?"

"No."

"My friend, he give you best price. Just look, not buy."

I said no more forcefully. The barman shrugged and carried on swabbing tables with an indescribably filthy rag. A dapper old Muslim in a fez, his gray beard dyed a hellish orange by years of henna, sat next to me, smoking cigarettes and drinking black tea from a glass. The nails on his little fingers were more than an inch long and had been painted with crimson lacquer apparently some months before.

"It is most tiresome to be bothered when you relax, I think?" he asked rhetorically.

I agreed.

"I perceived accurately, isn't it?" he continued.

"You did. Most observant of you."

"I think you are a man of taste, yes?"

Who could argue with a statement like that?

"I will show you some very rare and beautiful carpets," he announced, cutting off my inchoate objection with "But just for their beauty, you understand. Not to buy—just to see . . ."

I told him I had no time now or in the foreseeable future.

"Buy if you wish," he said. "But just look for the beauty." He sighed just thinking of it. "We are men who appreciate beauty, are we not?"

Exasperated, I paid for my drink and left. Behind me the old Muslim was saying, "Then tomorrow, my friend? I meet you tomorrow?"

I arrived at the bus station just after six-thirty to leave the Kingdom of Mysore (now Karnataka state) and catch the seven o'clock to Tiruvannamalai. By 6:50 there was still no sign of the bus, so I asked what had happened to it.

"Leaving 6:00 A.M.," answered a man with teeth that grew from his gums almost horizontally.

"No," I complained. "It's the 7:00 A.M. bus I want."

"Yesyes," the man told me impatiently. "Seven A.M. bus leaving 6:00 A.M. today."

"But that would make it the 6:00 A.M. bus, surely?"

"No, sir. Seven A.M. can leave at 6:00 A.M."

"What about the passengers?"

"They are informed by notice." He indicated a chalkboard covered in what could have been runes. After much persistence, I discovered that there would be another bus at 8:00.

"Luxury bus?"

"Complete luxury."

At 7:45 a bus was pointed out to me. Almost brand-new, it had darkly tinted windows, a huge air-conditioning unit on the roof, and reclining airplane seats.

"Only ticket holders allowed?" I asked.

The driver nodded proudly.

It was not even full as we pulled out of the bus terminal, conditioned air pouring like springwater over the deeply cushioned seats, and a shaded world passing by outside. I couldn't believe my luck. The deliciously icy air alone was worth the price of admission.

About half an hour out of town, the bus pulled into a small enclosure of chai stalls made of straw and rotting wood.

"Tea already?" I asked no one in particular.

As the driver opened the door onto a blinding landscape of white heat, he casually called out, "Change bus, change bus."

The other passengers obediently hauled their luggage from the racks and started to troop out. I reluctantly followed suit, muttering to myself.

Standing once more unprotected by luxury in the south Indian inferno, I blinked around owlishly, looking for the bus we were supposed to be continuing our journey in. The only vehicle visible was an exceptionally ordinary bus: open windows, a patchwork of amateur welding jobs all over its battered body, roof rack with the contents of a small town tied to it. As my fellow travelers began to climb uncomplainingly into this ruin, I wanted to pull them out, read them their rights, form a resistance front.

Cornering the driver while he slurped tea, I demanded an explanation.

"Bus change this place."

Why were we moved to an ordinary bus when we had luxury tickets?

"Luxury bus stop here. No permit going Madras side."

Dripping with sweat and fury, I plunked down on the hard wooden seat of the ordinary bus, which was still steadily filling up with locals. I gazed longingly after the luxury bus and my dreams of luxury gliding silently away—heading back to Bangalore to hoodwink more fools, no doubt. There was no point in asking why the bus had no permit to travel outside Karnataka state even though it claimed to be going far out of that state.

An elderly man with the body of a thin twelve-year-old edged toward the seat beside me. His testicles dangled a foot down the side of a thread-bare dhoti. So bad were the smallpox scars on his birdlike face that he might have once survived two barrels of buckshot fired point-blank. He sat down gingerly on the farthest edge of the vacant seat, as if I might not notice he was there, gradually sliding across until I felt the hard, bony knob of his pelvis press against my cushioned thigh. He wore a turban the size of a laundry bag, whose musty orange cotton tickled my ear when he moved. Plucking a giant beedie seemingly from his left armpit, he barely had the weedy cone smoldering before succumbing to a bout of cough-ing that doubled him up. Lungs finally subdued, disciplined, he sat erect, looking satisfied. Then he spat a wobbling golf ball of ocher phlegm on the floor. I peered down. The bolus quivered barely an inch from my foot. I looked over at him, expecting remorse. He sucked beedie smoke contentedly from a clenched fist and seemed not to notice me at all.

In the aisle, a goat was nonchalantly expelling several gleaming black pellets from below the raised stump of its tail. Some fell into the lap of a toothless woman wearing gold earrings as big and heavy as paperweights. She retrieved one pellet in shaking fingers no thicker than dead twigs, in-specting it with a connoisseur's eye. Then she kneaded it, flattened it, rolled it back into a ball, and tossed it to the floor.

The bus had not even moved yet. For a journey that would take pos-sibly twelve hours, this was not a good sign. After twenty minutes, the only vacant seat left was behind the steering wheel, and the aisle resem-bled a rowdy farmers' market. Everyone kept up a rasping monologue that continued to grow in volume because no one was listening to any-one else; babies howled; a spitting contest was well under way, the dust outside spattered with gobs of mucus and betel juice like crushed rasp-berries.

A man I bet myself a hundred rupees was the driver eventually am-bled from a chai stall across the dusty compound. Barefoot, he wore pajama-striped shorts, a soiled sleeveless undershirt riddled with gaping holes, and a tea towel wrapped around his head. This was the unofficial uniform of all south Indian drivers. Bounding with apelike agility into his seat, he looked around at the overheated ark-on-wheels that he captained, as if uncertain whether it was full enough to warrant leaving yet. Then he lit a crackling beedie, hit an air horn that almost ripped my eardrums out, and started up what sounded like the engine of an ancient combine harvester. After a brutal altercation with the gearbox, he had us smashing and swaying over ruts and rocks out onto the open road.

An hour later we had stopped five times to pick up a few more farmyards, two Tamil nuns, and a woman with an ass like a sofa. She made her way belligerently down the aisle, then lowered herself beside the man next to me. Soon she'd squeezed him practically into my lap, sighing mightily. She carried a huge plastic holdall, much repaired and reinforced with various kinds of string. From this she pulled a kerosene pressure stove, gave its brass torso a good pump, then placed it by her feet *and actually lit it*. After adjusting the roaring bracelet of flame to her satisfaction, she next produced an old aluminum saucepan tied in a cloth to hold its lid on. She unwrapped this, peered beneath the lid at what smelled like stewed moss in tamarind gravy, and finally placed it on the sputtering blue fire below. These exertions required that she angrily shift three hundred pounds of buttock until she'd achieved the extra room she needed for her culinary work. I was half out the window by now, and the little man had drawn his feet up and was perched on two square inches, like a squirrel, with his chin resting on his knees. The heat and smell from the kerosene stove grew unbearable.

"This is ridiculous!" I told the woman finally. "You can't cook a bloody meal on a bus. It's dangerous. It's probably against the law, too. Why didn't you bring a packed lunch?"

I felt like John Cleese in *Fawlty Towers*.

The woman gave me an evil, uncomprehending glare and went on unpacking a pile of *chappatis*, a stainless-steel container of lime pickles, and another of homemade yogurt. Then she bent to stir her pot with an absurdly small teaspoon, releasing a mighty fart as she did so.

"Jesuschristalmighty!" I exclaimed loudly, appealing to the other passengers for support.

No one knew remotely what I was going on about. Some even looked as if they wished they'd brought stoves along, too, glancing enviously at the steaming pot. Indians are punctual and fussy eaters, incapable of missing a proper meal. They are also deeply suspicious of food cooked by others.

The old man beside me did not seem in the least bit bothered by any of this. He continued to puff on beedies, staring blankly at the untamed expanse of scrub, rocks, and steep hills passing by, its color increasingly bleached by a climbing sun that was almost white behind the veil of dust usurping air and sky.

❦   ❦   ❦

> *The poor benighted Hindu,*
> *He does the best he kin do,*
> *Sticks to his caste,*
> *From first to last,*
> *And for trousers just lets his skin do.*
> —ANONYMOUS LIMERICK FROM THE RAJ ERA

I reminded myself that someday all this would seem merely funny. And I had to admire the woman's ability to set up an entire kitchen and dining table in what little space she could steal on a moving bus, without spilling a drop of anything or setting herself on fire. Within fifteen minutes, the stove was out and she was serving herself fresh hot vegetable curry with warm chappatis, sliced mango, pickles, and yogurt. The size of her prodigious lap came in handy. Nestled in the folds of her sari, every container had its place, and she seemed no less comfortable on a moving bus than if she were sitting at a restaurant table.

Then she spooned a selection of this ingenious meal onto a chappati and offered it to me. She fed the little old man, too, and we all munched away hungrily. Hoping she'd not understood a word I'd said during her cooking, I fished out some plantains I'd bought in Bangalore and divided them among us. All of a sudden, three strangers had become three friends having a picnic.

❦   ❦   ❦

> *All deeds are traps, except ritual deeds. Hence the need for selfless action.*
> —THE *BHAGAVAD GITA*

We pulled in to Tiruvannamalai just after nightfall. Even the long, cramped, bone-battering ride seemed to pass quickly. I think I actually managed a nap as well, head pillowed on my elbow, cooled by that illusion of wind the bus created as it sped, hooting, through the brutal summer day.

Some three hundred kilometers southeast of Bangalore, Tiruvannamalai rests on the edge of the Javadi Hills in the heart of Tamil Nadu state. It's an ancient realm, heart of popular Hinduism's dramatic evolution into its contemporary polytheistic forms; seat too of once-mighty empires, birthplace of great cultures that flourished when Europe was a nasty, brutish wasteland. It is also the site of countless bloody battles, the territorial line drawn and held against many would-be invaders. In the south there linger still faint glimpses of ancient India, that lush, rich, fabled land that drew the invading Aryans to it three millennia ago to live like the Dravidian inhabitants they found there. *Like* them, but not *with* them. The caste system these Aryans devised was, as its Sanskrit name shows, a color bar, with them on one side and the small, dark-skinned peoples they had conquered on the other.

Traces of that earthly paradise remain: an ordered society free of strife and of any extreme inequalities, blessed by a climate and land where nature gave all things freely in abundance, allowing time for thought, for philosophy, for the development of art and architecture. Most histories claim the Aryans from the Russian steppes brought civilization to the wandering hostile tribes of the subcontinent; yet an increasing body of evidence supports the traditional Indian view that civilization actually began in India, and the Aryans—like many after them—came to get it.

Fierce and forbidding as the central southeast is on the surface, its inhabitants seem not to notice the inferno their sun generates. Indeed, they thrive in it, even asserting that they would want to live nowhere else. Children of the sun? They *must* be, to love such a harsh parent. Temperatures over 113° Fahrenheit are not uncommon, falling on winter nights as far down as 72 degrees, exceptionally cold to natives.

Under cover of a seething darkness, Tiruvannamalai seemed to smolder as we neared it. Smoky, flickering yellow flames of oil tapers, the only lights apparent, added to the impression that one had reached the outskirts of Hades. This reaction was so very Western, and it dismayed me. A great deal of the medieval Christian imagery depicting Satan and his evil domain can be traced to stories told by travelers returning from the East without grasping even a shred of the richly complex cultures they had been exposed to—often for years. The talents of the Eastern mind, in its instinctive use of symbols, its affinity for allegory and myth, its genius for paralogic capable of extrapolating a treatise on philosophy from a single image, still both fascinate and baffle the plodding, linear West.

I bade farewell to my traveling companions, headed from the bus, and was suddenly besieged by shadowy figures with faces that gleamed in lamplight, each of them offering a service: hotels, taxis, friendship, merchandise. Beneath a nearby tree sat a man with no legs selling shoelaces. In a country where hardly anyone owns shoes, and the rest wear sandals, business must be atrocious, I thought. I purchased a set of black laces out of sheer pity, handing over two rupee bills and telling the man to keep the change. He wouldn't, and embarked on such a complicated process of sending an urchin to seek the ten paise he owed me that I started regretting the purchase. Nothing in India comes easy. A dozen chai stalls and nearby vendors could not break a rupee bill, so the urchin was dispatched farther afield, while the legless man called over all manner of passersby, until a fair crowd had gathered. Everyone had theories to help solve this problem. I kept trying to leave, but no one would hear of it. My problem must be worked out satisfactorily. You'd have thought they were tackling a Middle East peace proposal.

After twenty minutes, the urchin returned with two other urchins and a fat man wearing spectacles, which were held together over his broad, oily nose with electrical tape. The urchins seemed very pleased with themselves. The fat man rummaged in his shirt pocket and produced two square five-paise coins, which he triumphantly displayed to all but held on to tenaciously, embarking on a protracted discussion with the legless man, presumably about how the latter would eventually reimburse him. Some pretty complicated financial angles must have been proposed before the fat man finally handed the coins to the shoelace vendor, who inspected them dubiously for some minutes, obviously getting the economics straight in his mind. Then he passed them up to me, and I handed them on to the senior urchin, which no one appeared to mind in the least.

The crowd was still deep in debate—no doubt weighing the philosophical ramifications of it all—as I hoisted my bag and followed a wiry little fellow who promised me that his taxi was the finest on earth.

It turned out to be a *tonga,* a bullock cart fitted with the kind of roof covered wagons in the American Wild West possessed, but much smaller and made of wood. After five minutes of persuading this driver that I did not want to go to his friend's hotel—had already arranged to stay at the ashram of Ramana Maharshi, was absolutely 100 percent certain about this—we finally set off.

There is a scientific institute exclusively devoted to researching the improvement of the bullock cart in India. So far the boffins have come up with one noticeable improvement: fitting pneumatic truck tires to the cart. This particular vehicle, however, had undergone no such radical overhaul; its hand-hewn teak wheels wavered around a bowed axle, causing a boatlike motion to its passenger, complete with mild nausea. The tonga was painted in brilliant swirling psychedelic patterns, and the bullock itself was so extravagantly decorated with sparkling tassels and jingling bells that I felt like part of a traveling circus. Bullocks may be strong, but they are not fleet of foot. We moved at an agonizing pace, overtaken by cycles, cows, pedestrians, and anything else on the road.

A mother-of-pearl moon, all but full, had slid secretively up the velvet sky, plating rooftops with milky silver, scattering diamonds over shadowed fields. The pyramid silhouette of Arunachala, the holy mountain, loomed dark and massive at the edge of town, its wedge revealing just how full of lights and countless mottled shades of blue and purple the enormous night sky surrounding it really was. And beneath the mountain, glazed by a moonlight almost dripping from their stones, the soaring gopura of Tiruvannamalai's vast and ancient Siva-Parvati temple reached two hundred feet upward, like fists punching the envelope of heaven. Arunachaleswara was its potent, resounding name.

"Templetemple," the driver pointed out helpfully. "Too big, this one."

Too frequently means very in India; in this case, though, it seemed appropriate. The temple—all twenty-five acres of it—did appear too big for the small town crouching beyond its walls. Many call it the largest temple in all of India. Here in the south, where the cult of devotion and idols first emerged as a popular alternative to the Brahmin-dominated Sanskrit path of knowledge, endure most of the largest temple complexes ever built on earth. Only Egypt exceeds in grandeur the breathtaking work of early Indian stonemasons; unlike those of Karnak and Luxor, these Indian temples still dominate the lives of those dwelling in their shadows as they did several centuries ago, and, deep within the holy of holies, still house Hinduism's living gods. The idol is not God, Hindu scholars will tell you, but God is the idol. . . .

The road curved along one side of Arunachala's steep and sacred slopes, heading up an incline that soon slowed our festive bullock to a standstill. The driver steered by twisting the animal's tail. Now he cheerfully inserted two fingers into its anus, as well. This action caused immediate and sprightly acceleration, the beast fairly dancing off over the crunching gravel, shaking the tonga so violently my head took several savage cracks against the roof beams before I found a plank to anchor myself with.

❧   ❧   ❧

I saw no light save that which came from within my heart. Much as I battered my head in the mosque and looked for it in the temple.
                                                    —BAHADUR SHAH ZAFAR

Sri Ramana ashram, a collection of low buildings and a small *mandir* bunched at the foot of the mountain, glowed palely in the swarming night. Its gates were shut, and it seemed utterly deserted. Perhaps the place had closed. Its guru, Ramana Maharshi, had died back in 1950, so I did not expect to find crowds. But I certainly expected to find the place open.

Happy to have the driver's fingers out of its anus, the bullock yawned, proceeding to chew the ashram hedge. Leaping from his perch, the driver shouted something that sounded like *Beestiwallahpa!* and rattled the compound gates violently.

No matter where you are in India, someone is always around. Soon an old man with a lonely white tuft of hair sprouting from the crown of his skull, wearing only a ribbon of material held over his loins by a string belt, staggered from the shadows, muttering irritably. The driver explained things in a cantankerous tone, and the old man shone a feeble flashlight at me. He then grumbled at the driver.

"This old man, he priest-man," the driver explained cogently. "You go with him for you sleeping, hah?"

"Hah."

I followed our priest, who looked like the world's oldest Venice Beach boy, hobbling around in that jockstrap. Instead of heading into the ashram, he tottered across the road, down into a ditch full of long grass and brambles. Hidden in this jungle was a gate leading through a low fence into more jungle. He flung aside branches that lashed back against my face. The air thronged with things that droned, buzzed, flew, and, as I quickly found, stung quite efficiently, as well. I was tearing a cobweb the size of a Chinese fishing net off my head when the old man pointed at the door of a low white concrete building. A padlock of medieval dimensions hung from the door's bolt. He rummaged in his loincloth and produced a sizable key to prod at the lock until it finally clicked open. Almost throwing himself at the two sections of door, the old priest burst through them, flicking on a light switch. The tiny bulb throbbed its feeble light over quite a nice little room: two Spartan beds, a table, a door concealing what was presumably the bathroom. The old man handed me the massive padlock and its key and headed back into the night, grunting and hissing to himself.

I bolted the door, looking forward to a wash. My hair felt like the brittle synthetic material you stuff sofas with. The little door led indeed to a small room equipped with a tap, bucket, and well-worn squatter. I opened the tap, which dripped for several seconds then shuddered mightily, spewing out a torrent of orange mud before settling back to dripping. Light ebbed and flowed from another jaundiced little bulb, creating an unnerving impression of incipient eye trouble or brain failure. Disappointed, I sat, watching the tap drip. Without any warning, a stream of crystal-clear water suddenly shot out with the force of a fire hose, soaking the room and me. I hurriedly stripped, and washed with soap and bucket. Just as I'd lathered myself from hair to toes, the pitiful electrical current died. I was plunged into a darkness so complete I could see only atoms and molecules dancing. Remembering that there had been no windows, only a sort of recess near the rear ceiling, I stopped waiting for my eyes to adjust and continued my bath as a blind man.

Washed and very weary, I groped my way back and lay down on sheets that felt like hot sacks. Within seconds, something winged swept past my nose and something large buzzed near my right ear. Soon several smaller things had prodded red-hot needles into various extremities. I tore at the sheets and wrapped myself in items I could not identify, all of them, I suspected, woven from hog bristle. It would be a long night—not the long night you get when you can't sleep, but the interminable one that imprisons you because you keep waking up. At one desperate point I stumbled off the pallet and rummaged blindly through my bag for a box of mosquito coils I'd sensibly brought along, locating it with scarcely believable ease. It was the matches I couldn't find. And waking again after three minutes a decade long, I had the distinct impression someone was in the room, watching me. I shouted out, and was convinced I heard foot-steps tiptoe off through the walls, back into that endless night.

❧   ❧   ❧

I did not so much awake to find that a dim, cloudlike dawn light had re-turned form and substance around me as struggle back up to conscious-ness using my nervous system as rope, too wary of the mind's tricks to be convinced the night was really over. Boy, did I ache, and my body was spattered with red welts. Half the jungle had been guzzling my blood, throwing a booze-up at my place all night. I rubbed my puffed eyes. It took me some moments to realize that a very small man in a fur body-suit was riffling my bag, quietly picking out items of interest and putting them to one side.

"Oi!" I yelled, leaping up.

The monkey bared its teeth at me, grabbed a plastic tub of diarrhea pills, and bounded across the room to make a mighty leap for the recess in the far wall. Which was not a recess, I now saw, but a narrow rectan-gular opening leading outside. Safely out of reach, the monkey looked down mockingly, proceeded to open the tub, and started to eat its con-tents with relish.

I began to laugh. Two of those diarrhea pills did the trick; sixty or so would probably turn a monkey's bowels into concrete for a month.

It seemed to know something was up—I wasn't supposed to be laugh-ing—but continued crunching away. It was not alone, either. Three more pairs of mischievous eyes peered down at me from behind its back, no doubt assessing my potential as a victim.

I now realized how feverish I felt, wondering if these monkeys were malarial hallucinations. Then I noticed the sensation of molten lead swiftly gurgling out of nowhere and streaming through my guts. . . .

I made it to the squatter just in time, yodeling in pain as cramps and spasms exploded like land mines everywhere south of my waist. Sweat poured from my now-scalding brow like rain. All I could think of was the fat woman on the bus and her bloody food. Then I remembered the *pakoras* I'd bought in Brigade Road from a man who made them right there on a grimy wooden slab amid the blowing dust, open sewers, and diesel fumes, frying them in what could well have been used engine oil.

Half an hour later, feeling fifty years older, very humble, and as if I'd received an enema with Liquid-Plumr, I decided it was safe to venture more than a yard from the toilet facilities. I sincerely doubted I'd ever eat again as I crept out and headed toward the ashram, each step making even my hair hurt.

The tidy little compound bustled, people scuttling to and fro with stainless-steel pails, jasmine malas, bales of banana leaves, and straw brooms, their fists full of incense. What they were up to, I wasn't entirely sure. The average age here seemed to be eighty. Most of the withered old men were clad in scanty white loincloths, just like my priestly concierge the previous night, and all the women wore cheap white cotton widows' saris. Even ashrams have their own uniforms.

A glance at photographs of Ramana Maharshi himself explained much. Cropped white hair and beard, with a kindly face and deeply compassionate eyes, and all he seemed to have ever worn on his slender little body was a skimpy white loincloth. It made him look curiously babyish—an adult in a diaper.

An office labeled OFFICE struck me as a good destination. In it a burly Brahmin, his sacred thread making him look overdressed, looked up from the letter he was smoothing out on a tidy little desk.

"You can stay two days only," he stated rather severely.

I told him I only wanted to stay two days. Then I mentioned the monkeys.

"This is India," he replied. "Monkeys will be there."

I suggested that some bars or netting on the recess would easily prevent monkeys from being there. He waved this theory aside like a fly. Then I recounted the recent saturnalia in my guts.

"You foreigners are not able to eat our food."

I waited for sympathy, receiving only a casual suggestion that I might try eating solely curds and plantains for a few days.

"You may eat them in dining hall," he offered generously, rattling off the times when I could do so. "All times must be punctual," he cautioned. "This is ashram, not hotel."

Some malevolent entity was again striking matches in my lower intestine as I made my way into the mandir for a ritual the official had told me about. Small but opulent, this structure contained little more than a white marble tomb. I assumed it must be where the Maharshi was interred, but soon learned it housed the remains of his mother. The ceremony in progress was an offering of milk to her, who, in typically Hindu fashion, had come to represent the Mother. The cult of a guru is frequently self-contained. The guru becomes in effect your god, and his wife or mother or sister becomes your goddess. It's a family affair.

I knew little about Ramana Maharshi, let alone his mother, and felt like an intruder amid the hushed boredom of this ceremony. The cloying smell of steaming buffalo milk was also getting to me. The whole temple, with its extravagant profusion of white marble, began to make me think of milk. Then a white-hot shoal of starving piranhas thrashed in my colon without warning and I had to tear back across the road.

Ten minutes later, I staggered off the squatter, gasping. Only then did I notice the thorough ransacking my room had recently undergone. Everything once in my bag was strewn over the floor, much of it under the beds. Anything made of paper had been chewed or torn to shreds. A bottle of antibiotics had been smashed, the two-tone capsules scattered among shards of brown glass—obviously not as tasty as the diarrhea pills.

Wearily I scooped it all up, placing everything I possessed—smashed glass included—under the spare mattress. Flopping onto my bed, I fantasized awful revenges, dreadful traps, simian holocausts.

☙ ☙ ☙

I'd missed breakfast but I thought I'd give plantains and curds a shot at lunch. Another occupant was in the office as I passed, an ancient little man whose visage looked even kinder and more compassionate than photographs of the Maharshi's had.

He greeted me in a high-pitched voice. "Welcome, welcome, dear friend. Please sit down. Where have you come from, is it?"

I told him. He seemed delighted. "Oh, wonderful, wonderful," he kept repeating.

I eventually got around to the monkeys and my guts. He suddenly looked as if he were about to burst into tears, shaking his head.

"Dear, dear, how terribly *terrible!*" He paused for quite a while, deep in thought. Then he brightened. "Bhagavan says the mind is like monkey. . . ."

I nodded, familiar with the metaphor. For want of a better response, I told him I wished I'd been able to meet Ramana Maharshi myself.

The old man smiled sweetly. "Bhagavan is still here."

"Huh?"

"He is still here, with us."

"Where?"

He pointed behind me. *"There."*

I turned, not really expecting to see Ramana Maharshi.

The man laughed. "Let me take you to Bhagavan's room, and you will see."

I followed his astonishingly athletic little form out of the office. His step was light and springy, as if that happy old heart inside him had wings. We walked down a tidy series of narrow pathways lined with flowering shrubs to a neat and tiny whitewashed structure. He unlocked its flimsy door. Inside was a small and spotlessly clean space like some cramped student lodging. It was unremarkable in every way—except that time in there had stopped at 1950: a cabinet of medicine bottles from the forties; a rickety little pallet dating earlier; an Edwardian child's desk with yellowed papers, inkstand, and cheap nib pen; a chair even humbler than the one Van Gogh immortalized; some worn pieces of cloth crisply folded upon makeshift shelves. Not much else.

"This is where Bhagavan left his body," explained the cheerful old man. "I was with him, you know. . . . How many times did we lucky souls sit at his feet right here, listening as God's Truth poured from those dear lips. . . .

"Come," he urged. "Sit for a while. You will soon see that Bhagavan is still with us. Where would he go, hmm? Sit and ask all your questions. You will see how clearly he answers. Come when you are finished so I may lock the door." He paused, eyes raised, staring inside himself. "Unlock *your heart,* my dear friend, and Bhagavan will undoubtedly speak to you."

He shut the door firmly behind him. I sat on the smooth clay tile floor by the Maharshi's bare little bed. Birds sang outside in the molten-gold sunlight. It was almost cool in the room, though, cool and peaceful, and outside time. I noticed, among a few other meager possessions the Maharshi had owned, a worn steel pocket watch. What had he wanted with time?

❧   ❧   ❧

Who am I? Where did I come from and how? Who is my real mother? Who is my father?
—ADI SANKARACHARYA, SIXTEENTH CENTURY

Adi Sankaracharya's fundamental query really summed up Ramana Maharshi's meditational method. You dwelt relentlessly on these five questions, and, if your efforts were hard and sincere enough, you finally realized the Truth. The Maharshi eventually reduced the query to three points: *Who am I? Why am I? Where am I going?* It was the nondualistic path, the path of *jnana,* or knowledge. It required fierce and rigorous mental discipline. Perhaps that formidable intellect was what I felt still energizing his room. The end result of jnana yoga was supposed to be the realization that the Self, the universe, and God are one. The All is the One.

Sitting there in the peace and silence, cocooned within the Maharshi's energy field, such vast concepts seemed less forbidding to me, even accessible. A pleasant tingling pressure massaged my brain. I felt quiet and calm, untroubled by thought, almost part of the world, purified by the purity and simplicity of a man who had died where I sat, a quarter of a century before.

᛫ ᛫ ᛫

The millions of hours spent pondering over these questions in 'Samadhi'
in Himalayan caves have brought us no answers. No prophet, mystic, guru
or godman has got us out of the cul-de-sac of our ignorance.
—KHUSHWANT SINGH, *WE INDIANS*

Truth can be only experienced, never explained. Explanations need language, the subject and object of duality, and can thus never touch the nondual. Otherwise so unerring in his assessments, Khushwant Singh, one of India's greatest men of letters, is oddly, cantankerously limited when it comes to mystical philosophy. Of meditation he once said, "You can wake up a man who is sleeping but not one who is awake." And "Mystic exaltation is no more rewarding than euphoria produced by a slug of Scotch whisky."

Every cell that constituted me seemed to hum now, as if my entire being had just received a badly needed tune-up. The tranquil little room suddenly looked very familiar. I noticed birds were singing again. What really shocked me was that my watch showed two hours had just passed. I'd missed lunch—not that this bothered me or my alimentary canal. In a pleasant daze, I went to find that man from the office.

He was just walking from the mandir, and, seeing me, he clasped his palms in greeting.

"Was I right?" he asked, beaming.

I nodded, tongue-tied. He seemed to understand.

"Now you must visit Bhagavan's cave," he told me, producing a bunch of plantains. "You missed your lunch, so I brought you these. Oh, I am so happy you were able to come."

❧   ❧   ❧

The cave was reached by a fairly taxing walk up and around the steep side of Arunachala. As caves go, it was roomy; but, like most caves, it was also gloomy—a place of concentrated inner toil. The necessary darkness before the dawn, perhaps, but that did not stop there being something leaden and oppressive about it.

Ramana Maharshi is one of those Indian holy men within living memory whose genuineness no one seems to question. As with those of Ramakrishna, Yogananda, Shirdi Sai Baba, Aurobindo, Ananda Moya Ma, and Swami Ramdas, the Maharshi's picture is found in stores, homes, and temples all over India. Like them, also, he is dead.

We prefer religious figures this way, of course. It guarantees they won't shatter our illusions. They can't eat messily, or fart, or get ill, or look bored when they're dead. And, as I'd found with Sathya Sai Baba, living masters are also confusing—how can you reconcile their form with the Formless? Even the photographs most commonly seen of dead holy men are the most idealized ones available. Almost the only living holy man in India to enjoy a similarly universal respect as these dead ones is the Dalai Lama of Tibet. He doesn't seem to have offended anyone yet, except the Chinese government.

Even the most commonly seen pictures of Sathya Sai—who dramatically divides opinion—portray him with all the somewhat repugnant and ritualized formality of a temple idol. Most photographs of Ramana Maharshi, however, reveal him as all too human—although the best-known ones show wisdom and deep compassion glowing behind the veil of flesh. Teachers are more revered than worshiped; only gods make it as calendar pinups.

Maharshi's story is conventional by the standards of Indian mysticism: a difficult childhood, inner struggles, long periods of self-imposed isolation, austerities, meditation. Then the final realization, followed by a lifetime of living and teaching it.

A *jnani* is an exponent of the path of knowledge. Ramana Maharshi's dualistic philosophy is termed *advaita,* yet it is less forbidding and more human than most advaita teachings, because it contains many elements of *bhakti,* or devotional yoga. Yoga—bhakti and jnana and karma (self-less work) varieties included—means union with God. Like many *muni,* or silent teachers, Ramana Maharshi seemed to operate more through the effect of his very presence on his devotees than through his words. Sathya Sai seemed to work in a similar way at times on me, but everyone saw him differently. Indeed, he falls into no category. Maharshi wrote almost nothing. He may not even have known how to write. The books "by" him or about him tend to be notes and transcriptions of talks and dialogues with disciples.

He taught advaita by his own example, as well as through a sort of inner supervision of those meditation techniques he gave to his disciples. One of these techniques involved the Sanskrit mantra *neti neti*—literally "not this, not that"—with which one approaches Truth by listing what it is not. This is something like blotting out the information all your five senses give you and then seeing what is left of you and the world.

Such meditation practices require tremendous powers of patience and concentration. Scoffers should attempt these themselves before dismissing them. Most of us cannot focus the mind on a single thought for more than a few seconds at a stretch. Jnana yoga requires you to hold the mind steady for periods of twelve hours or more. You must devote many years of practice to it, too, before you can hope to make any progress or realization or transformation.

Popular misconception—even by Indians themselves—considers meditation a blanking out of the mind, a sort of waking sleep. This is not true. It is impossible to blank out the mind, even in sleep. One's babbling brooks and streams and rivers of thought vanish into the One Thought, the divine ocean that underlies the final Truth. True meditation is preceded by years of learning just how to concentrate correctly, so it may be better described as a form of superconcentration. A more accurate analogy compares the mind to a lake, thoughts being the ripples disturbing its surface. When the lake is calm, its surface becomes like a mirror, reflecting perfectly the heavens above it, no different from the heavens. Meditation is the process by which you calm those ripples.

Techniques vary: attending to each thought as it arises without pursuing any one of them; following the stream of thoughts back to its source; or supplanting all thoughts by supreme efforts of concentration on one single thought. Breathing and thought are intimately connected in this. Other methods can involve artificially controlling one's breathing; or focusing on the elusive point where inhalation and exhalation meet, like dwelling on that moment when the future becomes the past. Like eternity, the present exists outside time. So the eternal is the present. To live completely in the present is the sole object of meditation, the calming of the ripples, the one great mystical goal, the resolution of opposites, attainment of enlightenment, union with God, Truth, Love, nirvana, heaven, fulfillment—and ten thousand other concepts humankind has called the sole purpose of existence.

From the extravagant enigma of Sathya Sai Baba to the perverse and baffling actions of many Zen masters, spiritual teachers tend to defy our expectations for them. They may act in ways that can be deliberately off-putting (the alcoholism of Chogyam Trungpa) or repugnantly antisocial (the cruel humor of George Ivanovitch Gurdjieff). But our own expectations for such teachers are yet more conditioned mental baggage from which their teachings are designed to liberate us. The Hindus view the playfulness of Krishna or the bloodthirsty violence of Kali as *lila*—a divine game. The Vedas, the most ancient Sanskrit texts, believed by some scholars to have been handed down through an oral tradition thirty thousand years old, constantly emphasize the battle between clouds and rain. The thunder and the sunshine war, yet the sun ultimately emerges victorious. It is the battle between spirit and matter, the pendulum swing all of us experience between our higher and lower natures. This is lila, God's game, played out for his amusement—and thus *our* amusement, too.

Maharshi, however, did behave the way you expected holy men to: He lived a humble, disciplined existence, feeding the poor, aiding the sick, teaching those who wanted to listen, to learn.

He detached himself from any pleasures of the flesh. Similarly, beyond taking the few standard medicines I'd noticed still in his room, Maharshi detached himself from the pain of cancer in his later years. His devotees were understandably distraught, begging him to heal himself as he had healed others. "The body has decided to get sick," he would reply. "Why should I interfere with its decisions? What has it to do with me?" The long process of dying was really the last great lesson he had to teach them.

A few photographs show his emaciated frame in the final stages of cancer. He must have endured agonizing pain, despite his detachment. Those who were with him near the end describe him as allowing himself virtually to disintegrate before their eyes so that they would realize the nature of *maya,* the physical illusion, so that they would cease confusing forms with reality. Those who witnessed his actual death say it was like someone shedding an old coat. This final transition from physical to incorporeal seemed so effortless and undramatic that many refused to believe he had died. According to his philosophy, of course, he had not.

Those who got close to his corpse, riddled with cancer though it was, say it smelled of fresh roses even days after the final exit.

✤   ✤   ✤

The supreme bliss is found only by the tranquil yogi, whose passions have been stilled. His desires washed away, the yogi easily achieves union with the Eternal. He sees his Self in all beings, and all beings in his Self, for his heart is steady in Yoga.

Who sees me in all things, and all things in me, he is never far from me, and I am never far from him.

—THE *BHAGAVAD GITA*

I sat in Ramana Maharshi's cave, a dark and spacious recess about halfway up Arunachala and overlooking the vast Siva-Parvati temple. I wondered how a man made up his mind to renounce the world, to sit in silent meditation until he discovered Truth. How many of us even know what solitude is, let alone could volunteer for a lifetime of it?

When I walked outside, soon daunted by the dark and fathomless night of the soul, I stood gazing down at the temple. The place was more like a city, with courtyards within courtyards, vendors' stalls, sidewalk entertainers with performing animals in tow, and many people engaged in activities that seemed to have little connection to any Western concept of religion.

I saw it as charming, in a carnival and medieval way. From the inner shrine, where the mighty idols of Siva and his consort dwelled, radiated the great wheel of life, the worldly solar system spinning around its divine sun. Where the sprawling mess that was the town beyond fitted into this scheme of universal harmony, I was less sure.

My guts had miraculously recovered from whatever waged war on them, and I had no intention of missing another meal. I returned down the mountain path back to the ashram.

The dining hall was a barnlike hut with stone floors and white walls decorated with several framed photographs of the Maharshi, along with one of someone who resembled Phil Silvers. A calendar bore a colored image of Siva off on a hunting trip in the woods: a bow and some arrows, deer leaping across the background. He was muscular, this Siva— good definition. He also had profound hair, great style, in fact. And very expensive jewelry. He did not look like the Destroyer of Worlds. He looked more like a hairdresser from Manhattan. Below this groomed, ruggedly pastoral Siva, a boxed sign read K MOHAN: HYBRID SEEDS. END SEARCH WITH MOHAN SEED (FULL GARRANTY). There was a local address and telephone number for anyone tired of searching in vain for fully guaranteed hybrid seeds.

Ashram inmates sat in rows on the flagstones, each in front of a banana leaf that already contained a plum-size mound of lime pickle and another of lumpy salt.

You had to have your wits about you when dinner was being served here; this happened so fast there must have been a competition going on. Two men holding a container of rice the size of a garbage can ran to the head of each aisle of cross-legged diners, one rapidly shoveling rice onto the leaves with a utensil like an aluminum Ping-Pong paddle, the other dragging the container along ahead of him. These men were swiftly followed by four others, each carrying a ladle and a large, steaming pail. In seconds I had a foot-high mound of rice, much of it in brick-size chunks. It would easily have fed ten people. I'd barely broken down the lumps and formed a volcano with my rice when, in quick succession, four ladles splashed their contents into its crater: a pint of sambhar, a pint of rassam, a pint of dal, and a pint of vegetable curry in which I could not identify a single vegetable. I bolstered up the rice volcano's walls, sweeping slopes up to the summit. And just in time, for bearing down on it was another breathless crew with ladles: curd so thick you could hold it, buttermilk with large leaves in it, poured into a metal beaker, and finally a huge clod of okra cooked until the pods chewed like licorice. The Indians called them "Ladies Fingers."

❦   ❦   ❦

India has two aspects—in one she is the householder, in the other a wandering ascetic. The former refuses to budge from the cozy nook, the latter has no home at all. I find both of these within me. I want to roam about and see all the wide world, yet I also yearn for a sheltered little nook, like a bird with its tiny nest for a dwelling and the vast sky for flight.

—RABINDRANATH TAGORE

I had heard rumors from several sources over the past months about a reclusive yogi who lived in secrecy somewhere around Tiruvannamalai, yet could easily be found in a part of the town bazaar where pots and pans were sold at sunset each day. Since India teems with wandering sadhus, most of whom seem little more than charlatans and parasites who prey on the superstitions and charity of the poor, the very fact that a particular one was mentioned generally indicated that he was worth a visit.

The tradition of renunciation runs deep in the Indian psyche. Early in life a genuine seeker of Truth may choose this path, giving away all he owns, donning the ocher robe (the color of leaves that have detached themselves from the tree), and wandering the land alone, living off alms, performing the spiritual exercises prescribed by some pundit or guru. Such people tend to travel the great pilgrim circuit, from Badrinath in the Himalayas down to the island of Rameshwaram, close to Sri Lanka. In between are seven holy cities, several hundred temples, several thousand shrines, all manner of ashrams, thirty-seven million villages, and many many miles.

These sadhus are not supposed to beg; they should receive only what is freely given them. Few seem aware of this restriction about asking, however, even though much is freely given in this generous land where there is little to spare. Most large temples regularly feed renunciants and the poor—the gods can't use everything they're offered, after all—and every Indian is enjoined to give alms to the needy each day if he or she can. Sadhus also have a reputation in folklore for laying curses, which the more unscrupulous ones tend to play up. They are rarely turned away. You hardly ever see one who looks as if he's missed a meal in his life.

And for all Hindus, pious or not, the pilgrimage to holy sites is still what it once was in medieval Europe: a religious obligation that is more holiday than hardship to those who can afford it. Sadhus thrive on these spiritual tourists, who constantly replenish holy hangouts with more people eager to perform religious duties they may neglect back home.

Renunciation is also common late in life. A man who has fulfilled his responsibilities as husband and father retires from his job; he sheds all worldly possessions and heads for the open road, never to return. Indians fully accept that the last stage in one's life should ideally be devoted exclusively to God; we'd call it Alzheimer's disease.

Such spiritual wanderers as these, old or young, are not usually holy men, but seekers. They have nothing to teach. There are, however,

many accounts of the renunciant attaining enlightenment and getting promoted to guru status or better. The Buddha, for example, left his family
without saying good-bye, to search for Truth. Swami "Papa" Ramdas, a
postal official all his life, ended up as one of the most revered gurus in the
South.

☙ ☙ ☙

When a clod of earth, a stone, and gold become alike, serenity is achieved.
—THE *BHAGAVAD GITA*

Embroidered with gold like a wedding sari, the sky above Tiruvannamalai
around sunset had weight and substance, almost undulated in the breeze
above the huge carved gopura of the temple. I easily found the part of
the bazaar that specialized in pots and pans. Kerosene tapers burned like
flecks fallen from the flaming yellow banner fluttering over our heads,
throwing off a thousand reflections across the walls of copper tureens, jugs,
and woks, and dancing around a hundred steel *dekchi*s, chappati irons, and
rice double boilers. A faint aroma of bhang hung in the air, along with a
dozen spices, incense, and woodsmoke. Shadows clustered in the gathering gloom, and in these, men in lungis and undershirts conspired, puffing beedies, gossiping. Housewives, proud in rustling saris of Kanchipuram
silk, strode from stall to stall, finally hammering out deals for frying pans
or ladles or aluminum saucepans large enough to serve soup to multitudes.
A turbaned man with a mustache like buffalo horns strolled by, dragging
a sad, moth-eaten dancing bear muzzled and leashed. The man looked
dangerous; the bear had big black tears hanging rigid in the corners of its
eyes.

There were no yogis in sight.

I asked a vendor about Yogi Ramsuratkumar. The vendor tried very
hard to sell me a copper saucepan, coming down to a price so reasonable
I would have bought it had I not pictured myself lugging it around India
for years. I reminded him I had asked about the yogi, not the saucepan.
The man sighed, knowing he'd done his best. He pointed across the dusty
lane.

"Yogi is there," he said.

"Where?" I saw nothing.

"There only. You see . . ."

I walked across to what appeared to be a vacant stall. On a bench in the shadows sat a powerfully built man, perhaps in his late sixties—it was hard to tell—with a huge, graying beard. His dirty robes had something of ancient Rome about them. He was flapping a circular fan of some sort of dried leaf attached to a wooden handle, powerfully, urgently, as if the heat really bothered him. His hand moved in a blur below his face. A large, soiled rag worn bandanna-style was drenched in perspiration.

"Yogi Ramsuratkumar?" I asked, suddenly nervous.

He looked up with bright eyes that were full of an impish amusement, smiling and nodding his head.

"Oh!" he kept repeating. "Oh!" He stood, putting the fan aside and grasping both my hands like some dotty old uncle I hadn't visited in years. "Oh! You have come!"

I confessed it was true.

"From where?" he asked, an odd intelligence entering his voice and eyes.

His English was excellent, and, judging by the pale skin and the accent, he was certainly not from these parts, not a Southerner. His body, too, was different: large-boned, with sizable muscles in the legs, big feet, and large but slender and well-formed hands. A Bengali, I decided, mainly because he resembled the poet Tagore.

He bade me sit next to him and proceeded to fumble with a packet of Wills Filters and light a cigarette, smoking it furiously through his fist, the other hand working the fan again. I noted an old cloth bag at his feet, from which protruded three more similar fans.

"I didn't know yogis smoked."

He merely laughed, puffing and fanning with even more concentrated intensity. The actions seemed connected. He did not look like someone enjoying a cigarette so much as someone using an asthma inhaler.

I lit up a cigarette myself, but felt oddly uncomfortable smoking it next to the yogi. I soon dumped it surreptitiously, asking him if he always smoked. He had just lit a second cigarette from the previous butt.

"Only here," he replied.

I felt the curious sensation you get when you suspect someone can read your mind, or, stranger still, can inscribe on it what you are currently reading there yourself.

When his other hand was not fanning, I noticed, it was performing a rapid motion like counting the beads of an invisible rosary. Indeed, he was all motion. In anyone else it would have seemed neurotic, anxious, but with him it gave the impression of someone who needed to vent excess energy.

I asked where he lived and what he did during the day.

"This beggar lives out there," he replied, indicating the barren wasteland surrounding Arunachala. "He does whatever God asks."

"What *does* God ask?"

"What this beggar does is not important," he answered firmly. "What is it that *you* wish?"

I told him that I just wanted to meet him.

He laughed insanely and long, as if he'd never in his life heard anything so preposterous. I wondered if maybe he *was* just a beggar. Except he seemed more like a king in exile.

"Oh! Oh! Oh!" he gasped, coughing. "Is it so?"

"Yes. I'm really interested in what you people do. Where I come from everyone thinks that a man's duty is to work in the world . . . with others—you know, make it a better place and all that."

This definitely amused him. "Is it so?" he repeated.

"They'd say you were escaping responsibilities, you know—running away."

"There are many tasks in this world," he suddenly said, his voice calmer now. "Many jobs that must be done by those who God wishes to do them. . . ."

He went on to say, without once mentioning himself, that negative forces clustered around people in important positions, such as political leaders, and it was vital that they be protected from such negative forces while doing their jobs, otherwise wars and catastrophes would result. I gleaned from this that Yogi Ramsuratkumar's job was to build auras of protection around such people by exerting some sort of influence to insure that positive forces determined major events.

This struck me as an important job. It also struck me as absurd. Did it exist beyond his imagination? And if it did exist, why wasn't it very successful—considering the number of wars and catastrophes that were happening even as we spoke? I couldn't trap him like this, however, since he never referred to himself as anything but a beggar, a vehicle for God's inscrutable will. Who knew how much worse things might have been without whatever it was he did, after all?

"There was a great teacher" was about all he'd say regarding the past. "The teacher took this beggar and made him function for the will of God.

Just as a broken automobile can be repaired so the driver can drive it again. Is it true? The driver must drive—yes? So his automobile should function? A broken automobile is of no use to anyone—is it not so?"

I agreed. He wouldn't say who the "great teacher" was. I asked how one built an "aura of protection." He laughed once more, tickled to death. *At least,* I thought, *I'm providing the evening's entertainment.*

Without warning, he swatted a fly on the bare counter of the vacant stall with his powerful hand. He picked the creature up by a wing and gave it to me. I tentatively accepted it, trying to appear grateful, and examined the insect in the palm of my hand to see if there was something I had missed. Mangled, oozing, one wing buckled into a squashed abdomen, it looked like any other dead fly I'd ever encountered.

The yogi watched me intently, puffing and counting those invisible beads, a big, generous smile swelling through his high cheekbones.

"Very dirty," he said, nodding at the fly. "Put it there." He indicated the spot where the fly had just met its abrupt end. A tiny stain was still visible on the wood.

I tipped the speck down near the stain.

"What can death be?" the yogi asked.

I shrugged, not about to offer an answer to that.

"It is a question we are interested in—is it not so?"

I nodded.

"Watch." He pointed to the fly.

I watched the raisinlike blob, hearing the yogi's breathing become faster and faster—until it suddenly stopped. He then held up his right hand a yard or so from the fly, becoming incredibly still. This stillness was all the more dramatic after his perpetual motion—and it really *was* stillness. As I continued to watch, the fly started twitching, shaking its buckled wing out, then getting up, testing its legs with a few unsteady steps. A second later, it flew away.

The yogi remained motionless for another minute, then immediately became his old self again, lighting up and fanning.

My first thought was just how dead the fly had been. Surely I had seen enough dead flies to know the difference. This fly had been crushed, split open.

"How did you do that?" I asked.

He looked over through the gloom, the whites of his eyes sparkling. "Life is a force," he said quietly. "Death is the absence of that force—is it not so?"

"I suppose . . ."

"Fly needs less force than the human—is this true?"

"Probably . . ."

"Can this beggar not give the fly enough force to live?"

I asked how he could transfer his life force and how the fly could repair the damage to its body even if it received new life force.

"Is it not so that God can do anything he wishes?"

"Yes, but . . ." I stopped, because I had the distinct impression that the answers I was looking for weren't available. No words from this yogi were going to explain anything at all.

"Why do you come here every day?" I eventually asked.

"Did you not wish to see this beggar?"

I didn't want to seem ungrateful. I knew that whatever he was doing, coming to the bazaar when he did, I would probably not understand, either. I told him I was glad he had spared some time to talk to me. Once more he laughed uproariously.

"Can I give you anything?" I inquired.

This got a chuckle, too. Then he said, "This beggar needs nothing. God gives him what he deserves . . . but he deserves nothing really—is it not?"

I held out my pack of cigarettes. He laughed, looking at it as if observing something about it that I couldn't see. Then, almost coyly, he took a cigarette.

I told him to keep the whole pack, but he bluntly refused, looking somewhat embarrassed.

Then I asked about the holy mountain, Arunachala, and why it was holy. He seemed baffled, reluctant to answer. I asked if there was any cosmic advantage in walking to its summit. There usually is with holy mountains. Quite forcefully, he replied that it was better to walk around it.

"Around it?"

"Good exercise—is it not so?" he said.

"Which direction?"

This clearly did not matter. I thanked him, feeling I'd overstayed my welcome, and asked if I could come back tomorrow.

"Why would you want to see this filthy old beggar again?"

"I like this filthy old beggar. . . ."

"Oh! Oh!" He sighed, grasping my hands. "God is too good to this old beggar."

"Does Indira Gandhi have an aura of protection?" I asked, standing to leave.

"What God wills must be so—is it not?"

"Is she a client of yours?" *Client* seemed as good a term as any.

"What use is a filthy old beggar to a queen?"

It was an odd reply, one I thought about often in the years ahead. I thought of it the day Indira lay in a pool of blood and India seemed poised on the brink of an abyss.

I left Yogi Ramsuratkumar there, amid the pots and pans, beneath a seething night brimful of mysteries. My heart was well and truly splashed across the heavens as I walked back up to the silent ashram. Some moments you would not trade, even for another hundred years of life.

The One God manifests Himself in two aspects so that the world may be sustained and fostered, improved and cleansed. These two—the terrible and the tender—are the characteristics found together in every single thing on earth, for are they not all parts of the selfsame God?

—SATHYA SAI BABA

I started out early the next day to walk around Arunachala as Yogi Ramsuratkumar had recommended, deciding a clockwise direction had tradition on its side. Heading behind the ashram and off through scrub and rocks, I soon realized this other half of the mountain was not as conical as the Tiruvannamalai side. It sprawled off, descending very gradually into a series of steep, irregular rocky hillsides, and thus widened considerably more at the base than I'd imagined. Circumambulating it would take me a bit longer than I had calculated. There also seemed to be no obvious route. I'd assumed there would be, that the yogi's advice was conventional wisdom. But from where I stood, I wondered if anyone had *ever* walked around the mountain. I was at least a hundred yards from what looked like the actual base of Arunachala, which was as near as I could get because of the density of scrub in between. Even so I kept getting hooked on thorns like darning needles or scratched by something with clawlike barbed spikes disguised as flowers. The flora out here were outright vicious. Why had nature equipped these things with such hardware?

Cursing, I ripped another thorn from my pants and followed the path of least resistance. After an hour of this meandering, I had progressed less than a hundred yards. And the sun by this time was sucking up the rich hues of rock, earth, and foliage to stoke its boiler for another day of grilling the planet. It occurred to me that a hat would have been quite a sensible item to include in my Sri Ganesh Industries Pvt. Ltd shopping bag, along with my notebook, two plantains, box of Band-Aids, Hindi phrase book, and tape recorder. A bottle of water would have been even more sensible.

I sought out another stretch relatively free of carnivorous plant life and headed in approximately the right direction. A plume of smoke caught my eye, rising near a cluster of rocks the size of houses about half a mile away. Encouraged, I walked faster and more bravely, swinging my bat at bushes blocking the route I'd picked instead of trying to dodge them. Soon I came across five goats busily chewing leaves from the plentiful thornbushes. It must have been like eating credit cards, but they seemed happy enough, their eyes crazed with lust and late nights, their bearded throats bobbing.

Before long I could see some sort of habitation constructed in the shelter of those outsize rocks. A lurching stockade of uneven branches like bars surrounded three rudimentary huts of hewn logs and straw. It was the kind of place my ancestors in Wales probably called home thirty thousand years ago.

The smoke floated up from a dying fire near an open door in the middle hut. I skirted the fence, looking for an entrance—although anyone could have just walked through this pitiful barricade, or even over it at many points. There was no break in the fence. Reaching the other side, I called out some Hindi greetings listed in my phrase book under Common Modes of Greeting. Three brilliantly colored birds flapped out of a nearby tree, complaining bitterly about the noise, but there was no sign of life from the huts. I consulted the book again, shouting the Hindi for *My name is Paul, what is your name?* I hoped. I might have been asking if I could take someone's grandmother nude clod-dancing, for all I knew.

Still nothing. I was about to squeeze between two branches in the fence when from the nearest hut there emerged a man with dreadlocks that reached his knees and a beard substantial enough to stuff a king-size mattress. Apart from all this hair, he was completely naked, unless dust counts. He stared at me, and instantly I waved back, shouting more common modes of Hindi greeting. He retreated into his hut, reemerging thirty seconds later holding a long crooked pole with an orange flag hanging from one end—like something you'd find marking the greens of a Neolithic golf course. He stood clasping it neither aggressively nor defensively, but somehow ceremonially.

Who the hell is he? I wondered, smiling and waving. Sadhus didn't go in for farming, as far as I knew. I had thought none of the tribal people in India lived anywhere near here.

The man stood his ground, so I decided to risk clambering into the compound. He showed no particular feelings for or against this intrusion. Walking toward him, I held out one of my plantains.

He looked thirty-five at most, and his body was lithe rather than thin. But he had the eyes of a very old and tired man. Scarcely blinking, he observed my movements as if not quite sure what I was . . . perhaps not entirely certain that this apparition troubling him was even really there.

"Namaste," I said, no more than a yard away, thrusting out the plantain.

I saw traces of sandalwood paste in vertical lines above his nose, which presumably meant he was some sort of Vaishnavite—a follower of Vishnu the Preserver, not Siva the Destroyer. This cheered me.

He looked down at the plantain with some curiosity but made no attempt to take it. Then he said, very distinctly, *"Tat Twam Asi."*

It was Sanskrit, a mantra probably as old as the Vedas, meaning roughly You Are That. Was he making any kind of statement at all, or just repeating his mantra? All you can do with mantras is repeat them. I'd heard the Vedas being chanted in Sanskrit numerous times, and had picked up a fair number of words and phrases by now, but I could never imagine anyone actually speaking the language, which seemed designed purely for ritual purposes. Although I knew words for quite subtle philosophical concepts—such as those defining the difference between soul, spirit, self, and God—I had no idea how to say *I'm really thirsty, could I get a drink?* No one in the Vedic age appears to have had any use for language beyond listing an inventory of natural phenomena and reciting the virtues of God, or gods. You recited the virtues of God in order to persuade him not to destroy you and your world. In such a world, every sunrise was a profound relief.

I offered the plantain again and asked in English what the best route around the mountain was. . . .

"Tat Twam Asi," he repeated, turning and motioning me to follow him into the hut.

It would have been hard to refuse.

Inside I found an animal-skin rug and a kind of altar fashioned out of three smooth rocks with several small branches tied together on top of them. From the twigs dangled dozens of bones, dried flowers, and chunks of colored quartz, all clumsily knotted to ribbons of faded red cloth. He propped the pole with the orange flag against one of the two beams holding up this hut, then indicated that I should put the plantain on the altar. I did so gladly. He sat down on the hide rug, pointing to a spot beside him. I nodded more gratitude, sat down, and riffled through my Hindi phrase book. It was full of phrases about getting the wheels on your bullock cart repaired and various ways to ask questions about someone's relatives—*My sister has a red sari; what color is the sari of your auntie?*—but there was nothing about mountains, routes, or thirst.

The sadhu was now sitting erect in padmasan, legs folded like arms, soles facing up.

"Arunachala," I tried. "Tapas, me . . . Yogi Ramsuratkumar darshan . . . and the bastard told me to walk around it instead of up it, see?"

His eyes were half closed. He actually seemed more like a statue than a person—sitting here like this probably for years just repeating his mantra. He showed no sign of hearing a word I'd said, and no sign of reciprocating my attempt at communication with one of his own. He'd probably offered me the only thing he had, now that I consider it: the opportunity to sit and dwell on the meaning of You Are That for the next fifty years. I'm not sure anymore that this would be so odd a way to live.

"Well," I said, clapping my hands briskly. "Thanks *so* much . . . for everything." I stood, looking down at him. "You take care, and if the mantra works, do let me know, okay?"

"Tat Twam Asi," he suddenly said, not moving, his eyes still half closed, half looking at this world, half gazing into another.

I felt ashamed of having barged in on him uninvited. Whatever he was doing, did not need company, and he was not *obliged* to offer hospitality. If he'd wanted company he would not have moved out here, would he?

I crept out of the hut abashed.

❦   ❦   ❦

An hour farther into my hike through hostile vegetation, in heat like an endless series of burning veils swirling in flames on every side, I discovered a series of caves in the rear slope of the mountain. By now I was not so much thirsty as turning to dust from the inside out.

One cave had signs of human life around the yawning entrance: a mangled pack of India Kings, a dried-out folded leaf containing traces of rice, a few crumpled pages from *India Today,* and a square of old cloth draped over a rock as if to dry. Where there's garbage, people are never far away.

I wandered into the cave without thinking what I was doing. It was *really* dark in there, and I could smell incense burning in the hot, damp air, along with hints of camphor. Hospitals came to mind. The rock roof slanted down steeply in a funnel toward the source of these smells. Close to what the echoes of my footsteps told me was the farthest reach of the cave, I realized I felt the presence of another being. The minutest sound of breathing may have rustled the air before I sensed its presence.

My eyes had to adjust to the heaving, bulky darkness before I could more or less make out some sort of human form sitting not six feet away, as if sprouting from bedrock and more stone than flesh.

"Namaste," I said, oppressed by this fat, narcotic air and the twenty million tons of stone entombing us.

There was just the breathing and the almost inaudible thump of life's rhythm distinguishing itself from the great stillness surrounding it.

Then a voice like the churning of worlds boomed, "Siva!"

I got out of there fast.

By four-thirty I was staggering toward the edge of town, my brain shrinking with dehydration. At the first chai stall, via sign language, I downed seven Campa Colas, a Limca, two Gold Spots, and a fresh lime soda. When I could finally speak again, I ordered a fresh lime juice with Limca, and then another.

"That's better," I gasped to the proprietor, who looked impressed. He offered me another Campa Cola for half price.

"You have some thirst, isn't it?" he observed.

❖   ❖   ❖

Yogi Ramsuratkumar was puffing and fanning in his usual spot at sunset.

"I walked around the mountain," I told him.

"Oh! Oh! Is it so?"

"Have you ever walked around it yourself?"

"It is far," he replied. "The heat will make you ill."

"Thanks." I drummed my fingers on the bench. "So why did you tell me to walk around it instead of up it?"

"Who listens to this beggar?"

I decided against answering this and asked about the sadhus I'd met.

"Oh! Oh! You honor this beggar's heart."

He then told me the yogi in the cave was 768 years old. I found that very hard to believe.

He laughed insanely, repeating, "Hard to believe! Oh! Oh! It *is* hard to believe—this is so. . . ."

"Have you anything else to tell me?" I asked him. "I'm leaving to-morrow."

He then asked me what his name was. I told him. He made me repeat it nine times—possibly so that I would not forget it.

"Yogi Ramsuratkumar . . ."

"Oh! Oh! You are too kind to this old beggar. When you write about him, you must write only the truth. . . ."

"When I *write*—?" At the time I had no such intention.

He laughed, nodding.

Seventeen years later, I finally did just what he asked.

The old man at the ashram also seemed to know more about my future than I did: "I look forward too much for your book," he said.

"What book?"

"Are you not writing about Bhagavan?"

I shook my head.

"Then you please tell what is happening to you here. You tell so many people will come for the darshan . . ."

"The darshan?"

"Bhagavan's living presence . . ."

"It'll be difficult to explain the living presence of a dead man."

"For saints there is no death . . ."

I asked him about the mountain and the sadhus.

"You should not go that side," he cautioned. "There is no path, and these men have lived in the bush and caves now for many hundreds of years alone. They must *remain* alone."

"Many hundreds of years?"

"They perform austerities that give them great powers. These are things beyond our understanding."

I knew what he meant.

5

"A Flame of Faith . . ."

GOA, 1975-76

🌾 🌾 🌾

*In a small island near this, called Divari, the Portuguese, in order
to build the city, have destroyed an ancient temple . . . which was
built with marvelous art and with ancient figures wrought to the
greatest perfection, in a certain black stone, some of which remain
standing, ruined and shattered, because these Portuguese care
nothing about them. If I can come by one of these shattered images,
I will send it to your Lordship, that you may perceive how much in
old times sculpture was esteemed in every part of the world.*

—ANDRE CORSALLI TO GIULIANO DE MEDICI,
JANUARY 6, 1516

*T*he churches of Old Goa were already a hundred years old before the
Red Fort in Delhi or the Taj Mahal were built. The first Europeans
to establish themselves on Indian soil, the Portuguese were also the last
to leave.

From the late thirteenth century until November 24, 1510, when
Afonso de Albuquerque's armada finally captured it, Goa had been in a
tug-of-war between Hindu and Muslim rulers. Granada, the last bastion
of Muslim rule in Iberia, had fallen only in 1492, five years before Vasco
da Gama sailed in search of a sea route to the East. The Portuguese came
to India intent on repaying in kind those people who had subjugated *their*
land for nearly five hundred years, who had forcibly converted *their* people to an alien faith. There was a competitive fury to Christianize among
the various orders that established themselves in Goa, and not just the
Muslims suffered because of it.

The Portuguese started out quite reasonably. Although a religious
man, Afonso de Albuquerque was no evangelist. His only interference in

the religion of the natives was to ban the practice of *sati*—widow burning—which was not common in Goa anyway. What conversions he did authorize were carried out for practical reasons. His sailors had started shacking up with local women, (the women of Goa have always been irresistible to male European eyes), so he decided to legitimize these unions by ordering the women to become Christians. Afonso disposed of another problem with equal facility: He distributed among his men the Muslim women taken hostage from the grandees of Goa and those rescued from the massacre resulting from the battle. He decreed that any of his followers could "choose a woman that suited him and he would receive from the Governor's own hands a house and a few acres of land and the right to engage in trade." The offer was eagerly taken up. In a private letter to his king, Afonso confessed there was another, more pragmatic aspect to this action: "These women who marry go back to their houses and dig out their jewels and gold . . . I leave it all to their husbands."

For the next two hundred years, the Portuguese expanded their control north, south, and east; but this expansion soon met with competition from the British. Bombay was given as a wedding gift to Charles II, in 1661, by his Portuguese bride, Catherine of Braganza. But the inheritors of Afonso's conquest had a talent for falling back and consolidating, holding on to their possessions in Goa with such tenacity that they were finally and forcibly ejected only in 1961.

In the wake of the warriors came the priests. First the Franciscans, then the Jesuits, then the Dominicans, and lastly the Augustinians. It must have made their holy blood boil to find their old foes, the Muslims and Jews, openly and brazenly practicing their religions. A number of ex-Jews had come out to the colony, and although they had professed to be Christians back in Portugal, in Goa they showed a worrying tendency to revert to their old ways. The men of God set about clearing what one Dominican termed this "jungle of unbelief" with all the ardor of Amazon lumber barons.

Just like the mullahs who had marched into Goa two hundred years before with the Bahamani sultans, these Catholic clergy were prepared to go to any lengths to spread their faith. Initially they pestered the Portuguese king for special powers, and then they pestered the pope to pester the king on their behalf.

The first of these special powers arrived in 1540 when the viceroy received authority to "destroy all Hindu temples, not leaving a single one in any of the islands, and to confiscate the estates of these temples for the maintenance of the churches which are to be erected in their places." Five years later, the Italian cleric Father Nicolau Lancilotto reported that "there was not a single temple to be seen on the island." The island in question was Teeswadi, the main field of operations for the two priestly orders then on the scene. Once the islands of Bardez and Salcete were acquired, each order was able to stake out its own territory—the Franciscans clearing the "jungle" of Bardez, and the Jesuits going to work on Salcete. By the time the dominicans and the Augustinians arrived a few years later, however, there was not enough room for separate spheres of influence. A glance at the absurd profusion of churches standing cheek by jowl in Old Goa still conveys some idea of the spiritual excesses indulged in by these competing orders during their heyday.

This Olympiad of Christianization scared the hell out of the locals, and thousands of families—particularly high-caste Hindus—fled across the river. To them, the harshness of those Moghul functionaries still governing the adjacent territories must have been preferable to the rabid monomania of papist clerics. A saying still exists in Konkani, the language of Goa: *Hanv polthandi vaitam* (I'm leaving for the other bank), one half of its double meaning implying to this day that a person is rejecting Christianity.

The Hindus who remained were not exactly fighting to be converted, either. Although their temples had been razed, they continued to practice their religion in secret. More extreme methods were therefore instituted to bring the heathen into the church's loving embrace. Hindu festivities were forbidden; Hindu priests were prevented from entering Goa; makers of idols were severely punished; public jobs were given only to Christians.

Soon it was announced that it had become a crime for Hindus to practice their religion at all, even in the privacy of their own homes. The penalty was decreed to be the confiscation of all property. Those who informed on such crimes were to receive half the property confiscated. Also, Hindus dying without a male heir could pass their estates on only to a relative who had embraced Christianity. Finally, in 1560, all the Brahmins who were left were simply kicked out.

The missionaries obviously had no idea how resilient Hinduism could be, and indeed is. It had survived Islam's scimitar, and it would survive the sword that so much resembled the cross in whose service it was now employed. There had once been more than two hundred temples on the islands, and although every single one had been demolished, some of the idols had been saved. These were hauled out to the dense jungles of Bicholim and Ponda, beyond the borders of Goa, and installed in new temples. Although orders forbidding all Hindus from visiting these temples were issued, the borders were not well patrolled, and it was easy for whole families to slip through to attend wedding ceremonies or sacred thread rites.

Another law, making it "a serious offense to fashion, or even privately retain, Hindu religious objects," was similarly circumvented. Since houses were frequently searched without warning, Hindus started making paper cutouts of their gods, which could be speedily destroyed if the need arose. To this day, during the great Ganesh festival, for example, instead of the terra-cotta idols of the elephant god that other Hindus worship, the Manai Kamats of Panjim use paper silhouettes.

Death was no easier than life for Hindus in mid-sixteenth-century Goa. To them, the cruelest piece of legislation passed by the Portuguese prohibited cremation of the dead—an inviolably sacred part of Hindu faith. As a result, deaths had to be kept secret; the wailing grief of women had to be smothered; family members had to go about their business as if nothing had happened: children were sent out to play, washing was done, work was performed—all as usual. No suspicions could be aroused, and known informers had to be paid off, prying neighbors kept at bay.

In the dead of night, a boat would be loaded with firewood down on the riverbank; then the dead body would be placed on it, covered by more wood. The pyre would be set alight and the boat pushed out to drift on the river's current as the funeral party ran back into the safety of shadows. Naturally, the watchtower guards could hardly fail to notice the floating inferno. Whipped up by the sea winds, the fire would blaze fiercely and fast, soon sinking the boat and leaving the authorities able only to record one more illegal cremation.

The missionaries simply couldn't grasp that another people's faith could be as dearly cherished and deeply embedded as their own. Even those Goans who had converted still clung to aspects of their old religion. According to Richard Lannoy, Goa's cultural historian, the chapels that can be found in most Goanese Christian homes "are direct derivations from the culture of family shrines in Hindu homes." And the old Hindu caste system continued on, Christians who had once been from high-caste families rarely socializing with those who had belonged to lower castes. To this day, members of low and high castes almost never intermarry. Many descendants of those lofty Brahmin families who had converted even continued the traditional practice of giving annual donations to those temples that necessity had forced the Hindus to establish beyond Portuguese territory. Indeed, I was assured this, too, still went on, the Miranda family of Loutulim dispatching a sack of rice and a heap of coconuts each year to the Kavalem Shanta-Durga temple. The Gomes Pereiras, pillars of Panjim society, do much the same for the Fatorpa Mahamayi temple.

✢   ✢   ✢

I was accompanied on this trip in 1975 by two acquaintances from Canada, David and Esther, who were taking a brief vacation in India.

I knew we were entering Goa because I noticed a little shrine by the side of the road dedicated to the Virgin Mary. A fenced-off enclosure, it contained a garishly painted concrete statue garlanded with fresh flowers, surrounded by burning candles and joss sticks.

A dozen or so miles back down the coast road, near Karwar in Karnataka state, we'd passed a similar enclosure dedicated to the elephant god, Ganesh. It, too, had been garlanded and lovingly adorned with candles and incense. Fifty-odd miles farther south, outside Calicut, off the coast of what is now Kerala, there'd been another wayfarers' shrine. It consisted of a red concrete pyramid topped by a hammer and sickle. This, too, had been recently garlanded and decorated with burning candles and joss sticks. In 1975, as it has had on and off since then, Kerala had a Marxist government.

These shrines told you what territory you were in. From where the workers' symbol was worshiped, we'd traveled through a land protected by Siva's tubby mutant son, and had now moved into the realm of the goddess Mary. Crossing the broad Zuari River, we entered yet another sphere of influence. The architecture of Goa is unmistakably Iberian: broad, low roofs covered with curved terra-cotta tiles, faded ocher plasterwork, shaded courtyards, deep balconies and verandas. But Goa Velha, Old Goa, through which we motored first, was once called "The Rome of the Orient." Now it's an overgrown area of ghostly ruins, for the most part, far from the impossibly overbuilt walled-in city it must once have been. Only the most ambitiously conceived structures have survived, and these are all religious: convents, churches, seminaries. Of the thirty-odd buildings that existed when Sir Richard Burton visited in 1846, more than a dozen are more or less intact.

The most striking of these is the Basilica of Bom Jesus. Elevated from its status in Burton's time, Bom Jesus stands out because it is red—the lateritic slabs left unplastered—and because a line of soaring double-arched flying buttresses prop up its open side wall. What struck me most, however, were the thousands of people waiting in long, unruly lines to enter its mighty doors—on a Wednesday afternoon.

Our driver supplied the explanation: the "incorruptible" body of Saint Francis Xavier was currently on display inside the basilica—an event that only occurred every twelve years or so. People were waiting "for saint's darshan." We stopped the car.

With Saint Ignatius Loyola, Xavier cofounded the Jesuit order. The two of them had divided up the world as their spheres of activity, Loyola taking Europe, Xavier choosing a more ambitious project: the entire Orient.

Xavier embodies and exemplifies the bewildering contradictions of his order. Hardworking, deeply committed to elevating the human condition, compassionate, as he wrote himself, he "lived in a hospital, confessing the sick and giving them Holy Communion." Yet he also inflicted sadistic punishments on those who failed to conform to the standards he set. Although he pitied the slaves he saw marched through the streets of both Lisbon and Goa, he regarded them as heathens, pagans lucky enough to have received God's mercy and been delivered up to those capable of making Christians out of them. The Goans of the time saw the best side of Xavier in what little of him they saw.

They knew nothing of the part he had played in Portugal's Inquisition; nor did they know he had pleaded with his monarch, Dom Joao, to "order the establishment of the Inquisition in Goa."

Most of Xavier's mass conversions—during which he Christianized entire villages in a stroke—were performed in Kerala. It's possible he never carried out a single conversion while he was in Goa, spending his time there in the hospital and visiting the city's three prisons, which he described as "the filthiest, foulest dens on earth." He used to ring a little bell as he walked the streets, gathering around him children, workers, and slaves to instruct them in basics of the faith. Consequently, the memory he left behind was saintly indeed: a "flame of faith" befriending the friendless and bringing hope to the hopeless.

But Xavier could not have spent more than six months in Goa during the entire ten years he lived in the East. Arriving in May 1542, he had moved to Kerala by that September. The following year, he returned for a few weeks before setting off on a conversion spree that eventually took him, via Malacca and the Moluccas, as far as Japan. Nine years later, he returned to Goa, spending less than two months there before heading off for China—the land he felt he was destined to convert. His god clearly had other plans. Xavier died on November 25, 1552, on the island of San-chuan, near the mouth of the Canton River, outside the closed gates of the Middle Kingdom. He was accompanied only by a young Chinese convert who had adopted the name Antonio de Santa Fe.

This devoted servant solicited help to bury his master, deciding "to pack the coffin with lime . . . as it would consume the flesh and leave only the dry bones," in case someone decided they should be interred elsewhere. Either the lime was highly diluted or the coffin packed with another substance altogether, for when one of Xavier's dearest friends made the arduous journey to the island five months later in order to look upon the Jesuit father's face one last time, he found, after digging up the coffin, that the body was wonderfully preserved, Xavier looking as if he were "only asleep." Legends had by now already bgrown up around the man, many of the faithful claiming to have witnessed him perform miracles. This incorruptibility in death was instantly hailed as more proof of his sanctity.

Xavier had never expressed any particular fondness for Goa; he had chosen to perform his most strenuous Christianizing elsewhere in India. Goa, however, was the base for Portuguese activities in the East, and thus had the right to claim his body. In due course, Xavier's corpse arrived on the wharf of Ribandar. It was greeted with wild enthusiasm: fanfares rang out; people thronged the streets, shouting; the city's countless bells pealed "as in welcome to some great prince or conqueror." Accompanied in a procession led by the viceroy and his councillors, the body was initially installed in the chapel of Saint Paul's, which Xavier had helped found. Some days later, the coffin was opened and the saint, now sixteen months dead, was found to be still in an extraordinary state of preservation. For four days thereafter, his corpse was exposed to the public, drawing huge crowds. Collection boxes filled up, and a tradition began.

It was this tradition that was still in full swing in 1975. An opportunity to see the "incorruptible body" of a saint seemed to me too good to miss. The unruly lineup twisted around the side of the basilica and off out of sight into a grove of dense palms. I asked someone near the main doors how long they'd been waiting. Two days was the answer. I had assumed the profusion of bedding and cooking equipment was just the typical Indian aversion to traveling light and eating someone else's food. In this case, however, it was merely pragmatism.

My two companions, David and Esther, had already found India something of a trial by fire compared with the cosseted luxury their wealthy parents provided back home. They were not prepared to spend two days lining up to see a Catholic saint who'd been dead for four hundred years. Our driver unexpectedly provided a solution: For a hundred rupees each—to grease the palm of a priest—we could go straight in the back door. His offer was accepted.

The basilica's interior seemed rather vast and bare. In the poor light only the altar, a shimmering block of gold, stood out at first. Xavier's body rested in a side chapel, on a raised platform and encased in glass. We joined a short and highly excited line of people—Indian Christians, presumably, yet scarcely distinguishable from the devotees who thronged around the courtyards of Hindu temples waiting to glimpse jeweled idols, dripping lingams, sacred bulls.

Before long, we'd reached the glass case. The "incorruptible body," I noticed, was somewhat less incorruptible than it had been back in 1554. It was almost entirely draped in worn, dusty, ancient, and elaborate robes, like those a pope might wear on special occasions, only the head, feet, and one hand visible. His entire right arm seemed to be thrust out of sight behind his back. And these parts were barely more than a skeleton covered with what resembled the skin of an incredibly old and dessicated prune. They lay in a violently vulgar gold casket. Saint Francis's yellow teeth were so chipped he could have been chewing the Rock of Ages with them. Next to the saint's display case was another, much smaller one. Scarcely larger than a shoe box, it contained what looked like the petrified feces of some small creature. I asked the seedy, well-fed cleric who had cheerfully taken our rupees what the objects in the second case actually were.

"They are toes of the Saint Francis," he answered.

"Toes?"

"Correct."

"Why are his toes not attached to his feet? If you don't mind me asking."

"They are being bitten off by a nun."

"A nun?"

"A nun in ecstatic state."

In fact, I learned later, one of the toes was bitten off by a lady called Isabela de Carom when Saint Francis still lay in Saint Paul's chapel. The annals record that she "bit off a toe which she carried away in her mouth as a relic." Some years later another toe was missing. I even met someone whose family still possessed one of Saint Francis's toenails.

The mutilation does not seem to have particularly outraged Catholic authorities: The pope himself took a fancy to Xavier's right arm, apparently, requesting it be sent to Rome. It was not behind his back after all: it had been somewhere in the Vatican for the past three and a half centuries.

On March 12, 1622, Pope Gregory XV decreed Xavier's canonization. Two years later, possibly to ensure that the faithful did not chew off any more of him, the saint was transferred to his gaudy but protected permanent home in the church of Bom Jesus, which itself had to wait more than two hundred years for its promotion to cathedral status. Saint Francis Xavier proved to be an abidingly popular money-maker, and over the years the clerics learned much about show business.

In 1975 the holy event had something of the circus freak show about it. Rumor had it that the priests had summoned experts to see if they could prevent the saint from becoming a pile of dust—which he was certainly not far from being when I saw him. Each time they wheeled the body up from the crypt for public viewing, they hinted this might be the last time Saint Francis would be shown. I'm sure the saint still will be making his twelfth-yearly appearances when that glass case contains nothing but a heap of lavishly embroidered rags. If Goans thought about the role Xavier played in the persecution of their ancestors, I wonder if they would be so keen to continue hosting most of his remains.

In the capital, Panjim—or New Goa, as it once was—a place that resembles a Spanish colonial town like Port Antonio in Jamaica, we visited the picture gallery of the Institute Menezes Braganca. Among an uninspired collection of faded, third-rate canvases, I noticed a table bearing a plaque that read:

THE TABLE OF THE REVENUE BOARD WHICH IS SAID
TO HAVE BELONGED TO THE INQUISITION.

The golden jubilee of the start of Portuguese domination in Goa was celebrated in 1560. To help festivities get off with a bang, the authorities back in Lisbon had a special treat in store for their Goan subjects.

Xavier was undoubtedly not the only one to request the Inquisition—and he didn't live long enough to help supervise it himself. This holy terror was ostensibly not directed against those Hindus obstinate or foolish enough to remain in Goa, but rather was intended for those who had already accepted Christianity but were suspected of not observing the Christian rites with appropriate rigor and enthusiasm—or even of covertly practicing their old faith. The Inquisition, however, was determined to be fair: It took an equal interest in any Hindus it discovered indulging their beliefs, since everyone knew these beliefs were "magic and witchcraft."

But the Dominicans, who were keener about the Inquisition than the other orders were—and the other orders were hardly apathetic—took a special interest in the *revertidos,* the backsliders with their cutout idols and furtive cremations. The culprits would be tracked down and burned alive. *Auto-da-fé*—act of faith—was the lofty title given to this inhuman practice. Far from disapproving of the burnings, the viceroy, the man who had outlawed sati, attended them in pomp and ceremony with his entire retinue.

Many of Goa's new Christians had grave misgivings about the faith that had been shoved down their throats, and few could discard ancient beliefs and taboos as easily as their Portuguese masters felt they should. Language was partly to blame. Far from being interested in learning the Konkani spoken by their subjects, the conquistadores swiftly set about burning everything written in the language on the off chance it might contain "precepts and doctrines of idolatry." Indeed, fire appeared to be the final solution to whatever they did not understand.

The priesthood could also be fairly described as "Christian soldiers," since many in its rank and file were mercenaries. While senior clergy might be men of education and sophistication, far more had joined up in anticipation of the cushy and lucrative existence the profession offered—especially in Goa. The historian T. B. Cunha comments that "every sailor who came to Goa preferred to be a monk." Most such sailors were after a more material form of enlightenment, too. Not only were they intellectually ill-equipped to pick up a very foreign language in order to assist their flock of converts in understanding the intricacies of Christian dogma, many were probably unable to read or write their own language. These early invaders were not particularly well-informed about Hinduism, either: One group of soldiers cheerfully sat through a rite in the temple of the dark goddess of death, Kali, under the impression that they were congregants in the shrine of a local Black Madonna.

Although the Goans had been studying Portuguese and Latin in schools established by the clergy, few attained the degree of proficiency in these alien tongues necessary to grasp even the basics of the doctrinal texts foisted upon them. To the non-Christian, there are many aspects of Christianity that are perplexing and, in some instances, downright bizarre.

The church decided the best way of resolving these problems would be to start a reign of terror to frighten the savages into submission. Set up as a kind of tribunal, the Inquisition was headed up by a judge dispatched from Portugal. The "grand inquisitor" answered for his actions solely to the court back in Lisbon. Thus, along with two judicial henchmen, he interpreted rules he himself made up, and meted out punishments as he alone saw fit, often for crimes he'd invented. By the time all these ad hoc laws were codified, they filled a folio volume of more than 230 pages.

The palace in which these holy terrorists ensconced themselves was known locally as Vodlem Gor—the Big House. It became a symbol of fear. Recondite ceremonies were conducted in there behind closed shutters, locked doors. People in the street often heard screams of agony piercing the night. All the Inquisition's activities were conducted in strict secrecy, replete with impenetrably arcane terminology, fiendishly discrepant logic, antonymous questioning.

Children were flogged and slowly dismembered in front of their parents, whose eyelids had been sliced off to make sure they missed nothing. Extremities were amputated carefully, so that a person could remain conscious even when all that remained was a torso and head. Male genitals were removed and burned in front of wives, breasts hacked off and vaginas penetrated by swords while husbands were forced to watch.

So notorious was the Inquisition in Portuguese India that word of its horrors even reached home. The archbishop of Evora, in Portugal, eventually wrote, "If everywhere the Inquisition was an infamous court, the infamy, however base, however vile, however corrupt and determined by worldly interests, it was never more so than in Goa."

And it went on for two hundred years, with one brief hiatus. *Fides suadenda, non imponenda* (Faith must be the result of conviction and should not be imposed by force), Saint Bernard of Clairvaux had once stated, this becoming a church tenet during the early Middle Ages. But Saint Bernard was a nephew of one of the original nine Knights Templar and even championed this mystical order that itself eventually became a casualty of the Inquisition in England and France. Saint Bernard might have had more than a vested interest in curtailing the persecution of heretics. In any case, such enlightened attitudes generally had no effect.

The Portuguese viceroy in Goa happily condoned the burning of far more so-called heretics than the number of Hindu widows he saved from the funeral pyre by banning sati. Those subjected to diabolical tortures could also be counted in the thousands, and the abominations continued until a brief respite in 1774. Becoming a senior minister in Portugal, the marquis of Pombal, one of the few great liberals in a most illiberal land, ordered the Inquisition abolished. Four years later, he in turn was driven from his office and the evil immediately resumed, continuing, almost incredibly, until June 16, 1812. At that point, British pressure put an end to the terror, the presence of British troops stationed in Goa enforcing it. During this period, Portuguese power was finally waning, and the old colony gradually crumbled into decay.

The palace of the grand inquisitor was ordered demolished around 1830, most of its stones removed to be used in buildings then going up in the new capital of Panjim. The priests who turn such a handsome profit on Saint Francis Xavier's bones today are clearly happy to be rid of anything that might remind someone of the Inquisition their saint had requested be sent to Goa.

One of the very last acts the tiny state's Portuguese rulers performed was in 1960, erecting a bronze statue of their great poet Luíz Vaz de Camões in the middle of a vast grassy space between the moldering ruins of Velha Goa. Green and gold, full of a dancing, vibrant life, it contrasts starkly with the crumbling remains of Portugal's empire around it. It's as if those who had brought the Inquisition had wished to leave a more noble and uplifting aspect of themselves and their culture behind them, to remind Goans that the 450 years had not been all bad.

In December 1961, forced by Dr. António de Oliveira Salazar, the cryptofascist monkey then on Portugal's back, Indian troops marched into Goa, Daman, and Diu, the remaining Portuguese possessions, in a massive maneuver. The Indian government had negotiated with Salazar for fourteen years, trying to arrange a dignified withdrawal. Obstinate and paranoid, Salazar had refused to budge. Finally the Portuguese were ignominiously kicked out by the Indians themselves. Apart from some serious fighting in Diu, the military operations were practically bloodless. Perhaps determined that his nation would not quit Goa the way it had entered, Governor-general Vassalo e Silva pointedly ignored Salazar's orders to defend the colony with everything he had. He, too, one assumes, wanted to leave his own version of Camões's statue, his personal apology—even knowing that Dr. Salazar would most certainly denounce him as a traitor.

India has always been a bighearted, forgiving land. Newly independent in a new world, the subcontinent found little difficulty in ascribing its suffering at the hands of imperialist colonizers to a vanished age of kings and tyrants. With the death of Salazar, a poor man's Franco, and the reinstatement of parliamentary democracy in Portugal, the two nations soon became friends and equals.

Perhaps it is its brutal past that has made Goa a far more lenient and understanding place than anywhere else in India. That lenience and understanding drew me and my companions there in 1975, along with thousands of other Westerners looking for paradise. The bridge across the Mandovi River was still standing in those days, so we were able to drive from Panjim and its pungent, harrowing past, north into a lush world of waving palms, emerald rice paddies, and ten miles of the finest beaches on earth. Calangute was our destination.

We were visiting Ray, a friend of David and Esther's, then living in Goa. He was hard to find. The road to Calangute wound through dense forests of palms and luxuriant vegetation pullulating with exotic flowers. The occasional colonial villa, weather-worn, its curved terra-cotta tiles cracked or occasionally replaced by corrugated tin, emerged along our route, but even total ruins charmed us. The people looked as different from what I knew of the rest of India as the architecture: stout men with drinkers' bellies on motorbikes; women in printed cotton dresses, not saris, and comfortable enough with their gender to hitchhike or shout greetings to strange men. And the names painted on doorposts and store signs differed from the Hindu and Muslim names I'd become so accustomed to by then: Da Silva, Pereira, Da Costa, Miranda, Da Souza . . . There were also little bars everywhere, bars that sold alcohol. In a land still operating a par-tial form of Prohibition, this was a raving novelty in itself.

Calangute in the seventies was a tiny town of low buildings, deep ve-randas, sleepy amiability, dollar-a-week "hotels," and, near the sea, a me-andering strip of makeshift thatched huts designed to serve a new kind of foreign invader. Everywhere were what we still called hippies. And here they were not the grimy, pale-skinned, unhealthy dropouts of London or Amsterdam. Lithe, suntanned, hair tied in knots or plaits, rattling with ethnic jewelry, the men wore patterned loincloths so spare they were scarcely more than small bags stuffed with genitals. And the women mostly went topless, sarongs wrapped around their waists for streetwear modesty, to cover G-strings. The only footwear seemed to be toe rings. Jingling ankle bracelets made of tiny bells warned you the way Saint Fran-cis Xavier once had that Western influences were approaching. Outside the little straw cafés, or in the shade of restaurants with roofs but no walls, these latter-day conquistadores sat smoking ornate *chillums* or Rasta-size joints. The warm breeze was fragrant with hashish and pot day and night. Little wonder a dreamy lethargy seemed to have invaded these new colonists, who walked in slow motion, broke off conversations in mid-sentence, and stared at nothing in particular for hours on end.

I asked someone who resembled the guy in *The Blue Lagoon* if he knew where Ray and Debbie lived.

"Yeah," he replied, the accent perhaps Swedish.

I waited about a minute for him to elaborate on this.

"That's American Ray, right? Wiz the beard and the chick wiz big knockers?"

"Right," David cut in. "That's them. Where do they live?"

"I saw 'er dancing at zis party the other night, man," the guy contin-ued. "Wow!" He became lost in his own thoughts, and we had to lure him back to the present.

After fifteen minutes—it was like handling a three-year-old—we man-aged to gather that Ray and Debbie lived "on the beach, zat way . . ."

Off the little main road were various dirt tracks weaving through palm groves, past houses both grand and humble. A hundred yards off, behind a line of steep coconut trees and thick bushes, lay the beach and the crash-ing breakers of the Arabian Sea. Goan children, wide-eyed, laughing, screaming "Hal-lo, hal-lo, hal-lo," ran alongside the car. Pausing at a fork, we asked a woman in a ragged cotton smock if she knew a Ray and Deb-

bie. She was so beautiful, with huge almond eyes and perfect bone structure, that she could have been the toast of Paris couture runways. Shoo-
ing the horde of kids away, she pointed to a large walled enclosure with
a massive red-tiled villa and many flowering trees inside it.

"Mister Ray nice man," she said, her smile implying something more.
"Tell mister Ray you meet Isabella, yes?"

"Sure."

The wall had huge wrought-iron gates, which were locked. A sort of
mission bell hung to one side, and when rung was answered immediately
by two of the largest, fiercest, most unpleasant dogs I've ever seen in my
life. Frothing with fury, they snapped their bared fangs through the bars
at us, even their barking suggesting all the tearing and chewing they'd
like to do with our flesh.

"They were Gestapo officers in their last lives," said Esther, removing herself to a safe distance.

David rang the bell again, narrowly avoiding a set of jaws embedding
itself in his thigh. The ringing, gnashing, and barking went on for what
seemed ten minutes.

I suggested that Ray and Debbie might be out. As I did, a voice from
within the villa shouted that it was coming.

Ray had clearly just woken up, his eyes dazed and puffy, one side of
his neat beard flattened like a cornfield after heavy rain. He wore a gold
Rolex, a thick woven gold chain around his neck, and a floral sarong that
emphasized the slight stoop his slender brown frame was developing. One
word from him and the dogs slunk back, grumbling, into the shadows.
The rest of us exchanged hugs and greetings.

We were shown inside. It was dark, the shutters all closed, and the
overpowering smell of hashish wafted over us. When my eyes adjusted,
I found an Indian Aladdin's cave all around me. We sat at a long carved
wood table just outside the kitchen, from which we could see big spacious rooms full of Turkish-style cushions, embroidered and mirrored wall
hangings, mirrors in impossibly ornate frames, bronze and painted-wood
statues, low antique lacquer tables littered with objects d'art in jade, ivory,
gold, silver, and marble. Twenty antique muskets, their stocks inlaid and
filigreed, all of them more ceremonial than practical, formed a row down
one wall. Decorating another was a wheel of ancient swords of similar
opulence, the works of masters, some featuring gimmicks like built-in pis-
tols or a catch that transformed one sword into two. These were defi-

nitely not so ceremonial: Serrated edges on some guaranteed that the wound they inflicted would never heal; on others, dual grooves facilitated the quick withdrawal from flesh, channels to allow the blood to run away and down. Fine old *kelims* and huge silk palace rugs were strewn over the floor's large red tiles.

Hanging all over this dining space were carved wooden masks from Bali—this was long before they'd ever reached the West—and dozens of Indian miniature watercolors in frames, old ones, too, not copies. On closer inspection, I found each of them featured some scene from the *Kama Sutra:* turbaned men sipped sherbet daintily, their formidable penises partially embedded in the shaved vaginas of women wearing much jewelry and makeup and little else, who also sipped from golden goblets. The sex seemed as casual and almost inconsequential part of their time with each other. Other paintings depicted sexual positions so ingeniously complex that the woman often required three handmaidens to support her on her lover's proud erection. There was much fellatio, too, then women looking more like people enjoying an especially succulent and tasty delicacy. In one extravagant scene, a man penetrated five women simultaneously, employing penis, fingers, and toes, while a sixth woman held a mirror in which was reflected the bald and fleshy labia of the woman squatting over his lap.

But it was the eyes I noticed most in these scenes: They were dreamy and tender, usually fixed on the lover's dreamy, tender eyes.

> It is the breath of lip on lip,
> the caress of eyes, breasts, hips, buttocks, thighs
> in the beautiful embrace
> from which a child is born:
> learn it from the *kama sutra* and the world.
>
> —THE *KAMA SUTRA*

There were also many poignant images of postcoital embracing: A hand coils to cup an exquisite breast; a head rests in a lap, staring out at a night sky full of stars; bodies dark and pale rest within each other like spoons. The whole gamut of the sexual act seemed to be understood, accepted, equal, the man knowing how important it was to show that the love that fueled the lust became again just deep, desireless love after the physical act.

After the lovemaking is over
she may avoid your eyes
and act as though that abandoned creature,
whose body crushed those petals
on the bed, had been a different woman . . .

Then, making yourselves comfortable
upon rugs and cushions
spread out on the terrace
in the moonlight,
you may enjoy each other's company.

Let her lie in your lap
with her face turned up to the moon;
point out Polaris and the Morning Star,
the Great Bear and his seven *rishis,*
and tell her all the stories of the night sky.

—THE *KAMA SUTRA*

"Wild, eh?" Ray said, noticing my interest.

"Beautiful, too . . ."

"Here," he told David, "roll yourself a doobie. I'm gonna take a shower. Want some coffee?"

Everyone did, and Ray suddenly shouted, "Debbie!" at the top of his lungs, disappearing behind an appliquéd hanging covering a doorway. He handed what looked like a wicker wastepaper bin to David. It was filled with slabs of hashish the size of floor tiles.

"Shit!" Esther said. "There must be fifty grand's worth of hash in here. . . ."

"In this country it's probably fifty bucks' worth," David replied, finding some Zig-Zag papers and going to work.

It was then that I began wondering what exactly it was that Ray *did,* how he was able to spend so much time in Goa—and not on a dollar a day. The antiques in the villa alone had to be worth hundreds of thousands. Later I learned that what Ray did was export hashish oil to Canada.

I was standing, looking closely at an especially cunning, virtually impossible coital position, when the hanging parted and Debbie walked in. The guy from *The Blue Lagoon* had been right. Her breasts were unusually prominent, jutting in defiance of gravity rather than hanging, slightly conical too, ending in nipples an inch long that gave the impression of perpetually accusing fingers. She herself was small, with long fair hair bleached in streaks by the sun and tied up on her crown in coils like the rishis of old. She wore only a sarong, the most lavish one I'd ever seen: embroidered silk, handpainted with jungle scenes, and distinctly Balinese.

She, too, looked not especially pleased to see her guests, and acted out cursory hugs and kisses, then slumped over the table with a pack of Dunhills.

"Great paintings," I said, to break the ice.

"At least the men could get it up in those days," she replied irritably, lighting her cigarette.

I looked at Esther, who rolled her eyes. David was still rolling his joint with the concentration of a watchmaker.

"Coffee?" Debbie inquired.

There were three nods. She sighed, muttering to herself while slouching off to the kitchen.

David blamed our hosts' behavior on drugs as he lit up the slim, immaculate joint he'd rolled.

"What the fuck is *that?*" demanded Debbie, returning with coffee.

"Well, it isn't a Popsicle stick."

"It ain't a joint, either," Debbie grumbled, sitting down and picking up a lump of hash the size of a Victorian novel.

Before long she'd fashioned a joint that resembled an antique ear trumpet. Nearly a foot long, it spread from a half-inch tube out into a cone nearly six inches in diameter, and contained as much hashish as it did tobacco. Once lit, the thing smoked like a damp bonfire, showering the table with meteorites of glowing cannabis.

Ushering us out to a huge veranda furnished with rattan chaise longues and a well-stocked bar, Debbie left us with our coffee and the ridiculous joint, saying she, too, needed a bath.

"Big on washing, these people," I commented.

"I think their brains have atrophied," David replied.

"If they're smoking a few of these a day," Esther said, holding the massive firecracker of a joint at arm's length, "then I'm not surprised. What shall I *do* with the thing?"

"Throw it in the ocean. It won't fit the ashtray."

David carried it out into the sandy garden, dug a hole with his foot, and buried it. "Look at *that!*" he said suddenly, pointing up at the low tiled roof.

We walked unsteadily out into the incandescent light, looking up to where he'd pointed. Spread across ten feet of tiles were huge, fat slabs of what looked like toffee. I reached up to touch one. It was sticky. Licking the end of my finger, I tasted instantly something bitter, something familiar.

"Opium."

"Jesus!"

It was presumed, of course, that Ray had expanded the range of his exports. No one really minded a person smuggling hashish, but opium was something else again. Smuggling opium made you a drug dealer.

An edgy silence descended. We were the guests of a man who would go to jail for many, many years if caught in the West, or be executed if caught in parts of the East.

"What if they raid the house?" Esther asked. "We'll be accomplices. We'll spend sixty years in the Black Hole of Calcutta."

No one replied. If the slums of Bombay were where people who were merely poor lived, we could only speculate on what Indian prisons must be like. . . .

After half an hour—or what felt like half an hour—there was still no sigh of Ray and Debbie, so we decided to walk down to the beach. The dogs eyed us hungrily as we slipped out the gate, but obviously approved of our exit in principle.

Past fifty yards of palms, the beach appeared: a broad stretch of fine yellow sand stretching off for miles on either side. A deep, thrashing azure, the Arabian Sea heaved into frothing breakers that crashed clawing at rocks and shoreline, as if trying to drag the world back down into itself. This was indeed the very image of a tropical paradise—sky, sea, pristine sand, coconut palms. After Ray's stoned and claustrophobic museum, the beauty was especially liberating.

We were far from alone in Eden. On both sides, young Westerners sat or lay in pairs and small groups. Chillums were being passed around, guitars strummed, tablas tapped, discordant flutes blown. And not a soul wore more than the cotton equivalent of a fig leaf. I felt preposterously overdressed. Everything I'd ever heard about Goa was patently true. Little wonder Indian men were convinced all Western women were incorrigibly immoral. They, of course, knew that all men everywhere are irredeemably immoral; God planned things that way.

But the carefree Goans were different. They did not mind in the least. Although their women would never go topless, they had no objection to anything the hippies did . . . providing they paid their bills and caused no trouble. "Trouble" entailed coming on to Goan girls and hassling bona fide tourists. Goan men, on the other hand, jockeyed to get a Western girlfriend. It was a status symbol: It meant you were bound to get laid.

Yet many of the Goan men I came to meet with ferengi girlfriends seemed tragically out of their depth. Lost in conversations, all too often they boasted about how much whiskey they could drink, how much money they'd made, how fast their motor scooters could go, which Bombay starlets they'd met when film crews were shooting in Goa, and—this obviously the ultimate—how they'd be emigrating to Canada or the States soon. Few of them could afford the bus ride to Bombay, let alone the airfare to Toronto or New York. And they certainly weren't used to a world in which women called the shots.

The Westerners often made fun of them in ways they didn't understand. It was cruel, ungenerous, far from the ideals the Love Generation professed to hold. But in Goa, as in Haight-Ashbury, the dreams were corroding by the early seventies. "All You Need Is Love" had become "All You Need Is Dope," which was fast coming to sound much like "All You Need Is Dough."

"Hey, man?"

I turned to find a young, bronzed girl wearing a tiny patch of material held over her crotch by green thread attached to a woven silver belt. Her black hair was cropped like a Marine recruit's, giving her a tough, elfin appearance.

I nodded, and David and Esther involuntarily stepped backward.

"You a friend of Ray's?" she asked. The accent was southern: Alabama, perhaps, or Tennessee.

"Sort of . . ."

"Can you tell him Velocity needs to see him?"

"Velocity?"

"That's me. Can you tell him that?"

"Why don't *you* tell him?"

"Listen, man—" she tilted her hips and rested a fist on one in a faintly hostile gesture"—you gonna tell him, or what?"

"Sure."

"Thanks." She turned away, paused, then looked over one shoulder quizzically. "Wanna lay a coupla hundred rupees on me?"

"For what?"

"For *me*. Hey, it's no big deal, man. Either you do or you don't, right?"

"Right. I don't."

"Okay, okay. That's cool." She was thinking hard, and it didn't look easy. "You gonna come to the party tonight?"

"Wasn't invited."

"So now you are." She finally strode off, exaggerating the movement of her hips the way actresses do when simulating a sexy walk.

"Cocky little bitch," Esther commented.

Back at the villa, Ray and Debbie had clearly finished their complex ablutions, sitting on the veranda with liter glasses full of orange liquid, ice, and what looked like the contents of some orchid fancier's hothouse. An antique opium pipe lay on the table between them, wisps of smoke or steam still trickling up from its bowl. Ray now wore a silk kimono embroidered with mountains and dragons; Debbie had on diaphanous silk-chiffon harem pants and a small needlepoint vest open at the front to display a torrent of gold, silver, jade, ivory, and various jeweled necklaces.

"Maria!" she called, telling us to grab seats.

A stout and irrepressibly cheerful Goan appeared wearing an apron bearing the legend KING OF THE KITCHEN in huge red letters.

"Drinks, Maria," Debbie told the woman, rather haughtily, adding to David, "I have to check the dinner. You can't trust these people to do anything right." She rose, heading into the house.

The harem pants were utterly transparent.

Maria constructed three more florists' cocktails. Ray fiddled with a Revox cassette player—the most expensive ghetto blaster money could then buy, and something only sound technicians needed to purchase. Soon David Bowie was claiming he'd sold the world.

I mentioned that an Isabella had told us to tell him we'd met her.

"Yeah?" he said indifferently. Then he asked me, "Wanna fuck her?"

I shrugged, embarrassed.

"Ray!" Esther said reprovingly.

"What?" This annoyed him. "The guy's on his own, ain't he? I thought he might want a chick. All right?" He turned back to me. "She's dynamite—but you gotta make her have a bath first."

I nodded understandingly, then told him a Velocity said she needed to see him urgently.

"Oh, really?" he said, smiling. "Good. Very good. Efficient little worker, that Velocity."

He seemed unwilling to elaborate—and no one seemed to want him to. I added that she'd invited me to a party.

"You don't need *her* to invite you," Ray scoffed. "Any guest of mine can go wherever they want from here to Anjuna. Stupid bitch. I bet she hit you up for rupees. . . ."

"Tried," Esther told him curtly.

"Who is she?" David wanted to know.

"Just a smart little hustler who'll do absolutely anything—for the right price."

❧   ❧   ❧

Dinner was goat curry cooked in coconut milk. Ray had five servants, I discovered—two cooks and three maids—and he made them dress like French chambermaids to serve dinner. With the candlelight flickering across all manner of exotic knickknacks, I felt transported to another age. The feeling lasted until we set off for the party, walking beneath the stars along the edge of a roaring black sea, the wind rattling palm fronds, the smell of woodsmoke drifting out to mingle with the salt spray, and the faint thunder of distant drums sounding like the planet's beating heart itself. It was nice of Ray to inform us that the curry had been laced with hashish *after* we'd all finished our second helpings.

My legs were beginning to feel like rubber columns when we passed a clump of agitated, stumpy palms and saw far off the writhing flames of a vast bonfire spitting red stars up at the strong competition shimmering in that great cupola above.

At least two hundred people were standing, dancing, or sitting around the area where the bonfire crackled and blazed. Most were Westerners, but a few Goan men who'd grown their hair and been very busy threading dried beans and shells into bracelets and necklaces were trying very hard to look like part of the gathering, too. Instead, they looked dreadfully uncomfortable. Music belted out from a massive P.A. system set back near the shadowed palms and bushes, perched on raftlike rectangles made from wooden planks. Someone who sounded very much like Bob Dylan, but better, was singing something about twisted fate. It was only a week later that I learned it had been Dylan himself—a new album I'd never heard, called *Blood on the Tracks*.

Everyone knows you can't dance to Bob Dylan—you can't even hum him—but this didn't prevent the tribes of Calangute from trying. Silhouetted by flames like huge burning curtains, forms writhed and swayed, hair hanging or flying out in blurred halos, bells tinkling, beads and pendants and silver chains rattling. Scarves tied to heads and hands and legs waved like snakes; breasts and buttocks, some streaked with colored paint, all slick with sweat, rolled and shook and swayed.

Esther looked terrified, and David looked at the scores of seminaked women all around him—until he realized Esther was watching him.

"Woodstock—slight reprise," she hissed.

Ray had gone to talk to a couple who looked as prosperous as he did compared to most of the other white tribals. Debbie was nowhere to be seen.

"Feed you head, man," a skinny blond boy advised me, bobbing past, shaking matted curly locks, waving a smoldering joint the size of the Olympic torch.

Hashish was clearly just the aperitif here, too. Many people seemed unusually interested in their own hands, waving them slowly back and forth in front of their faces as if expecting soap bubbles to stream from their fingertips, indicating there were powerful psychedelics on the job.

Three hours later, a Dionysian frenzy was building in the air, something old and dark and decadent. Couples rolled languidly in the sand, exploring each other's bodies minutely, fascinated by every inch of flesh, of hair, of teeth, of clothes and jewelry. Lips and ears and eyes were touched with the wonder of beings who had never seen such things before. Some were making love—but with a strange and dilatory deliberation, pausing to gasp and shudder as waves of chemical euphoria gripped them. There were not only twosomes, but threesomes, foursomes, moresomes—great squirming piles of coiling limbs, heaving sinewy torsos, swinging breasts, shuddering arses, and twitching, proboscislike erections. There were also many solitary acts of sex. There were also cries of ecstasy, cries of yearning, cries of delight, cries of surprise, cries of sorrow . . . and cries of primal fear.

David and I swigged wine from a bottle someone had passed us, aware of whatever Ray had really spiced our dinner with now coming on far stronger than mere hashish. Colors were getting more serious, more colorful; strange echoes pulsed in the smoky air; the sand beneath my feet seemed oddly sentient, alive; and powerful electric currents ran up my spine, making me shiver with delight and smile involuntarily.

"That bastard," David suddenly said, his voice resonant, on reverb.

"I don't know," I thought I was saying. "I haven't visited the cosmos in ages. I'd forgotten how pleasant it could be. . . ."

He looked at me as if I'd been speaking Venusian. Then he started to giggle. The giggle became a laugh, doubling him over, splitting his face apart. It was a perplexing spectacle. Soon both of us just stood there laughing, as if that were our mission on earth: to stand there forever, laughing.

It was only after what seemed like ages that we became aware of another presence, other laughter. Esther stood a few feet away, pointing at us and convulsing with her own mighty hilarity. She tried to speak, but she'd obviously lost the knack, too.

Next, I wasn't laughing anymore. There was a ball of energy in my head that felt like a dwarf star rapidly outgrowing the little bowl of bone it had been confined to. I could feel its searing white light seeping through the fissures in my cranium. Surges of euphoria coursed up my spinal column and spouted in a fountain of rapture through the myriad channels of a glowing brain. I gasped, throwing back my head to gaze upon the flares of heaven, the starry signs, the twinkling messages that had been there, so plain, since the beginning of time.

As light as the light streaming through my nerves, I moved across the silken sand, down to where the sea heaved its dark skin over the planet's mighty beating heart.

"Can I watch you?" a voice said.

Crouched in the sand a couple of yards away, chin resting on knees, arms folded around calves, was Velocity. She looked about three years old.

"Yes, of course," I replied. It made me feel fatherly.

This prompted a bizarre conversation in which everything I said, the moment I'd said it, seemed to mean something else. Each sentence contained a sexual double entendre—but I realized it only after I'd spoken. Then the flesh melted off her tiny, elfin face, and I saw the skull beneath it, feral, mocking, vacant—dead.

I can't be standing here talking to skeletons, I thought, and abruptly walked off.

I found Ray.

"Having fun?" he asked, his smile making him look like Punch.

"Fun? Who's Fun?" I was convinced it was someone's name.

"She is," Ray said, pointing.

A beam of power shot from his finger. I followed it to where it had materialized a girl whose long, thick brown hair streamed with flowers. She danced like an incarnation of the thundering music, the pumping of her limbs keeping perfect time, even the rhythm of her breasts tracing a backbeat narrow and hard to master. . . .

"Swedish," Ray said.

The word meant nothing to me.

"They're living here," he added cryptically.

"Who are?"

"Yeah."

"*Who* are?"

"*Yeah!* Up in Baga."

Only the next day did this exchange finally make sense. The band playing live on the beach was in fact most of the Who, and they lived a few miles up the coast, near a place called Baga. I'd known Pete Townshend slightly in London, and was very surprised to find him the next day sitting opposite me in a Calangute bar.

The evening went on. Only as a miraculous dawn broke and the stars seemed to plunge into the black Arabian Sea did people begin to disperse. Esther and David seemed somehow changed—calmer, closer to each other. The three of us found our way back to the villa, and we sat on the veranda drinking fruit juice in silence, listening to the waves and the wind in the palm fronds, the cry of birds and distant babies, the barking of dogs, the calls of traveling vendors selling mangoes and jackfruit and coconuts and spices. It was all a fragile idyll that seemed as if it would break if we moved or made a sound. We had to be silent and let the wind speak. . . .

Ray and Debbie, both looking haggard, returned separately many hours later, going straight to bed. They did not reappear until early evening, and were clearly not on speaking terms.

Calangute did seem to be paradise. But after a while the veneer wore off. A few days later a tourist was found beheaded on the beach. No one thought Goans were responsible.

Some of the hippies there had been in India for several years now, had run out of money long before, had no way of getting home. I noticed many were beginning to look less like flower children and more like pirates. Teeth were missing—dentistry was a luxury none could afford—and cunning had replaced their innocence, a hardness sharpening their features. The girls became amateur hookers and thieves; the guys developed more dangerous criminal skills. Hotels were robbed; tourists were mugged; villas were burgled; dope deals turned sour. Now, clearly, people were being murdered, as well.

The Portuguese had left Goa nearly fifteen years before I arrived. But the hippies, in their own way, cared as little for Indian culture as their colonizing forebears had, also taking what they wanted from it and scorning the rest.

Freaks looked less freakish in India, too. Once you've seen a thousand naked sadhus running toward the Ganges covered with ash from the cremation grounds, garlanded with human skulls, dreadlocks daubed with cow dung hanging to their knees, nails driven through their tongues, and tridents in their hands—once you've seen this and not found it especially unusual, you're hardly going to get upset about a guy with shoulder-length hair and a beard who wears beads and floral shirts. Of course, the hippies mistook this for tolerance. They soon discovered how intolerant the Indians could be if provoked, however—which was why they gravitated to Goa, where the inhabitants were more confused about what to believe than actually open-minded. Again, the hippies didn't care what the locals felt or thought.

This disgusted me. These kids had no idea, either, how appalled the Indians were to see visitors from the affluent West begging on the streets of their desperately poor land. But India as a nation was then only twenty-five years old. Memories of the white masters were still fresh, especially in Goa.

Ray and his cronies were another matter, living like grandees, with the vulgar arrogance typical of the nouveau riche. Unaccustomed to servants, they imagined one treated them much like intelligent pets, assuming their menials were stupid if they didn't know the difference between a brandy snifter and a whiskey tumbler. They also imagined that having servants meant not doing a single thing yourself. By the time of our visit, both Ray and Debbie firmly believed that they were regarded as royalty by locals and white tribes alike. It seemed glaringly obvious to me that Ray's servants thought he was a lazy, pompous prick. And they considered Debbie a cheap tramp with the manners of an ape. But what bothered Maria and the rest most was the drugs. Ray flaunted his profession in front of these people; his ego made him believe his loyal Goan retainers would no more discuss what they saw in his villa than serfs would have complained about their feudal baron to his monarch. It simply didn't occur to him.

Nor did it occur to him that discussing the ins and outs of his business with me might not be such a good idea. He never asked me what I was doing in the subcontinent. Yet before long he'd invited me to see firsthand the whole process of narcotics smuggling between India and the West.

In retrospect, as I consider it, Ray was the missing link between the original hippies and the yuppies of the Reagan era. Drugs were the catalyst, the same bridge to materialism that had once seen traffic heading the other way. Ray, after all, had capital now, and had it in Swiss banks, too. Today he owns a major stockbroking business with offices in Toronto, Chicago, and New York. But it was a time-honored path he followed: the Kennedys, and many more—all of them owed their seed capital to the smuggling of illegal substances. This is not to say that Ray didn't pay a price for his easy money.

Velocity turned out to be a sort of bird-dog for mules, the runners who actually took the drugs home, risking seven years in jail for five grand and a plane ticket. She sniffed out likely prospects, hung out with them long enough to ascertain that they were reasonably reliable, and—this was most important—not cops. She groomed them, got them inconspicuous clothes and neat haircuts, then told Ray they were ready to go.

They never met Ray, or even heard his name mentioned, so if they were caught there was little they could tell the authorities. Velocity arranged for Ray to see them without being seen—because he would be traveling on the same plane with them, making sure they got through customs without a hitch, and without being set up by the drug squad to trap the person picking up their cargo. Satisfied all had gone well, Ray would follow them to a hotel at which his client had also booked a room. Then he'd wait until he was convinced the coast was clear, have someone collect the bags and pay the mules, then—and this was the only time he ever touched the dope—personally take the bags to his client's room, where he collected his money and immediately left. The chances of his getting caught were virtually nonexistent, as he smugly told me. His only problem was converting a hundred and twenty thousand Canadian dollars, cash, much of it in twenties, into American currency. Mission accomplished, he flew to Switzerland for another appointment with his banker.

Purchasing the hashish beforehand was something else he always did personally. He didn't want some mule getting ambitions.

I had imagined it would be fairly straightforward to buy hashish in India, since every other person I met tried to sell me some. I was wrong.

For a start, you didn't buy it in India; and it was not hashish Ray bought—it was hashish oil. And, he proudly claimed, he was the man who had taught the Pathan hashish lords how to manufacture the oil. This was what he promised to show me—his secret plant, deep in the North West Frontier Province of Pakistan. As Ray told it, he was treated like a deity up where the Hindu Kush formed a bridge between worlds, where the Orient began its slow metamorphosis into the Occident.

Ray and Debbie were a good argument for puritanism. Their relationship was so "open" it didn't even have horizons. Both screwed around prodigiously; Debbie boasting of the young boys fresh off the airplane she picked up and fucked—she emphasized this: *She* fucked *them*—and Ray bragging of more complex pleasures, many of them voyeuristic in nature, some involving local girls and animals. Money was clearly the antidote to the ennui and apathy that permeated their vacuous lives. Ultimately it would claim them both completely. Money's like that.

As the three of us bade farewell to our hosts, I promised I'd be in Bombay as we'd arranged, and that I was looking forward to a tour of Ray's underground empire and the opportunity to be shot by hostile tribesmen. It was almost guaranteed that I'd never see either of them again. Their short-term memories consisted of seconds—if their shorter attention spans even *provided* them memories at all.

⚜ ⚜ ⚜

We had to double back to Panjim if we wanted to get on the national highway leading to Poona, our driver informed us. It was a puzzling statement: Since he knew we were going to Poona, did he imagine we'd object to taking the only possible route there?

Rusty barges carrying iron ore from the mines of Mapusa lurked in the mouth of the Mandovi River, perhaps hesitant to risk the open seas again. An ancient cross beneath a roofed enclosure stood at the summit of a hill overlooking cashew plantations. A few people seemed busy with spiritual activities around it, lighting candles, placing flowers, praying.

I asked the driver if there was some special significance to the place. He replied that travelers stopped at the cross to pray for a safe journey. It was a tradition. I wondered if we, too, could stop. He said something about being late and sped on past. This depressed me.

Seeing the shabby remnants of Panjim's Portuguese past again, I remembered one relic that I'd apparently missed when we were first there.

I walked alone to the little chapel of Saint Sebastian—a man martyred by archers—set at the base of a small hill in the Fountainhaus area of the city. The interior was gloomy, confined, but illumined by multihued beams of light reflecting from a life-size and unusually realistic figure of Christ on the cross. It seemed too large for the simple little building that housed it.

This was the cross that had once hung in the grand inquisitor's chamber, the authority by which he had judged the accused, and the witness to the awful punishments that had followed his judgments. Its authenticity and its removal from the institution of terror to where it now hangs are amply recorded. Even old accounts of the torments over which it once presided leave no doubt that the Christ in Saint Sebastian's is the one from the hall of judgment in the Big House: Experts claim there is not another like it in all of Christendom. The head does not hang lifelessly, as others do; it is held upright, almost stiffly erect. The eyes are not closed in death or agony, either. They are open, almost painfully so, eternally staring, as if they had no choice but to see all the ways of this world—like those men and women whose eyelids were sliced away so that they could never shut out the living nightmares acted out in front of them upon those they loved. I wanted to believe it was tears, and not some trick of the light, that glistened in Christ's eyes, there in that dark chapel.

6

"We Should Share Our Sex Energies"

POONA, 1976

🌱 🌱 🌱

*I am a materialist-spiritualist. That is their trouble. They cannot
concieve of it. They have always thought that materialism is
something diametrically against, opposite, to spiritualism. And I
am trying to bring them closer. In fact, that is how it is. Your body
is not opposed to your soul, otherwise, why should we be together?
And God is not opposed to the world, otherwise, why should he
create it? . . . I teach a sensuous religion. I want Gautam the
Buddha and Zorba the Greek to come closer and closer, my disciple
has to be Zorba-the-Buddha. Man is body-soul together. Both
have to be satisfied . . .*

—BHAGWAN RAJNEESH

*Kabir says: 'The Master, who is true,
He is all light.'*

—RABINDRANATH TAGORE, *SONGS OF KABIR* (LXXV)

*P*andit Nehru once described India as "a madhouse of religions." Although more than 85 percent of Indians today are Hindus, he had a
point. The remaining 15 percent may be divided among six other major
religions—Buddhism, Islam, Jainism, Sikhism, Christianity, and Zoroas-
trianism—but that 15 percent is nearly 150 million people now, and *they*
make a lot of noise. Non-Hindu Indians also exert a disproportionate influence over their nation's affairs, often making up for lack of numbers
with higher visibility and greater spiritual ardor. In part this is to avoid
being swallowed up by Hinduism's tenacious eclecticism, of course.

The most significant fact about Bhagwan Rajneesh's formative years
is that his father belonged to a Jain sect founded in the sixteenth century

by a Calvin-like reformer called Taran Swami. Taran chastised Jains for succumbing to idol worship, and he urged a return to the belief in a formless, nameless nongod.

Born in 1931 in small-town Madhya Pradesh in the Indian heartland, Rajneesh read a lot of Taran Swami as a child. Raised in a minority within a minority, he soon came to identify with the saint's trials and tribulations, and saw himself also as a pure voice crying out in the impure and chaotic wilderness of Hinduism. Thus he, too, became an iconoclast; but his target was the demolition of all faiths so that he could replace them with a new one—his own. As a philosophy professor at a very minor university during his twenties and early thirties, with an M.A. from another such university, he knew what he wanted from philosophies and what he did not want. He also had an unerring grasp of what Western seekers of Eastern truths in the seventies wanted; and he learned how to give them precisely that. In a "madhouse of religions," the Shree Rajneesh ashram was more like a spiritual supermarket in 1976.

Poona is a pleasant city nestled in the hills about a hundred miles southeast of Bombay and more than three hundred miles north of Goa. Our car ran into some problems half an hour north of Kolhapur. As we bumped over the hump of a bridge, there was a loud thud, then the scream of metal grating over hardtop. The gearshift appeared to float freely through all five stations, engaging none, and the engine roared aimlessly when the accelerator was pressed. The driver pretended nothing was amiss, however, attempting to unobtrusively reengage a gear, any gear, as we gradually slowed to a halt near a grove of palm trees like every other grove of palm trees we'd passed during the hours of our trip north from Goa.

Indian drivers take breakdowns very personally. Without a word, our man got out and opened the hood. Esther had something happening in her intestines that increasingly obsessed her with finding a clean washroom.

"What *now?*" she hissed.

In order to give David the privacy in which to receive the regular allowance of verbal abuse that I sensed was overdue, I got out and joined the driver. He was poking at valves and wires the way motorists do when they know nothing about cars.

"Could it be the transmission?" I asked him—not that I know anything about cars, either.

"Some minor problem is there," he replied.

"Where?"

"These roads are too much needing repair."

I knelt to look beneath the vehicle. It seemed to be held together by mud and petrified grease. One thing stood out even to a technical moron like me: A long metal pole running from the engine to the rear axle was hanging down from the chassis, its front end burred from crunchy contact with the road. I asked the driver if this was a driveshaft, and if it was, should it normally be hanging down in this fashion. He crouched, peered, then wriggled like a fat snake underneath. At this point the car chose to start slowly rolling backward. I jumped into the driver's seat, pulling at the hand brake, which now appeared to be connected to nothing besides the floor. A scream came from outside. I stomped on the foot brake, leaning through the open window. The front left wheel had wedged against the driver's thigh. It look painful, but not serious. I asked him if he was all right.

"Put first gear," came an anguished muffled reply.

The gearshift felt like a wooden spoon standing in a pot of porridge.

Slithering out from underneath, the driver walked over to a ditch, clutching his right leg, as if searching the ground there for something he'd lost. Eventually he hefted a head-size rock and offered it to me through the window like a gift.

"Thanks," I told him, wondering if he'd finally lost what few marbles he might once have possessed.

"Place stone on brake pedal."

"David!" Esther growled behind me. *"Do* something. I can't sit here all day. . . ."

"Like what?"

"Like stop being such a fucking *nebbish!"*

I rejoined the driver, standing as men stand with troublesome machines.

"Shaft has disengaged," he announced, looking around perhaps for angels in a tow truck heading to his rescue. "Big problem."

I suggested that we'd better set out for a garage. He glanced at me incredulously.

"Garage not available."

"Back in Kolhapur?"

"Too much far . . ."

"We'll hitch a lift. . . ."

I don't think he understood the expression.

Just then I noticed the most terrifying vehicle of all the terrifying vehicles on Indian roads: a public carrier. Camouflaged in a riot of painted gods and floral patterns, its cabin festooned with charms, garlands, and shimmering tinsel ropes, and crammed with wild-eyed men in torn undershirts and tea-towel bandannas, chrome everywhere, more beedie-smoking lunatics clinging to its roof or on the hundred tons of boulders haphazardly stacked behind, this was a hooting, lurching catastrophe on twelve wheels—and it was traveling a hundred miles an hour straight at us. Since our car now blocked the road, this confrontation would be interesting. Public carrier drivers operate in a hypnotic trance, programmed to do one thing and one thing only: *drive*. Their reactions are nonexistent—which is why so many public carriers litter the ditches of Indian highways after having lost arguments with trees or each other. This particular stretch of road was basically one lane, with room for two vehicles to pass if each moved two wheels over onto the gravel shoulder. There was no room for this thundering juggernaut to pass. If anything, it accelerated, the air horn blasting to announce its presence.

"These lorry mens too much bad drivers," remarked our fine chauffeur, looking sheepish all of a sudden.

I told David and Esther they'd better get out fast. They retreated to a safe distance, where Esther resumed her recitation of David's shortcomings as man and husband.

I ran ahead, waving the carrier down. The air horn continued to blare steadily, dust flying up all around, as the huge image of a gnashing metal death lurched all over the road. Now another horn—sounding more like something from a clown's pocket—joined in. *Poop! Poop!* I thought of Toad of Toad Hall. *Poop! Poop!*

"I don't think they've seen us. What do you think?" I asked the driver.

He shook his head in horror, wringing his oily hands and hopping from foot to foot. I started jumping up and down, tearing off my shirt and waving it. The carrier was now a mere hundred yards off, still honking atonally. I was about to throw myself into a rice paddy when the pained yodel of desperately worn brake shoes pierced the air. The carrier swerved in several drastic loops, narrowly avoiding both ditches, and skidded finally to a halt not ten feet away. Emblazoned across its floral-patterned portico on a roof in fanciful script was the legend START EARLY DRIVE SLOWLY REACH ON TIME. Gandhi had probably once said it.

Ten men, all identically dressed in pajama-striped shorts, tattered urine-colored undershirts, pubescent mustaches, tea towels wrapped like turbans, beedies in mouths, no shoes, jumped out, babbling in one of India's 845 dialects. They were all small, with the bodies of twelve-year-old boys.

"Esther's scared," shouted David. "Are we safe?"

I was getting a little sick of Esther.

"They say they'll spare us if they can take the ferengi girl with them," I shouted back. "I told them no problem. Okay?"

I heard something that sounded like *schmuck!*

By now one twelve-year-old had shot under our car, beedie still fuming between his betel-stained incisors. I stooped to watch. Like an iron-pumper, he raised the driveshaft and, after moving it to and fro, suddenly smashed it upward, sliding around to give it a further mighty kick with his bare foot.

"Braaabrakkalladdamannapadlinnam," he urged the driver.

I doubted that this was how driveshafts that had fallen out should be replaced. But the driver regained his seat and started up the car. I heard gears engage again, and the vehicle lurched forward . . . then stalled. Bending down, the driver reappeared with the rock I'd placed over the brake pedal. He hurled it through the window and turned the ignition key again. This time the car moved forward with no trouble, stopping only when it reached the public carrier's bumper. The driver was smiling.

I thanked the little men profusely. They all grinned, looking the Westerners over with fascination. Then I asked the driver how much I should pay them.

"These are very poor mens," he said. "They are not needing money."

I gave the man who'd fixed the shaft a hundred rupees, then, seeing the looks of yearning on the faces of his colleagues, handed over another hundred, indicating that this was to be shared among the rest. It was probably a week's wages—but for me it was still only twenty dollars. They all seemed overjoyed, offering us beedies and asking me to take their photograph. One man, in a script that resembled the tracks an ink-logged spider might leave behind, painstakingly wrote what turned out to be his address on a flimsy scrap of paper—so that I could send him a copy of the photograph. Having sold my camera in Bangalore, I asked Esther to oblige. Grudgingly, she did. Then we set off again.

David and Esther dropped in Poona. They'd had enough. They would check into the "best hotel," then take a first-class train to Bombay. They couldn't wait to get that flight from Santa Cruz airport back to "civilization." They'd never return.

Alone once more, and heartily enjoying it, I had the driver drop me at a hotel near Shree Rajneesh ashram, bidding him farewell and a safe trip to Bombay. He looked at me balefully.

"Much trouble with driving shaft," he said.

I agreed.

"I am having to explain this trouble to boss, sahib. Boss too much angry. Now I am paying for repairs . . . so no money for family."

"I paid for the *repairs,*" I reminded him.

He looked at me with frustration.

"Bye." I walked into a place called something like the Sri Ganapati Meales Hotell.

"*Sahib!*" I could hear behind me. "*Baksheesh, sahib?*"

The Sri Ganapati Meales Hotell had a yellowed rectangle of paper pinned above the front desk. It bore a lofty thought from Mahatma Gandhi extolling the virtues of work—printed in wobbly type. Five old men sat in an office with huge dusty windows, drinking chai and chatting. They had clearly seen me. I waited some minutes, then hit a bell the size of a crash helmet, producing a muffled *ping*. Before long, I was reduced to shouting and rapping on the office windows. A man who claimed to be the manager informed me that the desk clerk was "away from station."

I waited. An hour later, the desk clerk returned, and half an hour after that I had filled out enough forms to obtain visas for most of Asia. Then another fifteen minutes elapsed while the clerk copied details from these forms into a vast ledger that could have been purchased in the nineteenth century.

"Don't you ever wonder what Gandhiji meant by work?" I inquired.

The clerk did not answer. Instead, he handed me a room key, demanding payment in advance. When I had surrendered about fifty cents for the night, he handed me a tissue-thin purple flier. It read:

Wonder done with naked eye

MICRO ART EXHIBITION
On
Rice grains, Til Seeds & Hair
by Shri T. NANJAPPA, B.Sc., B.L.
(63, Annasandrapalya, Vimanapura Post, Bangalore-17)
INTERNATIONAL FAME
Exhibited to BRAZIL, FRANCE & HOLLAND

"T.N.'S BELIEVE IT OR NOT"

Includes
- Splitting of HUMAN HAIR into 15 Parts (World Record)
- 572 letters on one RICE GRAIN (A to Z 22 times)
- Microcalligraphy of National Anthem on a RICE GRAIN
- Paintings of 13 Great Men on one side of a RICE GRAIN
- 1100 Landscapes and 130 Nudes on 5 x 8 inch Paper
- Carving of GOMATESWARA & BIRDS on RICE GRAINS
- complete BHAGAVAD GEETHA on 5 ½ x 6 inch Paper
- GEETHA SLOKA & GAYATHRI Manthra on COW'S HAIR & HOARD OF SUCH SPELL BOUNDING FANTACIES

"Thanks," I told him.

"Shri Nanjappa is also our guest," he informed me. "You are wishing to meet him?"

"Later."

"As you like."

A walk was what I needed, then food and sleep. I opened the padlock on the door bolt, which made me feel I had rented a storage closet, pushed open the door, and groped for the light switch. Two dazzling banks of strip lighting sufficient to shoot 25 ASA film at maximum shutter speed without a flash ignited. Perhaps their function was practical: to blind occupants to the galloping exodus of dachshund-size cockroaches that happened every time someone opened the door.

I stamped on one especially large brute with all the force I could muster.

I threw my bag on the narrow bed, raising a cloud of dust and the tinkling music of bedsprings. The mattress was as thin as gauze over the springs, which protruded at various heights. The floor was the kind of concrete that is mixed with chips of stone, marble, and something shiny—glass, perhaps—that is etched into a grid before it dries to simulate tiles. It, too, was so carpeted with dust that I actually left footprints. Huge scales of whitewash peeled from bare concrete walls on three sides, and on the fourth the windows lacked most of their glazing panels, all of their mosquito screens, and any trace of shutters or curtains. They gave out onto the main street below, admitting a stupendous level of noise. Another door dangling from one mutilated hinge opened into a bathroom far larger than the bedroom, but equipped solely with a stained squatter, a lone tap over a very used-looking red plastic bucket that was frosted by—I hoped—aqueous salts, with a brand-new green plastic *lota*—a pint jug used like a bidet—hanging from its coated lip.

The hothouse strip lights and gaping windows had attracted a fair swarm of airborne insect life by now, the room abuzz and aflitter. On my shoulder I found a thing so much like a leaf that I realized it had legs and feet equipped with sturdy hooks only when I went to brush it off.

I killed the lights, thrashing at the busy air with a frayed newspaper as I retreated into the hotel corridor. A faded print of *The Blue Boy* sagged crookedly in a frame someone had artistically decorated with shells decades before—when the walls had last been painted, no doubt.

"You are liking room, yes?" the clerk stated more than asked.

"I don't know how you guys manage to provide this kind of quality for such economical prices," I said. "Is *this* what Gandhian philosophy does when applied to business?"

"Gandhiji was not businessman," the clerk said earnestly. "He was great saint, isn't it. Mahatma is meaning great soul, you see. Gandhiji is spiritual father of India."

"Really?"

"He is *not* father of Indira Gandhi. Many foreigner they think because name is same that Gandhiji is father of Mrs. Gandhi. But *complete* error. This is because of *name,* you see. Both are having *name* of Gandhi, but . . ."

I cut him off. There was urgent business, I implied, and I had to leave. Reaching the door, I turned and asked if he liked Mrs. Gandhi.

"You are the devotee of Acharya Rajneesh?" he asked, suddenly grave, his voice as low as it could be and still span thirty feet.

"Not at all."

He relaxed visibly. "This Mrs. Gandhi is too much bad for India." He frowned, editing his thoughts. "She is enemy of Hindu religion. All our great men, our freedom fighters, they are now being locked in jail cell, isn't it? She has become like your Hitler: a *rakshasa*, we say. It makes my heart to ache when a great saint like Morarji Desai is in chains. Desai was good friend of Gandhiji . . ."

I edged out. Rakshasas were female demons. In illustrations they frequently resembled some of the singers on MTV. I certainly wouldn't mind running into a couple. Desai was hardly in chains, either; he was under house arrest, according to the newspapers, drinking his own urine to ward off illness.

❧   ❧   ❧

Fighting off hustlers, "guides," and vendors offering everything from "Ell-Yesh-Dee very pure quality" to pictures of Rajneesh so ineptly printed you needed 3-D spectacles to view them, I strode off into the seething night streets.

Soon I saw a sight that was to become quite familiar all over the West by the end of the decade: people in orange clothes, each wearing a long string of brown beads with a locket containing Rajneesh's photograph. The faces milling around Poona reminded me of those milling around Calangute beach: long hair, or big curly hair, for men and women, long beards, or big curly beards, for men alone. No one actually wore a uniform, but whatever dress code the ashram enforced obviously involved all clothes being dyed the same garish shade of tangerine.

The bhagwan had been in Poona for two years now. Before that he'd spent four years living in an apartment in Bombay. And four years earlier still he'd been teaching at the Mahakoshal Arts College of the University of Jabalpur, where he'd remained since 1958. Jabalpur is a small city more than 450 miles southeast of Delhi; neither city nor university has distinguished itself particularly during the course of its history. Rajneesh Mohan Chandra, as he was originally known, proved a notable exception in attracting attention. Students were drawn to him to the point of idolatry, not because he was a good teacher, but because he was a good *speaker*. Wisely, he quit his job when his activities as holy man became lucrative enough to make the move feasible. Soon he was Acharya (it means a sort of spiritual preceptor) Rajneesh. Before long he dropped all pretense of humility, becoming Bhagwan—which he translated as "Blessed One, though it also means God.

There's nothing like an ideologue whose time has come. After 1970, the bhagwan's staggeringly eclectic hodgepodge of faiths and philosophies, with its spiritual hedonism and utter lack of rules or moral base, took off like a presidential candidate who senses victory.

People—Americans, mostly—realize how attached they are to material comforts when they arrive in India to renounce materialism. In a country where many comforts do not exist to begin with, the awful realities of renunciation hit home. To rich kids who have tuned in, turned on, and dropped out on their parent's largesse, the average middle-class Indian lives in conditions of abject deprivation. Discovering that this deprivation is what many gurus in fact called materialism—and that what they termed renunciation means hundred-day fasts, forty-eight-hour meditations, sleeping on stone floors—is simply too much for these credit-card ascetics.

The bhagwan had often made himself unpopular by criticizing Mahatma Gandhi as a mob-pleaser, an idiot, a Luddite, and far worse things— a sure way to get yourself attention in India. As far back as 1969, he had shown he was no enemy of capitalism. Speaking in July of that year at Jabalpur, he said:

> Socialism is the ultimate result of capitalism. It is a very natural process. There is no need to go through any revolution. In fact, capitalism itself is a revolution that brings about socialism. Capitalism has shown, for the first time in the world, how to create wealth. I believe that in India socialism is inevitable, but fifty, sixty, or seventy years hence. India should apply all its best efforts to first creating wealth. The poverty in this country is so chronic, it has lasted for so long, that unless this country develops a capitalist system for the next fifty or one hundred years, this country will remain poor forever. Capitalism would make it possible to distribute wealth. At present, in the name of socialism, what we have for distribution is only poverty.

He evidently understood as little about economics as he did about spiritual philosophy, but he had the classic sophist's knack for semantic legerdemain. He could make naive claptrap sound positively Hegelian in its logical purity. And since he was exclusively an oral teacher—the list of more than one hundred "Books by Bhagwan Shree Rajneesh" listed in Rajneesh Foundation literature being transcriptions of talks and discourses—his primary audience was one more affected by style of delivery and his carefully choreographed, charismatic presence than by the content of the words floating through its ears.

This studiously contrived, carefully calculated stance—extrapolated from the iconoclasm of his childhood hero, the Jain reformer Taran Swami—achieved its objective in a snap. Soon Rajneesh had made himself a major target for the wrath of Hindu fundamentalists as well, especially the *shankaracharya* of Puri. This latter was an authority as august as, say, the archbishop of Chicago, but so belligerently orthodox that he was defending sati as recently as 1987 against what he termed a "reign of unreason" that was attempting to ban it. At the same time that the bhagwan was branded an antinationalist, he was rumored to be a CIA agent, too. All publicity is good publicity. An antiestablishment guru was, after all, the only kind of guru those fleeing Vietnam, Kent State, and Watergate were looking for, anyway. Thus the hybrid philosophy of "Neo-Sannyas" appeared. (*Sannyasi* was the traditional Sanskrit term for a renunciant who has forsaken all material possessions, living on offered charity alone, wandering, chanting the names of God, meditating, and often performing extreme austerities in the total isolation of remote caves.) The bhagwan instinctively knew this kind of self-denial would not appeal to his growing brood of Western fans.

He moved rapidly from teacher to "bhagwan," declaring himself a fully enlightened Buddha-like being. Devotees were not entirely docile in accepting this rapid spiritual promotion. In a collection humbly called *The Book of Books,* the bhagwan is asked bluntly why he calls himself God. With impressive candor, he answers

Because I am—and because you are. And because only God is. The choice is not between whether to be a God or not to be a God; the choice is whether to recognize it or not. You can choose not to call, but you cannot choose not to be. . . .

Another time, when asked if he considered himself to be God, the bhagwan's answer was slightly different:

No, sir, certainly not! Even if I were I would have denied it, because who will take responsibility for this ugly world? I cannot take responsibility for creating you! That will be the real original sin!

This typical explanation-by-evasion echoes the pronouncements of many of India's god-men: "I am God—and so are you. The only difference is that I recognize it and you don't . . . *yet.*" So who does that actually leave as God?

In the years leading up to Poona, Rajneesh embarked on a binge of "initiations," anointing his neo-sannyasis as palace guard. The orange clothes, a new name chosen by him, the japamala rosary bearing a large oval image of him, became the external signs of the initiate. Then there were the secret mantras and the prescription of various spiritual disciplines, mostly hybrid forms of meditation.

The 108 beads of the mala represented 108 methods of meditation, and, he claimed, these 108 were merely a start from which hundreds more methods would eventually spring. Why was his face on the locket? In another characteristically modest tome, *I Am the Gate,* he explained:

> The picture is not mine. Had it been mine, I would have hesitated to put it there. . . . The picture only appears to be mine; it is not. No picture of me is possible really. The moment one knows oneself, one knows something that cannot be depicted, described, framed. I exist as an emptiness that cannot be pictured, that cannot be photographed. That is why I could put the picture there.

Thousands upon thousands of photographs of the bhagwan must exist. His moist eyes are sometimes soulful in such pictures, pungent with a stagy wisdom, but most often they look predatory, steeped in a goatish lechery. In many he appears surrounded by women writhing about in a frenzy, his large, brutal hands pressing their energy centers—often conveniently located near breasts and groins.

I met his first true disciple, the first sannyasi he initiated. She was a somewhat pushy, arrogant woman. On July 1, 1970, she shed the name her parents had given her and became Ma Yoga Laxmi, embarking on an ambitious career of manipulating human foibles. The bhagwan seemed to have other interests in Ma Yoga Laxmi back then. He certainly did not cater to feminists in the fold when he said, "Always remember that Laxmi never does anything on her own. She is a perfect vehicle. That is why she is chosen for this work. . . . Whatever is said, she does."

The classic Indian wife on one level, or a brainwashed automaton on another, Laxmi could have been either, from my impressions of the woman. With the bhagwan's unswerving confidence in grooming her for her role as *éminence grise,* Ma Laxmi assumed greater and greater power and authority while those of her god and guru waned, his diabetes and asthma in the 1980s gradually forcing him into a seclusion that his be- lievers naturally viewed as a classic retreat into silence. Many great spir- itual leaders dissolve into the great Oneness this way in their later years. From their seclusion they teach on inner levels only, working from within the very hearts and souls of their devotees. Apparently.

But back in 1976, the bhagwan seemed nowhere near retreating— nowhere near acquiring the world's largest collection of Rolls-Royces either. He had, as photos revealed, aged drastically in two years. But the newly white beard, which was eerily similar to his father's, lent him a more venerable Eastern-sage appearance. He now looked much more in char- acter for the role he was about to play on the world's stage: messiah of the New Age.

❧   ❧   ❧

One small restaurant I entered contained clients who all wore the orange and the beads. My first thought, however, was that this implied the joint served food acceptable to Western stomachs. I took my Western stom- ach in, searching for somewhere to sit. The proprietor propelled me to- ward a table with one spare seat next to two young women and a man—all orange, all beaded. They seemed delighted by this intrusion and intro- duced themselves: Ma Rukmini—blonde, probably Californian, spaced out; Ma Tantra Ananda—dark, gypsylike, Brooklyn accent; Swami Hariprasad—a youthful Robert Stone, prematurely balding, a beard at least ten inches long but containing fewer than a hundred hairs in total.

They behaved like people who had recently smoked a bale of pot. What did they recommend one eat here?

"Near Bhagwan," Ma Tantra informed me, in a dreamy tone ill- suited to Brooklynese, "everything is good."

Her companions nodded profoundly.

I ordered whatever they had ordered, and asked about their experi- ences with the bhagwan.

"Love," Ma Rukmini replied, making the word sound more like *loot.* "Bhagwan gives us so much love."

Swami Hariprasad was a little more explicit, announcing in an accent as bland as the Midwest that had probably produced it that the bhagwan had put him in touch with energy he'd been repressing all his life. I finally gleaned from this that he'd been getting laid more in Poona over five months than he had back in Omaha over the preceding fifteen years.

I dug into my fried flatbread and some kind of curried mush composed mainly of potatoes. As conversation progressed, I gradually deduced that Swami and these two Mas had been enjoying three-way sex—a novelty that was "opening up their *chakras* to the *kundalini* energy" rising brainward from its lair in the base of the spine.

"You come for initiation?" asked Ma Tantra, fellating a spoonful of mango ice cream.

I confessed I'd come to study current developments in Indian mystical philosophy. It seemed better to lie than to get into the inevitable squabble over gurus.

"You gotta let go of that mind stuff," she informed me. "That's all crap, Bhagwan says. It's your mind that stops you *livin'* life. You're like in a lead shield—you know, those things what they use to keep out X rays in the hospital—and you can't *feel,* man. You gotta dump that fuckin' mind."

She asked where I was staying. I wondered why she wanted to know.

"Fuckin' shithole, that dump," she said.

I agreed wholeheartedly.

"Why dontcha come stay with us?"

I thanked her, saying I'd consider it tomorrow. We all arranged to meet the next morning at Bhagwan's ashram. They had to go home to meditate—or so they claimed—and I lingered over a coffee that had milk skin like an old condom floating on its surface.

Sickened by the sight of it, I ventured out shortly after, forgetting to pay. I had walked thirty yards down the garbage-strewn street when a voice behind stopped me. I turned around. Padding my way with a gait just short of a canter was a gaunt Western man, excruciatingly thin, sixty-something, dressed in a crumpled dark suit, a still more crumpled white shirt, and even, for God's sake, a tie.

"Vait!" he was shouting. "Yes, you, my friend! Pleece vait!"

The accent—all singsong uphill candences that made every word into a query—had to be Scandinavian.

"You verr not paying your eating bill," he told me, pausing to catch his breath. "Do not vorry," he added, finally aerating his blood again. "I haff pay for you."

I started rummaging in my pockets, but he grabbed my arm, saying he could spare fifteen cents without too much hardship. Then he introduced himself: Gunnar Otis, professor of psychology, University of Reykjavik.

He had the face of a cadaver. His cheekbones were wearing through his skin like translucent vellum penciled over with faint cartographer's contour lines. His nose was a plantain-shaped gray protrusion of something closer to pumice stone than skin; and his few wisps of dying hair looked as if they'd been torn off someone's aged fox-fur coat and stuck haphazardly on his skull.

I asked what had brought him to these parts. Gurus was the answer. He had visited every ashram known where there was still said to be a living master in residence. On one hand, he was researching the "psychology of discipleship," the factors surrounding human behavior under conditions influenced by proximity to those who claimed spiritual enlightenment—or even more elevated achievements. And, on the other hand, he was a keen believer in something called Kirlian photography.

"You might call ziss a subtle emanation of electromagnetic energy," he explained.

By the time he had finished describing the nature of his work, using metaphors and analogies drawn from everything from music to campfires, I had grasped that the human body is surrounded by an energy field that extends about an arm's length from the physical body (which is why anyone standing nearer to you than that seems aggressively intrusive); and that this energy field, or aura, represented in the past by artists as a nimbus gleaming from the heads of Christ and saints, or, in Indian miniatures, as a halo similarly distinguishing maharajas and holy men, can even be seen by certain individuals possessed of psychic vision. The auras differ from person to person; those of children, for instance, virtually identical in both boys and girls, change noticeably after puberty, males developing an elongated, phallic form, females a more oval one. The colors in an aura also reflect its owner's inner state, too much red meaning anger, and so on. Psychopaths and schizophrenics apparently emit a bewildering display of flashing lights akin to an electric storm. If a person is sick—or is going to be sick, and the symptoms are not yet physically apparent—his aura will distinctly lack the essential healing colors and look dim. Most important to Dr. Otis, the auras of great holy men are utterly different from all others: far larger, brighter, and composed of golden light

through which bands of healing rays—usually violet, orange, or blue—
are often visible, pouring out to envelop disciples or those in need.

The aura represented a person's subtler bodies, the ones that survive
physical death, and were thus more real than the material form, being
sheaths that surrounded still subtler bodies. All emanate from the soul.
The outside shell of the flesh was entirely influenced by vibrations flowing out from these other envelopes, not vice versa. The physical manifestations of disease and of temperament originate deep within those
ever-subtler sheaths. They are to an individual soul what the creation is
to God.

As for Kirlian photography, no matter how hard he tried, Otis was
unable to explain to me in lay terms how a camera could be adapted to
photograph auras. I did grasp that it concerned electromagnetics, but beyond that I understood as little as I do about Stephen Hawking's account
of what happens inside black holes.

Curiously enough, we seemed to have visited many of the same
ashrams. Dr. Otis considered Sathya Sai Baba the only god-man he'd
come across who appeared entirely genuine, and felt he merited much
further study. He'd shot superhigh-speed 16 mm film, he announced, that
proved Baba's materializations were not sleight of hand or trickery.

"Frame by frame ve examine dem. Derr frames are each fractions of
a second—understand?—so there iss not possibility of hand being faster
than eye. . . ."

He'd even shot low angles revealing materializations of japamalas that
showed, as the frames were studied one by one, the flash of light like a
hole into another dimension, from which the objects gradually appeared.
And several separate segments showed vibhuti ash materializations—one
clearly revealing a gap between Baba's hand and the place the vibhuti
poured from.

"It iss quite definitely transported from another dimension." He was
convinced. "Baba iss opening derr door to ziss dimension, but he makes—
how to say?—crack in time-space continuum with his energy force—yet
this opening is not actually connected to his physical body. Film shows
quite clearly a distance between the hand and the place where object appears. . . ."

Had this news bothered the physics faculty back in Reykjavik? Apparently not, I was told, physicists now being more open to the possibilities of anything being true, having watched every law they'd learned as

students gradually reduced to something true, if at all, only within a certain range of phenomena.

But what of the auras?

"The Sai Baba aura . . ." He seemed lost for words. "It was . . . well, quite extraordinary. Nothing like any other ever photograph. Even a psychic I am using said she never before seen such an aura. . . ."

This psychic had been so impressed that she stayed on with Baba. Dr. Otis's photographs, he told me, showed a massive egg of pure gold light extending several feet all around Baba's physical form, sometimes shooting out to surround devotees. During materializations it was full of white flashes and explosions of violet light. Furthermore, one picture taken during a darshan when Baba had stood still for longer than usual, writing in the air and twirling another finger as if churning worlds, showed an aura that spread out in vast rays beyond the entire temple compound, with a particularly bright and broad beam apparently shooting from his head directly upward and a great distance farther than the film could show.

"Like this beam vass maybe coming down as vell as up out of him," said Otis. "It vass like these old paintings off derr transvigured Christ, or angels appearing in derr heavence. . . ."

I told him I too had finally been forced to admit that Sathya Sai was possibly who he said he was.

"Like being around Christ himself," Otis replied. "Quite extraordinary. Such purity. So simple the message. Just love, yes? No nonsense, no one asking for money. Just derr message, this love. I must get back there wiss funding. This opportunity is so rare. . . ."

Siva Bala Yogi's aura, on the other hand, had been chaotic, he reported, bursting with a rather harmful and even violent energy that could damage those around him. He had achieved through yogic disciplines remarkable powers, Otis theorized, but they were not directed, not properly understood, and they probably interfered with any further progress in his own development. Otis had met a number of other yogis in the same situation: their austerities eventually unleashing massive forces, but forces that they could not harness, forces also in danger of turning dark. . . .

"Dark?"

"Power is negative, as well as positive, no? You are vamiliar wizz electricity? Zo . . . derr power go either vay. Problem iss, a person is not always knowing that derr light iss now darkness. . . ."

"Evil?"

"Come, come!" He slapped my shoulders with brutal ebullience. "We are not medievals. *Ignorance*—that is what we now call eefill, my vriend. Derr Nazis were not eefill. Dracula iss eefill, and very smart, too—but Nazis were ignorant barbarians, no? Only savages do eefill things—ergo diss iss mere ignorance."

Nietzsche was wrong. *Satan* is dead—and semantics did the deed. Which brought us to Rajneesh.

Otis clasped his forehead, groaning, "Ahyayayaya-yah! Derr man iss sick—physically sick, *and* mentally sick. . . ."

The bhagwan's aura, apparently, was like a tattered version of Joseph's many-colored coat: an astral rag upon a stick. The aura, Otis claimed, was cracked, a symptom he'd witnessed before, both in people who had damaged themselves with dangerous yogic practices and in chronic paranoid schizophrenics. The two seemingly had much in common.

In his opinion, the bhagwan either had schizophrenia or had performed exercises usually forbidden to all but a few. These latter generate energy so powerful that it wreaks havoc on the mental body and physical nervous system of those not properly prepared to handle it. The result is indistinguishable from forms of insanity that also include delusions of grandeur and the conviction that a person is God, Christ, or someone equally influential. An obsession with sex, he added, is also common in many such cases.

To the Icelandic professor, whatever was going on in the ashram provided fascinating material. Such borderline personalities, he continued, frequently exerted tremendous influence over those around them. Those drawn near were pulled into a mutual psychosis, transforming into little clones of their idol and frequently doing themselves similar forms of inner damage. Such a mass psychosis, Otis added, was found in Nazi Germany.

By this time we had reached my "hotel." Dr. Otis agreed to meet me the next day, offering a dry, cold hand. He looked like an embalmer or a mortician as he turned again into the throng of relentless hustlers. They took one look at that grim-reaper face, however, and decided not to press their wares on him. Crowds literally parted to let him through.

❧   ❧   ❧

Washed and abed, I soon noticed that the cacophony of screaming voices and blaring speakers blasting out Hindi movie songs so loudly you could hear the tin vibrating was not going to make sleep easy. I fashioned earplugs from candle wax—these candles a telltale sign that power cuts were *guaranteed*—and pressed them inside my ears. But without material to bind it, as in commercial plugs, the wax gradually gets softer and softer, soon flowing right up against the eardrum itself. This hurts savagely, and then the stuff proves hopelessly difficult to extract. An hour later, I was banging one side of my head to shake the wax loose, without any success, when, although half deaf, I heard three distinct raps on my door.

"Hi," Ma Tantra said. "Hope you ain't busy."

She pushed by me, looking around at my room in exaggerated horror.

"The pits," she decided. "Fuckin' rats wouldn't stay here."

"Cockroaches don't mind it."

"They don't mind a million rems of strontium 90, either."

This scientific know-how impressed me. I mentioned the problem I'd created in my ears.

"Lemme take a look." She made me lie on the bed while she peered into an ear, her breath warm on my neck, her hair cascading in a dark, fibrous tent over my face—a tent filled with the aroma of alien flesh and something that smelled like a mixture of linseed oil and sandalwood. It was not unpleasant. The bare legs beneath her loose orange smock were now astride my left hip.

She looked not unlike Cher does now. When not suffering excruciating pain from her hair clip, which was probing and scraping at my tympanum, I wondered what this nocturnal visit was all about.

After fifteen minutes, the pain was no longer bearable, and the wax was still in the crevice where it had lodged.

Ma Tantra's eyes looked soft and liquid when I finally sat up. She assumed a half-lotus posture on the bed.

"I felt this message from Bhagwan," she told me very seriously. "I knew he wanted me to come and help prepare you for his darshan."

"Really? How?"

"By sharing his energy with you."

I told her this was very generous, but could we do it tomorrow? I was very tired.

"Exactly. That's why I came. To raise your energy so you can be in tune with his Buddhafield."

"Buddhafield?"

"Love energy," she explained.

Then she removed her smock. Her armpits sprouted thick tendrils of black hair. But, entirely naked, she was on the whole even better-looking than I'd imagined she might be.

"C'mon," she urged. "Get natural, man."

I did. Then she ordered me to sit opposite her and breathe deeply with my eyes closed until she told me to stop. This took ten minutes, by which time the energy between us was tangible.

"Feel it?" she inquired.

"Definitely. Now what?"

"Now I want you to draw my Shakti force into yourself."

"How do I do *that,* exactly?"

The answer turned out to be much the same process by which I had drawn the Shakti forces of women into myself since I was fourteen. I could see why the bhagwan's religion was beating out its competition. I could also see the appeal it must have to Americans, who had by now turned Freud into a prophet and sex into the salvation that he had promised lay at hand. In Western terms, the bhagwan was the natural culmination and consummation of an era that started with the Pill, continued on through flower power's free love, women's lib, and finally gay lib.

Eventually, of course, along with everything motoring down the yellow-brick freeway of this brave new promiscuity, the bhagwan's Sex-ianity also screeched to a shuddering halt at the Great Wall of AIDS. Was this the Oz, the New Age Jerusalem that Rajneesh told his followers they'd find if they just followed the Path? By the mid-eighties he would be hermetically sealed from all that scared him—odors, people, life. Shielded by walls of bodyguards, daring to venture out only when safe within the bullet-proof luxury provided by one of his eighty-odd Rolls-Royces, the messiah was being frightened to death, it seemed, just like the religion of sexual freedom he'd come to give the world. It was AIDS, too, and not so ironically, that became his greatest dread, prompting the wall he continued building around himself even after he'd been hounded out of the States into exile. When the edifice was complete, he finally brought his personal terrors back to Poona, to die with him in that great empty hall. It's lonely at the top, and God is no one's employee.

ᴪ   ᴪ   ᴪ

"Does the bhagwan personally help draw out Shakti forces?" I asked Ma Tantra later. I'd been hoping she'd tell me to call her Linda or something, but she hadn't yet. Calling her Ma seemed out of the question now; and I wasn't certain about using Tantra on its own. She might not like that.

"Sometimes he blesses us with his grace," she replied. "His presence makes the Shakti force flow out more powerfully."

"You mean he's actually there when you have sex?" I tried not to sound surprised.

"If you've earned his grace. Bhagwan responds to us only as much as we respond to him."

"Have you . . . I mean, *did* you earn his grace yet?"

She had. So had Ma Rukmini and Swami Hariprasad. The three of them had sex while the bhagwan moved around, charging their energy centers with his hands. He blessed many people with this form of his grace, according to her. Sometimes in groups larger than three, too.

"You can't imagine the Shakti that builds in a room where fifty or sixty sannyasis are all tuning in to their sex force within Bhagwan's Buddhafield!"

She was right about that.

"Now we should perform Nadabrahma meditation," she announced.

"What?" I felt I'd drawn out enough Shakti for one night.

Instead, however, we had to sit cross-legged, facing each other, hands clasped, and hum. Ma Tantra lit the candle I still had part of in my ears, then burned incense that made the room smell like a hut where ham was being smoked over hickory. And we hummed together, covered by the soiled sheet, for quite a while. It made the wax in my ears vibrate unpleasantly.

Finally I thought I would be able to get some sleep. I was wrong. We had to do the "prayer meditation" first. This entailed sitting with arms outstretched, palms up, and head tilted back.

"You're gonna feel the *prana,*" Ma Tantra promised. "The prana energy. It'll flow down your arms. Then you're gonna shake—but you gotta think like you're a leaf in the breeze, y'know? Let it happen, man. Let your whole body fill with the prana. . . ."

And when I felt my whole body had filled with about as much prana as it could hold, I had to lean down and kiss the floor—so that the divine energy could flow into the earth, uniting heaven and the planet—which were also, Ma Tantra added, the same as man and woman, yin and yang . . .

"Sonny and Cher?" I suggested.

"Fuck *off!*"

Only the bhagwan was allowed to crack jokes around here.

This prayer meditation took another half hour. I did feel my arms shaking, from sheer muscle fatigue. Similarly, my body quivered a little, mainly because my arms were joined to it. Feeling I could justifiably kiss the rug of dust that amounted to my floor, ending this prayer meditation, I learned that the whole process had to be repeated at least six more times, "Or you're not gonna be able to sleep properly."

I doubted this, but there was no way out. Fanatics have to be humored, particularly fanatics whose Shakti forces you've just drawn out. . . .

Another convention of the society Rajneesh despised and had come to transform was sleep. He regarded it as a waste of time, according to Ma Tantra. After Shakti-drawing and our various meditations, there wasn't much time left to waste on it, anyway. After what felt like five minutes, she was shaking me, though ordering me *not* to open my eyes. This, at least, was no hardship. Then she ordered me to stretch like a cat, making sure I felt every muscle in my body receiving the command to wake up.

"Every fiber's gotta come alive."

I stretched reluctantly, the bedsprings beneath me protesting loudly.

"Now laaaaff."

"Laugh?"

The last thing I felt like doing at four-thirty in the morning, after less than two hours' sleep, was laughing. But this was the bhagwan's prescribed eye-opener: the "laughing meditation." So I laughed—*ho-ho-ho*—suddenly recalling the psychedelic laughter on Calangute beach with David. The more I laughed, oddly enough, the more amused I felt, and the more I felt like laughing, until I was slapping my thighs and weeping with mirth. Eventually I was gasping for breath, shrieking hysterically, tears in my eyes, hooting and howling for mercy, and I think this actually irritated Ma Tantra.

"You ain't takin' this seriously," she snapped, telling me to stop, that five minutes was enough, was all the bhagwan recommended.

"How can you take laughing seriously?"

She answered the question adequately with a weary glare.

❧   ❧   ❧

The address I gave the taxi driver was 17 Koregaon Park.

"Rajneesh ashramam?" He knew the place, all right.

The predawn light gave the impression one was viewing the world through the sort of blue filter used in day-for-night movie scenes. It was difficult to miss the ashram, even in this iridescent gloom: a huge sign in two-foot-high letters stretching above excessively ornate gates capped by odd looped crenellations read SHREE RAJNEESH ASHRAM. On either side sat large octagonal gatehouses with small circular windows like portholes. I supposed some attempt at style was going on here, Bauhaus, Moghul, or our house. The overall impression was of schizoid neo-utilitarianism—an architect commissioned to construct a Taj Mahal, then informed he'd be using concrete, not marble, for the job, and would have to dispense with the domes and minarets due to lack of funds, besides changing his original plans to incorporate windows that were the wrong shape and design but came very cheap.

Many orange and beaded young Westerners were crowding outside the gates, which looked as if they'd just been opened. Ma Tantra fled from the taxi, dissolving into the walking river of orange and hair. Perhaps she was embarrassed to be seen with someone in blue jeans and a cream khadi cotton waistcoat who had shaved—although not recently.

Pulled along by the flow, I eventually found myself in a large garden next to Chuang Tzu Auditorium. Inside it, at one end, on a white podium about twelve feet square and four feet high, sat an empty armchair. Plush and roomy, it was supported by the sort of steel column and splayed legs that typists' seats usually feature. This, I learned, was the bhagwan's chair. Once he had sat there himself, directing meditations personally. Now he did not, his chair handling the job on its own.

And this first group meditation of the day was something else. "Dynamic meditation," they called it. An hour later I had thought up far more appropriate names. The process had five stages. I was told this by Ma Yoga Parvati, a young girl with about ten times more hair growing from her scalp than anyone I've yet seen. A good foot thick and at least a yard long, its dense frizzled strands made her face seem unusually small—the face of a little child with rosebud lips peeking through a hedge. She wore a shapeless orange frock held up on her shoulders by two straps not much sturdier than sewing thread.

Stage one began before I'd realized it. All around me hundreds of people suddenly began breathing very fast and very noisily through their noses. Bodies started rocking back and forth in time to their breathing. Those who had colds were soon in trouble, since it was not just air that they started exhaling, and there was not a handkerchief in sight.

This segued into stage two—which frightened the hell out of me. People started screaming and jumping about, shaking their bodies violently. Some began to laugh or cry, as well, still screaming, though, and still thrashing around like angry slam-dancers on speed. I did not feel safe, but joined in to seem less conspicuous.

Beside me, Ma Yoga Parvati was beside herself with howling joy, her massive thatch of hair like a personal storm cloud swallowing her head. Her billowing frock soon floated slowly down into a tangerine puddle at her feet, but she didn't appear to notice, flailing away with still wilder fury.

I looked around to see that the entire horde was also upping the tempo, many others also freed of their clothing. People were bleeding by now, either inadvertently scratched by the frenzy of others, or victims of their own thrashing limbs. Ma Parvati's nose bled profusely, blood dripping onto her chest, from where droplets were flung off splattering others. A flash of red dots decorated my waistcoat and one arm.

But suddenly we'd reached stage three. The uncontrolled tumult metamorphosed effortlessly into everyone jumping up and down, their arms raised high, great hammering shouts of *Hoo! Hoo! Hoo!* blasting from upturned mouths.

Hoo!—the sound seemed to come straight up out of the groin. The bhagwan, I read later, dismissed the traditional Hindu primal chant of Om, the original word, as in the opening of Saint John's Gospel, calling it irrelevant to the New Age he had ushered into being. *Hoo,* claimed Rajneesh, emanated from the sex center, unleashing an energy of joy, the creating force itself, the vibe of tomorrow's sexy world. *Hoo! Hoo! Hoo!*

The unmistakable presence of gale-force lust throbbed in the air. And it built. Ma Parvati and her sisters were now jumping for orgasm, or so it seemed. The *hoo*'s got faster, sounding more and more like groans of mounting pleasure. In places, men and women jumped in unison, face-to-face, groan matching groan in an exhibition of mating techniques by some unknown species.

Instantly the hundreds of lust-leapers stopped, froze stock-still in their tracks. The only sound was dreamy, labored breathing, sated post-passion gasps, satisfied sighs.

This heaving frozen silence seemed to last for close to twenty minutes. Then, like some bizarre Quaker congregation, one by one people called out their love for all present, hugging each other. They started to sing and soon to dance to the dozen songs going simultaneously. There

were tears; there was kissing; and at least one couple proceeded to cop-
ulate in an ingenious position right there on the grass.

"Is it over?" I asked Ma Yoga Parvati, who'd just disengaged herself
from the eager embraces of a man old enough to be her grandfather.

She looked out from the jungle on her head, saying in a Marilyn Mon-
roe voice, "It's only beginning."

She seized me in her bloody arms and plastered her lips over mine.
Coming up for air, I noticed vast smears of blood from where her breasts
had been squashed all over my waistcoat. I took the garment off and offered it to her as a rag to clean herself up with.

"You just arrived, didn't you?" she said.

I confessed this was the truth. She thought about it for some moments,
lifted one breast and studied it with curiosity, then said, "We should share
our sex energies, then. You gotta get your vibes adjusted to Bhagwan's
love."

"Well, maybe later, Ma."

She promised that she'd been "deep into tantra" and could really help
me along the road to bliss. I'd had too much "bliss" already. Ma Yoga
Parvati smiled and shrugged—it was my funeral—turning to greet a man
who looked like the Anglican Jesus: blond, blue-eyed, and inordinately
clean.

Now that the "dynamic meditation" was over, people were wandering around or off toward other buildings. Here, it seemed, you couldn't
say no. You *could,* of course, leave. But if you stayed, you'd be saying no
to God.

I realized only much later why the hotel desk clerk had asked if I followed Rajneesh before telling me what he thought of Mrs. Gandhi. The
bhagwan was safe as long as Indira remained in power. He was a sup-
porter, and, more important, he could influence a sizable number of voters. Also, I heard, his support took a still more tangible form—campaign
contributions.

Only the following year, when that hard-core Gandhian Morarji Desai
shed his chains and moved out of house arrest into the prime minister's
office, did the reasons for Rajneesh's enthusiasm for a Nehru dynasty become apparent. A crackdown on foreigners visiting Poona soon began.
Suddenly the newspapers splashed scathing articles across their pages de-
nouncing the bhagwan as a pervert, a fraud, a greedy charlatan.

Then, a few months after Mrs. Gandhi was reelected as India's prime minister in January 1980, a Hindu fundamentalist got up during one of the bhagwan's discourses, shouting out that Rajneesh was maligning his religion and these insults could no longer be tolerated. The man tried to run at Bhagwan's podium and before the ashram guards could grab him, he hurled a large knife at Rajneesh. That the knife clattered harmlessly on the floor, nowhere near its target, who was reported to have continued his talk unfazed. Official Foundation accounts have the knife missing the ashram's god by a mere fraction, and insist he did not blink or miss a beat in his discourse throughout the entire incident. The managing trustee, Ma Yoga Laxmi herself, pulled out all the stops in a farcically hyperbolic press release, characterizing the business as an assassination, comparing what the bhagwan had suffered to Buddha's stoning, Mahavir's torture, and even the murder of Mahatma Gandhi—the man Rajneesh had often and openly reviled.

According to an eyewitness, however, the bhagwan was never in any danger, and his reaction was hardly "unfazed." He shook, and his voice quavered as he tried to continue his talk, which veered off into semicoherent rambling in which he blatantly insulted Hinduism yet again.

A year or so after the so-called assassination attempt, and a couple of arsons and explosions in Foundation buildings around the country, Rajneesh moved himself and his Dionysian crew to America, under the pretext of seeking medical attention. Unfortunately, U.S. immigration laws did not have a special category for gods seeking American citizenship, although they did contain a clause about entering the country under false pretenses and not leaving it when a visa has expired.

California's contribution to human development in the ashram seemed to be well represented and doing a roaring trade. Encounter groups, primal therapists, Reichians, gestalters, bioenergeticists, Rolfers, even humble exponents of massage—all were there, and many more exotic flowers besides. All had the bhagwan's personal blessing and wholehearted endorsement. In fact, therapy was another mandatory activity for the orange troopers. Clearest of all, though, was the guru's intention to keep Westerners happy. If it was therapy, sex, and rock music that did it, then therapy, sex, and rock 'n' roll it would be. It's true he denounced drugs publicly, but then it's also true that half the neo-sannyasis I came across were stoned from dawn to dusk on whatever they could lay their hands on. And there was much they could lay their hands on in Poona. The bhagwan had let the genie out of the bottle, all right, but he had not yet tried to put it back in.

A buzz of excitement suddenly seemed to flow through the orange crowds. Now, I was told, I was going to see the man himself. A good deal of shoving and barely concealed aggression went on as orange legions packed Chuang Tzu Auditorium, everyone wanting a piece of floor as near the bhagwan's podium as possible.

The bhagwan's residence in the ashram was called Lao Tzu House. It virtually adjoined an enormous hall with a roof supported by a forest of pillars—Chuang Tzu Auditorium. Elsewhere, there was a Buddha Hall. I imagined that before long the bhagwan would have buildings named after spiritual heroes from Tokyo to Tulsa, as long as they were not Hindus or Muslims. He rarely mentioned foes in his talks, which were otherwise eclectic in their scope of spiritual reference. Only Krishna had some appeal for him: He liked the story about the blue god making love to sixteen thousand milkmaids by the river beneath a burnished full moon.

In a publication titled *Dimensions Beyond the Known,* a transcribed talk concerns Rajneesh's childhood—his favorite topic—a romp through the Hindu concept of the *gunas.* There are three gunas: *rajasguna* (activity), *tamasguna* (inactivity), and *sattvasguna* (purity), and all they really represent are states of mind or qualities present in varying degrees and proportions in every person at any given time.

Rajneesh struck me as an extraordinarily indolent character. Clearly his parents and family had had the same impression when he was just a kid. Of course, they weren't to know that little Raja Mohan Chandra was not really lazy. He explains:

The first years of my life were spent like Lao Tzu, in experiencing the mysteries of the tamasguna. My attachment to Lao Tzu is, therefore, fundamental. I was inactive in everything; inactivity was the achievement sought by me. As far as possible, nothing was done—only as much as was unavoidable or compulsory. I did not do so much as move a hand or a foot without a reason. . . .

In my house, the situation was such that my mother sitting before me would say, 'Nobody else can be found and I want to send someone to fetch vegetables from the market.' I would hear this as I sat idly in front of her. I knew that even if the house was on fire, she would say to me, 'No one else can be found and our house is on fire, who will extinguish it?' But silently, the only thing I did was watch my inactivity as a witness, in full awareness.

A lot of the bhagwan's devotees, sitting around me now in the Chuang Tzu Auditorium, looked as if they'd spent much time themselves also exploring the mysteries of the tamasguna, stretched out on a stained mattress, Pink Floyd at warp ten, the sole "unavoidable or compulsory" activity being to roll another joint.

Swami Hariprasad squeezed down next to me. He looked like someone who'd jumped straight out of bed and gone for a five-mile run before breakfast. Everything was crumpled, sweaty, out of place, including his meager allotment of hair. I wondered if he might be unhappy about my drawing out his Ma Tantra's Shakti for half the night. Perhaps he needed that Shakti for himself.

"Have a good night?" he asked, clearly telepathic.

I nodded, hoping this nod seemed noncommittal.

"She's a helluva lay, no?" This seemed more like Theodore Pringle talking.

I agreed, hesitantly.

"The women here are unbelievable, man." He sighed, barely able to believe the unbelievable himself. "See that chick there?" He pointed out someone who might have been Morticia Addams's little sister.

"Yeah."

"Go for her, man. She does this yoga thing with her legs you won't believe. She's got muscles in her snatch like fuckin' hands, too—they virtually jerk you off in there."

I wasn't sure whether this would be something I'd like.

"Hands, hmmm?"

"A fuckin' *noose,* man—I *swear.* Just tell her you feel her vibes are right to help loosen up your kundalini—she'll go for it, I promise you, man."

"You don't take all this seriously, do you?"

He turned and examined my eyes for—what? He decided to look puzzled. I made it simpler: Wasn't he here just for the women, the sex?

"Oh, *man!*" He groaned theatrically. "You're still locked in that guilt thing, aren't you? You don't understand who Bhagwan is, what he's bringing to the world. Sex is pleasure is love is giving is sharing is . . ." He ran out of analogies. "There's nothing wrong with joy, man. It's our birthright, Bhagwan says. The union of man and woman is a symbol of the joining of heaven and earth. . . ."

"Yin and yang?" I suggested.

"Exactly!"

"Who is 'heaven,' then? The man or the woman?"

He muttered something about not getting literal-minded with symbols.

Just as Theo was offering to sell me some "unbelievable Thai stick," I saw the bhagwan hobbling across a distant section of garden, and pointed him out to Swami Hariprasad.

"No, man!" He laughed. "That's not Bhagwan. It's Dadda, his father."

I looked more carefully. The man did appear more like someone in his mid-seventies than his mid-fifties. But the bald head and white beard matched pictures I'd seen of Rajneesh perfectly. Little more than two years before, during the Bombay period, he had resembled the young Allen Ginsberg: balding, but compensating for it with long black hair and a glossy sable beard so vast it would have made Walt Whitman look clean-shaven. Now he'd caught up with Dadda, at least as far as hair went, who was twenty-three years older than his son.

Swami Theo told me that Dadda was now his own son's disciple. Indian children traditionally touch their parents' feet as a sign of respect; now, however, it was Dadda who had to touch Rajneesh's feet, as any other disciple did. He wasn't Dadda anymore, either, although everyone seemed to refer to him as Dadda still. Since October 15 of the previous year, Dadda—who was actually Babulal—had been Swami Devateerth Bharti. The whole business obviously satisfied the bhagwan, because he mentioned it often. In a series of transcribed talks on Jesus, with a title like some all-singing, all-dancing Broadway version of the gospel story—*Come Follow Me*—the bhagwan had this to say:

Jesus' father never came to Jesus to be initiated. John the Baptist initiated many, but his own father never came to be initiated. Krishna's father was not a disciple of his. My father is rare—not because he is my father: he is simply rare.

Dadda did not look so much rare, I thought, as old and sick. He was only sixty-eight at the time, but would die three years later.

"Try one," Swami Pringle urged, thrusting a Thai stick in my blood-stained waistcoat, which he suddenly noticed for the first time. "Christ! What *happened*, man?"

"Fight," I told him. "Vampires ripped my flesh."

"No shit?"

Just then a wave rushed through the auditorium, everyone raising pressed palms. The bhagwan had arrived.

A catlike presence, slinky, slow, yet looking capable of pouncing swiftly and suddenly, he did resemble Dadda—a rejuvenated Dadda, a Dadda pumped full of sheep's fetal tissue and rare herbs in some outrageously expensive Swiss five-star clinic. He, too, had pressed palms, bowing slightly, returning the greeting the way very serious Shakespearean actors sometimes applaud their audience while it applauds them.

According to my diary, it was language that the bhagwan had on his mind that mourning in Poona. After the mock humility of this entrance, he sat in his cushy CEO's chair, leaning back with hands still clasped, looking around at the swamp of adoring faces. He was either far tinier than I'd imagined, or the chair was much too big. His posture wasn't great, either—particularly for a man who supposedly meditated most of the time (although, I subsequently read, he actually told people that meditation was not particularly useful—it was just something to do that killed a bit of time and did you no harm).

Slumped back, staring, he took deep breaths—as if calming himself. For a man of forty-five, he was definitely not aging at all well. He looked more like eighty-five, and his hair had lost its color in strange ways. His beard now looked as if the remains of several meals had congealed in it, dripping halfway to his chest. And the hair below that gleaming naked dome of a skull had turned snowy white on the sides, but was still black beyond his ears, giving the impression that he wore a fluffy little angora scarf to keep those ears warm. His most prominent feature was huge hooded eyes, exopthalmic—a thyroid problem, perhaps?—and ringed with dark circles that spoke of secret excesses, late nights, tenacious partying. Or possibly just fatigue and illness.

The eyes were very sparkly, however, maybe because a spotlight had been positioned to illuminate the area he occupied, even in broad Indian daylight and inside an auditorium without walls. These were also gloating eyes, hungry eyes, eyes that wanted something from you. He'd probably spent a lot of time in front of a mirror, practicing with these eyes. He knew how to open the lids so that, framed by white, those eyes could pierce. He knew also how to close the lids and appear to be gazing upon another world, a hidden realm.

He understood the value of silence, too. In fact, he ended up realizing that he had more impact when he didn't speak at all than he did when doing nothing but speak, announcing on April 10, 1981, his intention to remain silent for the rest of his life. But this maquette of silence was quite a hit with fans even in 1976. All around me people were smiling serenely, basking in the bhagwan's presence. Swami Pringle even sighed longingly, like someone getting a massage.

I tried to tune in to Big Silence, but the bhagwan's face kept making me think that he was simply wondering what on earth he'd talk about today. His audience looked just as thrilled to hear him not speak as they did when he finally began to test the microphone, offering it an alternative to silence.

"In the beginning was the word," he said, in a slow, measured, and pleasantly clear voice.

I thought we were in for a trek through Saint John's Gospel. I was wrong. Having let this phrase sink in for some seconds, Rajneesh continued, "But this is total nonsense. There was no word in the beginning, there was only silence. In the beginning was the silence—this is how this writer should have begun." Saint John, he informed us, didn't know what the hell he was talking about—nor did most of his fellow gospelers. They'd never known Jesus, never been "initiated" by him, never really understood what he was all about. How could there be a word in the beginning, the bhagwan asked, looking around incredulously until people laughed along with him at poor Saint John's ignorance. The bhagwan himself had given a practical demonstration: He had not begun with words. If there was a word way back when the world was just a glimmer in eternity's eye, then there must have been someone or something to speak it, he continued confidently. Who or whatever that someone or something was would have preceded the word; ergo, the word couldn't have been in the beginning at all, could it?

What's more, who or what existed to speak that word must have been preceded by who or what created him, her, or it.

Rajneesh let this logical tour de force sink in. That Creator, naturally, turned out to be the Great Nothing he was so fond of. And what a perfect partner the Great Nothing seemed to be for the Great Silence. But, and there's always a *but,* before the Great Nothing there had existed the cause of the Great Nothing. This cause, this parent, turned out to be Silence. . . .

"Dead religion," Bhagwan pronounced, referring to Christianity. After all, Jesus had only a paltry *twelve* "initiates"—what could anyone possibly hope to achieve with such a bantam staff? The bhagwan slyly noted that he himself had forty thousand initiates, and would soon have many millions more. Jesus had failed miserably. Transforming this obdurate planet was an epic task, requiring the services of some spiritual superhero—a man like himself, the bhagwan.

Hinduism received a severe drubbing, too. It believed in Om as a first cause. Wrong again. These ancients were such fools. Unlike the bhagwan, they had no scientific approach. Our speaker was all science. Now we finally knew the truth.

Somehow, the bhagwan had now gotten around to the topic of language he had originally promised to illuminate nearly an hour before. Ancient sages thought words held power in their vibrations, their sounds. This was preposterous, said the bhagwan, laughing heartily. Everyone else laughed heartily, too. Words had no more power than farts—he used this old noun—since both were simply noises produced by the body. Jesus was also called Emmanuel, Rajneesh informed us, pointing out that this was really "I Am in You All," and thus a word with real meaning. Abraham and Sarah in the Old Testament, he stated, were clearly Brahma and Saraswati of the Hindu pantheon. Possibly, Rajneesh mused, the whole Bible was just snatches of Indian mythology some traveling merchant had picked up and then regurgitated for friends, a compulsive diarist then jotting it down in a quire of dried goat skins. The bhagwan laughed. Everyone laughed. I could not tell how seriously he took any of this, or any of us.

Moving right along, he was suddenly recounting what he described as "one of the great novels of English literature," a story about some fellow who built a house that fell down, depressing him so much that he set sail for unknown lands and discovered an island populated by children who seemed much happier and better organized than anyone he'd met back home. From this point, the plot degenerated into a series of zany adventures involving this unknown hero, the children, a band of pirates, a princess, and, finally, a kindly old sea captain. Everyone smiled knowingly at the happy ending. I wondered which of English literature's great novels the bhagwan imagined this was.

But he was on a roll now. To his credit, he genuinely seemed to enjoy reading. I heard names like Tolstoy, Jack Kerouac, Plato, Confucius, and the Pied Piper all mentioned in quick succession. Still, the bhagwan definitely had the gift of the gab, and unshakable faith in himself.

You can spot a real living religion, the bhagwan confided, by the fact that it attracts young people. More than 90 percent of his audience, I'd say, were under thirty. Old people, Rajneesh assured everyone, were interested only in dead religions. These, the bhagwan suggested, were just like flowers: They bloomed and then they died, and only old people were attracted to dead flowers. And, he added ominously, his ashram was no place for old people. I wondered about poor old Dadda. People "old in their spirit" ruined the vibes.

It occurred to me that old age scared him. He spent the last minutes of his discourse discussing Mahatma Gandhi's repressed sexuality and how it had atrophied the poor old man's brain. He'd tried hard to get a little action with young girls in his later years, the bhagwan hinted, but Gandhiji had discovered that sex was the answer he'd been looking for all along far, far too late in these later years. His "channels" had dried up, and he'd forgotten what little he had ever known about women.

This sexual ignorance was really why Mahatma Gandhi had been assassinated. His killer apparently had had absolutely no intention of killing the father of his nation, or anyone else, when he got out of bed that fateful day. According to Rajneesh, Gandhiji had beamed out mental forms that made his killer go into a trance, obtain a gun, and then blow away a man he actually idolized. The assassin had been as horrified by what he'd done as everyone else. This was why Gandhiji had forgiven him just before he died. The killer had never mentioned "possession by mental forms" in his defense, either—as far as I knew. But, as with everything that came tumbling out of the bhagwan's venerable beard, it wasn't even worth pondering over whether it was true or not.

Years later I remembered Rajneesh's discourses when I scanned Adolf Hitler's *Tabletalk*. Fortunately, Rajneesh didn't have the Führer's resources behind him, so the havoc he was able to wreak remained negligible.

After two hours of this I felt like tearing my hair out and screaming. Everyone else rose as the bhagwan left the podium and vanished behind curtains, just like the Wizard of Oz. They paused in a profound and blessed silence. Then, apparently, it was time for breakfast. But Dr. Otis placed a ghostly arm on my shoulder, asking, "Vell? How you like your virst glimpse of derr bargvaan?"

"I'd rather memorize all of Wordsworth's *Ecclesiastical Sonnets* than sit through *that* again for two hours."

Apparently Otis had managed to arrange an audience with the bhagwan. And I could come, too, as his "assistant." He needed help to set up all his equipment for aura research.

"Whose aura are we researching?"

"His." He rubbed his dry bony hands gleefully.

"I doubt that."

"Vass promizzed," he assured me.

❧   ❧   ❧

Having lugged several heavy metal cases half a mile under blistering sun, I eventually found myself sitting with the sepulchral Icelander in a sort of waiting room at Lao Tzu House. Many orange folk hurried through the corridors, trying to seem busy with matters of great cosmic significance. Several of them looked like Mob assassins in disguise. These watched us with eyes that crackled and fizzed.

"Don't make any sudden movements," I advised Otis.

All he did from that moment on, of course, was make sudden movements, flipping open cases, hauling out wires and plugs and canisters and meters and a pile of very technical-looking stuff that resembled what you'd probably have after dismantling the instrument panel of a jumbo jet. I wondered how long it would take to put whatever it was back together again.

"It iss togezer," otis told me, somewhat defensively. "Basically."

"Excuse me, brother," said a six-footer with perfect teeth and biceps like thighs. He filled the doorway. "Would you mind telling me what all that is?"

Otis did not mind in the least, but the six-footer looked no wiser as he ambled off in his size-fifteen sandals, brows clenched together.

He returned some minutes later with two even larger men and a small dark-haired woman who looked as though she'd just eaten something truly vile. She did all the talking, in a nasal New York whine. Otis explained his life's work once more.

"That right?" the woman kept saying. "Yeah? That *right?*"

Finally she muttered something at the three hit men, and they meekly vanished.

"You foller me, 'kay?"

Staggering under the weight of Otis's boxes and cases and stuff, I followed her, and Otis followed me, carrying the smallest case of all. We ended up in a windowless room, newly decorated but bare apart from some extremely expensive-looking yet vulgar armchairs that stood on linoleum simulating irregular-shaped tiles in garish hues, most of them variations on a theme of orange.

"You can set ya shit up here, 'kay?" the woman announced.

She stood watching as I tried to look like a man who's been around miles of wire, piles of meters, tons of plugs and gadgets all his life. Otis crawled about like the skeleton of a Great Dane, demanding resistors and capacitors and blue wires, red wires, white wires, and even wires that seemed alarmingly free of any colored covering at all. Soon we had what looked to me like the aftermath of an explosion in a television factory. Otis looked pleased. Then he found his plugs did not match the room's sockets. He tore off these plugs with his bare hands, stripped wires with yellowed incisors, then emptied out an old cigar box full of clips and screws and things with tufts of frayed wire on them. He stamped on this box forcefully, making the woman jump with fright, and then selected fat splinters from it. He wrapped his wires around these and thrust them into the sockets, receiving at least one vicious electric shock by so doing. Finally, he slapped on switches, and needles began to float in their illuminated windows.

"Yeah?" said the woman, when Otis announced that he was ready. "That right? Wait." She disappeared.

I told Otis that the mangled heap of wires and boxes didn't look much like a camera to me. He seemed perplexed, then explained that it wasn't the camera. It was something that measured electromagnetic waves—maybe. The camera was in the box he hadn't opened yet. It apparently required no setting up.

Two unreasonably beautiful orange women floated into the room, followed by the New Yorker. Both were young, fresh-faced, and very clean-looking.

"Stand *here*," the New Yorker told us, pointing at a spot on the linoleum near the beauties.

Otis and I obediently scuttled over and stood. *Surely not?* I thought.

And for once I was right. One blonde leaned very close to me and began sniffing. She sniffed in circles around my head, then began to work her way down, gradually kneeling as she sniffed almost every inch from crown of head to grimy toes (I had been asked to remove my battered loafers before entering the building). Otis underwent the same treatment from the other woman, looking very entertained by it.

I glanced at the New Yorker, who seemed to be supervising this very seriously.

"Bhagwan has allergies," the New Yorker announced abruptly. "He can't stand odors or clones."

"Clones?"

"Coll-lones," she said pointedly. "Or poy-fumes. He's very sensitive to gross material vibes."

Finally, these two sniffers swept out in the same unearthly silence they had maintained since arriving. The New Yorker next brought in two of the big, suspicious men and closed the door. The five of us stood staring at each other in strained and noiseless uncertainty. Then, some minutes later, an inner door opened without warning and the bhagwan stepped daintily into the room, smiling. Two more harrowingly attractive orange women glided in his wake. The room was somewhat overcrowded by now, but no one looked as if they intended to leave.

We all pressed palms, and the orange people bowed.

"Scientists," the bhagwan stated more than asked.

Otis and I nodded.

"Then we are professional brothers," announced the bhagwan, looking pleased with himself. "It is a science that I am bringing—you know that?"

"I haff been vorking viss derr aura, Bargvaan," Otis said, a trace of reverence trickling through his hyperborean voice.

"Derroara?" mused Rajneesh, clearly having no clue what this meant. "Interesting. And now you wish to take sannyas from me?"

"Take some tests, Bargvaan," Otis elaborated. "And take pictures."

Now neither man understood what was going on.

The bhagwan came and stood about a yard from me. His big, moist eyes searched mine, reflecting an inner unease that I found profoundly disturbing. He looked up, his eyes nearly vanishing beneath oily, toad-like lids. I assumed that this meant he was consulting the Great Nothing, or that I should be aware that the Great Nothing and he were on very intimate terms. He was not so much especially small as particularly frail and delicate.

"Hmmm," he murmured at last, returning his attention to me. Unblinking, his eyes were now trying to do something, to get a relationship going with my eyes. It wasn't working, and the bhagwan began to look irritated, as well as nervous. His breathing became labored and his breath smelled like decaying fruit—sweet, yet deadly.

"You," he ordered, "sit. *There.*" He pointed to the ground beside one of those pricey tasteless armchairs.

I hesitated. Before I could react, he'd sprung on nimble feline feet to sit in that same armchair. I thus found myself not a foot away from his elbow. He leaned onto the chair's padded arm, peering down at me, enjoying the advantage in height.

"Ph.D.?" he asked, his tone vaguely mocking.

"D.Phil., actually," I replied, unease poisoning every cell within me, heart thumping.

"De*file!*" he added, giggling more than laughing, looking to his straight men and women for backup.

All in orange laughed heartily at me, as if I were a hired clown.

"Defiles the mind," Bhagwan confided, his oddly cruel yet soulful face very close to mine. "I want only no-mind here. Close your eyes. I am the Murderer of Minds."

I felt scared. And stupid. Everyone had sat by now, and all were looking at me. Otis huffed and puffed a tad, clearly not used to so much sitting on hard floors and anxious to continue his work. I closed my eyes.

I heard the bhagwan's voice whispering phrases that I was unable to hear clearly enough to understand.

Next I felt his thumb reach over and push hard into the space just above where my eyebrows met and my nose ended. It felt hot and moist, and I had to struggle against it to avoid toppling over.

"You!"

I opened my eyes. The room seemed to glitter slightly, and the bhagwan's face had a smug look about it, a look of satisfaction—the satisfaction of having taken revenge.

"Yessss," he purred. "Much better to have the mind minded by the master, yes?"

I made no reply. He turned to his courtiers, smiling a see-what-I've-done smile. They smiled back lovingly.

"You!" He was referring to me again. "I think you stay here. You have died. I have given you another birth. Now you are mine, my swami." He considered something, index finger to temple. "Swami Dharma Rumi," he told me with a smirk. "That is your name in my ashram. And my ashram is all this world. I have much work for scientists to do. Much work."

"Professor Otis has some work he'd like to do, Bhagwan." I thought I'd better get that in.

"Ah, yes!" The bhagwan chuckled. "This old man—what is it *he* wants, hmmm?"

Otis attempted a brief summary of Kirlian photography, auras, and electromagnetic waves, concluding with his intention to show the world the wonders of the bhagwan's unique energy, on eight-by-ten prints and in living color.

The bhagwan smiled at some private joke, prodding the wires sprouting from a contraption nearby with his immaculately pedicured toes. He did it in the manner of a man removing a slimy length of seaweed from his path.

"With *this?*" he asked, raising amused eyebrows.

Otis confirmed that, but was interrupted by a great pealing chime of mad laughter that clattered out from somewhere high in the bhagwan's throat, eliciting the predictable response from his minions, one girl covering her mouth to suppress hysterical shrieks of mirth.

"You plug your wires into this body," the bhagwan informed Otis, shutting off his own laughter as if he possessed a switch that controlled it, "and you will have no more tools to use on those who may need them. This energy cannot be measured, Professor. Can you harness the light of a million suns and measure *that?*"

Otis looked frustrated.

"No, no, no, my dear scientist," the bhagwan continued. "The impossible is not possible for you, yes? This is foolish science. What man thinks he can measure the Eternal? Does the Nothingness possess specific gravity? Can you photograph *that?* Can you weigh it? Can you put it in your petri dish and observe it? Can you exhibit the Great Silence in a glass museum case? You cannot even *understand* it, my dear old man. Can you? I think there is no Nobel Prize for ignorance, is there?"

Then he stood. So did all the orange people. He walked toward the girl who had almost laughed herself incontinent, placed an arm around her shoulder, and lead her toward Otis. He then ran the palm of his hand down from her neck over her body.

"Old man," the bhagwan said to Otis, "here is the energy of life. Here is the only subject you should be researching. Otherwise you will die without ever knowing you were born. Science of life, not science of death. Look at your old body, sir. The life is ebbing away. Do not waste the little time with dead things. You must *experience*—that is true science. Observer must merge with observed to know what is observed. You must leave this place. But you will return when what I am saying to you starts burning in your heart. Yes, you will come back when you are ready for me."

He pressed his palms—the gesture was promptly returned—and moved toward the door by which he had entered the room. Suddenly he turned back, pointing a lazy finger at me. "You will stay, my Rumi Swami. I will see you tomorrow. This is now your home. I am your father. I am your mother. You are my son. Is this not what you came to hear? Hmmm?" He laughed out loud and was gone.

"Get *him* outa here," the New Yorker ordered her hit men, indicating Otis. Turning to me, she added, "Happy boithday. I wanna see you at 3:00 P.M.—*sharp*. Goddit? You need clothes. Whatever Bhagwan want you to do, you get to hear from *me*, 'kay?" She knotted her brows, running through a mental list. "Yeahyeah! Ya *do* realize ya pal 'ere can't come back inside the ashram, right?"

I nodded.

"Yeah?" she said absently. "Rightrightright! We're all so fuckin' blessed, ain't we?" She spun on a heel and shot out.

✤   ✤   ✤

Outside, I tried to console Otis. But he wasn't bothered.

"See? He vass too scared ov being caught out, vassn't it?"

"What a fucking asshole" was my assessment.

The doctor in Otis diagnosed paranoid schizophrenia without a shred of doubt.

"Mad," he muttered. "Mad and quite dangereuse. I sink zat, yes. Zat iss my opinion."

We ate a very bad meal in a restaurant that imagined it served Western food. White sauce coated almost every dish—we were grateful that it hid what we were eating.

In his hotel room, I finally got a look at the Kirlian photographs. They resembled gasoline stains in puddles. Ones showing fingertips, however, were more easily recognizable: four little stains in an arc, with a slightly larger fifth stain slightly below them and to one side. Otis knew all about the varying colors and shapes, and I had to take his word for it. Kirlian photography? Who knows?

It was already two-thirty as I packed my bags, wondering, while washing off the dust I'd collected just by touching anything in my fifty-cent room, if I had time to see the entire Prado emblazoned on a single grain of rice, or whatever it was. I decided to go.

Then there was a rapping on the door. I hid in the bathroom, noticing a huge albino lizard lounging high up on one wall. Could the bhagwan have some sort of telepathic powers? He did have a terrifying sense of humor. I heard the unlocked door burst open. Ma Yoga Tantra flew through the air, gripping me in a steely embrace.

"I *heard!*" she announced.

She'd heard right, too. And she wanted a piece of my Shakti force, since it was suddenly worth having, now that the bhagwan had personally recharged it, or refueled it, or whatever she believed he had done.

"Listen," I said, "I must be honest with you . . ."

On the way out, the desk clerk gruffly demanded about three cents for a Campa Cola I had no recollection of ordering. I would have paid thirty dollars if he'd waived the lengthy and complex receipt he spent fifteen minutes practicing calligraphy on before allowing me to run all the way to the bus terminal.

7

"I Like Too Much the Phfit-Phfit"

BOMBAY TO SWAT, 1976

ψ ψ ψ

Who or why, or which or—what—
Is the Akond of SWAT?
If he catches them then, either old or young,
Does he have them chopped in pieces or hung,
or—SHOT—
The Akond of Swat?

—EDWARD LEAR, "THE AKOND OF SWAT"

I lost my bet with myself that I'd never clap eyes on Ray and Debbie from Goa again. I found them ensconced in an extravagant suite in the old wing of Bombay's Taj Mahal Hotel. Their room, with its regal furniture, four-poster bed, twirling ceiling fans, and broad balcony, lent the couple additional radiance, making them less like minor feudal potentates and more like vacationing Westerners from a more leisurely and elegant age. In his rumpled linen suit, Ray could have been visiting a tea-planting relative; and Debbie, in a tight little cocktail dress ending in a froth of ruffles at the knee, with a matching turbanlike object held on her head by a giant emerald pin, could have been his Jazz Age gaiety girl or moll, the two of them enjoying an illicit fling. As long as they kept their mouths shut, this rather pleasant illusion remained.

Ray had not forgotten his promise to guide me on a state visit to the forbidden empire he claimed to preside over. First, though, he wanted to show me Bombay as I'd never seen it. He seemed very busy, however—so busy that much of my day was spent alone with Debbie, or rather waiting for Debbie to get herself ready to go outside. Not that "going outside" generally meant actually leaving the hotel.

I would sit, drinking several cups of tea on the balcony, watching ships

cleave the heavy brown waters of the Arabian Sea. When Debbie's outfit, hair, and makeup finally coalesced into something she deemed tolerable, we descended to the lobby, taking tiffin in the Shamiana, a huge
coffee shop designed to look like a billionaire's tent—then went no farther than one of the many exotic boutiques on the lavish white marble
floor.

These boutique owners welcomed Debbie reverently, behaving as if
the queen of England had just materialized. They would produce chairs,
send minions off for tea or fruit juices, and present their wares like oblations to a conquering deity. I never saw her leave a shop without buying another three-pound chunk of silver in the form of a bracelet, or
ordering another outfit to be made from hand-embroidered silk so gor-
geous you could have framed it just as it was. The day she told the Taj
vendors she was leaving, many had real tears welling up in their dark eyes.
But, she added after a suitable pause, she'd be back in a month or so.

Ray, too, was greeted as Ray Sahib by all and sundry, fawned over,
offered special merchandise no common tourist would ever dream existed. Vendors told him about fabulous jewels some financially embarrassed *nawab* wished to part with anonymously, or invited him to partake
of forbidden and very secret pleasures.

An establishment located behind the Taj, named after and run by a
certain Ahmed Joo, was the most favored of all Ray's favorite haunts. Beyond its unassuming exterior, past heavily curtained doors, the store concealed a special room at the rear. It was reserved for big spenders like Ray
Sahib. Mint tea or cardamom coffee was served beside soft and monstrous
armchairs; hookahs were proffered, with dark, oily tobacco marinated in
molasses smoldering upon glowing charcoals; and items never on display
were reverently borne from locked cabinets and oh-so-slowly extracted
from ancient cases so they could be appreciated in silent awe. Ahmed Joo
himself, a dignified and elegant old Muslim *pukka* sahib, supervised these
rituals, deriving as much pleasure from the treasures he displayed as his
customers doubtless did. Treasures they were, too: a Victorian model train
with five carriages, wheels that worked, doors that opened, carved entirely from ivory, every minute detail accurately and painstakingly included, even the very seats looking as soft as cushions. A steal at
$15,000—Mr. Joo was virtually *giving* it away. Ray bought it on the spot
and, I learned a decade later, sold it to a New York dealer for $95,000.
A maharaja's state *tikkaghari* (horse-drawn carriage) in miniature, made

from forty-three ounces of eighteen-karat gold, studded with emeralds, rubies, pearls, and diamonds, the four horses pulling it carved from ivory and gilded, its little coachmen made of ebony and jade, a cloisonné coat of arms set into each door, which opened to reveal an interior entirely handpainted with hunting scenes by someone who must have possessed superhuman eyes or have gone blind completing the work.

A man known only as Sirdarji was another of Ray's biggest Bombay fans. He was a *banya,* a moneylender, and appeared to own a somewhat sinister and splendidly decayed area of the city, fond of employing the phrase *banya ki raj,* which meant something like "rule of the moneylender." He also owned people: They *owed* him, and thus, until they paid up, he *owned* them and whatever was theirs, including wives and daughters. The Sirdarji was also an art dealer who specialized in erotica. This was where Ray had purchased his miniatures and where he made some more arcane acquisitions.

Early one sultry evening, we were sitting in Sirdarji's "office." This air-conditioned room was paneled in faded teak and furnished with expensive reproduction sofas and chairs that might have suited an emperor's throne room but here screamed at you in gilded vulgarity. Walls and shelves were strewn with both original and fake erotic paintings, sculpture, and objects d'art, all depicting variations on the sex act that boggled the mind.

A gold-and-ebony pipe of opium laced with cocaine was being passed around while Ray exchanged dollars for rupees at nearly double the government-enforced bank rate. From a locked drawer in his great gilded whore of a desk, Sirdarji hefted bricks of banknotes, stacking them in towers before him. He loved money the way Ray did—loved the *idea* of it, the satisfying weight and bulk of six-inch-thick slabs of big bills bound with string or rubber bands.

Both Ray and Sirdarji adored playing the *burra* sahib, the Big Man—someone the Raj had trained the little Indian man to recognize instantly and treat with stereotypical fawning obsequiousness.

"I'm gonna show my friend here the Cages tonight," Ray announced, rolling up a sheaf of hundreds to shove into a pants pocket, smiling a foxy smile.

"Ach!" Sirdarji threw up thickly veined and brutal hands. "He does not want those grass *bidis,* do you, my good friend?" He flashed a mouthful of gold teeth at me. Grass bidis were country prostitutes.

"My *friends!*" Sirdarji exclaimed, magnanimously sweeping jeweled fingers up toward the heavens again, as if about to grant us half a kingdom. "You will do me the honor of taking my *bibi khana* as if it were your own. As you are aware, Ray Sahib, I have only the best girls. Tell him, tell your friend that Sirdarji's bibi khana is the best in all of the Bombay. You like white girl—you take her. Chinese girl, Turkey girl, Sudan girl, India girl, America girl—yes, my good friend, you take her. You take *all* . . . if you are *takra!*" He shook a clenched fist, making it clear what takra meant. "Everyone just like Shahzadgai—I promise you, good friend. *Puh Kher raghli* . . . Always it is so for friend of Ray Sahib at my house."

He was speaking Pushtu, I discovered from Ray later, saying the women in his personal whorehouse were all like princesses, and that we were welcome there, welcome to all his girls—if we were "strong" enough, that was. Pushtu was the language of Ray's underground empire. For the first time, I found out that the place was called Swat. The state of Swat. I'd never heard of it, although the name instantly conjured up swamps and plagues of mosquitoes in my mind.

"Sirdarji's from Swat," Ray explained. "His real name is Rahmani Khan, see? Khan means chief, and so does Sirdar in Hindi. He's a Swati khan. Thousands of acres of *zmaka,* rich as . . ."

He trailed off, thinking. I expected him to say "rich as *me,*" but words often eluded him. Where the hell was Swat? I imagined we were going somewhere near the Pakistan-Kashmir border. Finally, after Ray's extremely vague description, I located the place on a large, ancient British map at the hotel, using a magnifying glass. It was up in an area that here resembled a bent finger crushed between Afghanistan, Soviet Central Asia, and China. The capital, Saidu Sharif, did not even appear on this map. Indeed, north of a place called Malakand, which itself was just southwest of the area identified as Swat, the next major city on this map was somewhere named K'a-Shih—and *that* was at least a hundred miles inside the Chinese border. I mentioned this to Ray.

He laughed. "That's the way I'd like to keep it, too. Don't want tourists messing things up. Tourists bring in government; government brings in cops; cops bring nothing but fuckin' trouble."

He claimed he'd instructed his "people" to make sure that anyone resembling a cartographer was to be given "fuckin' uncooperative cooperation." Swat, he told me at least thirty times, was "the Switzerland of the

East." I still pictured it, however, as a malarial swamp, famous solely for being where the first flyswatter had been invented.

But this conversation took place later. That night, in spite of Sirdarji's exhortations, Ray insisted on taking me to the Cages. A street in an exceptionally hectic and shabby area of Bombay, it was devoted entirely to the business of two professions: dentistry and prostitution. The dentists occupied second-floor walk-ups, and the prostitutes plied their trade from . . . well, cages. Where other shops might have had walls and doors, these "brothels" had bars, just like Hollywood jail cells. Behind them, often peering out, hands gripping the metal rods like prisoners, were the hookers. Many were village girls purchased from their parents and little more than thirteen or fourteen. They were grotesquely made up: eyeliner applied with a jumbo Magic Marker; eyelashes half an inch thick and curling out practically to their ears; crimson rouge, unnatural on dark skin; and a heavy dusting of white powder, ostensibly to hide this skin color, but actually emphasizing it in a macabre way. Their lips, too, thickly daubed with red, looked purple, like the lips of dying people. Their clothes glittered, sewn from the same crackling fabric used to dress the ethnic dolls sold in airport souvenir shops. Rather than the cloth-of-gold it was meant to suggest, it reminded me of Christmas tinsel.

Beneath this finery the caged women frequently displayed pudgy, misshapen bodies; doughy, waiflike faces; and pathetic stares. They did not seem unhappy. Instead, a mood of Fellini-esque gaiety prevailed along the rows, pink little tongues flicking suggestively through the bars, forefingers humping fists decorated with patterns in henna like dried blood, grimy little breasts revealed and squeezed as if proving their freshness. And everywhere we walked, the cackling laughter and calls of *Hey, American: fikky-fikky, sucky-sucky . . . Mister! Sahib! Nice girl, good girl . . . Sahib! You like? Best girl, good girl, clean girl . . .*

A ferengi would be the best catch any of these girls could make—for the pimps who owned them. They had to pay back the money their parents had sold them for originally before they would ever see a rupee of what they earned on their backs or their knees—and probably none of them knew much about accounting. Used up at eighteen, they would end their days begging, if disease did not claim them first. The average life span for India's poor is still well below thirty years—as it was in nineteenth-century London.

"Buck a fuck," said Ray, as we walked down the sad row of cells. "Deal

of the century. Actually, for a buck you could fuck the whole cage twice—
if your dick hasn't festered down to gristle after the first three. . . ." He
brayed laughter, some of the hellish dolls laughing back, laughing with him.

I told him this was awful, sad and awful.

Fortunately the produce on display that evening did not strike a match
in him. Bored and irritated, he eventually suggested a drink and promised
something that would amuse me.

Behind the Taj Mahal Hotel, in a gloomy Victorian sidestreet, was an
establishment called the Diplomat, a cheap hotel where less affluent Westerners liked to stay. It had a bar, but this bar, for mysterious reasons, was
installed in a building adjacent to the hotel, with its own entrance. It also
lacked any windows. The blast of almost icy conditioned air reeked of
mildew and tobacco when we stepped in. Whatever cooled it desperately
needed new filters, a major overhaul, and a good soak in disinfectant. As
always, Ray Sahib was treated like a deity. Two bloated Indians were virtually thrown from their table, to retreat with their pint bottles of King-
fisher into a corner while a shoeless bearer swabbed the puddles of beer
they'd left with a rag he'd just employed to wipe the ashtray. Then the
manager personally dusted off the chairs he offered Ray Sahib and me
with his own handkerchief.

"I am always too much happy when Ray Sahib come," this manager
informed me.

"Seen Franco lately?" Ray asked him.

The manager nodded grimly.

"Same room?"

He nodded grimly again.

"Great!" Ray slapped my hand, informing the manager, "My friend
here is a connoisseur of scum, Kumar. Think he'll enjoy Franco and Sophie?"

Ray evaded my questions, pointing out various people seated in the
room. The other customers were all either debauched, villainous-looking
Indians, or Westerners who, judging by the profusion of their ethnic silver and flowing silk, were slightly wealthier than the average hippie, but
still members of the species. Ray identified each customer to me in a low
voice, describing his involvement in drugs or vice of various kinds, or
both.

"Small-time punks" was how he assessed them all.

Whiskey sours arrived—not that I'd ordered one—and Ray seemed
suddenly anxious to gulp them down and leave.

I suddenly wished I was back in Puttaparthi. Safe.

We returned to the Diplomat, where Ray Sahib was grandly received, proceeding by means of a shuddering, claustrophobic elevator up to the fourth floor. The corridor smelled like the bar, but was warmer. Ray knocked on a door, from behind which blared a track from *Exile on Main Street.* Then an accented and muffled voice hollered at us to piss off.

"Franco!" Ray shouted, knocking louder.

The door opened a crack, and a pale face with an appalling complexion peered out.

"Eet's Raymondo!" Franco shouted to someone in the room, flinging open the door and grabbing Ray in an eager embrace. Ray roughly extricated himself and brushed at the sleeves of his immaculate suit.

Franco stood before us, wasted, gaunt, an unruly nimbus of black curls surrounding a ravaged face, clad only in creased black cotton pajama pants. I guessed he was in his early twenties. The pants' drawstrings hung loosely below a spidery tuft of pubic hair. Running like stations on a subway map along the veins of his arms were red welts and sores and ugly scabs.

The room was a sordid junkies' lair more vile than anything in William Burroughs's imagination: numerous blackened teaspoons with bent stems rested on ledges and tables, containing rolled-up pea-size cotton balls or the insides of cigarette filters stuck in the bowls by brown scum; spent matches burned down a fraction from the end were also scattered over every surface; so were clothes that needed a thorough burning. Several tumblers full of murky pale pink liquid held hypodermic syringes that belonged in medical museums. The Rolling Stones thrashed and barked from a cheap cassette recorder held together by Scotch tape.

Stretched out like an exhausted swimmer in a turbulent ocean of sheets stained with everything from blood to curried grease lay Sophie. Barely twenty, if that, unaware of her lank and matted long blond hair, she turned a once-pretty face toward us, its skin drawn, haunted, her weary eyes experienced. Wearing only a ragged cotton dressing gown minus belt, she made no attempt to conceal the purple bruises that floated like clouds over a sky of almost translucent skin, from her thighs up to a wedge-shaped one above her left breast, and a cirrus line of coin-size smears descending in an arc from nape to throat.

She tried to greet Ray enthusiastically, but the falling cadences of her weary French accent just made her words seem all the more lifeless.

"Did you bring anything, man?" asked Franco.

Once introduced, I ceased to exist for either of our hosts.

Ray pulled a plastic film canister from his jacket, holding it up between thumb and forefinger like a magician about to demonstrate a disappearing trick.

"Oh, man! Dat's grade . . ." Sophie became nervous with excitement.

Franco reached for the canister, but Ray smoothly flipped it over his shoulder, catching it behind his back with the other hand. He must have practiced the move.

"A little matter of price, Franco," he said.

"Sure, man. Sure—whatever eet is . . . what you want? We do nuzza run, yes?"

Ray tugged at his neat beard, simulating deep thought.

"Maybe your frenn?" suggested Franco. "Sophie—Ray's frenn?"

"Sure. No problem," said Sophie, hauling herself up from the bed and taking unsteady steps until she stood about a foot away from me. "Anysing you wanting?" Sweat droplets gleamed like pins driven into her brow. She placed a shaky hand on my chest, sliding it down and around until she squeezed my waist.

I wasn't sure what to say. Ray pulled her away roughly. She barely reacted, flopping back on the turmoil of sheets.

"Not good enough, Franco," He said, now tossing the Kodak canister from hand to hand. *"Not good enough."*

Franco's eyes had widened, and his breathing quickened. "Juss name eet, Ray. *Please,* man! You know me an' Sophie, man. You *name* eet, yeah?"

"You just did," said Ray, brushing spent matches from the edge of a table and sitting on it.

"What, man? What I name?"

"You, *man,"* Ray told him, the words delivered in slow installments. "You . . . and . . . Sophie. *Now."*

Swallowing audibly, Franco turned in circles and banged at the springy black mop on his head.

Ray turned to me, smiling, and confiding in a low tone, "You see? Franco has a problem. He's pumped so much shit into his arms that he hasn't got it up in as long as he remembers. But poor Sophie here—she has to fuck anyone and everyone in sight just so Franco can support his little problem. Not fair, is it? So now I think it should be Franco's turn to fuck his girl, don't you?"

There was a slight pause.

"No fuck, no luck, Franco, old pal." He flipped the canister, catching it in a jacket pocket held open without even taking his eyes off the Frenchman. "C'mon, be a *man,* Franny. Show her you care, go on! It'll make a change from beating her up—won't it, Sophie?"

I confess the scene was morbidly fascinating. Franco's humiliation lasted half an hour, Sophie frantically striving to divert his tenaciously single-minded junk-craving cells with every trick she knew. Sweating and shaking, Franco struggled to accommodate her. Furious, Sophie cursed him in an impenetrable argot, the only word of which I caught was *tata:* "queer," or "faggot."

"Enough!" Ray snapped, springing off the table to slap Sophie's bum. "You find yourself a man, babe—*really,* I mean it."

"Man," Franco pleaded. "Doh do diss to me, Ray. C'mon . . ." His expression was naked and vulnerable, the eyes wide and helpless like those of a rabbit caught in oncoming headlights.

"Pack ya stuff, Sophie," Ray said, still watching Franco. "I'm gonna save your life for you."

Sophie tried to plead, but Ray told her to shut up, do what he said. It took her under a minute to fill a ratty holdall with some rags, a small painted box, two worn paperbacks. She pulled on a cheap, creased *kurta* and matching baggy pants.

Franco had fallen to his knees, begging for his life.

"But . . . whatta bow *me?*" he kept almost sobbing. "Ray? Whatta I *do,* man? I do anything, man. You *know* me, man . . . anything!"

"You can't even do anything for yourself, Franco," Ray said in disgust. "What the fuck could you possibly do for *me?* Jesus, you pig—you can't even get it up anymore. Here." He threw the Kodak canister across the room. "Why don't you shoot the whole fucking lot in one go and save everyone a lot of trouble?"

Dragging Sophie with him, Ray ushered me from the room.

"I cannot leave 'im," Sophie said in the elevator.

"That's why I'm *taking* you," Ray told her, smoothing a strand of hair back on her head. "Because you can't stay with him either. Anyway"— he hissed out a laugh"—old Franco's in for a big surprise." He paused to make sure he had maximum attention. "That wasn't junk."

"What wass eet?" Sophie jerked her head up to stare at him with terrified eyes.

"Pharmaceutical mescaline."

⚜   ⚜   ⚜

Ray handed Sophie over to Debbie, with orders to fly her to Zurich, put her in a clinic. When she was cleaned up—he wasn't sure . . . maybe send her home?

"Nah," he decided. "I'll meet you both in Geneva early next month, all right?" He patted Sophie on the head as if she were a child. "I like to see what I'm paying for." He told Debbie to buy her some clothes—good ones—get her hair done, her face done, get the lot done. "Then," he added enigmatically, "who knows? I might find you another life. . . ."

The next evening, Ray and I were in New Delhi. Very early the following morning, we touched down on the tarmac at Amritsar, capital of the Punjab.

While waiting for our baggage to travel the ten yards from airplane to terminal, I noticed something that puzzled me. As I studied a board announcing flight schedules, I discovered that the tiny airport, scarcely inundated with domestic traffic, also had one international flight every week: direct to and from Birmingham, England. This seemed highly unusual. It was only when Sikh separatism, and the wave of terrorism associated with it, became worldwide news in the 1980s that I remembered and understood what this stray scrap of information meant.

Rumors and allegations abounded about exactly where and how Sikh separatists were obtaining all their funding and weapons. Britain and Canada topped the list of suspects. A direct flight from Birmingham, a city with a huge population of immigrant Sikhs, to Amritsar, a city hosting nothing but Sikhs, would have simplified the process of shipping arms and any other form of assistance from Britain to the Punjab. With tacit approval from the British government, the only problem would be Indian customs officials, which, in Amritsar, of course, meant Sikh customs officials.

"Divide and conquer" had been the imperialist modus operandi on entering *and* on quitting India. An overly simple answer to communal strife between Hindus and Muslims then threatening to escalate toward civil war, the Partition of 1947 displaced 11.5 million refugees all over India, and created a Muslim nation in two parts separated by a thousand miles, West Pakistan and East Pakistan (now Bangladesh). Nowhere was this upheaval, created by a cartographer's almost arbitrary line, more acutely felt than in the Punjab, which was ripped in half. While very many

Muslims elected, tellingly enough, to remain in India, virtually no Sikhs or Hindus imagined they would be safe in Pakistan. As a result, entire villages emigrated overnight, hundreds of thousands of their inhabitants murdered as they tried to escape, or caught in bloody attacks on the over-crowded trains and buses that were supposed to carry them out of harm's way. And before long India and Pakistan were continuing this "communal strife" anyway. By 1965, it was an international issue—one called *war*.

Nehru and his daughter always favored the Soviet Union over the U.S. With India's alleged nonalignment then, and Pakistan's duplicitous foreign policy, opportunistic but sliding ever more steeply toward the arms of oil-rich and fundamentalist coreligionists, Britain, the old puppet master, and its eager American apprentice, sought a buffer zone between the Soviets, the willfully unreliable closet-Marxist Indians, and the still unknown quantity of an emerging and virulently anti-Western Islamic world stretching from West Africa to Indonesia.

More portentous still, in the eyes of Western multinational capitalists, was the appearance of atomic weaponry. First it surfaced in India; then, it was suspected, in Pakistan. Coupled with the ever-present and allegedly ever-growing Soviet nuclear arsenal, this conjured up a daunting vision to outside vested interests. Foreign powers could not fathom the intentions of these new nuclear powers, and they were annoyed by the fact that none of them had any base any longer from which to observe and control it.

The Punjab seemed to represent neo-imperialism's only opportunity to correct this omission, and so it was seized. Then it was instantly dropped like a hot roti when the Soviet Union vanished—Sikh dreams of Khalistan, an independent homeland, teased, then abandoned.

All is now *relatively* quiet on the northwestern front. There are no more of those direct flights to and from Birmingham.

❧   ❧   ❧

For some reason, I'd never thought that the Golden Temple would really be made of gold, but it is (which is probably why it's surrounded by water and the fiercest armed guards I could ever imagine seeing).

Eight years after I was in Amritsar, on June 5, 1984, Indira Gandhi ordered Indian troops to oust Sikh militants from the Golden Temple, which they had turned into a fortified headquarters. It was the anniversary of the martyrdom of Guru Arjun Dèv, the temple's founder, and thousands of pilgrims were inside the sacred precincts paying homage. After five days of continuous fighting, those militants still alive finally surrendered. Some five thousand people died, most of them innocents caught in the crossfire; the great temple's archives were reduced to ashes, and many of its ancient holy structures were irreparably damaged, including the four-hundred-year-old Akhal Takhat. This domed temple had recently been used by the revolutionary Sikhs' leader as a fortress headquarters, though it was ostensibly seat of the supreme religious council.

Those who had encouraged the militants and their increasingly bloody quest for Khalistan, the "Land of the Pure," did not care about the awful consequences of their self-interested actions, did not care about the Punjab or the Sikhs at all, now that their buffer zone was no longer crucial. Besides, this was not the first massacre the British had been responsible for in Amritsar.

✣   ✣   ✣

The Punjab was isolated, cut off from the rest of India; a thick veil seemed to cover it and hide it from outside eyes. There was hardly any news, and people could not go there or come out from there. Odd individuals, who managed to escape from that inferno, were so terror struck that they could give no clear account.

—NEHRU, *AN AUTOBIOGRAPHY*

In the early evening of April 13, 1919, a platoon of Indian soldiers commanded by Brigadier-general Reginald Dyer was ordered to open fire on an "illegal assembly" of some twenty thousand people gathered in the Jallianwala Bagh to hear speeches and devotional poems. The British officer had been sent to impose martial law in Amritsar after numerous violent anti-European incidents there indicated a building opposition to colonial rule. It was Baisaki Day, the beginning of one of the Punjab's most important religious festivals, and, in 1984, most of the crowd were pilgrims from outlying districts who could not afford to stay in hotels and were camped out in the Bagh, several acres of walled-in wasteland that were "gardens" in name only. The crowd panicked as gunshots cracked on all sides, the soldiers blocking their exit. When the smoke had cleared, more than fifteen hundred men, women, and children lay dead, dying, or wounded.

Like much that went on in the colonies, this event was shrouded by

Foreign Office bureaucrats in London in a conspiracy of silence and secrecy that lasted nearly sixty years. To the Indians, who quickly learned
the truth by word of mouth or from eyewitnesses, it provided more welcome evidence that the revolt against the Raj, allegedly crushed back in
1857 during the so-called Mutiny, was still alive, leading to independence,
gaining momentum day by day. Nehru knew it; and so did Mahatma
Gandhi, who said: "Plassey laid the foundation of the British Empire, Amritsar has shaken it." Many historians believe that Dyer's troops fired the
first shots that blew out the jewel in the crown of their own empire.

The "Granary of India," as it's known, the Punjab did seem lush, green,
and fertile compared with most of the subcontinent, as Ray and I drove
past groves, orchards, and lavishly irrigated rich dark soil, heading for the
medieval walled city that had seen more bloodshed and turmoil during
its four centuries than it had peace and harmony. Punjab means land of
five rivers—the Ravi, Jhelum, Chenab, Sutlej, and Beas, all arterial life-
lines flowing from the western Himalayas. They quench the insatiable
thirst of those abundant Punjabi plains before meeting as one in the
mighty Indus and eventually pouring away into the Arabian Sea.

Not only the landscape looked rich and orderly. Within twenty minutes I'd seen more tractors than I had in all of India in two years. The
heavy machines rolled through fields dense with ripening wheat, snowy
cotton, and mustard, and chugged past the emerald squares of luxuriant
rice paddies, along the perimeters of leafy sugarcane plantations thick as
jungles.

The people, too, looked prosperous—the men big, strong, handsome
in their glossy beards and immaculate turbans; the women graceful, proud,
more self-assured in their billowing *salwar-kameez* pantsuits than their shy,
nervous Hindu counterparts farther south. Warriors by necessity—their
symbol the crossed swords of temporal and spiritual authority—the Sikhs
were respected by the Raj officers far more than the "effeminate Hindus," and came to be disproportionately represented in the British Indian
forces, then remained so in their nation's independent military. Their
affinity for machines and their love of cars has made them the drivers of
India—and made the word *asti* (slow down) one of three entries in the
Hindi dictionary every tourist must learn very quickly. Clearly close descendants of the invading Aryans, who found a haven of plenty in the

Punjab, the Sikhs are warriors in everything they do: They eat with the voracity of Ghengis Khan's Mongol troops; they walk with an innate power and virility, moving like men accustomed to respect; and they speak like men used to giving orders that are obeyed.

Behind houses along the paved lanes in the Punjab stand well-maintained coops stocked with fat chickens, and neat sites, where corpulent pigs jostle and snort contentedly. There is an air of confident control over the villages.

Just before I arrived in India, the Sikhs had been warrior chieftains in another kind of revolution. If not for ruinous droughts and the so-called world oil crisis, India would have achieved her goal of producing enough grains to feed the entire population. And the credit for this Green Revolution went largely to the hardworking Sikhs of the fertile Punjabi plains.

In 1976, after the tumult of the past, and blissfully unaware of the bloodshed to come, Amritsar rested as calm and placid as that mirror of the azure sky, the waters of the Pool of Tranquillity itself.

The Pool of Tranquility is a manmade lagoon where pilgrims bathe, and after which Sikhism's holiest city takes its name. In the center of this lagoon, accessible only by a narrow causeway of white marble more than two hundred feet long, stands the Golden Temple, Mecca for India's more than thirteen million Sikhs, the physical center of their world. It is a structure of unearthly beauty, a shimmering vision entirely covered in copper gilt and gold leaf, with inner walls of near-translucent marble inlaid with semiprecious stones in designs as intricate and as surpassingly magnificent as those found in the Taj Mahal or any other supreme achievements of Moghul architecture. The plasterwork and mirrors on the ceilings shower the interior with flashing stars reflected from candles and oil lamps, or from the sun itself reflecting off the surrounding waters. Its founder, Guru Arjun Dev, described his temple as a ship built to carry the faithful safely across the oceans of ignorance of this world.

Ray, who had been in Amritsar possibly several dozen times, had never seen the temple before, and, what's more, had no desire ever to see it.

"Sikhs give me the creeps," he explained. "You should see the size of the fuckin' knives those guys carry. Go in there, pal, you'll be fuckin' *salami* in ten seconds."

He said he wanted to visit a friend. I wondered who this would be. As always, I had to be content with finding out when it was too late to get out.

Overhead, in the high blue air, kite hawks deployed downwind. On the crumbling stone roofs of houses lining a labyrinth of narrow, muddy lanes, vultures scanned the world below for courses for their endless dinner party. Filthy and depraved-looking, hunched in feathers that resembled shredded academic gowns, they reminded me of a sadist who'd once been my housemaster at school.

The air was pungent with spices. Hunks of simmering warrior food in vast copper pots that squatted over charcoal braziers. Wherever I looked, there was a different kind of face floating along in the river of humanity in the bazaars: cheerful Tibetans come to trade their woven carpets; an entire range of hybrid Occi-Oriental mugs from the various Soviet Central Asian regions; sly, hawkish kissers from Kashmir with Shrewd Negotiator all but stamped on their foreheads; ill-tempered, swarthy Iranians, seemingly ready to kill to close a deal, if that was what it took; and little impish Nepalese, disarmingly shy and using this innate inoffensiveness to their advantage.

The only major railway stop between that panorama of nations and races spreading out north of India and the subcontinent's capital, New Delhi, Amritsar has always been a meeting place of worlds. And where worlds meet, much is traded, not all of it legal. Besides the silks and spices, the ivory and copper, there was wool—pashmina wool from the downy-soft throats of Himalayan mountain goats, and just as eagerly sought out in Amritsar as it was up in Srinagar, Kashmir. But the towering, burly figures, with their aggressive beards and stately turbans also wore leather bandoliers plugged with shells in a forbidding X across their chests, holding the rifles that required these shells in a forbidding X across their chests, holding the rifles that required these shells like scepters, symbols of office. It was probably not wool *they* were trading. Booze, guns, hashish—it all came through Amritsar. And hardly a week passed without some Indian newspaper reporting a shoot-out between such smugglers and the border guards, who were their occupational hazard. It was not always the border guards who emerged victorious.

"Pathans," Ray mentioned, pointing out one walking arsenal nearly seven feet tall. "Pathans or Swatis, most of 'em."

I could see why few people wished to travel into Swat.

After a meal of stewed bones with a pleasant man called Singh—which in the Punjab was much like introducing someone as "person"—Ray bought a collection of seventeenth-century Tibetan coins from him, then announced that we ought to visit a whorehouse he knew with Burmese girls who would "tickle your heart with their tongues—*from the inside.*"

I declined an offer at last. The longer I remained in India, the more romantic my ideas about sex seemed to become. Instead, I arranged to meet Ray later, heading off to the temple—not guessing that this was the last time I'd see it looking essentially the way it had since the late sixteenth century.

❧   ❧   ❧

By early evening, Ray and I were in Lahore, one of innumerable cities referred to—usually in awful irony now—as the Paris of the East. Crossing from India into Pakistan, the first thing I noticed was how much more run-down the place looked compared to the land connected to it before Partition. Squat, crumbling structures, potholed roads, hardly a sign of those few concessions to the late twentieth century that were visible in much of India, especially power and communications. Far from being an Oriental Paris, Lahore—much of it, anyway—was a shambles of heat-blistered rubble, makeshift mud brick or cracked concrete huts, and over-grown expanses of dessicated weeds. It seemed nearly deserted, too.

The Intercontinental Hotel's five-star modernity merely emphasized the decay outside; but even it seemed afflicted by a sinister stasis that made you feel you were disturbing the staff. And this staff regarded us with deep suspicion. Passports were held for police inspection; all movements appeared to be monitored—as if the only reasons for Westerners to be here were the wrong reasons. I felt distinctly uneasy, but Ray shrugged it off as he shrugged everything off, announcing that he had "some business to take care of."

Left alone, I entered the freezing, deserted bar and drank a couple of doubles to relax me. This was an Islamic state, so alcohol was served to foreigners only. A personable old bartender with British-style military mustaches asked me enough questions to justify his trust, then proceeded to tell me how General Zia was ruining the country. I was cautious with my answers, not certain that I could justify *my* trust.

"This city was once so full of life," he confided. "Nightclubs, singing, laughter . . . Now it is dead. No life. We do not like this *sharia,* Islamic law. It is not for our people."

Zia's piety, I heard, was a sham—something designed to impress his oil-rich fundamentalist pals in the Middle East. He was spending all the country's money on mosques—just for show—the most ambitious named after him and currently under construction. Zia did not seem to be a popular dictator.

"He killed our beloved Bhutto." The bartender sighed. "We can never forgive that. He was a wonderful man, Bhutto."

I asked why a Muslim would object to the enforcement of Islamic prohibitions against frivolous activities—like having fun. The bartender, however, was an Indian Muslim at heart, preferring the looser, less censorious Islam he'd grown up with to this state-imposed puritanical form. He genuinely seemed to miss the old days.

Ray had rented a two-bedroom suite, and on his return we sat watching American TV shows—ones crudely edited by Islamic censors—and eating room-service food.

"Lahore's still a wild place," Ray volunteered. "But you gotta know where to look." Even he confessed, however, that it was wise to keep your nose clean in Pakistan.

The next day, we drove the two-hundred-odd miles to the twin cities of Rawalpindi and Islamabad—this latter the newly constructed capital, a showpiece of modern structures as contrived and artificial as most modern cities designed and built from scratch. Along bleak, broad boulevards lurked a lot of evidence of the heavy military presence—telltale signs of a nervous dictatorship. The threat of another war with India made it nervous, as did the threat of a coup from within. Every available surface was plastered with posters and pictures of General Zia, looking, with his rakish mustache and heavy-lidded eyes, like some roguish thirties matinee idol on opium.

Dropped at another Intercontinental Hotel, we ate a bad lunch there, then hired another car and driver to take us on to Peshawar, another hundred miles northwest. Ray told me he didn't want our movements to be easily traced.

We were heading up into the hills now, through landscape that was bleaker, while less arid, occasional groves and relatively fertile fields visible beyond roadside irrigation ditches, the air cleaner and slightly cooler. Approaching the Attock bridge, we encountered a checkpoint, as if we were crossing some kind of frontier. Soldiers looked at passports, compared their photographs to their owners, asked cursory questions. Then we were waved on into the North West Territories, where the jurisdiction of Pakistan's government takes a backseat to the tribal laws and customs that have prevailed for as long as anyone remembers. It is ostensibly another land, inhabited by another people: the Pathans. Tall, pale-skinned, hawk-nosed, many even with green eyes and red hair, the Pathans have no racial connection to the small, dark folk in Hindustan—their term for everything east of the Indus. Their reputation as some of the fiercest, most dangerous warriors on earth stretches back to the fifth century B.C. And the Soviets were soon to experience their talents in the mountainous tribal lands of Afghanistan, just across the Khyber Pass, a mere dozen miles west of Peshawar. Their law, the Pukhtunwali or Way of the Pathan, derives as much from revenge and tribal feuds as it does from ancient codes of hospitality to strangers. And this latter quality owes more to pride than to generosity.

The Pathans refer to themselves as Pukhtun, Pushtun, or even Afghan. Pathan is the Hindi form, itself corrupted by British Soldiers into Paytan. Some fifteen million of them, divided among as many as one hundred distinct tribes, comprise the largest remaining tribal society in the world today, occupying 100,000 square miles of land that straddles the Afghan–Pakistani border. This is still referred to as the Durand Line, after Sir Mortimer Durand, who signed the treaty with the Afghan amir, Abdur Rahman, that in 1893 separated Afghanistan from British India. The Pathans then simply ignored the border, as they do now. Thousands of the nomadic Ghilzai tribe migrate annually from the Afghan highlands down to the plains of Pakistan. Some quarter-million nonnomadic tribesmen still cross back and forth over the line every year on private business, even though Pakistan has officially "sealed" the border. No official in his right mind would dream of questioning them or asking for papers, let alone refusing them.

I noted the many tea shops as we drove through the hectic streets of the old "native quarter." They employed vast and ancient Russian copper samovars, around which clients congregated. We, on the other hand, were heading into the Peshawar cantonment, opposite the Kisakhani Bazaar. The permanent military station spread beyond what was then the Pakistani Frontier Corps' headquarters in the huge round Sikh fort. Built in a style that could be termed "Victorian Pathan," the cantonment lined two sides of a broad, tree-lined boulevard, its massive bungalows set far back from the street, their walls a yard thick, with small, deep-set windows positioned just below the high ceilings of their rooms—a precaution against snipers.

Dean's Hotel turned out to be our destination, a sprawling collection of single-story structures laid out across gardens ablaze with flowers over three or four acres. Ray instructed me to write a phony name and destination in the guest register.

"The fucking thing is copied out ten times a day by a dozen different intelligence agencies," he claimed.

Any foreigner in Peshawar is even more suspect than any foreigner merely in Pakistan: No one ever came to Peshawar for anything so innocent as tourism. Ray warned me to avoid even the most innocuous conversation with strangers, and to act doggedly like a tourist.

We dined that night in the hotel's sepulchral restaurant beneath a full-size lithograph of George VI. I had not wanted half our meal; we were bound by Dean's tradition to order the five-course dinner: mulligatawny, fish, roast lamb, curried beef and vegetables, and a rather bizarre apple pie spiced with something that tasted like pine-scented disinfectant. The management of Dean's prided itself on its traditions. Many of the "bearers" and other staff still there in 1976 had served under the Raj. Since then they had exhibited the distinctive British qualities of inflexibilty and punctuality, and, alas, British notions of what constituted good food.

Later on we strolled into the old city, with cameras around our necks and guidebooks conspicuously in our hands. The old *serais* tucked along the base of the crumbling walls now mostly housed aging cars; but the great caravans coming in from Bokhara, Samarkand, Herat, Meshed, and Kashgar had once unloaded their cargoes of carpets, spices, weapons, and beaten copperware there.

We stopped for *qahwa* in the Chowk Yad Ghar, the central square. Qahwa means coffee in Arabic, which must have confused many Arab travelers to Peshawar, where the word refers to the Pathans' national drink, a light, delicate Chinese green tea. This is not what you should order if you're in a hurry.

An astoundingly wizened character with a Long John Silver wooden leg first washed out a battered tin teapot with water drawn from a samovar the size of a steam engine, and flung a stream of rust-colored muck into the dusty street. Then he threw a fistful of tea leaves into this pot, added about an inch of hot water, and swirled the pot above his head with enormous grace and skill, repeating the same process twice before filling it up with boiling water, shoveling in a couple of ounces of battleship-gray sugar, and finally placing the pot on top of glowing charcoals. When its contents began to boil, he tossed a few cardamom pods into a wooden mortar and smashed them with a gnarled pestle; he pulled the pot off the charcoals, sniffing its contents with a nose like a puffin's beak, contemplating it seriously and, satisfied with it, tipping in the crushed spice. Back went the pot on the charcoals again, to be removed a few minutes later, subjected once more to the Nose's opinion, and finally placed with two cups on a tray, which was slapped down on our table with a flourish.

It almost shocked me to learn that the cost for all this showmanship and teamanship was about ten cents. Ray muttered something to the old man that I didn't catch. A small boy was immediately dispatched on an errand of some sort.

The people passing in the street reminded me of those Mountstuart Elphinstone described in 1809. He was the first Englishman to visit Peshawar. "Men of all nations and languages in every variety of dress and appearance" walked the streets, he wrote, remarking particularly on the Peshawaris in their "white turbans, white and blue shirts, and sheepskin coats," the Persians and Afghans in their "brown woolen tunics and silk or sheepskin hats," the "Khyberees with the straw sandals and the wild dress and air of their mountains," and the broad-faced Hazaras, with their little eyes, "remarkable for their want of the beard which is the ornament of every other face in the city." Nearly two hundred years later, I also observed just "a few women with long white veils that reach their feet."

"Come," Ray suddenly said, pulling me up. "Let's be tourists."

We ascended a steep winding hill that was the Street of the Silversmiths. Flanked by tall, narrow three-or four-story houses, it shrank to ten or so feet in width, leading like a canyon up to an Aladdin's cave. Oil lamps cast a jaundiced glow over the piles of heavy anklets and curtains of necklaces displayed in the open storefronts. About halfway up the hill, lit by a high-wattage moon like some silversmith's vision, gleamed the minarets of the Mahabat Khan mosque.

"The Sikhs used to hang Pathans from them," Ray informed me, adding, when this had sunk in, "Two a day . . . they say."

Beneath the shimmering minarets, in the middle of a broad tiled courtyard, rested a dark, still pool, the night breeze blowing cool off its surface even in the heat of summer. Men with vast turbans, their fearsome countenances accentuated by black beards, white beards, red beards, glided around this area, occasionally kneeling and bowing in prayer on a profusion of bloodred carpets.

"*Salaam aleikum,* Ray Sahib," growled a low voice behind us.

I turned to see Ray embraced by a massive and dangerous-looking fellow—four hundred pounds of Pathan. The man wore an immaculate brown shirt that billowed over baggy pants, which in turn crumpled down onto incongruous black patent Gucci loafers. He also reeked of cologne. A neatly trimmed beard framed his broad, cruel face, with its protruding bloodshot eyes, and, most unusual here, his head was bare.

"I Hadji," he announced, when Ray introduced me.

His name, I learned, was actually Waris Khan, but he liked to be called Hadji, since he had made the *hadj,* or pilgrimage to Mecca. More importantly, too, the name protected his identity—as being called Singh would have in Amritsar. He looked around suspiciously, then urged us to follow him at a distance of several feet.

Through a dark labyrinth of narrow streets he led us, until we turned a corner to find a new Toyota sedan waiting with black glass windows, doors open, engine running. With one glance to check that no one was in sight, Hadji bundled us into the plush backseat, slammed the door, and climbed into the front beside a driver wearing more traditional Pathan clothes. The stench of cologne inside was almost suffocating. Hadji pulled an atomizer of Paco Rabanne from the glove compartment, sprayed his burly neck extravagantly, and offered it to us.

"I like too much the *phfit-phfit,* he explained, *phfit-phfit*ing the roof. "It give good cool to body, yes?" Then he smashed a cassette into the tape deck, and as Bob Marley loudly maintained that no woman should cry, we shot like a runaway roller coaster through streets and alleys not much wider than the car, and pitch-dark.

"I like too much the Bob Mally," Hadji announced, cackling, and thumping the dashboard in time to the music's beat with fingers as thick as country sausages.

Fifteen minutes later, I deduced that we were passing through some kind of suburb: laneways of low houses set behind walled enclosures, clumps of trees visible inside them. Our car swerved into a narrow alley, and men swiftly shut large gates behind us as we slammed to a halt within what looked like a fortified compound. After my prolonged encounter with Paco Rabanne, I was relieved to clamber out. The first smell to greet my nose was hashish. Not burning hashish, but simply hashish. There must have been a ton of the stuff nearby. From the shadows emerged several ominous turbaned figures X-ed with bandoliers and cradling semiautomatic Kalashnikovs.

Salaam aleikums sounded enthusiastically from all sides. Ray embraced each of the men, then individually introduced them to me with a handshake. Pathans are very formal with introductions, and very egalitarian, too: It is considered a major insult not to introduce a guest to even the humblest servant. And major insults are not something you want to hand any Pathan, especially one you employ.

Beyond a pair of massive and ancient double doors rose a flight of stone steps. We were shown up these and then led into an open second-floor courtyard furnished with low cushioned sofas and a huge, ornately carved table no more than a foot high. More weapons were propped in corners, and from a peg in a worn leather holster hung the kind of handgun Clint Eastwood claimed could knock a wall down. Ray threw himself onto the cushions as if he owned the place, and I sat myself somewhat uncomfortably at his side. Hadji barked orders to various men, who disappeared through the numerous doors leading off the courtyard. Above, in the unfamiliar night sky, stars raged, strange constellations striving to snare the blazing wedge of moon in their jeweled web.

Through one door stepped an excruciatingly shy woman, swathed in folds and layers of material from head to toe and bearing an elaborate copper teapot and glass cups on a tray. She set these on the table and scuttled off. Hadji opened a monstrous cupboard and hefted a duty-free-size bottle of Chivas Regal from it, slamming it down before us.

"Cheee-*vass!*" he roared. "I like too much this whisky."

With tea and whiskies, we listened to Hadji's account of exploits with "dancing girls" in Lahore. Then Ray opened his camera bag and extracted some gifts for his host: twenty-odd envelopes that turned out to contain reels of eight-millimeter porno films; two cartons of Dunhills; four atomizers of Paco Rabanne; and a Cartier wristwatch.

Hadji examined the photographs on the film packages with professional eyes, occasionally laughing dangerously and calling over some henchmen to take a look. These other men obeyed reluctantly, glancing over at Ray with faintly disapproving eyes. Pathans have curious attitudes toward women: chauvinism mixed with worship and almost fear. To see women engaged in acts they would not expect even prostitutes to perform, and engaged in such acts *while being photographed,* disturbed them.

Hadji called for a projector. Then he asked Ray, "Next time you bring Hadji real America girl, yes?"

"Got just the one for you," Ray replied. "Getting her all prepared right now, as a matter of fact."

Sophie? I wondered.

"She have the yellow hair, yes?"

"She does now."

Another armed man dragged in a huge wicker hamper. Inside it were slabs of hashish the size of bridge tables. He broke off pieces from different slabs and handed them to Ray, who cracked them apart and sniffed the fresh, greenish resin inside.

"But now we smoke this one," Hadji announced, pulling a different chunk from his pocket.

Ray informed me that *this* was the finest hashish on earth. "They only make a few kilos a year," he explained. "And it ain't for sale."

What Ray bought was the second-best grade; and even that, he claimed, was a thousand times better than anything anyone else was selling in America or Canada. He selected the slabs he approved of while Hadji rolled a Western-style joint, emptying a Dunhill and restuffing its tube with hashish and tobacco. The sweet odor soon wafted around the courtyard.

The stuff was so strong I soon had hallucinations about being in some scene from the Arabian Nights; then things began to veer toward the paranoid, as I wondered how safe it was to be lounging around with all these armed tribal dope dealers. The whisky began to taste like burning honey, and, as porn films flickered into life on the peeling plaster walls, I asked Ray how long we'd be staying here.

Not long. After a mumbled conversation with Hadji, he rose, beckoning to me. The original driver took us back to where he'd picked us up. Feeling very vulnerable and conspicuous, I plodded beside Ray back to Dean's Hotel. Next day we'd be "heading north." To Swat.

❧   ❧   ❧

We checked out and took a cab to the Peshawar bus terminal. Ray enjoyed being secretive, and I'd long since stopped questioning him; it only gave him the satisfaction of being mysterious. But somehow public buses did not seem to be his speed. We stood with our luggage, Ray peering around for spies, assassins, narcotics agents, as various people besieged us with offers and requests. Suddenly Hadji's blacked-out Toyota cruised to a halt nearby, and Ray shoved me inside.

"Salaam aleikum!"

"Aleikum wah salaam."

Hadji had the renovated air of a man who's had a bestial night and little sleep, but has had a rigorous shower and changed his clothes. He'd presumably just showered in Paco Rabanne.

We sped off, soon joined by a white Range Rover, which tailed us.

"Do not worry, my friend," urged Hadji, indicating the Range Rover. "This are my people."

Heading north into the Malakand Pass, we began to leave the barren moonscape of the Khyber behind to enter a more Alpine zone of steep, pine-covered mountains, each one seemingly higher, as if we were climbing a vast staircase. At the end of these enchanted valleys is the mightiest massif of mountains on the planet. When I finally saw it, rank upon rank, tier upon tier of enormous frozen peaks, I had the impression that there could not possibly be anything beyond them. It felt as if I'd reached walls at the end of the world.

Approaching a tiny town called Dargai, Hadji hauled a package wrapped in newspaper from beneath his feet and handed it to Ray. Inside were two thin white cotton sheets. Above, on a ridge, I could see an old British fort with four stark square towers.

"Checkpoint coming up," Ray said, handing me a sheet. "Throw this over yourself." Through the sheet I could see well enough. A stately soldier with waxed mustaches leaned in Hadji's window, shaking his hand.

"*Suh hal day?*" he asked. How are you?

"*Takra!*" replied Hadji, laughing lewdly, showing his clenched fist.

The man gave the two sheeted figures on the backseat the most cursory glance, waving us on.

"*Khudai de mal sha,*" he called out. May God be with you. Compared to Urdu or Hindi, Pushtu was an alien, unfamiliar tongue, a tongue with something grand and ancient about it.

Soon we removed the sheets.

"He think you my *khaza*," Hadji explained. Khaza means woman or wife. "I tell him Hadji have too much khaza for one car." He laughed himself into a hideous fit of coughing, the anguished barking of lungs weighed down with kilos of cannabis resin.

Now the icy waters of the Swat River were tumbling along furiously below the roads, and the pine-covered slopes on either side became steeper.

My carnal heart is an Afridi, who cares nothing for religion.
Its good thoughts are few, and it is very much given to wicked-
    ness . . .
The call of the muezzin is not to be heard anywhere in the
    Afridi land,
Unless you listen to the crowing of the cock at the dawn of day.
                    —KHUSHAL KHAN KHATTAK, SEVENTEENTH CENTURY

Hadji eventually revealed, with some pride, that he was an Afridi, a member of one of the fiercest of the Pathan tribes. Much later I remembered the story he told while reading Khushal Khan's poetry. Many years ago, he announced, a *pir,* a Muslim holy man, had come from India to visit his people. He told the Afridis what dreadful sins they had committed, pointing out that in all of the Afridi lands there was not one single tomb of a saint where they could worship.

"My people, they were *too* much impressed by this old pir's words," said Hadji, growing implausibly grave. "So they are *killing* him, and now this holy-man tomb is too much popular place of worshiping. . . ." He burst into another lung-ripping bark of laughter.

I came across the same story in 1992, in an account written by some British traveler in the 1850s.

"The Church Hill," Hadji suddenly announced, pointing vaguely to his left.

There were hills everywhere—none, however, with churches, or indeed any kind of buildings, on it. I did not pursue the comment. Only later did it dawn on me that what Hadji must have been referring to was Sir Winston *Churchill.* Churchill had seen his first real action out there as a subaltern in 1897, using the material to launch his literary career with an action-packed book published in 1898 as *The Story of the Malakand Field Force.*

The Malakand Pass, or Staircase, as it would be more appropriately named, connects mother Pakistan and what were then the three princely states of Swat, Dir, and Chitral. But the lush, fertile valley we were entering—so very Swiss, as Ray had rightly said—seemed like another world altogether, a Shangri-la secreted outside time. Malarial swamp it most certainly was not.

Yet Swat has been very much *inside* time. The valley was site of Alexander the Great's battle at Massaga, recorded by Arrian and Curtius in their histories, and of other battles fought by the Macedonian armies, too. Between 500 B.C. and around 800 A.D., Swat—taking its name from the river, known in Sanskrit as Sweta, or "white"—was the Udyana, the "garden" of Greco-Buddhist culture, and a good candidate for the hidden mountain paradise of traveler's lore. The Moghul emperor Babur mentioned it as "Swad," but essentially nothing is heard about the place from the fall of Buddhist civilization until nearly a millennium later. By then the Yusufzai tribe, from Afghanistan, were migrating through Peshawar and north, pushing the inhabitants of the valley, whoever they were, east across the Indus, while they settled in the fertile paradise themselves.

Hazrat Abdul Ghafoor was the notorious akond of Swat, immortalized by Edward Lear. Of course, the Swatis themselves revere his memory for very different reasons today. A Yusufzai warrior-saint, the akond led his tribes against British forces commanded by Brigadier-general Neville Chamberlain, grandfather of the future prime minister of England. The akond's grandson, similarly, would become ruler of Swat. This campaign culminated in the historic battles of Ambella in 1862. The akond—also known as Saidu Baba—died in 1877, and was interred in a shrine in the exquisite mosque at Saidu Sharif, which would become the state capital. Both of the akond's sons having died in battle, no obvious leader emerged, and anarchy reigned for the next forty years. In 1897, when the tribes rose en masse against the British, the *mulla* Mastun, called "the mad mullah" by the Brits, declared a *jihad,* a holy war, from his village in the valley. He had one of the few boys he taught in the little mosque school proclaimed "king of Delhi" and marched with them off to war. Three days later he'd managed to gather some twenty thousand local tribesmen around him, and they attacked British installations in the Malakand Pass and elsewhere. After a week of bloody fighting that saw a few hundred casualties on both sides, Mastun vanished back to his village, wherever it was, as swiftly and as enigmatically as he had appeared.

The state of Swat was finally founded by Miangul Gulshahzada Sir Abdul Wadud, a chieftain of the relatively petty Safi tribe. He also happened to be the akond's grandson, and was known affectionately as Badshah Sahib. He ruled successfully for twenty-three years, thanks to both his family's saintly reputation and his own genius for organization. He had had to carve out a state from scratch, building forts at either end of the valley, installing telephones and other innovations that brought Shangri-la into the communication age and made invasion by other tribes a thing of the past. Knowing a good thing when they saw one, the British quickly recognized the new progressive state and its enlightened ruler. On December 12, 1949, during the upheaval following Partition, Badshah Sahib turned Swat over to his son, Major-general Miangul Jahan Zeb, H. Pk., H.Q.A., C.I.E.—whatever the abbreviations mean. Liaqat Ali Khan, then Pakistan's Prime Minister, installed him as *wali* of Swat. Swat was the first state to accede to Pakistan, immediately after independence. Although not precisely independent in status, the state ran its own affairs, with its own army of ten thousand men, a police force of two thousand, and its own civil and criminal laws and system of administration.

In 1976, the wali was Miangul Jahan Zeb's son, Miangul Aurangzeb, who had previously been A.D.C. To the commander-in-chief of Pakistan's army, then an elected member of Pakistan's National Assembly, from Constituency NW-18. Like his father, he ruled Swat with a legion of advisers, secretaries, *munsheer*s, *qazi*s, *hakim*s, and *tehsildar*s. Still a princely state within Pakistan, Swat then meted out justice through a mixture of Islamic law, custom, and the wali's orders—although Pakistan's central government managed foreign policy pertaining to the area. In effect, the wali presided over an advisory council of forty members that included ten Swati officials and advised the ruler on matters of state. It also acted as a legislative body. Membership to the council was by public elections held every three years. Fiercely independent in nature, at least, Swat had no income tax, and its annual revenue of some three million dollars in 1976 came from land revenues, forests, import and export, customs and excise, and minerals. With this relatively small sum the state paid for its own militia and police, the upkeep of all its hospitals and medical facilities, and its schools, as well as maintained 450 miles of road in excellent condition—all with no outside aid. Most Swatis supported themselves as small landowners and farmers, harvesting two crops a year, and as beekeepers, which was Swat's largest cottage industry. More than seven thousand families still produce over two million pounds of honey and pure beeswax annually. The state grew all its own food grains and exported the surplus to Pakistan.

Education was free and, while not mandatory, encouraged; needy students were even provided with free books and uniforms. Medical treatment was also free then, with sixteen well-equipped hospitals spread over the four thousand square miles of the state, twenty dispensaries scattered around the villages, as well as a mobile dispensary, a leprosy clinic, and a veterinary hospital. The entire population of just less than one million seemed to know how lucky they were, too.

None of this, of course, was thanks to Ray. As far as I could make out, Swat seemed blessed with rulers of exceptional ability and dedication. The wali was a busy man, his duties ranging from general administration of state affairs to trying personally and passing judgment in civil and criminal cases, reviewing cases, hearing appeals, applications, and petitions, interviewing members of the public to hear their grievances, and even inspecting all new state construction sites. Whether for some junior state employee's house, a school, a road, or a bridge, no final payment was ever made to the contractors before the wali had personally inspected the work and okayed it. This explained why everything looked well built, well maintained, and reassuringly solid after the crumbling architectural bedlam of Pakistan.

Swat's beauty deepened as we drove into its heart, past albescent snow-capped peaks, plunging rivers flashing and foaming over rocks, broad, verdant valleys, dense, lush forests, and tall legions of evergreen firs patrolling the lower slopes. The temperature was cooling, already a pleasant 79 degrees Fahrenheit, which, after Peshawar's low hundreds, seemed cooler still, especially in this clear, clean mountain air. All year round, apparently, the moderate climate ranges between 45 and 85 degrees, dipping slightly lower at night from November through February, the winter months.

"So," asked Ray as we passed another landscape of beguiling elegance and opulent beauty, "how d'you like my little kingdom?"

"Nice."

"Hadji and me are thinking of deposing the wali," he then announced. "Yeah. Make Hadji the wali and me his minister of pleasure."

Hadji roared with laughter. "Yes! Good, Ray Sahib! *Wali Hadji,* I like too much this. But we must fight war, take Shameem Valley—womans there *too* good," he explained for my benefit. "Too much beautiful, the Shameem womans."

Just north of Swat, beyond the Lawari Pass, which connects the states of Dir and Chitral, is Kafiristan. The only people in this area to resist Islam, the Kafirs are light-skinned, fair-haired people who still practice an ancient form of "paganism" abandoned elsewhere. Only a few thousand of them survive now, but the extraordinary beauty and passion of their women is legendary to the Pathans, who locate the fabled "Valley of Shameem" somewhere just east of the Afghanistan border, north of the town of Drosh. To Hadji and his men, the place existed as a pleasure dome, a place to imagine forever rather than ever actually see.

This plan to depose the wali, however, seemed to be something more than a joke. I hoped the two of them weren't planning to attempt a coup while I was there. It seemed the classic gangster's dream: a land of your own, where you made the laws, where no one could interfere with your whims.

A few years later, though, the wali *was* assassinated. The old Swat is no more.

Four hours after leaving Peshawar, we were pulling into Saidu Sharif, still capital of Swat in 1976. With a population of less than twenty thousand, it was hardly surprising to find the place wasn't very large. Cheek by jowl with sturdy stone dwellings boasting elaborately carved lintels and window frames rose newer concrete structures, some bizarre and fancifully space-age in style. Two towers flanked the Jahan Zeb College like gigantic monopod bar stools, with open staircases that streamed down and around the outside.

Hadji and Ray considered stopping, but Ray preferred to keep his low profile. So we continued northeast and climbing. After about twenty miles, we reached Khawazakhela and turned right onto a dirt road that ran level for a while, then started the most drastic ascent up a 1-20 grade incline of hairpin bends. A few inches farther the rock face fell sheer all the way back down to the emerald valley. After ten miles we'd snaked up to an elevation of seven thousand feet, emerging onto a terrace that overlooked a breathtaking view, clear and uninterrupted all the way up to the vast opalescent mass of the Hindu Kush, with the borders of Russia and China just beyond. There were passes there at sixteen thousand feet—between twenty-five-thousand-foot peaks—where camel caravans still traveled to and fro with their cargoes, both licit and illicit.

"Home sweet home," sang Ray as we veered off down a track toward a broad and distant copse of pine trees.

I looked at him, hoping my expression seemed puzzled. *This* was the heart of his "underground empire"? A mountaintop?

"The village actually *is* called Shangla," he told me. "Just a coincidence, though. Shangri-la's a valley, isn't it? Probably Kashmir, anyway."

The track wound through the pines, and several hundred yards within

I saw a clearing with a high-walled compound. The stone houses in it looked ready to survive anything less than a direct hit with nuclear weapons. Hadji's driver honked, as did the Range Rover behind us, and Pathans wearing traditional medieval Swati caps and thick vests over baggy shirts and *shalwar* pants, every man clutching a rifle, rushed out, hauling open the massive wooden gates before us. We pulled in, the gates were swiftly closed, and Ray embarked on elaborate cheek-kissing and introductions. After the warmth of the car, the air into which we stepped chilled us.

Into the throng came a bony Westerner, thirty-something and balding, his fair hair sprouting in untidy fronds that hung over wire-rimmed spectacles and a pinched nose.

"This is Gunther," announced Ray. "He's my scientist—aren't you, Gunt?"

Gunt nodded blankly. I never once saw him smile. A flaxen-haired girl holding a child of perhaps two and indeterminate sex stood in a doorway. Mrs. Gunther, I assumed, with baby Gunther.

Packing cases were being unloaded from the Range Rover, and, introductions completed, Ray ushered me into what he termed his *"dharbar* hall."

This was a single huge room hung with elaborate woven Swati fabrics, and furnished with a low mammoth bed strewn with huge, bright cushions; several carved armchairs; tables; and cupboards—one of which contained state-of-the-art stereo equipment. Inside a building with five-foot-thick walls, it spoke of loneliness.

The whole point of the remote outpost, I learned after a meal of bread and mutton curry, was a building at the rear of the compound. For some reason it made me think of a high-tech moonshine still, with its elaborate equipment. All of this was wired to banks of car batteries. Most noticeable, though, was the reek of hashish. This was where Ray manufactured his hash oil.

"The trick's in the filtering," he told me more than once.

When the Pathans tried manufacturing hash oil on their own, they neglected to use pure charcoal filters and ended up producing something that smelled, looked, and smoked like old engine grease.

"You can't even *give* the shit away," Ray yodeled incredulously. "That's why Gunther's here."

Dozens of portable typewriters in injection-molded cases were conspicuously piled in the laboratory. Here was yet another of Ray's "tricks." The cases were hollow, with about half an inch of space between the inner and outer layers. He drilled two small holes in them, filled them up with oil, resealed the holes with epoxy resin, and painted over the wounds to conceal them. Each case held nearly three kilos of hashish oil.

"Two mules and four cases per trip," he announced grandly. "One hundred and twenty grand. Not bad for a day's work." The oil fetched ten dollars per gram, wholesale.

"Don't customs people wonder why someone is carrying so many typewriters?" I inquired.

"Nah! They don't really *look* like typewriters, do they? They could be any old hand luggage."

To me they looked like typewriters.

That night I wandered out into the pines to gaze up at the raging inferno of stars above me. As he subsequently proved, money was all Ray ever saw in Swat. When money could be made in Toronto and New York, he never had the slightest urge to return to Shangla.

"Too fuckin' *boring,*" he explained years later on another continent. He waved at the city skyline beyond his penthouse office windows. *"That's* where the action is. I feel sorry for those poor assholes over there, I really do. They *dream* of being here."

Most of them did not dream of being in North America, I noticed. They were fascinated with it, true, but they were happy where they were. They saw no need to travel any farther than the Indus River. Even as ruler of Swat, Ray would have been bored.

⚜   ⚜   ⚜

We left the next day, after Ray had inspected a dozen typewriter cases ready for export. Gunther's wife would soon take them to Lahore, where the mules would pick them up, either carrying them back across the border and flying out of Delhi, or proceeding on to catch an international flight from Islamabad or Karachi.

Hadji's Toyota drove us to Lahore. The next day we were back in New Delhi. Lounging in a hotel bar, Ray pointed out a young couple sitting with beers. Both looked unnaturally neat and tidy, as well as drawn and tired.

"My mules," he announced, with the pride of a horse breeder.

The two had apparently picked up four typewriter cases in Lahore, and would be taking a Lufthansa flight to Frankfurt the following morning. Ray was taking the same flight.

"It's the best," he explained. "You stop overnight at Frankfurt but the luggage goes straight on to the Toronto flight if you want, so you don't have to go through kraut customs. And when you arrive in Toronto it looks as if you're coming from Germany, so the narcs aren't as interested as they would be if you'd come from Dope Central here. The chick's cute, no?"

Ray had fun with his mules, he wanted me to know. Sometimes he chatted with them during the flight. He even hinted that he was an international narcotics cop just for fun, just to see how they'd react. Of course, they had no idea who he was, no idea that they were risking seven years in jail to make him richer. Ninety percent of Ray's shipments got through. And thus Ray got very rich—rich enough even to go legit. If you consider commodities trading honest work, that is.

8

"If I Didn't Want You to Leave This Place, You Never Could"

BANGALORE TO VENKATAGIRI, 1977

❧   ❧   ❧

If everyone wants to be a ruler, who is there to be ruled?
A ruler may have a few villages only to rule over but a beggar has
all the world to beg in.

—TELEGU PROVERBS

*M*y experiences with Ray depressed me. I felt I'd lost track of my purpose in coming to India, so I returned to England to resume doctoral studies. Before long, though, tired of modern academia's limits and its myopic view of spiritual matters, I looked for ways to return to India. Sathya Sai Baba just wouldn't leave me alone. Waking and sleeping—in dreams—I felt a profound need to return. Oxford University was no place to be if you wanted to explore ways of reining in the mind. Bangalore University, on the other hand, had possibilities. I accepted a position there lecturing on Shakespeare.

Although my sole experience of Baba had been in Puttaparthi, he spent much time near a place called Whitefield, an Anglo-Indian community where he had started his first college. Whitefield was a mere twenty-odd minutes from Bangalore.

Brindavan, as the college-ashram was known, seemed cool and peaceful compared to Puttaparthi's raging inferno. The very first day I sat there waiting for this Brindavan darshan, Baba told me to go over to his house. I assumed this meant an interview. It didn't.

Crammed into a room the size of a Volkswagen bus, I asked the dignified old gentleman next to me what he did for a living. He was president of India. A few yards away was the prime minister, Narasimha Rao.

He wasn't the prime minister then, of course, but he would be by the time I visited India in 1992.

When Baba entered, we all stood, and he inspected us like a general with very substandard troops. I was informed by Dr. Gokak—then one of Baba's chief aides—that I could teach at the Brindavan college in my spare time. In return, I got to sit in Baba's house whenever I wanted to, or whenever he was there. This, I came to realize, meant that I saw a far more personal, human side of him, occasionally being jarred back to reality when he materialized objects and vibhuti inches from my nose, or sit, suddenly still, remote, with eyes that saw into undreamed-of realms. Eyes that saw all.

Over a period bordering on several months, all he ever said directly to me was "Yes, yes . . . very happy." It was open to many interpretations.

As before, the material life gradually overwhelmed the spiritual one. If there was anything that became clearer, it was again the utter necessity of realizing Truth within. Like other teachers, Baba *did* operate on inner levels—nothing else explained the intensity of one's inner life around him—but, in so doing, he made it very clear that his physical presence was now more of a hindrance to me.

The interior experiences I had over this time are beyond the scope of this book and my talent, but, once again, they finally flung me back into the world, the real battlefield of the *Bhagavad Gita*. That was where one had to apply the lessons learned inside. Simultaneously, my interest in India broadened now. The more I read, the more fascinated I became by the sweep and majesty of its very long history, the intricacies of its culture and society, both good and bad, and the ways the past coexisted with a present that most people still saw as the foundation for the country's future.

"Now," I said to my students at the University of Bangalore, "you've all read Shakespeare's wonderful tragedy *Macbeth*—so, before we start examining why it's so wonderful, does anyone have any questions?"

A resonant silence descended upon the acoustically challenged room, broken only by a creaking of chairs, the gurgle of metabolic processes, and the short-circuiting of brain synapses. Faces looked as if I'd caught them masturbating.

Then a voice said, "If the Macbett is believing these sadhu womens when they are telling him he will be the raja, why is he not also believing them when they are saying his children will not take crown because the Banko's issues, *they* will be taking crown?"

It was the most intelligent question I'd ever been asked about *Macbeth*. Students I'd taught at Oxford were always more interested in whether Lady Macbeth and the witches had a conspiracy going, or if Macbeth could be fairly described as a paranoid schizophrenic suffering from delusions of grandeur and hallucinations.

I looked at the list on my massive desk. There were five columns: *Sl.No. . . . Name of the Students . . . II Language . . . Caste . . .* and *Remarks*. I looked down the list.

"Sunderasan C.N., isn't it?"

"No, sir. I am Bhagvanulu, sir." He sounded hurt.

Sunderasan's second language, I noticed, was listed as Sanskrit. Where had he picked that up? I soon found the correct name. It spanned half the page, flowing into an adjacent column: Nunna Sathyanarayana Bhagvanulu. His second language was Telegu, and his caste was described as Kamma (B. Co.).

"Very good, Nunna," I told him, wondering how far down the hierarchy Kammas were. Most of my students were listed as Brahmin. And hadn't the caste system been officially abolished, anyway?

It took me a while to discover that there was a quota system operating in Indian colleges, as well as a vestigial caste system. They were obliged to take a certain proportion of local students, whether these students were up to university standards or not. This meant that more than half my class consisted of sophisticated, urbane rich kids from Delhi who spoke fluent English, and often nothing else, and poor kids from the surrounding villages whose second language, I soon learned, was often also their only language. For people who would have big problems reading Dr. Seuss, it seemed rather cruel to be asking them what they thought of Shakespearean tragedy. Yet, as Bhagvanulu's question proved, *Macbeth,* with its tribal feuds and supernatural phenomena, was something south Indians in particular could relate to. Macbeth himself would probably have felt quite at home out in the more remote parts of Andhra Pradesh or Tamil Nadu. There were still tribal feuds and witches in 1977, and still are.

My teaching duties were hardly onerous. The job turned out to be a sinecure arranged by an Indian academic I'd met in England in order for me to study his country's literature and culture. My lectures on Shakespeare consisted of my explaining plots and leaping around acting out scenes. Try summarizing Shakespeare's plots sometime; half of them don't make sense. I'd overlooked this aspect of his work when I was studying the plays myself. Staggering coincidences were often the only way he could come up with any sort of conclusion by the close of act five. I ended up playing all the parts myself to spare all of us the agony of Raghunabdhan V.A. (Kannada; Balijiga B. Co.) or Vasudeva Murthy R. (Telegu; Neygi F.C.) stumbling through *wouldst*s or *perchance*s. We spent an entire hour on "Thrice the brinded cat hath mew'd." No one seemed able to understand why the greatest writer in the English language did not appear to write in English at all. When I told them that many words no longer meant today what they meant in the late sixteenth century. I had the distinct impression that my students assumed this meant Shakespeare had been semiliterate. Adding that the Bard occasionally appeared to make up words, or adapt them, using nouns as verbs, for instance, and that the dictionary was devised after his death, confirmed their suspicions about the rudimentary state of English culture a mere four hundred years ago.

They'd been taught that Indian civilization had been going strong for more than thirty thousand years now, and many believed Vedic sages possessed nuclear weapons, radar, and magnetically powered aircraft equipped with cannons. Translations of the Vedas do in fact contain, in somewhat obscure stanzas, words that can be translated as "airplane" and "electricity." But the translation of Sanskrit, like that of Egyptian hieroglyphics, seems to be a fairly personal business. One well-known Bengali scholar eschews the word *translation* altogether, his books stating that they have been "transcreated" from the Sanskrit.

"Why is the Shakespeare making these play in five act only?" asked Subramanian R. (Sanskrit; Brahmin F.C.).

This, too, had never occurred to me before. I told him it was a legal thing—Elizabeth I insisted all plays have five acts, violators subject to execution by big axe. Subramanian R. found this an eminently reasonable answer.

They were so well behaved, these students, so polite, that they began to irritate me. This exemplary behavior, I came to see, made up for their salient and prodigious laziness. The first essay I sat down to mark con-

sisted of one single sentence: "The Macbeth is play by english genius
Sheikh Spiro he was knowing king and some bad peoples they are not
wanting this man to be their king so forest is walking to kill him."

Maybe teaching wasn't my forte.

It was at the university that I met the *rajkumar* of Venkatagiri, a prince
who had some kind of financial relationship with education and religion
in south India. His father had been one of Sathya Sai Baba's earliest devotees, although the rajkumar did not seem to be particularly favored at Brindavan. This prince was a thin, hunched man in his fifties, with bulging
eyes, a nose like a boomerang, and an air of always being cold—something no one ever is in that part of the world. He also kept inviting me
to stay at his palace: "You must come as guest at my palace," he'd say.
"My family have been rajas there for more than one thousand years, you
see." The two statements seemed related.

The idea of staying in a "palace" was more than usually attractive to
me at this point. My time around Baba, once more, seemed to be suddenly over. And *King Lear* was next on the academic agenda. I couldn't
face attempting the plot synopsis.

The crumbling colonial bungalow I'd inhabited now for some months
was also beginning to oppress me. With its rotting rattan, its brimming
septic tank, its eight dilapidated servants who barely managed the work
load of one part-time man between them, it was a place I dreaded returning to at night. The electricity supply was so erratic that I often had
to prepare lectures by candlelight; and when it did work, the plugs and
switches frequently provided shuddering 240-volt shocks. Food was kept
in contraptions like bird cages suspended from the rafters, to prevent rats
getting at it. Giant ants constructed extraordinary adobe skyscrapers up
the walls overnight. And once, out of the corner of my eye, I saw something moving up *through* the tiles. It was a small snake, which, after I'd
drowned it in Flit, I learned was deadly poisonous. Yes, a palace was exactly what I needed.

"My father owned one thousand horses and three hundred elephant,"
the rajkumar told me.

He kept adding these tidbits, whetting my appetite for life at the
palace. Returning there himself, finally, he gave me his address and phone
number—Venkatagiri 1—urging me to call whenever I liked.

It was now nearly summer, and the sun had once more turned the brilliant blue sky to a burning mist of pale gold dust. The heat effectively

halted the working day by 10:00 A.M. Along with everyone else, I'd been rising at four, often delivering a lecture at five, when it was still pitch-dark outside, having lunch at eight, then spending a delirious day splayed beneath a ceiling fan that turned precisely three and a half times per minute, when the current was available.

When the shade on my veranda finally registered 123 degrees Fahrenheit, I decided to call Venkatagiri 1. This took three hours in the swarming, sweltering post office and provided me with a line about as clear as you get from two tin cans joined by a length of string. I thought it was the rajkumar that I eventually spoke to, and I thought he understood I intended to visit him, but I wasn't certain.

The morning I was due to leave, my septic tank overflowed. With the incredible heat, the smell was sumptuous and overpowering. I pointed out the problem to Bogan, the alcoholic old crook allegedly in charge of the bungalow and its other seven helpers. He seemed horrified that I would suggest *he* could involve himself with such an unclean task. While packing, I heard his raucous, rasping voice adopt the tone it employed when dealing with those he considered inferiors. Then there was a shout and a mighty splash. Going out to investigate, I found two dark, skinny men up to their naked chests in the reeking tank, cheerfully shoveling its indescribable contents into wicker baskets, then leaping out in dripping pajama-striped shorts, hoisting the dribbling baskets onto their heads, and bearing them off somewhere. They soon returned and plunged back into the pit with cries pitched somewhere between sheer delight and utter horror. Bogan watched from a safe distance.

"Sweeper mans," he informed me, indicating the sanitary experts. Harijans, he meant—Untouchables. For the first time the word had some meaning for me.

✢   ✢   ✢

The air-conditioned express train out of Karnataka state and through the rich green rice paddies of Tamil Nadu to Madras was easy enough. The bone-rattling bus ride north into the baked rocks of Andhra Pradesh, wedged in with the usual solid wall of humid human flesh, chickens, goats, and two baby camels, was the only thing it could be. For nine hours.

I'd stayed overnight in Madras, visiting the fort where Robert Clive had begun working, in 1744, as a clerk for the East India Company at a salary of £5 (about $9.25) per year. By all accounts, he found the job unrelievedly tedious. Not fifteen years later, Clive, still technically an employee of the Company, was also its landlord, and feudal lord, too. As first governor of Bengal, defeating the local nawab at the decisive battle of Plassey, he became the bridge between the commercial presence of John Company in India and the imperial presence of Great Britain.

He returned to England in 1767, a very rich man indeed. In fact, as some complained, perhaps too rich a man. In an age of colonial plunder and state-sanctioned thievery, there were still limits on what was deemed proper for any individual to make, as opposed to what was deemed proper for the Crown and Company to make, and a resolution was proposed in the House of Commons that Clive had "illegally acquired the sum of [$500,000] to the dishonor and detriment of the State." The resolution was defeated, however, and another passed: "That Robert, Lord Clive did, at the same time, render great and meritorious services to his country." Something clearly nagged Clive's conscience, though, because eighteen months later, on November 22, 1774, depressed and wracked with pain for which he took opium, he sat on his toilet and slit his throat with a penknife he'd used only minutes before to sharpen the quill of a houseguest who wished to write a letter.

Information about local transport being more than usually scarce, I had no idea how difficult it would actually be to reach Venkatagiri, which was not featured on any map I could find.

Nine punishing hours on the first bus seemed to take me far out of my way, although I kept being assured this wasn't so. Then another packed oven on wheels deposited me in a forlornly beautiful town called Cuddapah, on the banks of the Penneru River: ancient ornate temples, stone ghats leading down to a broad expanse of lazy cobalt water that slid through and fed the land like a great artery. Nothing had changed here in several hundred years.

The whole area south of the vast Krishna River—a natural boundary delineating south India proper, everything between the Deccan and Sri Lanka—was once the seat of an enormous and now largely forgotten empire. The Venkatagiri rajas, I later learned, had once been part of this, vassals to monarchs who controlled an area larger than the Austrian empire, ruled from the city of Vijayanagar, "City of Victory." Numerous fifteenth- and sixteenth-century European visitors declared it a marvel with which no Western capital could compare in size, prosperity, and magnificence.

Vijayanagar was founded in 1336 A.D., when Edward III reigned in England, a date that marks the transition of ancient India into modern India. Before this time, the whole of the southern subcontinent was dominated by Hindu kingdoms so old that their origins are lost in the miasma of time. We know of them only through references in Buddhist edicts carved in rock 1,600 years earlier: the Pandiyans, lords of Madura; the Cholas, also great temple builders and based at Tanjore; and many others, among the least of which were the rulers of Venkatagiri. But this often glorious past, in its old form, vanished forever with the founding of Vijayanagar.

The empire arose for pragmatic reasons. Muslim leaders increased their persistant efforts to conquer all of India, and even stepped them up, their feared and hated forces amassing just north of the Krishna River. The feuding Hindu principalities forgot their differences out of sheer terror, and united under the leadership of the warrior-kings of Vijayanagar, who for the next 250-odd years held the enemy at bay, becoming the saviors of the South.

All that now remains of the City of Victory are the ruins lying forsaken near the tiny village of Hampi. Even the name Vijayanagar has vanished from memory. The first Western contact was commercial and indirect; the Portuguese on the western coast battled various forms of opposition solely to secure Vijayanagar's maritime trade. When the empire finally collapsed in 1565, the prosperity and influence of Portugal's base in Goa declined with it, never again to achieve the heights it had before the middle of the sixteenth century. Abdur Razzak, a Persian envoy writing a century earlier, informs us that then the king of Vijayanagar reigned as absolute ruler of the South, from the Arabian Sea to the Bay of Bengal, and from the Deccan down to the Indian Ocean: "from the frontier of Serendib [now Sri Lanka]," he adds, ". . . His troops amount in number to [1,100,000] . . ." Even as far back as 1378, in the opinion of Firishta, "in power wealth and extent of land" the raja of Vijayanagar appeared to be vastly superior to his contemporary, the Muslim Bahmani Sultan, who ruled the Deccan. History is written by the victors, and Islamic historians have played down the two and a half centuries of Vijayanagar military humiliation the Moghul invaders suffered—in the same way that the 1857 War of Independence was called the Indian Mutiny by British imperialists.

When I finally visited the Hampi ruins of the City of Victory nearly fifteen years later, I came across Portuguese chronicles describing the forgotten empire in detail. In 1977 even those whose ancestors had once been part of it knew only the most cursory facts.

I inquired in Cuddapah—little more than fifty miles southeast of what remained of Vijayanagar—about the Venkatagiri bus, only to learn that there *was* no bus to Venkatagiri. In fact, it seemed there was no transport of *any* kind to take a traveler there. Looking at the address scrawled on a card the rajkumar had given me, I began to wonder if his palace was in Nellore District or a district called Vellore. Both existed, but Vellore was a hundred miles southeast of Nellore, and Cuddapah, thirty-odd miles from Nellore, was presumably in that district.

Eventually I gleaned that I was some twenty miles northeast of Venkatagiri, the bus having been the wrong one, or there being no other possible route to take. Used to such vagaries by now, I asked more forcefully how a traveler who really *wanted* to reach Venkatagiri, who absolutely *insisted,* might achieve this. People twirled upturned palms with outstretched fingers in a typically south Indian gesture of hopelessness. I could have been asking how to get to Kansas City. After an hour of hiking through vicious, blistering heat, up and down the baking, dusty streets, I managed to locate a man who was believed to own a car—although he himself did not appear to share this belief. He did admit he had a friend who knew someone who *might* be able to assist. After many glasses of chai, and many false leads, we found a man who possessed an assemblage of steel and rubber that one could, at a stretch, have called a car. I had little faith in its ability to move, however; the engine groaned and strained for ten minutes before erupting into an emphysemic sort of life.

A couple of hours later, daubed from head to toe in dust and grime glued on by my own sweat, I was finally bouncing into Venkatagiri. The place made Cuddapah look like Brasilia. If it had changed at all in eight hundred years, there was little to prove it, beyond what might have been one crooked, sagging telegraph wire. Bazaars choked in swirling dust like dirty mist; flamboyant, irreparably decayed temples; shimmering heat mirages; narrow streets mobbed by cows, by turbaned men in stained khadi dhotis, by women in brilliantly colored saris who covered their heads while revealing the family wealth in their cobblestone-size gold earrings. Everywhere there was that bittersweet sense of crumbling splendor, none of it more crumbling or more splendid than the colossal edifice of the palace itself. The size of a large Oxbridge college, surrounded by a forbidding thirty-foot-high wall, this edifice dominated the center of town. In fact, it *was* the center of town.

My "taxi" swerved, hooting, through a massive entrance, past the kind of gates built to keep ancient Muslim armies out, and screamed to a halt in a bleak, flagstoned courtyard of awesome dimensions. There followed a loud and acrimonious dispute over money, the driver eventually pocketing my rupees with a sullen scowl, then navigating his rattling heap of exploding metal back out into the swarming streets.

Toasted between the pitiless sun and roasting flagstones, I looked around. A man in ragged white pajamas eyed me suspiciously from the shade of an archway, but when I called out the nature of my business, he disappeared, muttering to himself and hawking as if there were mud in his lungs. After several minutes' wandering in search of something resembling a main door, I found a shamefully fat man with walleyes, who beckoned me up a worn granite staircase. I wondered in passing just how long granite would take to wear. My guide ushered me along dim, corroded corridors and finally into a small room furnished with filthy old steel folding chairs and a picnic table. Here I found the rajkumar seated with about ten other men, all of them dressed identically in creased, baggy white pajamas.

At first he acted as if he'd never seen me in his life, although, on the other hand, he did not look unduly surprised by the sudden appearance of a Western stranger. Maybe they were always dropping in. I felt obliged to remind him of our great friendship in Bangalore, his kind offer, my phone call . . . He motioned for me to sit. After that I never got over the feeling that he didn't know what the hell I was going on about.

We sat, the whole dozen of us, on the creaky unstable chairs in uncomfortable silence. At least *I* was uncomfortable. Indians are quite capable of not saying anything to each other for considerable periods of time without feeling remotely ill at ease.

The room did not strike me as palatial. Its walls had probably needed a good dusting and a coat of whitewash when Robert Clive was still poring over the East India Company's ledgers. They were bare, apart from three yellowed photographs in buckled frames of men standing over dead tigers and a curled calendar emblazoned with the image of the Tirupati idol, Lord Venkateswara, a burly space alien inordinately fond of ostentatious jewelry. The fat walleyed man abruptly reappeared bearing a bowl of what looked like red sponges soaked in pink Day-Glo fluid. I thanked him profusely, feeling more in need of a bath than food, gamely picking up the stained spoon. The stuff tasted like chunks of watermelon in an 80-percent solution of sugar. It was so sweet it was almost bitter. I had to put the bowl aside after two mouthfuls. The fat old man picked it up and pushed it back into my hands, making a bizarre squeaking noise at me.

"What does he want?" I asked the rajkumar.

"He wants you to eat it all," my host replied jovially, adding, "This man is my personal servant, you see. He is looking after me since I was a boy. But he is deaf-mute—no hearing, no speaking, isn't it?" He leaned toward an unpaned window and, after a good rasping hawk, spat through it.

I had no wish to be impolite. Reluctantly I forced the excruciatingly mushy lumps down. Throughout, various other men kept ambling over to the windows and spitting tumultuously out or blowing noses with their fingers and flinging the wobbling results down into the street below. No wonder people outside covered their heads. When I'd finally swallowed the last lump, I felt an arm like a whip with fingers dart from behind and swab at my mouth with a damp, fetid old towel.

"You *see!*" the rajkumar exclaimed. *"Now* he is happy, this old man."

The manservant scooped up the bowl and shuffled out, looking more content with things. I mentioned that I might like to freshen up, since I'd been traveling since 4:00 A.M. through a fog of dried mud in 120-degree heat. The rajkumar, now looking my way as if he vaguely recalled me from somewhere, announced "You can stay in my son's bedroom— he is away." He made this sound like an incomparable honor. There was, however, he added, one drawback: That bedroom was located in the *purdah* area of the palace. All the women of the family lived there, and they had not only never left the palace in their lives, but had also never before met a man they weren't related to. I would have to be led through the area by a eunuch who could warn any loitering women to clear out of my way. "And," the rajkumar added magnanimously, "you can use my personal bathroom."

This is more like it, I thought.

The old deaf-mute led me down various terminally wrecked and be-grimed corridors and more decomposing staircases until we reached a huge wooden door in what I guessed was the subbasement level. He strug-gled with a bolt as thick as my arm and eventually heaved open the door to reveal what I assumed was a stable of some kind. Beckoning me in-side with a squeak, he indicated a barrel full of water, a hole in the mud floor flanked by two footprintlike indentations, a gnawed plastic jug, and a teeny wooden stool upon which lay a couple of tattered towels. He smiled paternally, gesturing at all the facilities, then left, hauling the door closed behind him.

I stood assessing things for a few moments. *This* was a maharaja's bath-room? Something brown and furry shot behind the barrel. Just above eye level was a hole with broken and rusted iron bars, through which I kept seeing various swathed legs pass by: I was looking out, I realized, onto one of the town streets. . . .

Feeling a sinister twinge in my guts, I washed, ladling water from the barrel with the plastic jug, much as I did back in my bungalow in Ban-galore. Except my bungalow was in better shape than this palace.

Somewhat refreshed, I was led, not by a eunuch but by two twelve-year-old girls, identical twins, in soiled and threadbare saris down some very dark and narrow corridors into the purdah area. Here all the win-dows were screened with carved wood dotted with tiny peepholes—to enable the royal ladies to look out while remaining unseen. One of these corridors must have been the kitchen: It was black with soot and scat-tered charcoal fragments, strewn with dented aluminum pots and pans, the flagstones suggesting that cooking was performed on wood fires right there.

My room, the princely chamber itself, boasted a narrow springy cot, a bookcase crammed with torn old Rex Stout, Mickey Spillane, and Agatha Christie paperbacks, one bare light bulb dangling dangerously close to the fly-splattered blades of a prewar ceiling fan, and a minute bedside table that nearly collapsed when I placed my toilet bag on it. There sim-ply was no room in the room for anything else. Apart from laser beams of sunlight piercing the purdah screens for a few hours in the afternoon, the place was oppressive. That and the stupendous heat made me feel I was in a medieval prison cell—the Black Hole of Venkatagiri.

I lay on the dry lumps of my bed for what seemed hours, reading about a murder I knew damn well the vicar had committed. (He hadn't, as things turned out.) It grew extremely dark, and my bulb pulsed spasmodically—as did something in my intestines. I was beginning to think they were connected when, without warning, the little twins arrived bearing a bowed tray between them. They set it down on a fissured Formica table out in a kind of antechamber, swiftly retreating into the shadows. The food was a greasy black mass of something I could not identify, partly because of the ferocious, blistering spices it contained. I pondered the folly of this trip, eating listlessly with my fingers. I do not know when I noticed the rajkumar standing silently over me. He had a way of appearing without noise or warning, and he watched me eat with interest, as if observing a pet, without saying a word, even in response to my greeting. At length I told him that if this was a bad time to have come, if he was too busy, I could always come back later in the year. . . .

He gave a rather deranged and lopsided smile at the suggestion, then said, "You know, if I didn't want you to leave this place, you never could." With that, he vanished in the direction of the royal ladies' quarters.

He was dead right, I decided, feeling distinctly uneasy. I was not remotely hungry now, and I left the thing on my plate, fully expecting it to jump up and run off howling into the night. I went back to my cot to read. This proved difficult beneath the creaking fan and a haze of flies, but I tried to lose myself in the mystery novel. Before long, I began to suspect the behavior of the handsome gamekeeper. When I awoke, I noticed two things: The fan and light no longer functioned, and something red-hot, with teeth, was gnawing its way through my bowels. I needed a washroom—*fast*. My watch claimed it was 2:30 A.M. The palace lay unnaturally dark and eerily silent around me. Oblivious of anything beyond the searing pain down below, I padded back through the labyrinth of corridors in my underpants. I should have unraveled a thread on the way in. . . .

Once I made it beyond the purdah quarters, a high-wattage moon illumined the stone maze sufficiently for me to grope my way back to the rajkumar's personal washroom. I wondered what everyone else used. Finally squatting down over its pit, feet in the slimy footprints on either side, I stifled banshee howls as a torrent of what felt like lava almost propelled me through the roof. Not even the incessant patter of very tiny feet all around could disturb the relief earned through enduring the alternating bouts of agony.

What happened next, however, definitely did: I heard the heavy door scrape open and saw the bulky silhouette of the deaf-mute manservant peer in, as if searching for something. His eyesight obviously wasn't in much better shape than his other senses, because he soon withdrew and I heard the door close. This was followed by the sound of a massive bolt being drawn across the outside.

"Hey!" I yodeled, almost slipping into the evil pit. *"I'm in here!"*

Nothing.

"Hey! Oi!"

When the spiteful, biting spasms in my lower east side had subsided, I washed myself wearily with water and hand. I'd long since ceased missing toilet paper—it didn't trouble me in the least. But the prospect of spending a night in this dungeon with whatever else inhabited it *did* trouble me. I tottered over and tugged at the unyielding bulk of the door. It was not about to budge. Briefly I contemplated running at it with my rugby shoulder, but I soon faced up to facts. Finally I looked up at the small barred rectangle: Surely I could squeeze through it, no? A few minutes' investment of tearing flesh and fingernails and I'd slid over all manner of vile and slimy things, pushed aside bars that crumbled into sharp flakes of rust, and found myself outside the palace walls, in a forlorn and dormant thoroughfare. Trekking along in the security of towering shadows, I soon reached a yawning recess that looked like the main entrance. Its mighty gates were closed. There was no doorbell, and the anguished thumping of my fists brought not even a hint of response. Plodding on in search of an alternate entrance, I came across part of the palace wall that, with the aid of a vendor's cart, a conveniently situated tree, and some stone protrusions, looked fairly possible to climb over. Feeling, in my damp, soiled underpants, like some crazed old Tarzan, I bounded from cart to branches and then protrusions, managing at length to drag myself up and over onto a parapet—scraping off only half the skin on my knees and chest in the process.

Hanging from my hands, I let myself drop to the ground. It was a good deal farther than I'd imagined—such things usually are—and my right foot hurt savagely from the impact. Hissing curses, I stood to find out where exactly it was I'd landed. A walled second-floor courtyard was the answer—but a courtyard littered with the forms of women swaddled in saris sleeping unsheltered on flagstones beneath the heavens.

This was not good for a foreigner wearing only y-fronts. This was bad—very bad. Even trusted old retainers were forbidden in the purdah quarters.

Expecting some shrill, panicked voice to raise the alarm at any moment, I tiptoed past snoring rolls of tangled cloth, edging around the courtyard's perimeter. Miraculously, I came across a doorway that led right into my own princely chamber. I peeked out. No one seemed to be shrieking for the guards, and I was able to enjoy the sight for a moment. There was something ancient and beautiful there: the moonlight on exquisite faces, saris muted in color and lacquered with silver.

I spent the entire next day stretched out in my oven with Mickey Spillane. I timed the spurts of current that moved my fan overhead, to see if there was any pattern to Venkatagiri power cuts. There wasn't. I counted the holes in my purdah screens: one had 235, the other 198. Soon, I considered, I'll be marking off the days in batches of seven on the wall. The two ragged twins brought more food, or perhaps had recaptured the same food. They giggled at me shyly. My Telegu vocabulary consisted of phrases like "Hello," "How are you?" "Good-bye," "How much is that?" "You must be out of your mind," and "Fuck off." In vain I tried to ask these twins where the rajkumar was, and what I might expect in the way of freedom. I had no intention of touching the food, which appeared to be oddly sentient that day, content to watch me from where it squatted malevolently on its chipped plate.

Late the next day, two men with untrustworthy eyes and lived-in dhotis materialized at my bedside, gesturing for me to follow them. I followed them all the way to a neolithic Jeep, finding myself suddenly driven out of town, trailing clouds of dust. Perhaps they were taking me to the Madras bus. I did not have my luggage, though, and I also lacked sufficient skill in mime to convey this detail to my escorts. We tore recklessly through the parched wilderness of massive rocks and anorexic trees for about fifteen minutes; then we swung on two wheels off the cracked hardtop and onto a sandy goat track. We were heading toward an abandoned colonial mansion surrounded by extensive low outbuildings.

"Cricket club, cricket club," the driver informed me with fantastic enthusiasm, nearly slamming into the remains of a bullock cart before slithering to a halt by what termites had left of the veranda.

Double doors leading into this dessicated ruin of a house were suddenly thrown open from inside by a weary man with legs like old plumbing. Inside, the place echoed resonantly. Its floorboards were riven with cracks and bulging from decades of unrelieved aridity. The walls were hung with dozens of faded sepia photographs, in crooked and mutilated glassless frames, of people playing cricket in another era. My minders flung open the clacking shutters on the far side, pieces tumbling off, to reveal an extensive area of uneven ocher sand dotted with rotten posts from which clung shreds of netting.

"Cricket pitch, cricket pitch," the driver announced, proudly waving an arm at it all.

I tried to look suitably impressed. A little later, strolling the grounds, I realized that the long, low lines of partially collapsed outbuildings had been stables. Hundreds of stables, for the old raja's hundreds of horses, I presumed. I saw no horses, however, and no elephants. The shattered stalls, with only a hot wind blowing through them to break the silence, made the place seem all the more abandoned and sorrowful. The rajkumar had talked of the past in the present tense.

Returned to the palace, I was immediately shown into what was patently the rajkumar's bedroom, where he sat cross-legged on a gigantic and dangerously unstable four-poster job, holding court. Several prosperous-looking men, with paunches that could easily have housed a sack of grain each, sat around him on the bare stone floor, soliciting princely approval for business schemes or intervention in vexing matters. My presence was studiously ignored, although the deaf-mute brought me chai in which a large flying ant was swimming lengths.

"Tonight we shall visit tennis club," declared the rajkumar sometime later, after his court had dispersed.

"If you're too busy—" I started to say. He cut me off.

"No, no, not at all. I have full program set up for you."

The tennis club proved to be not far from the palace, and, unlike the cricket club, was still more or less functional. We traveled the short distance there in an aged Ambassador that had frilly curtains on wires around its rear windows to keep out the sun and seal in its heat. It was like being in a mobile dollhouse. On several very hard courts, people in modern-looking gear played inept and languid games, often with the net.

The rajkumar and I sat watching these efforts from a courtside table. We sat with a pleasant man to whom I was never introduced, sipping Campa Colas and discussing education, a subject the pleasant man had strong and knowledgeable opinions about. He suggested that the current system needed a thorough rethink, the introduction of a more structured syllabus, and a more disciplined approach to what was taught. He was right about this. It was the closest I had been to a normal conversation in many weeks, and I was enjoying it. As the light faded and the insect chorus of yet another suffocating tropical night tuned up, the rajkumar abruptly stood—the pleasant man was in midsentence—announcing it was time to leave. Back in the springy leather seats behind those preposterous curtains, my host said, "You see that man we were talking to?"

I nodded—not that I could now see anything.

"He is going to prison tomorrow. He has been embezzling funds, you see. . . ."

I gathered that this would be as big a surprise to the pleasant man as it was to me. The rajkumar did not elaborate on the man's crimes, staring in silence at his thumbnails.

That night he watched me eat again, suddenly announcing that he currently had many problems and, as if the news would astound me, little money to deal with all of these problems.

He sighed. "Too much of troubles."

The abolition of the Indian princely titles, in theory, and the privileges associated with them, in practice, left him in an awkward situation. The local people, so remote from the realities of contemporary India, and so conservative, so attached to tradition, still regarded him as their ruler, and still expected all that this had always entailed. When his children married, for instance, he was obliged to provide everyone in Venkatagiri with new clothes. Fortunately for his peace of mind, the disastrous condition of his palace scarcely seemed to bother him. "So many problems," he kept repeating.

One of these, I was almost shocked to hear, was the fact that he was having an affair with a Tamil movie starlet. The problem, though, was not fear of getting caught, as I had imagined. It was guilt. As I knew, he was a devotee of Sathya Sai Baba. Now, out of pure shame, he could not face seeing the family guru.

He was full of surprises that night: He announced in nearly the next breath that his wife and daughters wished to meet me, but I should realize they were shy and not used to meeting strangers. When I discovered that they had never met any strangers before, probably because they had always been behind the walls of purdah *throughout their lives,* I found this perfectly understandable.

Following him into the forbidden area, past the "kitchen," where ragged old crones were indeed then cooking more black stuff in even blacker pots placed on wood fires burning randomly on the bare flagstones, then past my cell, we ascended a short staircase into a comparatively opulent zone. There I was seated on an exquisitely carved ebony sofa inlaid with ivory and mother-of-pearl. There was nothing wrong with it that a gallon of furniture wax couldn't have fixed.

His two daughters had the huge almond eyes and delicately pointed features familiar in so many classical south Indian miniature paintings. Fragile beauties, they were indeed somewhat taxingly shy, constantly veiling their giggles in folds of sari. When they spoke, their English was good, and they were charmingly excited by my visit. The rajkumari, on the other hand, a huge, pasty, and ungainly mass of silk-swaddled flesh, held herself aloof and uncommunicative to the point of what would be interpreted in the West as outright hostility. I could see why her husband had taken up with his starlet. The power of the purdah sat at some distance in this unnerving, pungent silence, while her daughters answered my questions and began, even more eagerly, to ask their own.

Yes, it was true that they'd never left the palace and probably never would. No, this did not trouble them. One girl—neither looked more than sixteen—hauled out an elaborately bound photo album and, placing it chastely between us, showed me her wedding pictures. The wide-eyed bride stood in a stunning crimson sari that must have had a kilo of gold thread embroidered around its borders. She had eye makeup that made Elizabeth Taylor look like Golda Meir, and wore a huge pearl-encrusted nose ring joined by gold and ruby chains to filigree earrings festooned with diamonds and emeralds. She looked nervous, however; the eyes were like those of a frightened fawn. On one page a large picture showed her weighed down by this costume and entering a large, square white bag. It was almost a tent, in fact, with a long zipper that presumably closed its entrance. The marriage rites, she told me, were performed while she was in this bag. She had never seen her man until *after* they'd been pronounced husband and wife.

What was it like when they finally unzipped the bag and she found herself face-to-face with the fellow she'd be spending the rest of her life with? She giggled, hiding her face, blushing.

"I thought Mummy and Daddy made *very* good choice," she replied eventually, still hopelessly embarrassed.

Somehow, I couldn't imagine her having a sex life at all. She went on to say, as if answering this unspoken question, that she was so far still very happy with her parents' choice of spouses. I suspected that the rajkumari's silent but forbidding presence had more than a little to do with this answer. (I was wrong, as it turned out—"Mummy" spoke not a word of English, which also probably accounted for her silence.)

The wedding seemed to have been very involved, and exceedingly long, both bride and groom resembling temple idols during a marathon puja, beginning to look bored and very weary after the first hundred photographs, then merely dazed. I guessed the heat and the heavy outfits took their toll as the festivities continued. After the ceremony itself, there had been numerous tiresome-looking formal functions—you could hardly term them a party—such as Princess Di and Prince Chuck once endured. No one appeared to be having any fun. I sensed an air of absolute chaos behind the vivid colors and the exotic rites. In one sequence, the rajkumar, dressed like Yul Brynner in *The King and I,* handed out saris and dhotis to his loyal subjects. Men on one side, women on the other, the people of Venkatagiri sat lining the main street for as far as the eye could see in both directions. Although these clothes were not silk, and more Zellers than Versace, they were still new—packaging and labels visible. I discovered Venkatagiri's population exceeded ten thousand. After the free clothes came another tradition: free food, the sweating rajkumar now seen ladling rice and curry onto banana leaves. I assumed he hadn't served all ten thousand meals personally. What with this, the wedding itself, and a more lavish function for about two thousand private guests, not to mention gifts and a dowry, the rajkumar's coffers must have suffered a dreadful plundering. It was a good thing Prohibition still existed in Andhra Pradesh.

I asked about the expense. The little princesses said only that "Daddy" had many responsibilities. I supposed they knew little of the world beyond their purdah quarters.

Except movies. These girls lived for movies. Mainly Indian movies, of course—screened for them privately. Movies were their sole source of contact with the outside world. Indian movies hold no mirror up to life; thus, I wondered what exactly the girls imagined went on beyond the palace gates. All singing, all dancing, all fighting, all sex—such was the content of virtually all Indian movies, apart from the few that were all religion, all singing, all dancing, all fighting, and a little subliminal romance.

I asked them if they'd like to live the way people in movies lived. More giggling, more whispered consultations between them. It dawned on me that they thought I was asking if they wanted to live the way movie stars did off-screen. They clearly read the scandal-mongering, shameless, and salacious gossip that comprised movie mags like *Stardust* (IS NEETU CAR-RYING KUMAR'S BABY?) and were not quite sure how to answer this.

"Movie world is most unreal" was the eventual reply. "These stars are not understanding that movies are being fantasy only. But they are living same life when not acting, isn't it? This is why they are having too much of troubles. *Very* bad. Always problem with the marriage, isn't it?" They looked earnest.

It sounded like something their father had told them. I could see this life of sexual liberty, of liberty alone, for God's sake—something they could not even imagine—both fascinated and terrified them. They were so secure in their small and ancient world, yet it was a security that made them terribly vulnerable and insecure, as well. And what if one day all this ended, their small and ancient world collapsed, forcing them to survive in shark-infested waters with the rest of us?

They knew nothing of the changing society around them, of the "Emergency" Indira Gandhi had proclaimed nearly a year before, and which, still in place, was beginning to undermine her popularity. Opposition leaders had been arrested, strict censorship imposed on the press; Indian democracy itself was suspended and in grave danger of being permanently replaced by a dynastic totalitarianism. Yet the little princesses of Venkatagiri were hardly aware of it. I wondered, the following January, if they had heard that the country had elected a new prime minister, Morarji Desai, a man who drank his own urine for its curative properties and advised others to do the same. The influence of Marx is always just below the surface in Indian politics. If it isn't Karl, it's Groucho.

What did interest these girls, however, was Bombay and Hollywood—the two movie meccas seemed to be interchangeable in their minds. I was a visitor from the Outside World, and for them, I came to see, this Outside World was all one immense and exotic place. National boundaries meant nothing to them. Beyond the gilded, if now somewhat tarnished, cage of their confinement, they pictured only various kinds of astonishing freedoms.

I did not have the heart to tell them what most people's lives were really like out there. The wonderment and childlike enthusiasm in their huge, bright eyes struck me as the most precious possession this life offers anyone, and not something I had any desire, let alone right, to tamper with. When the rajkumari growled a few words in Telegu that no doubt amounted to "That's enough, girls," I saw the disappointment in those eyes. They made me swear I'd ask their father if I could come back—they had lots more they wanted to show me, they promised, and lots more questions they wished to ask.

To my utter amazement, quite early the next morning, the rajkumar appeared, informing me that he had arranged a complete tour of the palace for me, with himself as guide.

As I traipsed after his loping, lanky form through endless musty corridors, across bare upper courtyards in various states of ruin, and into countless shabby rooms that resembled long-abandoned garages, my heart sank. I felt deeply sorry for the man, living still on memories of times he'd barely even known himself. With all his retainers, relatives, hangers-on, and the antique deaf-mute—who even squeezed the toothpaste onto his master's brush for him twice a day—the rajkumar now lived scarcely better than the least of his subjects. He did have a kind of power, true, largely owing to Venkatagiri's remoteness from the authority of central government, but it was really just the power to solve problems at his own expense.

On the far side of the palace was a small free-standing structure with steps leading up several feet to its only entrance.

"Bhagwan Baba used to stay here when he was just a boy," the rajkumar told me mournfully, presumably suffering another twinge of remorse about the starlet. "My father was his devotee since the very early days. Many miracles we saw Baba perform here. Many miracles."

His father had even been given one of the lingams Baba materialized during a Sivarathri festival. I asked where it was now. The rajkumar wasn't sure, didn't seem concerned.

"Bhagwan's room has been kept just as it was when he left it," he told me with a measure of pride.

Since everything in the palace had been left untouched since it was built, as far as I could see, I wondered why he found this so unusual. I asked if I could look inside the room, but he said the key had been lost years before. I peered through dusty windows—the only ones I'd come across here that were actually glazed—seeing a tidy and thoroughly unremarkable room: one small bed with a white cover and tangled skeins of mosquito netting hanging like sails from a frame, a side table, a desk. Considering that Sai Baba had last stayed there in 1943, the place was in remarkably good repair, and still a definite improvement on the rotting cavern where the rajkumar currently slept, held court, and spent most of his time.

Crossing a nearby courtyard, I noticed the man I had first encountered on arriving at the palace, the one who'd run off when I announced my business. Seeing us now, he dodged behind a column, peering round it with mad, furtive eyes. Who was he?

"He is cousin," the rajkumar confessed, adding that the fellow had "some mental sickness." This "sickness" necessitated his confinement in a distant wing of the palace on occasions, I learned. Confinement actually meant being locked up.

"Forcibly?"

"He must be kept on bed with chains."

"Oh . . ." I felt I'd rather not know what the cousin was liable to do during such periods if he managed to escape from his chains and prison.

The tour was starting to depress me profoundly, when we finally arrived at two imposing and ornately carved wooden doors. Surely whatever lay behind them had to be grander than the warren of old garages we'd been visiting.

"Darbhar hall," announced the rajkumar grandly, throwing open these vast doors to reveal a room of spectacular proportions, lined on either side by a colonnade of towering alabaster pillars. These led toward a raised dais upon which perched a solid silver *jula,* a kind of swinging seat two yards square suspended from an intricately worked silver frame. It was like a piece of garden furniture commissioned by Kublai Khan. Padded with moldy crimson velvet cushions and bolsters, it swung on gilded chains and had to contain a ton of silver, every inch of it swarming with bas-relief scenes from the *Ramayana* and flowing patterns inlaid with jewels and gold. This was where the rajkumar's father would have sat holding *his* court—particularly on holy days and other special occasions. Clearly no one had sat in this jula for decades. The cushions looked as if they would disintegrate into dust if even touched.

Beyond the soaring pillars, in roomlike areas where guards and servants once would have stood, ceilings had literally collapsed in places, lying in untidy heaps of rubble no one had bothered to clear away. But all over the large central area facing the royal dais had been placed the family treasures—presumably for my pleasure. A dozen servants bowed as we entered, all of them out of sync, and beamed with pride.

Sorrow would have been a more appropriate response. Everywhere posed victims of the most untalented taxidermist ever to have possessed sawdust and a sewing kit: faded dusty tigers so long and thin that they resembled giant weasels; gazelles proportioned like obese ostriches, bursting at the seams in places; panthers as flat as woolly crocodiles; crocodiles you could have mistaken for charred logs; and a bear, with perhaps a square foot of fur left on its entire body, that appeared to have died of fatigue and old age. The rajkumar's ancestors had certainly wreaked havoc on the local wildlife in their time.

I asked him if there were still tigers left in the area. He shook his head, as if puzzled by such a wry turn of events, certainly not connecting it with his moth-eaten little zoo of corpses.

More than just the fauna had been neglected. Astounding items of furniture, carved and inlaid, were also near extinction, gasping for wax, savaged by the climate, intricate marquetry buckled and bleached, pieces missing altogether. Some of it was even the work of European masters: Sheraton, Chippendale—signed, too, for all I knew.

Then there were solid-gold statues of gods, an army of them, two feet high, wedged in beside enough yellowed elephant tusks to build an ivory tower with. Ceremonial costumes glittered dully with silver and gold threads. Studded with gems, they now hung limply on deformed tailor's dummies, dust probably the only thing holding them together—the weight of all the precious stones and metals that had once been their glory now their undoing.

I gawked in amazement, hoping the rajkumar would see fit to mention the sorry condition to which his magnificent past had been reduced. Instead, he showed a boisterous and almost obscene pride in every object he pointed out, explained, attributed to this or that ancestor. I supposed that, like his father before him, he was so accustomed to displaying these treasures and hearing flabbergasted sighs of awe that he had not perhaps noticed the obdurate toll the years were taking. I recalled the way he'd presented things to me back in Bangalore. He hadn't lied; it seemed he only saw what used to be. Perhaps the drastic contrast between past and present had also slightly unhinged him—although, judging by the cousin who needed chaining down from time to time, a good deal of inbreeding was also splashing through the family gene pool.

That night he had arranged for us to watch old sixteen-millimeter home movies. The projector was set up beneath the stars in a courtyard, the screen a bare wall daubed with scaly whitewash. Our projectionist turned out to be the mad cousin. I did not like having him behind me. But, after burning several yards of film, then getting a sleeve caught in the machine's teeth, he encountered another hitch: a power cut. No one seemed too upset, including the rajkumar, who confessed that he'd never seen for himself what the thousand crusty canisters of film, now piled up in a corner, contained.

I was composing a diplomatic speech about having to leave—wondering if I'd ever be allowed to—when my host suddenly announced that he was driving to Madras the following day and could take me along. If I wanted to go, that is.

I felt quite sad saying farewell to the little princesses, and they seemed sad to see me go. The thought of leaving them to spend the rest of their lives watching their world literally fall apart around them haunted me for months. I still think of them there, watching Bombay videos, reading the movie mags, dreaming.

※   ※   ※

The last time I saw the rajkumar of Venkatagiri was in a restaurant in Bangalore. It was a warm December night, and he came over to my table, wearing a thick sweater, hunched and shivering, complaining about the appalling cold. We exchanged small talk that seemed oddly strained and formal. Perhaps he regretted letting me inside his life, telling me about his financial woes, his Tamil starlet. Then I noticed, far back at a corner table, the portly form of a shabbily elegant woman, staring around at the other diners with abject terror in her eyes.

"Isn't that your wife?" I asked him.

"Yes. Wife is there," he replied, as if he'd forgotten she was.

"Is she all right?" She didn't look it.

He grinned his cartoonishly deranged, toothy grin, his nose virtually spiking his chest, and his eyeballs almost squashed against the lenses of his glasses. Then he said, "She is little nervous, isn't it? You see, this is first time ever she is traveling outside palace."

Perhaps there was hope for those daughters of his after all.

Rob Howard, a photographer friend of mine, visited Venkatagiri in 1991. Dacoits had broken into the dharbhar hall a few years previously, stealing the entire menagerie of stuffed wildlife. Little else had changed, he said. I still wonder what those bandits did with that taxidermist's nightmare, and why they wanted it.

PART TWO

The Nineties

A physical object may be at one point in space at one moment and at either the same or a different point in space at a later moment. We imagine that somehow the points in space persist from one moment to the next, so that it has meaning to say whether or not an object has actually changed its spatial location. But Galilean relativity tells us that there is no absolute meaning to the "state of rest," so there is no meaning to be attached to "the same point in space at two different times." Which point of the Euclidean three-dimensional space of physical experience at one time is the "same" point of our Euclidean three-dimensional space at another time? There is no way to say. It seems that we must have a completely *new* Euclidean space for each moment of time!

—ROGER PENROSE, *THE EMPEROR'S NEW MIND*

I am quite prepared to admit that, being habitual liars and self deluders, we have good cause to fear the truth.

—SAUL BELLOW

Prologue

My initial experience of the spiritual life was bewildering. There were times when I wished I had never heard of Sathya Sai Baba, wished I had never taken LSD that summer's night by King Arthur's castle so long ago. The Path is not easy. But as William James said in his "Paradox of Volition," when faced with a series of choices, always choose the one that seems most difficult, because it is the one that can teach you something.

As the years passed and I became more entrenched in the material world of credit cards, mortgages, and families, it became harder and harder and then all but impossible to consider returning to life in an ashram. But I did return to India, always, however, avoiding Bangalore. After nearly twenty years, the impression that Sathya Sai Baba had made upon my heart remained, occasionally bursting out in vivid dreams or subtly turning around my inner self at the most unexpected moments.

I always saw things in black or white terms, like the old rhyme

> *The devil was sick, the devil a monk would be;*
> *The devil was well, the devil a monk was he.*

But I'm learning to see things in shades of gray . . . or possibly pastels.

I went back and forth, each time creeping nearer the place I feared. But who is it we really fear? To me India was and is the Empire of My Soul, of The Soul.

Each time I visit her, I grow a little closer to the one I yearn to know. It gets a little easier—until it once more seems unbearably hard, that is. Yet at least I know enough to know that I am utterly ignorant.

I've always liked the metaphor of the empty bowl—yet I wonder why, just because it is empty, anyone feels it must therefore be filled. It is, though. Indeed it is.

PWR
January 1996

9

"Many Ghost Here . . ."

JAISALMER, 1990

❦   ❦   ❦

The wives of Rajput warriors often chose jauhar *and leapt into the fire when defeat for their men seemed imminent. At the* jauhar *before the fall of Jaisalmer in 1295 . . . no less than 24,000 women are said to have been burned to death.*

—SAKUNTALA NARASIMHAN, *SATI*

*O*ne hundred years before Marco Polo passed through this area, traveling the Great Silk Route from Europe to China, they called Jaisalmer the Golden City. Indeed, in the late afternoon sunlight, it did seem to be a deeper yellow than the bleached and arid desert through which I'd been driving for several hours with another photographer friend, John Bentley. Bentley had not been to India before, and was suffering badly from culture shock, jet lag, and the apocalyptic hangover we both shared after a night of duty-free to reduce the weight of our luggage. . . . He lolled beside the driver, groaning occasionally, in too much pain to open his eyes, let alone take photographs.

It was a monotonous landscape. A monochromatic one, too: flat sand and sparse bushes, broken every now and then by a hectic, ramshackle one-street town, or by small, almost African villages of mud-and-thatch huts upon which wild peacocks perched, the beauty of their plumage confounded by the screeching ugliness of their cries. Moghul emperors had once used them instead of guard dogs for these very cries, and for their extreme aversion to strangers. All I'd seen for most of the day were stray camels nibbling at what few minuscule leaves the desert could produce; wiry black goats with crazed eyes, hopping daintily among the rocks; ragged gangs of women and children singing happily as they broke stones in a futile attempt to repair the narrow, snaking hardtop that often disappeared entirely beneath desert sands. It came as a mighty relief to see in the quivering distance the imposing outline of the Golden City's great fort, set high on its craggy plateau—even if that first impression was of a gargantuan series of children's sandcastles. Getting closer, though, I thought it resembled old pictures of medieval Jerusalem or some of the Crusader forts in the Holy Land.

The rulers of Jaisalmer, the Yadava-Bhati Rajputs, believed themselves to be descended from the moon, via the divine lunar lord Krishna, including for a thousand years among their many titles "Guards of the Northern Gate." Remote, impregnable, and now close to the volatile Pakistani border, Jaisalmer remains India's northwestern gate, though no longer a key city on the Silk Route. That disappeared when the British constructed the port of Bombay. From its historic prominence as a hectic metropolis like Peshawar, crossroads between East and West, Jaisalmer has become one of the least-visited great cities in India: scarcely changed since the Middle Ages, with its winding cobbled lanes, ornately carved overarching houses, open sewers, and sense of vulnerability to attack that the immense walls and fortifications emphasize.

The abiding reality for the ancient Rajput warriors has always been the great Thar Desert, an inhospitable expanse of shifting sands, scrub, and rock covering most of Rajasthan state and protecting its desert kingdoms from their enemies while threatening to engulf them itself. It was this desert that Bentley and I had come to explore. And there was, unfortunately, only one way to do it.

When we eventually reached a hotel that called itself a palace but was in fact a converted camel stable, the photographer was more interested in exploring his bed.

✢ ✢ ✢

Dawn. A fragrant mist rolled through the quiet streets, almost rose-tinted beneath a huge shimmering sky. Bentley was standing, staring at the jumbled mound of photographic equipment on his bed, when I opened the door. He did not look good. His mustache sagged as if too heavy for him to carry, and he must have lost twenty pounds since I'd last seen him. He didn't have another twenty to lose. I asked if he was ready to head out.

"Yes," he said, uncertainly. Then he bolted for the bathroom. It sounded as if someone were running him through with a saber in there.

Our cameleers were waiting—dignified old Rajput men carrying mustaches like the photographer's but lighter, counterbalanced by the regal, intricately tied yellow turbans peculiar to the region and emblematic of the Golden City. A sense of history, and a pride in it, run deep here, each man full of family tales about chivalry, about valor in war.

Leaning at 45 degrees to support his bag of equipment, Bentley looked as if he might weep when he saw the camels.

"We *ride* these things?" he croaked.

I couldn't imagine a worse punishment for a man in his condition either, but I just nodded cheerfully. We arranged for a cameleer to sit behind him—supposedly so that he'd be free to take pictures, but really to make sure he didn't faint and plummet to the ground.

He gasped in horror as the camel raised its hind legs, dipping drastically before straightening up onto all fours. These cameleers knew their job, though, and knew their camels so well that they could identify them from footprints alone if necessary.

It was a perfect morning for a caravan, if you were able to enjoy it. "Hoppy," our guide, rode in front, and trundling ahead of him, soon out of sight, was a camel-drawn wagon with supplies. In the low, bright sun, we composed a vibrant and timeless image: the handsomely dressed Rajputs; the camels covered with appliqué blankets in riotous colors, their saddles huge, exotic contraptions of leather and brass. The tiny silver bells around their necks sparkled with saffron light, and jingled—a practical reassurance to desert travelers that companions were not far behind.

The camels had an elegant rocking gait. Watching the one ahead, I found its big oval feet unusually charming as they squashed down onto soft, thick pads, taking curiously light and dainty steps with long, shapely legs that had the fur on them decorated with carefully shaved zigzag patterns. Haughty beasts they were, however, regarding passengers, drivers, and all passersby with a measured disdain.

They liked to trot occasionally, too, perhaps to prevent the normally soporific rhythm from putting them to sleep the way it did their riders. They're not called ships of the desert for their charm, I suppose. And all ships have to weather out the odd storm at sea. The desert is nothing if not an ocean of liquid stone.

Soon the city, with its waking hubbub, faded far behind us, and the enormous peace of the lone and level sands descended on all sides, the sunlight gentle, still, even in April, cooled by scented breezes left over from the night. But a pleasant 60 degrees began its inexorable climb with the sun toward the low hundreds. The long shadows cast by the rocks were the sole definition in a surreal void, slowly crawling into the sand along with the lizards and what few other signs of life there were.

Sweating profusely, ghastly pale, Bentley swayed in his seat, lens caps untouched, the odd strangled sigh escaping his blue lips. I stopped asking him how he felt. It seemed heartless to pretend he might be perking up when he was so patently perking down with each roll of the saddle.

Our first stop was Bada Bagh, four long camel miles away, where *chattri*—royal cenotaphs—marked the cremation sites of Jaisalmer monarchs going back six centuries. I thought of Shakespeare's line "Bare ruin'd choirs, where late the sweet birds sang," and of Wordsworth's "The Ruined Cottage." There was a silent and lonely desolation about that eerie place, set though it was in the midst of a rich oasis with abundant orchards and verdant rice paddies. It was not even really a graveyard, but it felt like one. Ashes were removed after cremation and scattered over the sacred river Ganges. The tiny red henna handprints I'd noticed left on the wall by those taking their final journey through Jaisalmer fort's Sati Gate showed that not only dead princes had been burned out here. Living princesses, according to the custom, attained divine status by throwing themselves, or in some cases being thrown, onto their husbands' funeral pyres. Though it is outlawed, some villagers continue the practice to this day, particularly in Rajasthan. There are shrines to the *sati mata* worshiped across the country, one of the latest dating to 1987. Knowing that these young girls were often in an opium-induced haze when they were burned alive does nothing to mitigate the abomination entailed. It was this sad horror that I felt still hanging over the place. The tradition persists for even less exalted reasons: Generally the dead husband's relatives encourage it with great enthusiasm; otherwise they have to support his widow for the rest of her life. To this day, no one wants to marry a widow in village India, and husbands are still frequently decades older than their brides.

Hearing all this was the last straw for Bentley. He crept off to the shadows of a cenotaph interior and lay on the cool stone floor, breathing heavily, waving away all offers of drinks and medication. Even the cameleers muttered anxiously among themselves, pointing to where the photographer had crawled looking as if he'd decided an empty tomb was exactly where he needed to be.

I wandered the avenues of chattris, worried and not sure what to do. The Moghul architectural style of the cenotaphs, high on raised stone platforms, with their ornately worked, slightly drooping ribbed stone canopies, their magnificent octagons of monolithic fluted columns, had remained virtually unaltered for more than five hundred years. Each bore an inscribed tablet bearing the death date of the monarch in whose memory it had been erected. Yet the last maharajah commemorated here— cremated, alone, in 1982—had only a crude low brick wall for a memorial, sloppily fenced in with rusty barbed wire, containing only somewhat mysterious earthenware pots and two sad little faded photographs in cheap frames.

"No skilled craftsmen and no money now," Hoppy explained mournfully.

It seemed a partial truth. The real explanation flapped in the prayer rags tied to the fence wire by those faithful few who still believed their maharaja was a god, able now to answer petitions from his new throne in paradise. Although the princely titles have officially been abolished, the royal families of today continue to command a deep loyalty and respect from their subjects—now called voters—that threatens the modern democratic political process. The real truth about this humble tomb was that lavish funerals and the erection of cenotaphs affirming the divine status of rajas are discouraged by the nervous commoners running New Delhi.

The quasi-Marxist inclinations of Nehru and his daughter, Indira Gandhi, sought to undermine all traditional Indian institutions that threatened their power. And, in once-mighty kingdoms like those of Rajasthan, religion is linked to royalty in a potent medieval combination that frustrates the modern central government. For instance, maharajas are made into members of parliament, elected by their voter-subjects with overwhelming majorities in no-contest races. The simple fact, however, is that the princes and nawabs often did far more for their subjects and kingdoms than the new government can, now that the wealth is more evenly spread. And memories in India are long.

Bentley adamantly refused to move from the cool gloom of his mausoleum. I asked Hoppy what he thought could be done. Our schedule was tight: We needed to ride on if we were to make camp by nightfall. Eventually it was decided that one cameleer would ride back to the city and arrange a Land Rover to pick up Bentley—to cremate him, to take him to the hospital, or, if he was up to it, to drive him out to meet us.

I felt dreadful about leaving him in a cenotaph, of all places, but I was certain, having had my unfair share of "Delhi belly" in the past, that he'd soon recover. He was just at that stage where death and recovery are all one: Whatever it took to stop the agony would have been perfectly acceptable to him.

✧   ✧   ✧

Name: Boodul. Age: 25. Caste: Chuttry.
Date of burning: 4 August 1822.
Remarks: The woman burnt along with the corpse of her husband. She had only one child, a girl 13 years old, well provided for, and she was not pregnant. The chief and other police officers were present and I myself saw and spoke to her a few hours before the sacrifice. There was no legal impediment to her being burnt . . .
—EXTRACT FROM OFFICIAL BRITISH RECORDS FROM A SATI, 1822

And so I went off with Hoppy. Weaving through the primeval landscape, I had the oddly comforting sensation of having been there before, and in less tranquil times. Vivid images of violent battles fought in the swirling dust kept flooding my mind: the screams of wounded camels, the thunder of another charge, the clash of swords, the bloodcurdling howls and groans of the wounded, horns blowing, horses rearing, commanders yelling orders through biting clouds of sand. It was all so clear that it could have been happening around me in some other dimension. Perhaps time was an illusion, and everything that ever was or would be happened simultaneously in zones piled within each other, boxes within boxes, like a Chinese puzzle.

The seat of my loose cotton pants was beginning to feel like sandpaper against my arse by the time we rode into Rankunda, a dilapidated but still-functioning temple complex dedicated to Krishna. The point of this stop was partly to visit a deep well, surrounded by palm trees whose fronds swayed listlessly in the kiln-dry air. Our camels politely waited their turn to drink, while other scruffy, rowdy beasts, who belonged to some traders who looked more like bandits, jostled each other roughly to get at the murky water hauled up by rope in big leather buckets. Enigmatic creatures, camels really can survive, if necessary, like Christ, for forty days in the blazing wilderness without a drink. I was having trouble lasting forty minutes in the heat that now enveloped our bodies in a suffocating shroud.

Wondering what sort of business a temple so far out here could possibly get, I roamed its courtyard, where polished flagstones reflected the heat like mirrors and burned my bare feet. An ancient Brahmin with bottle-thick spectacles wandered in circles, mumbling his mantra, a set of withered testicles flopping outside his threadbare loincloth like a money pouch.

"*Hare Krishna,*" I said, but he didn't even hear it . . . or see me.

Vultures squatted on the domed roof of a shrine, hunched and ugly, waiting for death, which can come suddenly and unexpectedly in deserts. The whole place felt as if it had been stranded, left behind by time, which waits for no man and certainly hadn't waited for that old priest. Of course, the point of ritual is that it is action and inaction at once—action outside time, thus timeless or meaningless, depending on how you view it. According to Hindu scriptures, its very lack of meaning is what gives it meaning—it is freed from motivations of ego, and thus is pure, selfless devotion. God likes that sort of thing.

Soon we were off again, threading our way now through patches of thin cactus like giant asparagus. Vegetation, when there was any, was scant and scattered, mainly tropical thorns. The only flowering plants in the area are shrubs and wild grasses that manage to survive for a few months after the rains. We passed dessicated remnants of babul, neem, jal, kunta, and rohira. When they could, our camels paused at the occasional adar tree for a few slow mouthfuls of slim but succulent leaves that seemed to affect them like catnip, inciting a friskiness totally out of character.

The vicious little skirmish between my saddle and my butt was heating up nicely now, like the day itself, and my legs began to join in a chorus of various other bodily gripes. The next five miles were the longest yet, as the land on all sides melted into one white haze, the hypnotic pace and the cocoon of singeing air wrapping me in a pleasant narcosis. This was assisted, admittedly, by the pea-size ball of opium I'd eaten to deaden the pain in my arse. Opium is the drug of the desert, transforming those long hours of nothing but blinding sand and rocking camels into a reverie of cooler places, of trees and water—a nomad's heaven, just as you find in the Holy Koran. It's good for curing the runs, too. And it's also still a bit of a social problem in this part of the world. But all I thought of was our next stop, Ludarva, and the prospect of lunch, then a shady siesta. . . .

❧ ❧ ❧

The Bhatis, who once ruled this blasted bleak realm, traced themselves back to Lord Krishna, of the Yadav clan, based in Mathura, south of Delhi. When the Yadavas migrated from Mathura, it's believed, some traveled west into the desert regions of what is now Rajasthan. It's possible that this mass exit occurred after the great Mahabharat war, enshrined in myth and in the world's longest epic poem, the *Mahabharata*. According to bardic oral histories, the Yadu chieftains were not especially talented at war, and had trouble maintaining their power. They kept being driven still farther beyond the Indus. Eventually they returned, having honed their military skills, and are thought to have settled next in the Punjab. There the clan's chief, Gaj or Gajpat, son of Raj, constructed their first capital, a fort named Gaznipur—near Rawalpindi in modern Pakistan. When Gaj died during a battle with the king of Khorasan, the clan was forced to uproot itself yet again, heading into the southern Punjab. Several generations passed before another chief, Shalivahan, built his people a new capital at Salbahanpur—probably Sealkote now. This new leader was obviously worth waiting for, because before long he appears to have conquered the whole Punjab, and is even said to have recaptured the clan's old fort of Gaznipur.

Later on, during the reign of one Baland, the Bhatis faced great trouble from invading Turks, who gained control over considerable areas of their territory—including, yet again, Gazni. The clan in fact derives its name from Baland's son, Bhati, who seems to have possessed those military skills so much in demand but so rare in its leaders. In keeping with well-established tradition, though, Bhati's son and successor, Mangal Rao, was attacked by the current king of his old home town, Gazni, then forced to flee his kingdom and hide out in the desert.

Sometime around 650 A.D., things finally began to look up for the Bhatis. They defeated the various Rajput tribes they found, decided they liked the Thar Desert after all, and made it their permanent home.

Things seemed to go well for a few hundred years, until another catastrophe struck. During the reign of one Vijayraj, the warlike Varahas, always a nuisance, proposed that the two tribes end their bitter century-long feud with a matrimonial alliance. They offered their princess to the

Bhati heir apparent, Devraj. Vijayraj trustingly accepted this magnanimous offer, and a splendid wedding was soon held in the Varaha kingdom. Sleeping off the effects of what must have been an extravagant feast during the night following the marriage rites, the wedding host slaughtered virtually the entire Bhati contingent. Only Devraj, helped by a Brahmin priest, managed to escape alive, returning to regroup what was left of his forces back home. He needn't have bothered. Soon after, another horde of murderous tribesmen swept out of the desert and attacked the Bhati fort of Tanot, built in 731. This time the Bhatis seem to have been left all but extinct. Given their lack of military prowess, one is surprised only that this hadn't happened sooner.

But Devraj, who was either very lucky or a dreadful coward, managed somehow to escape this massacre too, getting taken in by a Buta chief who was one of his mother's brothers. This uncle gave Devraj some land, where he constructed a fort named after himself: Devrawal. Here he built up sufficient military might to avenge his father's death, and, astonishingly, even went on to capture Ludarva from the Ludarva Rajputs, subsequently shifting his own capital there. He became the first Bhati to assume the title "rawal." Little good it did him. He was killed soon after that in an ambush by the Chenna Rajputs while he was out hunting.

Things quieted down for a generation, but life was never dull for long for the Bhatis. Devraj's grandson, Bachchraj, had to put up with Mahmoud of Gazni. A ruthless and bloodthirsty Turko-Afghan freebooter, Mahmoud managed to invade India no fewer than seventeen times between 1000 and 1027 A.D., devastating Hindu cities and temples from the Yamuna to the Ganges, destroying anything and anyone that got in his way, and stealing almost everything else. To this day, Mahmoud of Gazni's name is synonymous with Muslim brutality and barbarism in the minds of many Hindus. Even the appearance of enlightened Moghuls like Akbar the Great was never able to wipe this bloodstain from the Hindu image of Islam.

Ludarva was a trifle that just happened to be in Mahmoud's way while he marched toward greater treasures in the Gujarat. He reportedly captured and sacked it in twelve hours. As always, though, the Bhatis soon regrouped, recovered. Bachchraj was succeeded by Dusaj, who was in turn succeeded by Vijayraj II. He seems to have made a more useful marriage than most Bhati rulers, taking for a wife the daughter of the Solanki ruler, Siddharaj Jai Singh of Patan. With the marriage came also a title for

Ludarva: "Gateway of the North." After his death, around 1176, his son
Bhojdev ascended to the throne—there presumably *was* one again by
now—but had to put up with his wicked uncle, Jaisal. Another advantage still left over from his father's marriage was five hundred Solanki
bodyguards. This force managed to thwart Jaisal's grab for the throne, but
not for long. Jaisal quickly formed an ad hoc alliance with the ruler of
nearby Ghor, obtaining for his efforts the use of troops that finally enabled him to storm Ludarva, kill Bhojdev, and seize the crown for himself. In keeping with traditional Bhati strategic know-how, Ludarva is
situated on an open plain. Having had personal experience of this shortcoming of the city as a defensible base, Jaisal shifted his capital to a hill
not far away, founding the fort of Jaisalmer. Unfortunately, he died before much more than a gateway for the structure had been completed.

Knowing this background made the bleakness of Ludarva all the more
poignant when we finally rode into the scattered ruins that are all that remains of it nearly a millennium later. Riding past a dried-up tributary of
the Kak River, we'd passed the mournful wreck of an eleventh-century
Sati Mata temple, the shrine to some unknown princess who had thrown
herself alive onto her husband's funeral pyre and become a goddess. A
beautiful young girl, dressed in her wedding sari, her husband's corpse
cradled in her lap as flames surrounded her . . . The image is powerful.
But nothing is left now except stones overgrown with weeds. Not even
her name has survived.

We finally dismounted, however, by something still very much sur-
viving. The magnificent Jain temple at Ludarva was founded two centuries before Christ, and still functions in excellent condition, though, as
with the Krishna temple we'd passed earlier, I couldn't help but wonder
who it still functioned for. Outside, a priest who looked old enough to
have helped build the place sat on guard, his long white hair hanging
down and mingling with a beard like a bleached privet. Above his head,
fixed to the wall, a sign read USE OF EGGS, MEET AND VINE IS STRIKLY PRO-
HIB HEER. He might have looked like Santa's great-great-grandfather, but
he was a real stickler for rules and regulations. Fully prepared to remove
my shoes in the temple, I wasn't prepared to be strip-searched until this
guardian was convinced he'd found every scrap of leather on me and removed it. Wallet, passport pouch, belt, watch strap: He confiscated the
lot before opening his gate.

Jainism, which resembles Buddhism, is also an offshoot of Hinduism, founded largely in reaction to the bewildering proliferation of Hindu deities (up to thirty-six million now, by some counts), as well as the depressing harshness of caste restrictions designed to discourage intermarriage. Originally, the caste system reflected the divisions that exist in any society: the kinds of temperament and the various tasks suited to varying capabilities. It was not the rigid and tyrannical structure it later became. Once the system had permitted movement, even marriage, between castes. By the time of Jainism, however, it existed solely to preserve an elite status quo in power, restricting opportunities to all but the chosen, and creating along the way a nearly subhuman race of outcastes, people not even allowed physical contact with caste Hindus.

Mahavir, Jainism's enigmatic founder, along with the twenty-four *Tirthamkaras*, or teachers, who preceded him during the current cosmic cycle, is represented in the religion's temples by identical Buddha-like seated figures of white marble, with unnervingly beady inlaid eyes. Coupled with curious plaques covered with innumerable pairs of tiny molded feet, the result, I couldn't help thinking, confused the outsider every bit as much as the profusion of gods and goddesses in any Hindu temple. Since all the little feet and all the idols are indistinguishable from each other, it doesn't really seem to matter which of them represents Mahavir himself, and which his predecessors. Little is known about these latter, although one is said to have been Krishna's cousin. The images are bathed and subject to devotions, much as Hindu idols are, but they are not worshiped. Jainism is essentially atheistic, teaching that man ascends to the supreme state of consciousness and omniscience through the help of Tirthamkaras and by ascetic practices alone. No creator-god exists to intercede. The Jains, and particularly the Jain saint Rayachand, deeply influenced Mahatma Gandhi's earliest formulation of his socioeconomic philosophy, with its foundations in truth and nonviolence.

Every religion needs its distinguishing features, of course, and in Jainism these include a reverence for all life that transcends the wildest dreams of the most pedantic and pious vegetarian. Many of its two million adherents in India today wear surgical masks to prevent their accidentally inhaling and thus murdering bugs; some carry brooms to sweep the path ahead clear of insect life as they go on their rather slow way. Jain temples, consequently, are often havens for rats, snakes, and various kinds of bird life. Many Jains, somewhat incongruously, are now bankers and extremely wealthy merchants. Thanks to the affluent Jain

Trust, the extraordinary temples in and around Jaisalmer are immaculately preserved. In its preserving zeal, unfortunately, the trust has frequently gone a little too far: for example, *rechiseling* eleventh-century sculptures to make them, in the words of a Jain I spoke with about this, "fresher."

Stepping past its ancient, authoritarian sentinel, I entered the cool and silent temple interior alone, aware only of peace and stillness—until I noticed the extremely large cobra lurking in a shady corner and watching me disapprovingly with black pinhead eyes. It looked as ready as the guardian to enforce any breach of protocol. A soft breeze and pale, yolky sunlight filtered through carved marble latticework as I trod warily around the snake, hearing birds fluttering and gibbering in the eaves. I felt I'd disturbed more than just wildlife.

Suddenly I was face-to-face with the giant image of Mahavir, serenely posed cross-legged in his sanctum, with ruby eyes set in solid gold and oddly watchful, as if that whole veined, translucent marble body were inhabited. Even the hoopoe bird perched irreverently on the idol's massive head could not detract from the still and powerful dignity of its ghostly form.

Behind the shrine, in a cluttered recess, hung a small clothesline bearing a large, worn length of linen cloth; on a ledge sat a small, cracked mirror and a metal bowl containing an antique straight razor. The old guardian probably lived here. I tried to imagine his life among the snakes, the rats, the birds . . . and the vast supernatural image of perfected man, taunting, reprimanding, encouraging.

☙ ☙ ☙

The Chohani queen, with sixteen damsels in her suite, came forth. "This day," she said, "is one of joy; my race shall be illustrated, our lives have passed together; how then can I leave him?"
The Bhattiani queen proclaimed, "With joy I accompany my lord . . ."
The Choara rani, Tuar queen and Shekhavati queen did likewise. For these five queens death had no terrors . . . The countenances of the queens were radiant like the sun . . . As the flames rose, the assembled multitudes shouted, "Khaman, khaman" (well done) . . .
—LT. COL. JAMES TOD, ANNALS AND ANTIQUITIES OF RAJASTHAN,
DESCRIPTION OF SATI BY FIVE QUEENS OF THE RAJPUT POTENTATE
AJIT SINGH, WHO DIED IN 1724

Lying in that twilight zone between sleep and waking, after a lunch of bread and fruit beneath the shade of a sacred peepul tree, I thought about that old temple guardian, about the difference between one man's life and another's. Crows bounced like evil little black kangaroos around the remains of our food; bulbuls and robins cringed beneath leaves, out of the heat. The city had moved on, but the temple remained. In India, the past refuses to die, undisturbed by new realities. On all sides the lunar desert now flowed around Ludarva's lost and lonely monument to faith, a lugubrious ocean of shifting, bone-white sands, indifferent to God and man.

By midafternoon the brutal ball of fire above had lowered itself and once again tamed its strength, splattering gold like nourishment over bleached, thirsty land. I felt we had been riding forever by now, making no progress, passing the same rocks, the same nervous chinkara, the same cautious desert foxes, hearing the same mynah bird mocking us with calls of *There they are again, there they are again. . . .* We'd covered only twelve miles that day—as good as making no progress. Hoppy finally pointed to a distant plume of smoke scribbling up across the high blue air.

Reaching the camp, I dismounted and walked like a tortured cowboy toward the anomaly of a table and chairs in the middle of nowhere. Bentley was ensconced there with a bottle of beer, smoking and chatting with the other cameleers, looking quite recovered.

"What kept you?" he asked.

I washed off a kilo of sand and joined him, watching the cameleers pile more dried camel dung on the fire, preparing to cook.

"Literally shit-hot, eh?" Bentley commented, nodding at the fire.

An especially talented sunset was at work on the giant canvas above us now, daubing streaks of purple into the golds and oranges already overlaid on its Prussian-blue base. Bentley had made a miraculous recovery the moment he saw the Land Rover, he claimed, enjoying a pleasant ride out to the camp via another route. He'd even taken some photographs.

By the time an extraordinary quantity of food arrived on the table, it was all but dark, a mystic twilight teeming with ill-defined forms all around us, illumined more by something held now within the sands than by anything given out by what was left of the sky. And in the center of this powdered nether sky, the campfire glowed like a dying subterranean sun.

"You like . . . here?" inquired Girdhar, head cameleer, gesturing at this magic spectacle.

I nodded.

"Yes," he added, sighing philosophically. "Yes. City no good. Here you have peace. In city no peace. A man, he need peace . . . like the camel he need food." He laughed.

I asked him about his family, his life. His wife, he said, was "finished." He meant dead. "I also finished soon."

"No . . ."

"Oh, yes," he replied matter-of-factly. "All men finish soon. Only desert never finish."

"Cheerful bugger, isn't he?" commented Bentley.

Above us now arched a huge basalt dome studded with stars like nails made of diamond. The table creaked with food: goat curry, a hill of rice, raita, and spiced vegetable dishes of numerous kinds, including an odd-looking but delicious regional specialty made from the tender, twiglike wild beans that are one of the few edible plants capable of growing in the barren dust of Thar. The myriad flavors were all smoky and exotic, their taste enhanced by the unfamiliar constellations raging overhead and by an invigorating coolness floating in from shadows that flapped like massive shrouds beyond our circle of light.

Only memories of sati sounded a savagely discordant note in this extravagant tranquillity. It was one aspect of traditional Hinduism that I couldn't even begin to understand. Love and fire seem to be the poles between which many religions function, though. Presumably Saint Francis Xavier was able to feel the love of Christ in the flames of the Inquisition.

❈   ❈   ❈

All actions of a woman should be the same as that of her husband. If her husband is happy, she should be happy, if he is sad she should be sad, and if he is dead she should also die . . .
—*SHUDDHITATTVA* (APOCRYPHAL HINDU TEXT, c. 800 A.D.)

It struck me that these cameleers genuinely liked us gringos, serving food and performing even the most menial tasks with the tenderness more of parents than of servants. It seemed so out of character with their warrior past, and I mentioned this. The fact that I was British had something to do with it, apparently. People I'd encountered all over India had sung the praises of the Raj days to me. Originally I took this as a desire to please, a sad remnant of years of colonial brutality and oppression. I suggested this to Hoppy. His reply took the form of a truncated history lesson—a lesson he felt I'd never learned.

Jaisalmer had been one of those princely states that had not participated in the 1857 Indian War for Independence—the Indian Mutiny in Western history books. In reality, it was India's first attempt to rebel against colonial subjugation. Bahadur Shah, the last Moghul emperor of Delhi, reportedly dispatched a letter to Maharawal Ranjeet Singh, ruler of Jaisalmer in 1857, urging him to crush the contingents of British soldiers in his state and then bring his entire army to reinforce the troops at the court of Delhi. Bahadur promised Ranjeet great rewards for such obedience. But the maharawal remained loyal to the British government, even providing reinforcements for the massive British mobilization from Sind to Kota. Thus the administrative affairs of the maharawal's state came to be even more strongly influenced by the colonial government than they had been before 1857.

This was why an anti-British attitude upset Hoppy. Also, as our host, he felt obliged to avoid subjecting us to anything distasteful, not comprehending that someone could actually disapprove of his own nation's behavior. In any case, the Rajputs, with their proud warrior traditions, admired the British for their military excellence—something that in their minds far outweighed any trifling political or ethical concerns. They'd been proud to fight with such a great army, not to mention to be on the winning side against states and peoples with whom they had warred for generations themselves. The shrewd British had manipulated these ancient suspicions and enmities among the princely states very skillfully, dividing one against the other in order to rule both. The same tribal grudges still underlie mind-boggling divisions in Indian politics and the hostilities among states today—particularly over issues of language and education, issues at the core of all nationalism.

Hovering over us, but not joining us—a host's duty, not servility—Hoppy made another valiant effort to change the subject.

"My ancestors fought here against the Turks," he announced. "Hundreds of years ago. Perhaps on this very spot . . ." He looked around to see if this had grabbed our attention. "You know," he continued more enthusiastically, "they ate *amal*—opium—before going into battle, so they would not feel their wounds."

I could relate to that.

"No," Hoppy went on, assuming he hadn't been believed. "It's true. There are stories of Rajput warriors fighting on for over half an hour after their heads had been cut off. . . ."

"We got junkies like that in New York," Bentley added.

"No, no," Hoppy protested. "It is true. They felt nothing, and their bodies would just keep fighting. . . ."

Opium, he told us, was still very much part of traditional life around Jaisalmer, and in ways one found hard to compare with the use of illegal drugs in the West. It was the custom, for example, to present a ball of opium to every guest at a wedding.

"No wonder your weddings here last so long . . ."

Perhaps thinking he had gone too far in presenting his people as a bunch of dope fiends, Hoppy tried to backtrack, saying these customs were really only practiced now by village people. This was familiar to me. Village people in India are blamed for everything the Western sensibilities running New Delhi cannot condone or stop. I observed the dreamy patience of our cameleers and said nothing.

Unlike most Indians, these Rajputs would not talk much about religion. It was far less a part of their lives than seemed plausible. I wondered aloud why this might be.

"Perhaps here opium is the opiate of the people," Bentley whispered.

No one offered any other explanation. Hoppy muttered about "modern times," and Girdhar coyly said something to do with what a man had in his heart. The real answer, I suspect, lay in the inextricable link that had once existed between the raja, his army, and the religion both fought for. The great Hindu epics concern themselves almost exclusively with this same trinity. They even make it seem the very core of the religion itself, to the point that, for warrior peoples, the removal of rajas and their private armies took away most of their religion's meaning. Philosophy is wasted on a soldier who has no war to fight.

As we ate, our weariness turned into silence. And no silence is like the silence of deserts—not utter, but vast, the multifarious tiny noises within it so much tinier in the desert's mass. Somewhere far off, a hyena cackled at its own joke. Then, floating in from those billowing shadows, came a few shy local villagers, offering to entertain us.

It felt like an ancient pleasure, sitting there filled with food and relaxed with weariness, watching a dance accompanied by the mournful, atonal lament of some old song that told the story being danced. Every muscle in my body glowed rather than ached. The moon peeped out from behind a marbled sheen of low cloud, silhouetting the sphinxlike forms of our aloof camels as they lay, legs folded at impossible angles beneath them, noisily regurgitating their dinner, gazing dispassionately at something invisible beyond our pulsing cocoon of firelight. The world felt as if it were finally at bay, and a pungent alchemy was now at work transforming the inner self. We'd gotten even with that tyrant Time. Almost.

❧   ❧   ❧

As the wind drove the fierce fire upon her, she shook her arms and limbs as if in agony; at length she started up and approached the side to escape. A Hindu, one of the police who had been placed near the pile to see she had fair play and should not be burned by force, raised his sword to strike her, and the poor wretch shrank back into the flames . . .
—FANNY PARKS, *WANDERINGS OF A PILGRIM*

During the hushed depths of a dream-wracked night, a vicious sandstorm hit, the flysheets of my frail little tent flapping like dragon's wings at my head. I scrambled around, tying knots, pulling poles upright and trying to sink them deeper into the sand. Outside, a howling white wind enveloped everything in a coarse, swirling mist of stone. Voices called out in the chaos; tent pegs were driven down by unseen hands.

There was something thrilling about it all. As flashlights carved through the rushing cloud of quartz, a shouted debate of disembodied voices heightened the wildness: Should we try to get out before it got any worse? Were we safer staying put? Had anyone checked on the camels?

"I'm not moving!" Bentley shouted to someone. "I'm not taking forty thousand dollars' worth of Leica shit out into this!"

We decided to tough it out where we were, zipping up flyleaves, anchoring anything loose with luggage. Lying back with the fury throbbing at our flimsy canvas walls, I felt like a fetus imprisoned in a malevolent womb, to be disgorged any moment into a world of perpetual night and tempest. Perversely, I was delighted, shriven.

Sleep must have come, as it always does eventually, even to prisoners. I awoke from infernal nightmares to find a world all the calmer after its mighty temper tantrum. In a predawn aura, the desert lay once more serene, the morning star a cool magnesium flare fired far up into the steel-blue east like a message of reassurance from the universe. Our place in it was secure once more. The cruel, barbaric wind of several hours before that had wanted to tear our hearts out and erase all works of man had worn itself down to a humble, geriatric breeze licking penitently at the coral flames of our breakfast fire.

"Big storm," said Girdhar, concealing a smile. "I think you much frighten, hah?"

Bentley and I gave him macho shrugs.

"No fear," he reassured us. "Only wind, only sand. Possible only to live or to die. *We* live." He nodded to emphasize this warrior's truth.

"That's a pretty black-and-white philosophy you've got there, pal," said Bentley. "Where does crippled or blinded fit in?"

"Still you *live,*" the cameleer replied. "Blind man, crippled man—still living. Dead man dead. *Finish.*" He slapped his hands.

As the sun's huge, florid head peered over the horizon, looking as if it had had a rough night itself, and a thousand black shadows, sharp as swords, slid out from beneath stones and rocks, we were saddling up again. Girdhar silently passed me an extra blanket for padding.

Miraculous recovery or not, Bentley was having no more of camels. He cheerfully elected to walk alongside us. After two hours, he was still walking contentedly—looking like advance infantry with his camera always poised for action—and had won a mysterious respect from the cameleers. For them, walking seemed as remarkable as riding camels was to us.

By now we'd reached the edge of a steep plateau, and the village of Jajiya. As I dismounted, I heard cries behind me and saw Hoppy and Bentley both pointing with horror at my butt. I looked over my shoulder, to see a bloodstain the size of a dinner plate spreading out like a ragged rose around the seat of my pants. Initially I thought of ruptures, of hemorrhages, of diabolical parasites. But, dodging behind a bush to take a closer look, I saw what you'd probably find after sitting on a hot plate, then sitting on it again after the blister had formed, and finally taking an electric sander to it. It didn't *feel* that bad, thanks to the opium. I squeezed antibiotic cream over a cotton scarf, fashioning a kind of enormous diaper from it. Then, changing pants, I forgot about it. There was no other option.

Jajiya turned out to be a unique little village. Constructed of thick, curving mud brick, the walls of its courtyards and impeccably neat thatched huts were all coated with a mixture of cow dung and mud that had been combed into complex swirling patterns. Even the sand laneways and alleys looked as if they'd been raked and smoothed that very morning. These were low-caste people, I learned, which is probably why almost nothing seems to have been written on their kind of folk art. An additional aspect of this art's charm—to me, at least—was its ephemeral nature. The mud-and-dung murals disintegrated or were washed away when the rains came, just as the very homes themselves would need constant additions, alterations, and repairs as the climate eroded them or families outgrew them. This kind of art simply expressed pure joy in its creating, in its decorating.

Peering into various dwellings, I found myself often warmly welcomed inside. Here, too, these humble huts had a tidy dignity that was almost heartbreaking. Each one I saw was immaculately clean, neat to the point of minimalism. And each contained in its main room something that I'd never encountered in India before: a sort of built-in rococo shelf unit molded from white clay and inlaid with coin-size mirrors. No two were alike; their twisting organic forms were as similar, yet as different, as human faces.

"My mother make this," a small boy proudly explained in halting English, displaying the series of shelves that grew from one wall, a collaboration of nature and man. On each shelf, behind curved crenellations almost like fat leaves, were piled the family possessions: folded clothes, cheaply framed photographs of relatives and prints of gods, and ancient alarm clock, a couple of plastic toys.

"Your *mother?*" I looked at the shelf unit's extravagantly writhing pediment—forms adapted from nature, improved, then studded with sparkling mirrors that made light dance around the small, dark room.

"This *tradition* for our people," the boy elaborated, clearly pleased by my reaction.

I wondered how these shy, happy folk lived out here with nothing but their camels and goats, on what seemed to be the edge of human history, in such an unfriendly wasteland of stones, shells, fossils—still in many ways resembling the seabed it had been a few million years ago. But then, we all live on the edge of human history. And where there had once been nothing *but* water—nature loves irony, of course—now there was only the once precious well, its muddy depths often drying up entirely as subterranean streams shifted their course. When this happened, the whole village would have to move on or die. For all I know, Jajiya may no longer be there at all now, its murals and mirrored shelf units already dust in the desert, rain on the ocean. . . .

Barely an hour or so farther on, incendiary air biting through my thin cotton pants at that masterpiece of a saddle sore, we passed one such village exodus, now merely a camp of skinny, depressed camels and ragged, weary nomads, their crimson turbans and saris the only color we'd seen beneath this pitiless white sky. Grimy, bright-eyed children ran screaming toward our caravan, demanding rupees, pens, even empty pop bottles, and throwing up clouds of dust. A sly-looking man, his mustaches like the silhouette of a diving swallow, produced a flaccid snake from a battered basket at the foot of my camel, proceeding not so much to *charm* the sorry reptile as to hit it with a stained old gourd pipe.

"Where are your people heading?" I asked him.

"That way, sahib," he replied, gesturing east with his head.

"That way?"

"To water, sahib. We have no water in our village. Maybe we go to city for job."

"What would you do there?"

He shrugged. It meant he'd do whatever he had to.

"Will you return to your village?"

"Village gone now, sahib. These peoples having no home now."

Girdhar rode up beside me. Two or three barked words from him made the man hastily fling his wretched snake back in its wicker cell and run off.

"Big cheats, these people," Girdhar told me confidently.

"They say that their village ran out of water."

"Too much lazy," he replied. "Need water, then well must be there. These people too lazy to dig new well."

Girdhar had firm ideas about things, and particularly about people. Few ever came up to his standards; and nomadic peoples always seem to frighten those who cannot imagine a permanent life on the road.

Perched now on a camel again, out of necessity, Bentley was clicking his shutters furiously, capturing images of a people who could easily have blended into any place or period over the past four millennia. As a result, he had an ocean of desperate humanity lapping at his feet: three or four generations of these displaced villagers demanding pens, waving snakes, grabbing at saddlebags, shouting for money or pop bottles or clothes or absolutely anything that the rich ferengis might discard their way. After tossing cigarettes, gum, paper clips, coins, and whatever came to hand, Bentley reloaded cameras, changed lenses, focused and clicked, focused and clicked, like a man in a furious trance. It was not images of bare-forked mankind at his feet that interested him, however, but the camp beyond. It was clearly not the sort of pastoral nomad encampment Girdhar had claimed; it was an entire village that had truly just upped and moved. Beds, pots and pans, crude wardrobes, water storage tanks, yokes for bullocks, cages packed with squawking chickens, plastic washing bowls, even desks and chairs and a filing cabinet, and much, much more, were lashed onto wagons, piled in tarpaulins, or still strapped to the bowed backs of camels. Anywhere else these people would have been refugees; here they were merely victims of nature's capriciousness, accepting their lot and moving, to start all over again.

Girdhar's attitude was incomprehensible to me. I could see him trying to push these ragged and homeless people away from his camels, and he knew I was not happy with him. Later, when Bentley had been persuaded to cap his lenses and move on, Girdhar claimed he'd only been thinking of our safety.

"Doesn't the sight of your own people in desperate need bother you?"

"These peoples not my peoples," he replied hotly. "They are big thieves and cheats . . . very lazy peoples. . . ."

"Aren't they just really very poor people?"

"Poor because lazy," he replied bluntly, adding after some thought, "Dirty peoples, too."

Dirt never means *dirt* in India. It means caste. To Girdhar, these people were doomed, destined, *cursed* to be what they were, to suffer what they did. And nothing should or could be done about it. I felt he thought I was insulting him by even comparing him to such people. As far as he was concerned, they belonged to a different race. Even Mahatma Gandhi, revered by all, quoted ad nauseam, had never really been listened to by those who still revered and quoted him, had never managed to get the message across. Untouchables might have become Harijans—children of God—but they were still untouchable. And few were touched by their plight.

After another hour's ride beyond the chaos and desperation of those dispossessed people, and still out of sorts with each other, we came to one of the haunting abandoned villages that once belonged to the Paliwal Brahmins, a now-vanished subsect of the priestly caste who seem, among many other things, to have been pioneer socialists. When we stopped to rest and feed our camels, we took the time to roam through silent, deserted streets that, like Pompeii and very few other places, had the odd feel of somewhere everyone had decided to leave forever at once—urgently. A sudden hot wind worried noises from the few bare trees, making me feel the inhabitants of this modest yet elegant little settlement were merely hiding, would run out again at any moment down the paved lanes, or chant once more within the shadowed shrines of their small, exquisitely carved and subtle temple.

Because it had been evacuated overnight, the place had succumbed to nature utterly and all at once, every part uniformly decayed. Somehow this made it look whole and unified in its ruin, rather than actually ruined. Where *was* the meaning of buildings in which no one now lived, which nature had reclaimed? And what sad or edifying stories did these particular ones yearn to tell us strangers disturbing their solitude? Why, for example, had they been left so abruptly?

Not very much is known for sure about the Paliwals' origins. A branch of the Adi Gaud Brahmins, they came from eastern India and claimed descent from a certain Maharaj Haridas, who was the personal priest of Krishna's wife Rukmini. Lord Krishna is said to have granted Haridas a special favor, the gift of vast areas of land in the Gujarat, where he founded a city he named after himself, Haripur. The community that grew up here around his many descendants expanded and prospered over the centuries, producing powerful landowners who allegedly gained an unequaled expertise in agriculture—unusual for Brahmins. Several generations later, at least one segment broke away, deciding to migrate to Pali—south of what is now Jodhpur, in central Rajasthan—thus becoming known as Paliwals.

The Paliwal community, too, seems to have thrived in Pali. They remained there for a long time, fortifying the city with strong defensive walls, and building up a widespread reputation as an exemplary community, upholding ethical and moral standards that many in the priestly castes had long ago left by the wayside. As a result, many of the more idealistic Brahmins from all over India gradually descended on the city, each individual or family receiving financial and material assistance with which to establish a self-sufficient and dignified new life. No Paliwal was allowed to be poor; each member of the community was expected to help any newcomer by providing bricks to build a house, and money to buy a cow, as well as land to farm. Thus the population grew. Their agricultural know-how, and the wealth it helped accumulate, naturally began to attract the attention of various plundering tribes, like the Mer and Meena, who began to make life at Pali hell. Unable to combat this menace effectively, the Paliwals finally sought protection from the Marwari ruler, Rao Siha, whom they apparently encountered as he was returning from a pilgrimage to Dwarka, sacred city of Krishna. Siha had little trouble making mincemeat of the marauding tribesman, but his actions seem to have been far from selfless. After the Marwari king had returned peace to Pali, he captured vast tracts of land surrounding the city, and finally even the city, too, for himself. Clearly, you don't ask a thief to catch a thief.

Continued attacks from Muslim tribes sweeping in from the west forced the Paliwals to abandon Pali sometime during the thirteenth century and look for more peaceful pastures, one group of them moving west, into Bhati territory. For the next few centuries they seem to have moved around quite frequently, as discarded monuments all over the area show, before finally establishing themselves in eighty-four villages near Jaisalmer.

After such a long period of upheaval, surprisingly, they then settled in much as they had several hundred years before at Pali. By the seventeenth century they had built up an enormous agricultural base, growing staples like wheat and lentils, as well as cultivating orchards. And they branched out into various kinds of business, even trading with foreign countries. Their strict moral code and the principle of helping any member of the community in need reestablish a dignified existence seem also to have continued unchanged. But their growing wealth brought with it increased political influence. Several Paliwals entered royal service, holding key government positions; and there are numerous instances of Paliwal wealth assisting the Jaisalmer maharawals, upholding royal prestige in times of need.

All went well until the advent of the *dewan* Salim Singh, a Machiavellian character who used internal dissensions in the state after a series of weak maharawals to bolster his own power, even proposing that the dewanship should in future be hereditary. He tried to cement his own relationship with the vital Paliwals—essential to the coup he no doubt had in mind—by asking for the hand of one of their daughters in marriage. As rigid proponents of caste, regardless of rank or influence, the Brahmins snubbed him. This aroused in Salim Singh a fury that earned him a reputation as the incarnation of evil. He began to oppress the Paliwals by every means at his disposal, confiscating property on the slightest pretext, and taxing them excessively and mercilessly. Every inch as proud as any dewan, the Paliwals met briefly and secretly to decide their future. The next day the inhabitants of all eighty-four villages simply walked away from their homes, farms, and businesses. They disappeared into history. Salim Singh, it's worth noting, narrowly avoided assassination by the succeeding maharawal, only to be poisoned in 1824 by his own wife.

The tale of the Paliwal Brahmins remains as odd and as moving as the villages they deserted. Most of these have been uninhabited ever since. Looking around the empty streets, peering inside rooms where only animals and shadows lived now, and walking through small, exquisite temple courtyards, I noted their abundant prosperity. For one thing, they had used a fine quality of stone and had employed carvers skilled in working it. But everywhere, too, I recognized the austerity of this vanished sect: No house was larger than any other, and no secular dwelling compared remotely with the temple's restrained and dignified grandeur. The Paliwals had regarded each other as equals—that seemed clear, even mandatory—but none of them had questioned the supremacy of the god under whose rule alone they could all be equal. That such people, with such principles and such detachment from worldly success, could simply walk away from it, *on principle,* is rare in any nation's history. The most extraordinary thing about the Paliwals is that no individual names have survived to overshadow their collective identity.

That night we made camp beside the crumbling temple and empty echoing courtyards of another Paliwal village, under another star-splattered jet-and-sable dome.

"It's just like they leave only yesterday, no?" Hoppy said over dinner, indicating the dreadfully silent village beyond, its smooth masonry now silvered with moonlight.

"Where did they go?"

"Good people," Hoppy replied, scratching his stubbly chin thoughtfully. "They just vanish . . . like many good things of the world." He gazed away across the shifting sands.

"Many ghost here," Girdhar announced, quite seriously.

"Jesus!" Bentley complained. "Let's get off death for one night, eh? Don't you guys have another topic?"

I asked Hoppy what he felt about the caste exclusivity of people like the Paliwals.

"Now very greedy . . ." The answer was predictable.

"All lazy," Girdhar threw in, illustrating this with a story about a Brahmin who now made his living by smoking.

"Smoking?"

Apparently the man in question sat somewhere in Jodhpur all day long, smoking a hookah, dressed in traditional robes, so that tourists could photograph someone in traditional robes smoking a hookah—and, of course, pay for the privilege.

"Are Brahmins allowed to smoke?"

This brought a chorus of complaints: They weren't allowed to eat themselves into airships either, but they did; they weren't allowed to use temple funds for personal use, but they did; they weren't . . . Well, the gist was that they lived like parasites from the sweat of those who worked. These men, I felt, saw their own caste—now independent workers more than warriors—as sandwiched between parasites: the Brahmins, the Harijans, what was the difference? None of them believed for a moment that the universe any longer needed priests to chant mantras every dawn to prevent it collapsing. With sewers and flush toilets ever more common for city folk, could the usefulness of Harijans as sweepers of excrement be similarly viewed as also all but over?

"But you said the Paliwals were good people . . ."

Ah, came the reply, but that was then, and this is now. Had these cameleers been in the dewan's private army a hundred years earlier, they would doubtless have viewed the Paliwals as just as more threatening variety of parasite, hungry for power and obtaining it through financial skulduggery. . . .

Before turning in, I wandered through those quiet houses, where the crosier's curve of faith still seemed to run in the walls. Modest and orderly even in their ruin, they were perhaps homes for the ghosts of lost and tranquil times. The only threatening presence here was us, or the world we represented, the world that destroyed a better one in creating itself, perhaps from the chaos left from that lost one.

Everywhere you looked in India, there was evidence of a past that had attained mythical heights. From philosophy to architecture, few civiliza-

234 EMPIRE OF THE SOUL

tions have left such an awesome record. It was reputed to have made even the gods jealous of humanity. And now the place that once had all the answers—from the meaning of life outlined in the Vedas, the Upanishads, or the *Bhagavad Gita,* to the zenith of architecture in the Taj Mahal or the great temples of the South—India had now become the place that had only questions. It questioned its past, even, but most of all it questioned its future, and questioned whether it *had* one.

❧   ❧   ❧

A dawn suitably dark with deep, embattled clouds hung over my last hours with the desert and the camels. A Land Rover arrived to speed Bentley and me, as if by time machine, back to Jaisalmer. The city was all too near. And all too modern after the ageless sands and the wreck of human dreams they still contained, and whose stones they would soon wear away, back into more ageless sands. OPIUM IS BAD FOR BODY read a Hindi sign by the road. It hadn't been too bad for mine—which was, however, beginning to feel bad without it. The sign seemed to affront ancient ways that had proven their worth, affronting, also, the desert itself, the wilderness where many Rajput souls had proved their worth, or found their deepest solace.

"A drink is what you need, pal," Bentley rightly observed.

After dinner we roamed the silent, twisting cobblestone streets, peering in on other people's lives, until a pack of wild dogs chased us back to our camel stables.

10

"There's Bloodletting As We Speak"

CALCUTTA, 1992

❦ ❦ ❦

To all Gentlemen Seamen, and Lads of Enterprize, and true
Spirit. Who are ambitious of making an honourable Independence
by the plunder of the Enemies of their Country. The DEATH or
GLORY Privateer, a Prime sailing Vessel commanded by
JAMES BRACEY mounting 22 six pounders, 12 Cohorns and
twenty Swivels and carrying one hundred and twenty Men—will
leave Calcutta in a few days on a six Months cruise against the
Dutch, French and Spaniards.
The best Treatment and Encouragement will be given.

—HICKY'S BENGAL GAZETTE, SEPTEMBER 8–15, 1781

The *Bengal Gazette,* as its front page still showed in 1781, had originally been the *Calcutta General Advertiser.* Ads like the one above convey the atmosphere of Calcutta in these early days more efficiently than
many entire books. The British established their first settlement in the area
at Hugli, or Hoogly, in 1640; but it was not until Robert Clive's decisive victory over Sirajuddowlah, the local nawab, at the battle of Plassey,
or Palashi, in 1757 that the British became absolute rulers of Bengal and
gained their first real foothold in India. Calcutta became Britain's imperial capital in the East, and the base for the famous East India Company.

The era of John Company marked a time of state-sanctioned free-
booters, or merchant princes, as they preferred to be called. Immense fortunes were made in the lawless climate, and Calcutta's architecture
reflected this, much as that of Venice, another pioneer multinational cor-
poration, did. Both cities existed to make a statement of power and prestige as much as anything else. Neoclassical palaces sprang up along the
banks of the Hoogly River, as the Ganges is called at its delta, and the
city's extreme opulence impressed all who saw it, as it was supposed to.

When the Raj officially arrived, a more imperial style—grander but less ostentatious—was adopted, and the city grew to look as much like a weirdly regurgitated London as Bengal's climate would allow. Yet, just as there is something dark and sinister about Venice, so Kipling's City of Dreadful Night reeked of greed and ruthless commercialism. Its inhabitants were undeterred by plague and pestilence from pursuing their business interests for well over two centuries, filling the coffers of the Company on London's Leadenhall Street and then, later, of His Majesty's Government. And these coffers were nowhere near as full as they might have been, either, much loot remaining in sea chests belonging to the white *nabobs* who represented the Company in Council House, on Calcutta's Clive Street, or presided over gigantic feudal fiefdoms spread across remote areas of the country. Even Clive himself, Bengal's first governor, called Calcutta "the most corrupt place in the universe." He knew what he was talking about, being chief among those who helped create and enhance the city's dubious reputation early on.

That enigmatic figure, Edward Lear, the poet, painter, and idiosyncratic mystic, arrived in Calcutta on December 21, 1873, to spend three weeks there before leaving for Darjeeling and the holy mountains that obsessed him on January 8. He spent the day of January 5 in the lavish gardens of what would soon become the renowned Tollygunge Club, painting a view of the place. Lear found the city a little hectic for his sensibilities, dubbing it "Hustlefussabad." And his view of his hosts and those he met—whose gluttony appalled him—is enshrined in one of those limericks for which he is best remembered, if least understood:

> There was an old man of Calcutta
> Who perpetually ate bread and butter,
> Till a large bit of muffin
> On which he was stuffin'
> Choaked this horrid old man of Calcutta.

Like North American bootleggers and assorted mafiosi, the Raj that John Company had metamorphosed into sought to distance itself from its origins under the guise of imperial legitimacy. When the Suez Canal opened in the 1860s, the P & O Lines shipping company swiftly moved its headquarters to Bombay. Half a century later, in 1911, the Raj followed suit, shifting its administrative base to New Delhi. But even decades later it was Calcutta where fortunes still were made. When the British finally left

India, the city retained far more of the essence of the Raj than Delhi, Bombay, or Madras, and continued to host the twentieth-century avatars of merchant princes, now called international corporations, until the red flags of Communism waved in the city streets. Only then were the ghosts of Empire exorcised forever. The violent Naxalite faction also frightened many Indian businesses out of Bengal, and Calcutta plummeted into a decline unequaled in any peacetime urban history—as if finally consumed by the dark forces that had erected it.

When East Pakistan—which had once been much of East Bengal—became the independent nation of Bangladesh, in December 1971, India found herself in military occupation of the fledgling country, and on the brink of war with what had been West Pakistan. This meant that Calcutta found itself a mecca for around ten million Bangladeshi refugees fleeing war, flood, and famine. Thus began the second and worst wave of what *could* be called a "housing problem" in the city. It wasn't really a problem, since problems can be solved. It was a living nightmare that turned Calcutta into the biggest slum on earth. The first wave swept in after independence, as Hindus arrived, fleeing the eastern portion of the newly created Muslim state. The housing problem was, as most social problems tend to be, in reality, a poverty problem. In 1981, the population was estimated at seven million; today some put the figure closer to twenty-five million. That's almost the total population of Canada.

✤ ✤ ✤

"Oh, darling!" said Lady Sinha, when I telephoned her from Delhi. "Things are very bad. You'll find the city has deteriorated dreadfully."

I found it hard to imagine Calcutta any worse than it had been when I last visited the place, in 1975. But these weren't the only things that were bad for Lady Sinha: Her son, Sanna, the Hon. S. P. Sinha, was dying with cirrhosis of the liver.

Back in 1975, her husband, Lord Sinha, had still been alive. His father had been the only Indian granted a *hereditary* peerage by the British government, for services rendered, and the privilege remained a useful asset to the family, even after Independence. Calcutta was one place that could say in all honesty that "things were so much better when the British were here." Indeed, the upper classes of Bengali society in countless ways happily filled the vacuum left by the Raj, continuing many of its institutions exactly as they had always been—apart from the signs that once read "No Indians or Dogs Allowed," that is.

Lord and Lady Sinha then lived in a palatial house with high white walls and a manicured and well-watered lawn, upon which peacocks roamed and around which rosebushes bloomed. Inside were all the trappings of the Raj: eighteenth-century British furniture polished like glass; gleaming Georgian silverware; portraits of governors and nawabs in gilt frames; silk Persian rugs; heavy brocade drapes with gold-tasseled sashes; swollen down-filled sofas; mahogany humidors full of Cuban cigars; and engraved silver boxes stacked with Dunhill cigarettes. And two of the most beautiful daughters I'd ever clapped eyes on.

At the time, the city outside looked as if it had been alternately flooded and thoroughly burned several dozen times. The streets teemed with hand-drawn rickshaws and closed carriages like stagecoaches pulled by the skeletons of horses. These were the only vehicles able to navigate the flooded streets in monsoon season. Wherever you looked, emaciated figures in rags held snot-nosed babies masked in flies, with arms thin as garden hoses and bellies swollen from starvation. On every available surface someone had painted the hammer and sickle or plastered a poster announcing revolution, death to the rich. I sympathized. But back in Lord Sinha's cool and spacious oasis, the time had frozen at 1928. A dozen servants did everything but wash and spoon-feed us. Death to the *poor* was what they feared.

Early one evening, two decades ago, we sped through the outrageous summer heat behind smoked glass in the air-conditioned cool of Lord Sinha's chauffeured Mercedes, heading for a drink at the Royal Calcutta Golf Club. It is the second oldest golf club on earth. Bearers in immaculate starched white jackets greeted the Sinhas as if they were gods. And, like most wealthy Indians, Lord Sinha treated menials like menials. Everyone knew where he stood, though—and every system needs order, according to its rulers.

When the sleepy fellow who carried over our tray of gin fizzes managed to spill one, Sinha snapped angrily at him in Bengali, as if the man had deliberately spilled the drink. Then he turned to me, shaking his head and sighing.

"These *blacks!*" he said. "They'll *never* learn. . . ."

Blacks? I recall thinking, noticing as if for the first time that Lord Sinha was no darker than I—and that the bearers *were* black. Caste, of course, means color. South or north, the high-caste Indians were all big-boned and pale-skinned; and hard labor was the province of small black folk.

❧ ❧ ❧

Huge clouds the color of bruises hung over the Ganges delta as I landed in Calcutta on July 17, 1992, spilling rain in torrents so heavy you were drenched in half a second. This brooding darkness in the sky at noon made the city feel doomed, saturated in its sin.

"This country needs a dictator to sort its problems out," a businessman from Delhi had informed me on the plane.

"What, like Stalin?" I'd replied.

"No," he said. "Like Hitler."

I thought of his words now as I passed through the city's streets. Lady Sinha was right: Calcutta did look worse. There were now many grades of slum, sprawling for miles in every direction on the outskirts and occupying any and every available patch of land in the city itself. Some homes were fortified tents; others were buckled and sagging structures improvised from scrap corrugated tin, flattened-out gasoline cans, oil drums, palm fronds, bamboo, and various wooden containers still bearing stenciled names. Entire families camped around damp, smoldering fires under old burlap awnings tied to trees on muddy patches of open ground—sometimes those in the middle of major roads. A river of people holding umbrellas like a funeral black Chinese dragon miles long flowed down every sidewalk. Washing hung out hopelessly on the railings of balconies in crumbling low-rise buildings made from concrete that was more like phyllo pastry than any building material. Traffic jams started miles from the downtown area, an angry honking chaos of lurching rusted steel. The humidity was malarial, making me feel hot and cold at the same time. It penetrated to my bones, where it clung like the clammy hand of death.

It must have taken courage to build a new five-star hotel in a city closer to extinction than any I've seen, but the Taj Bengal had opened anyway a few months before, the only new structure Calcutta had seen in years. With its soaring five-story lobby and elegantly ingenious employment of interior space, the place was not just a marvel, but a refuge from the blasted decaying horror outside. Only the thought of Lady Sinha's house made me feel like leaving my room, with its view over the Maidan and the Victoria Memorial—the only building the city bothers to maintain at all now. Irony gets tiresome, ironically.

The address was 7 Lord Sinha Road, which I assumed was what it had been in 1975. I couldn't remember. A dingy, narrow side street untidy with sidewalk vendors and mounds of garbage, it did not look familiar as my car pulled off the main drag and bumped over potholes like tank traps. Nor did the festering three-story edifice whose drive we turned into, coming to a halt beneath a peeling, sepulchral monsoon porch. An ancient marble plaque set into stone the color of old bloodstains bore the legend THE HON. S. P. SINHA.

Beyond rusted sliding concertina bars and through the massive door was a gloomy, musty-smelling hall last decorated around the coronation of King Edward VII. To one side, a smaller door bore a crude sign announcing the offices of several doctors. An old man in a crocheted Muslim cap had been watching rain fall into an ocher puddle out on the porch when I arrived. Now he watched me with the same diffident interest.

"Lady Sinha?" I inquired.

"Ah! Top floor, top floor," he replied enthusiastically. "You will take stairs please."

Since scaling a drainpipe appeared to be the only alternative, I gladly took his advice. Huge and hewn from dark oak, these stairs must once have been grand; now they were forlorn, creaking in protest at having to work at their age, the banisters sticky with decades of sickly damp and poisonous mildews. I passed more officelike doors, plodding through the suffocating air until I reached the top floor, where a low gate closed off the stairs from a dim landing. This was definitely not the house I'd visited in 1975. The corridor I now faced had yellowed paint blistering or coming off in huge scabs everywhere. The woodwork was shabby, and a threadbare runner snaked down the grimy floor, off which were doors closed by tattered old curtains. I called out.

A broad-faced, cheerful woman dressed like a nurse appeared from behind a rag, opened the gate, and let me in. She shouted something unintelligible down the corridor, while a small dog was going the right way about getting a swift kick in the skull.

Lady Sinha appeared in a far doorway. An elegant, beautiful woman, she'd barely changed in twenty years, except for dark circles beneath her eyes and an expression of utter sorrow and fatigue on her face. After hugs and kisses, she ushered me down to a sitting room. Tragically dilapidated, its paint cracked into large pockets, the room was thick with a hopelessness and despair that emanated from every object, from all six sides: from the chewed rug and the geriatric sofa and chairs; from the cluttered dusty cabinet packed with the little mementos of a lifetime; from the tarnished silver frames bearing photos from that parallel universe where people just like the Sinhas also lived, but looked young and happy; from the yellow net curtains that would dissolve if washed; and from the broad, stained expanse of balcony visible through open French doors and looking onto another of those hideous concrete towers that march across every Indian skyline.

"As you can see, darling," Lady Sinha—Anjoo—said in a mournful cadence, "things have changed since you were last here."

She'd been up all night with her son, who'd been vomiting blood. He refused to go to the hospital, so they'd hired a nurse to look after him. It wasn't the best arrangement: He'd bribed the driver to smuggle in supplies of booze, which he had hidden all over the house now. He refused to eat, and spent most of his time fighting with his younger sister, Manjoola, when he was not in a coma.

"She's an alcoholic, too," Anjoo told me frankly, shaking her head and sighing.

What the hell had happened? Manjoola drank and was divorced. Sanna was not only divorced, I learned; he'd been accused by his ex-wife of trying to murder his children—in fact, he'd set fire to the house after falling asleep with a cigarette in his mouth. He was even separated from another woman with whom he had a child he wasn't allowed to see. His daughter had disappeared, apparently wanting nothing to do with any of her family. The other sister, Anjoola, was divorced, too, but at least she didn't drink, and now lived happily with another man.

Twenty years before, this family had been rich, beautiful, and titled, and every door in India, if not the world, had been open to them. I asked about the old house.

"Oh, yes," Anjoo said. "Of course, darling, you knew us *there*. . . ."

It sounded as if she were talking about a previous incarnation. The old house on Camac Street had apparently belonged to her husband's company. Lord Sinha had probably not been as clever with money as he thought he was.

An ancient, toothless woman wearing spectacles an inch thick crept out from an adjacent room, clutching her sari as if cold. This was Anjoo's mother, and I think she mistook me for someone else, because she greeted me as if we were dear friends.

Manjoola and Anjoola appeared, wearing loose cotton frocks, their hair coiled up untidily—anything to thwart the unbearable humidity. Time had been fairly kind to them, too, and for an alcoholic, Manjoola looked pretty good, apart from the telltale potbelly even a loose smock couldn't hide.

I asked Lady Sinha about another old friend, one I'd assumed was long dead now.

"No, darling, Sudhadi's still alive. She's ninety-three, but she's still all there."

"Hah!" scoffed Manjoola. "If you have time to listen to her entire autobiography every time you talk to her, I suppose she's all there."

"I'm eighty-seven," proclaimed Lady Sinha's mother, her lips and gums working like those of a large carp. "We are women of the century, Sudhadi and me."

"Call her, darling," Anjoo urged. "I told her you'd call as soon as you got here."

Her mother took my hands and whispered confidentially, "He was blessed of God, you know. And he was more than a son to me."

"Who?"

"Daddy," Anjoola explained.

I phoned Sudhadi. A man answered, telling me to wait. I waited ten minutes, hearing vague noises through the cackling static.

"It takes her a while to get to the phone," Anjoo added.

Eventually Sudhadi's familiar voice sounded. I wasn't sure she could hear me, though—or that, if she could, she knew who on earth I was.

"This city is dark," she said, her voice quavering with the weight of its message. "There's bloodletting as we speak."

"Bloodletting?"

Manjoola snatched the phone from my hand and tossed it to her mother, snapping, "Mummy! The poor chap's just got here. He doesn't want Sudhadi rambling in his ear all night. You know she can't hear a thing."

"Except her own voice," Anjoola agreed thoughtfully.

"I haven't spoken to her since 1975," I protested.

"Well, she's worse *now*," said Manjoola, sneaking out of the room.

There actually *was* "bloodletting" in Calcutta that night. Police clashed, as they say, with demonstrators protesting price hikes they couldn't afford. The police are no nastier in India than they are anywhere else; they're just less restrained and worse paid.

"It's all *such* a mess." Lady Sinha sighed into the receiver.

"Once she starts talking," Anjoo's mother explained, "she does not like to stop."

"I think you probably have to be very interested in yourself to live that long, isn't it?" remarked Anjoola, igniting another Wills filter.

They were lost without their daddy, Anjoola confessed. Forced to move back into the old family home, they'd rented out the bottom two floors and sold off the garden for the monstrosity that now blocked whatever view they'd had. There was another family home, out near Shantinekitan, where the poet Tagore had once established his artists' colony-cum-ashram, but that home was "a ruin." The last time they'd visited there was with Daddy's ashes.

Their lives had stopped with Lord Sinha's death. Everything, the way Anjoola told it, had begun to disintegrate around that time. They were lost without a man at the helm. The only man left was less capable than they were of doing anything. Sanna had been so overshadowed by his father and grandfather that he felt incapable of ever matching their standards, sinking deeper into drink, drugs, and gambling.

The grandmother kept nodding agreement as Anjoola puffed away on her cigarettes for the next hour and a half, filling in the blanks of twenty years. Manjoola, clutching herself as if in pain, paced up and down, muttering. And Lady Sinha hunched over the phone, occasionally turning to roll her eyes at us.

I pictured them all sitting here like this, night after night, waiting, wondering, totally lost, while the swarming city growled and burned and collapsed around them. By the time I'd returned to my refuge at the Taj Bengal, I was thoroughly depressed. So I treated myself to one of the best Chinese meals I've ever eaten. In Calcutta, food *is* the meaning of life.

Once upon a time, when gods still walked the earth, King Daksha, the father of Shakti (or Sati, or Parvati), wife of Siva, decided to perform on of the epic Vedic rituals called *yagna*s. He invited everyone to attend the elaborate rite, which probably took months to complete—everyone, that is, except his son-in-law, Siva. Shakti was so heartbroken by this insult to her husband that she died while the yagna was in progress. Hearing this tragic news, Siva was furious with grief. He came like the wind, devastating the yagna, scattering its spectators; and taking up Shakti's lifeless body on his shoulder, he began to move in the dreadful steps of the great *tandava,* a dance that commences the destruction of all creation. Naturally, this alarmed the other gods, and they realized they had to move quickly. They had to take Shakti from Siva so that he would be forced to spare creation or lose his eternal consort along with it. The Great Preserver and Sustainer of Life, Vishnu, was sought out, and the god was persuaded to hurl his *sudarshan chakra,* a sort of whirling Frisbee of pure energy. It instantly severed Shakti's body into fifty-one parts. These he scattered all over India, to conceal them from her distraught husband. The Egyptian myth of Isis and Osiris is satisfyingly similar.

Shakti's right toe fell in what is now Calcutta, on the spot where the Kalighat temple stands, making the place one of fifty-one *pitha*s, the most sacred of all destinations for pilgrims. To those who worship Kali, devourer of human skulls, the most fearsome aspect of Siva's consort, Kalighat is the holiest temple in the world.

Thus, Calcutta is the city of Kali, active force of a god of destruction, of death—the destruction and death that are essential to life. To Christians, no image was more terrifying and repugnant than that of Kali— who was at one point a focus for *thuggee,* the dreaded cult of ritual assassins who strangled their victims in the goddess's name. More recently, a gun-toting female Robin Hood figure, feared by the rich and loved by the poor villagers her gang shared their loot with, also worshiped Kali, remaining loyal to the Terrible Mother even after she finally surrendered to the authorities, who had failed to capture her after years of trying.

Near the Kalighat temple stands Mother Teresa's mission, one of many institutions in Calcutta that have taken Kali's destruction, her City of Death, and from it have allegedly created a City of Joy. Mighty opposites rule this world. In this clash of opposites, Calcutta is the most truthful city on earth, exposing all the wounds, the scars, the festering sores, the realities we in the West hide away as if they did not exist. Calcutta shows what poverty and social injustice really are. And that truth is a savage beauty making Calcutta one of the most vitally alive and uncompromisingly *real* places in a world veiled by Maya, illusion. It's also why tourists rarely visit the place now.

I traveled across town to the Kalighat temple to pay my respects to the Fierce and Terrible Mother, and to ask the goddess's help for Lady Sinha.

The present structure, built around 1790, is singularly devoid of any architectural interest. But in the early evening it thronged with devotees waiting to catch a glimpse of Kali Ma, to have her darshan. A maze of crowded bazaars surrounds the building, practically concealing it. Vendors offering puja articles, lockets, incense, dashboard minishrines in plastic, and countless other mementos of Kali Ma yelled out offers as I passed. Lit by flaming kerosene tapers, this was an Oriental Vanity Fair, a dangerous meeting place of greed and the most ferocious form of God ever yet conceived by humankind.

As I was expecting, a young Brahmin accosted me, offering to perform pujas and show me the temple. I kicked my loafers beneath a stall and followed him through muddy puddles barefoot, stopping at a stand selling the items necessary for approaching the deity. You never approach deities empty-handed. A coconut, a few yards of jasmine flowers threaded on cotton, a few sticks of incense, and—Kali *is* a woman, after all—some large glass bangles. The price?

"One hundred and one rupees," said the vendor.

Five rupees was what these items were worth, so I complained bitterly.

"Okay, friend," he relented. "One hundred rupees."

"This for goddess Kali," my Brahmin reminded me, hinting that Kali had no time for cheapskates.

I paid up and followed the fellow, in his loincloth, thread, and shaved head but for a tuft on top. Our first stop was a small shrine that contained a stunted tree with a profusion of little branches to which many small red rags had been tied and bangles attached on suitable twigs.

"Name of person making request to Kali Ma?" the Brahmin demanded.

"Lady Sinha," I told him.

"This is your name?" he asked, not particularly surprised.

I couldn't be bothered with an explanation, so I just nodded.

"Repeat after me," I was told.

He recited a series of Vedic invocations, with me repeating them after him, line by line. He seemed pleased with my Sanskrit pronunciation. After each invocation, we placed incense beneath the tree and bangles in its branches, and then I tied a little rag he gave me to one twig. Finally, yodeling at full volume for Kali's grace, I smashed a coconut open on a specially provided rock, spraying its milk over the tree and throwing chunks of meat onto an aluminum tray. Then sacred water was poured over my head, and the Brahmin led me off toward the main shrine. A thick crowd of people stood on tiptoe and craned their necks for a glimpse of the goddess as they swarmed around the bars walling off this enclosure. The Brahmin beckoned, a knowing smile on his face, taking me up some steps, around to the front of the shrine, and to a point where, if the huge silver doors were opened, I'd get a good view of a real goddess.

My personal Brahmin roughly elbowed several shriveled old men aside, dragging me to where some of his colleagues held the doors closed. He told me to place the flowers on a tray one of them held, which contained a flickering camphor lamp.

"Must offer Kali Ma some rupees," said the Brahmin knowledgeably.

I put a ten on the tray.

"Five hundred minimum," I heard.

"See what she'll do for ten," I told him. "We're in a recession, you know."

His expression implied it was my funeral.

Suddenly, the two gatekeepers flung open their doors and there, staring out at me some ten yards away, swatched in floral garlands, was Kali Ma herself. Three piercing red eyes gleamed from basalt pupils, her face was jet black, a huge gold nose ring protruded from the two white dots of her nostrils, and her broad golden tongue cascaded out from a line of sharp gold incisors and hung two feet down over rows of flowers. The whole idol was draped in bloodred robes two yards wide, and sat in an enclosure surrounded by a low wrought-iron fence. Behind it a solid silver arch framed the whole haunting image. The glimpse lasted no more than a second before the doors were heaved shut again. It doesn't do to let people become too familiar with their god.

The Brahmin examined my eyes to assess how impressed I was.

"Thanks," I told him.

There is always an odd power to these idols, a sense of something alive, something tangibly real. And why not? God can be anywhere she likes.

"Come," he urged, clearly pleased.

We skirted the shrine, ascending some stone stairs to a small platform overlooking a courtyard. As I looked below, a man brought an axellike sword down on the neck of a goat, severing the animal's head in a single stroke. Other Brahmins seized the goat's body and sprayed the blood pumping from the raw pink hole where its head had been all over a series of low walls bearing stone effigies. An excited crowd gathered round, chanting and smearing themselves with blood, then uttering a great cry to Kali.

"You want sacrifice the goat," the Brahmin asked me sincerely.

"Well . . ."

"Five thousand rupees only," he hastily added. "Then you get the god's blessing for sure. *Guaranteed.*"

"I don't have that much on me now."

If I'd been certain that Kali's blessing *was* guaranteed, I probably would have gone for the goat. Lady Sinha wasn't a vegetarian.

"Then you come back in morning with money," my Brahmin said cheerfully. "Come, I show you my office."

The temple was packed by now, chants roaring out all over the place, a dozen pujas being performed simultaneously, and regular gasps of awe and adoration uttered as the great shrine doors were opened yet again. I followed him through the mud, located my shoes, jammed my filthy, wet feet into them, and then followed him through ranks of holy-knickknack vendors to a tiny cubicle in the side of the temple wall.

"This my office," he announced, proffering his business card:

> PUNDIT H.K. SIVAN
> (Kalighat tempel side)
> pujas, wedding, scared thread
> goat sacrificing, horroscops
> tax problem solved, busines blessing

I paused at "scared thread": The sacred thread ceremony was a sort of Brahmin's first communion.

"What's this about tax problems?"

"I am study business for one year," he explained with a measure of pride. "So people have some problem with the tax paying, then are coming to me for solution."

He made me swear to return for my goat the following morning at nine sharp. I asked him if he'd ever spent time alone in the shrine with Kali.

"I have wash Kali Ma many time," he answered, beaming.

"Washed her?"

"Yesh. Each week the Kali Ma she washing and taking the clean clothes."

"What's under all those flowers and robes?"

He grew serious, looking down.

"Only the Brahmin man he can know this thing," he informed me. "Brahmin peoples very pure, isn't it? Not eating of meat, performing the mantra each day."

"But you kill the goats . . ."

"Yesh, yesh—*killing* but not *eating*. Low-caste people, they eating the meat." He sounded faintly disgusted.

"But surely it's the killing part you're supposed to avoid?"

"Killing the goat for Kali Ma, not for the eating." He grew defensive. "Kali Ma she like too much the *blood*. Brahmin peoples they doing the kill of goat for Kali Ma, so goddess she too much happy for them."

"If you studied business, why didn't you go into some kind of business?"

He twirled his upraised palm and clucked his tongue. Indians ask why a lot less than Westerners, partly because they're more fatalistic and partly because they find it absurd to question the course a life takes of its own accord. Only in our culture does "fate" invariably have sinister connotations.

"You like horoscope?" he asked, indicating an astrological chart pinned to the wall of his cubicle. "I tell you all thing in the futures, yeh? So you have good understanding of complete life to come."

"I prefer surprises."

"You come here nine, remember?" He thrust a packet of red powder, a gift from Kali, into my hand.

"Thank God, darling!" Lady Sinha laughed later. "I think we save the goat sacrifice for a last resort!"

She placed some of the red powder on Sanna's forehead, assuring him that Kali was now on the job. Anjoo was oddly grateful for this little gesture.

The next day Sanna seemed better, too, asking for food—something that hadn't crossed his mind or his lips in weeks.

God loves those to whom He can give the most, those who expect the most from Him, who are most open to Him, those who have most need of Him and count on Him for everything. . . . The greatest sin is the lack of love and charity, the terrible indifference to those on the fringe of the social system, who are exposed to exploitation, corruption, want, and disease.

—MOTHER TERESA, *SPIRITUAL COUNSELS*

The world sees Mother Teresa differently from the way people in Calcutta do.

"There's an element of selfishness about her," said Vinod Lal, a social worker now tackling the AIDS pandemic about to sweep over Calcutta's long-suffering poor. "Her concerns are religious, not social. With her fame, she could raise a fortune talking and making appearances around the world. Money is one thing that would guarantee progress in the war against poverty here. If she really wanted to change things, she'd leave the work to others and raise money. But that's not what she's about."

Words like *stubborn, arrogant,* and *self-centered* cropped up in a number of conversations I had with Bengalis about Mother Teresa. *Mother Teresa!* I thought I'd better go and see what she was about myself.

Mother Teresa founded her order, the Society of the Missionaries of Charity, when she came to work in the Calcutta slums in 1948. Its objectives were simple: to live and work among the poorest of the poor, relieving suffering and expecting nothing in return. For more than thirty years she carried on this work in relative obscurity, until she was "discovered" by a world hungry for something or someone to believe in. People like the former atheist and Catholic convert Malcolm Muggeridge saw in her the image of a living saint, and thus began her meteoric rise to international prominence, recognized by a Nobel Peace Prize and countless other honors. Indeed, she did fit the bill nicely, her tiny bowed frame, luminous eyes, and simple, self-effacing speeches about love approximating most people's idea of sanctity. Movies were made, showing her fishing discarded babies out of trash cans, nursing the dying, feeding the poor, housing the homeless, and always talking about the world's real hunger: for love. Despite her fame, she continued to dwell in the Shanti Nagar slum, where she'd lived since coming to India. When the city of Calcutta generously gave her a free bus pass—the only gift she ever kept for herself—the world marveled that someone more famous than the pope still traveled by public transport. No illusions were shattered. No one would have been terribly surprised if Mother Teresa bought a Lear jet or hung out at Studio 54. People would even have said she'd earned the right to enjoy her fame. But in such a cynical age, it was still a plus to find her choosing to ride the bus around her slums in the same old fifty-cent cotton sari.

I arrived at the Mother House, her headquarters, just before 5:00 P.M., as I'd been told to do. The only new building in sight, Mother Teresa's mission-control center resembled a European convent: keeplike, few exterior windows, a formidable door in the side of one wall, and a large bell hanging to the side. I rang the bell, feeling like a medieval pilgrim seeking shelter. A peephole slid open, and a pair of smiling eyes asked my business.

The door was opened by a disarmingly pretty Indian nun dressed in the familiar Mother T—style blue-bordered white sari. Inside was a wide courtyard surrounded by neat little dormitories, with a chapel at one end and offices at the other. It was in effect a convent, although not all the inhabitants were nuns; some were novices, some were poor women being educated, and some were volunteer workers. There were, however, enough nuns to make me think every other person was the mother herself, since the outfit and the way it was worn, covering the head, were as inseparable from her as Mao's jacket was from him.

I was told "Mother" was still out at a meeting, but I could wait. The meeting was to discuss the AIDS crisis. No one knew how long she would be. I was wondering if she still traveled by bus as I was shown into a Spartan room where a rather severe middle-aged nun was at a table, apparently teaching a young local woman to read. I sat down on a wooden bench at another table, watching the late-afternoon ration of monsoon rain suddenly smash down like a convention of waterfalls on the stones outside the open door.

"The-*enn Jee*-zuss sa-*eed* . . ."

"Sedd! Sedd!" said the nun severely.

Surely the Bible wasn't the best book for beginners. When the nun looked down, following her bony finger along the text, her pupil glanced over and, catching my eye, grinned mischievously. Clean clothes, regular meals, and a place to sleep were obviously worth enduring the life of Christ—as uneventful as that life must seem compared to the tales of Hindu gods she had probably grown up on. The lower castes and the Harijans had always been conversion fodder, a profession of human equality being all any religion needed to gain a substantial following in India.

On one wall hung a large framed photograph of Mother meeting the pope. John Paul II looked happier than she did.

"A ma-*ann* huh-*oo* wass bl—bla-*ee* . . . blah-*inn* . . ."

"Blind!" snapped the nun. "A man who was *blind* . . . Continue."

It was agonizing to hear, and I felt grateful when the reading lesson was over and both teacher and pupil disappeared into the steam outside. On a bookshelf were twenty-nine copies of a treatise on prayer by some French cleric, three other Bibles, a fifteen-year-old *National Geographic* magazine, and an English dictionary that began at the tail end of B: *buzzard, buzz bomb, buzzer, buzz saw, by, by-and-by, bye, bye-bye, by-election, Byelorussian* . . . I began to feel sleepy, reading the introduction to *Prayer*, which stressed that the activity was not supposed to be a shopping list of desires you wanted God to fulfill.

☙ ☙ ☙

To become a saint, one must suffer much. Suffering begets love . . . and life among the souls.

—MOTHER TERESA

"Who wants to see Mother?" a crackly old voice snapped.

I looked up to see the curtain covering an inner door briskly swept aside by a tiny, robust figure clutching an enormous bone rosary in her hands.

Mother Teresa was clearly good at making entrances. She also seemed far less shy and frail than she did on film, with some impressive warts on her nose. At eighty-two, she was more vigorous than many people half her age—like me—and there was a certain tenacity in her manner I had not expected.

She gripped my hands firmly with hers, saying, "Very kind of you to come all this way. What do you want?"

We sat, and her gnarled and fissured fingers constantly counted the huge worn rosary beads, causing an incessant clacking noise. I imagined the thousands of similar meetings she must have endured, wondering what I could do to make this one a little different.

I started off with a pretentiously convoluted question about how she dealt with Hindu concepts of karma and the philosophical differences between Catholicism and the main Indian faiths.

"I don't know about any of that," she replied gruffly. "All that is important is prayer and love in action. People suffer in different ways all over the world. There is such a hunger for love everywhere. Love—that is what matters."

That pretty much answered all the questions on my list. I asked if Catholicism was important to her.

"It is important to everyone," she replied. "Not just me. But it is all according to the grace God gives each person."

"So it doesn't really matter which faith you belong to?"

"No." She seemed alarmed. "It matters very much for the individual. Once someone begins to seek God—through His grace—then he must look in the right places. Otherwise he leaves the road. You know, Gandhi once said if Christians lived the way Christ taught, then there wouldn't be any Hindus remaining in India."

"I doubt if he meant it literally . . ."

"Oh, yes," she said sternly. "Christians are the light of the world."

"Do you find the poor more appealing than the rich?"

"We owe so much to the poor. Only in God's heaven will we know how much we owe them—because, you see, they help us to love God so much more."

"That sounds like you're using the poor to get closer to God."

She merely shrugged.

"What makes a saint, do you think?"

She brightened at the mention of this topic, saying, "There is a great price to be paid. You must renounce everything. You must overcome many temptations, and there will be struggle, even persecution. And always sacrifice, sacrifice, sacrifice. The price of loving God is your whole self."

"Are you saying that your work with the poor is really connected to your desire for, er . . . perfection?" I was going to say "sainthood," but thought better of it.

"The poor are God's gift to us," she said obscurely. "They are the way to learn love—through caring. It is not what we do that Christ cares about, you know. He cares only how much love we put into whatever we do. In your country there is spiritual poverty—that is an even heavier burden, you see. It is so hard to see God's love in your country."

"Well, at least we aren't fishing babies out of garbage cans. Not often . . ."

This seemed to raise her hackles. "What is suffering?" she demanded. "It is *nothing!* But when suffering is sharing the pain Christ Himself endured, it is the most wonderful thing—a beautiful gift, you see. It proves the love of God, who gave His son out of such great love. The suffering relieves the sin—that is why it is such a beautiful gift."

"That's pretty much the way the Hindus view karma, isn't it?"

"To be a saint," she continued, "means tearing away anything that is not God from yourself—every false desire. You remove it and purify the heart. You give up your own will—all the petty things you want—and you live in the will of God."

"But if your concern is the poor, there are so many contradictions in your faith that ignore the real situation here, aren't there? I mean, are you against contraception and abortion?"

She tut-tutted, the rosary zipping through her busy fingers with noises like a hectic pool table. "It's not 'for' or 'against,' " she told me. "No one should attempt to end life, because that is God's life in us. He hears the scream of the unborn child killed without even a chance of entering the world."

After we went back and forth on the subject briefly, I asked how she felt about things like the Inquisition. She kept harping on love. It suddenly occurred to me that she did not really care about the poor at all—except as a way to achieve her own spiritual fulfillment. The thought surprised me with its irreverence.

"Are you consciously trying to be a saint?"

"I share the passion of Christ," she said, looking at me angrily, beads clacking. "If you wish to share this with us, you come to the service in our chapel this evening . . . to praise God with us. Then you will see what we do here."

I told her I'd heard that Jerry Brown had worked with her as a volunteer, and since he was still an American presidential candidate at that point, I asked how he'd held up.

"Brown?" she repeated. "There are so many volunteers. Let them all come. They come and work, though. No one comes here and does not work. They must be willing to work. . . ."

"To suffer, you mean?"

"It is all for the love of God."

"Is it, Mother? Or is it just more vanity—as Ecclesiastes would have said?"

She rose abruptly, glaring at me. Her feelings weren't hurt, I felt—but her pride was.

"Thank you," she muttered, hastening back through the curtain from whence she'd appeared.

"Hi," said a lazy American voice.

I looked up. A young red-haired girl in baggy salwar-kameez was sorting through a pile of mail on the windowsill.

"Hi. You're a volunteer?"

"Just for nine months." She mopped the sweat on her freckly brow. "Are you a missionary?"

"Sort of. How are you finding it?"

She narrowed her eyes. "Can I be honest?"

"Ideally."

"Half the problem here is laziness. *We'd* be this poor if we were as lazy as these people."

"You think Mother sees it that way?"

"Mother's *Mother*—she *likes* doing everything for them. . . ."

I asked if that meant she liked them helpless and grateful.

"Maybe it does. . . ."

"Are you disillusioned?"

She screwed up her eyes, shook her head, sighed, then said, "Yeah. But that's okay. I wanted to believe in fairies once, too."

"So . . . no *Saint* Teresa?" I smiled at her courage.

"No Santa Claus, either . . . What I *have* learned is that we've got to get used to just being people—with all faults. We've gotta stop putting each other on pedestals . . . because we keep falling off."

"God?"

"Yeah. God. What was it John Lennon said God was?"

"A concept by which we measure our pain?"

"Let me say it again. . . . Shit. Don't you wish John was still around?"

I did. I do. I wished her luck.

"You know what?" she called after me. "She gets high on converting them, I *swear.*"

☙   ☙   ☙

Some time later, I read Mother Teresa's words on the function of missionaries.

A Missionary is a carrier of God's love, a burning light that gives light to all; the salt of the earth. It is said of St. Francis Xavier that "he stood up as a fire, and his words burnt like a torch." We have to carry Our Lord in places where He has not walked before. The Sisters must be consumed with one desire: Jesus. We must not be afraid to do the things He did—to go fearlessly through death and danger with Him and for Him.

. . . he stood up as a fire, and his words burnt like a torch. How could Mother Teresa use such words about the man who'd requested the Inquisition come to Goa? Yes, Xavier's words burned like a torch, all right.

✣   ✣   ✣

I wanted to go to the famed Bengal Club for dinner. Lady Sinha's son was vomiting blood again, and I didn't feel the family needed a guest on its hands. The Taj's manager, Mansoor, a delightful man, told me the venerable old club—founded in 1827—was open only to members and their guests. He'd happily take me himself, he said, but his own membership was still pending. Mansoor thoughtfully considered how to get me in. He remembered that the general manager was a member and could have taken me as his guest. Unfortunately, he was away on business. I found it hard to imagine any Indian institution being so inflexibly rigid as Mansoor seemed to imply, even though I knew the Calcutta clubs operated pretty much on the same lines as they had during the Raj.

Mansoor came up with a solution: He'd get the GM to fax him a letter authorizing me to dine at the club as his guest in absentia.

Armed with the precious document, he escorted me in a car to the massive Victorian edifice. Winds and rain roughed up our car as we drove through dreadfully bleak and forlorn streets in a preternatural twilight, banded darknesses teeming with eyes. Even the luminous dome of the Victoria Memorial, that last gesture of imperial might, was plunged abruptly into darkness as we approached it. The floodlights were left on only until the *son et lumière* was over: Calcutta couldn't afford to waste anything, particularly light.

Floods had knocked out the Bengal Club's phones, so we had not been able to discover in advance whether the fax tactic would work. An entire antique switchboard was on its side in the dingy lobby, being overhauled, as we entered. Overall, the place now reminded me of some seedy government office. We climbed tired wooden stairs that had once shone with wax, as countless old photographs attested. Mansoor suggested we stop in for drinks, in case he recognized someone else who could take me in to dinner. The famous bar was another disappointment; it looked and felt like something from a run-down no-star hotel off the Bayswater Road. Several small clutches of men sat with their beers in silence around the nearly empty room, barely looking up as we came in. The tired, musty atmosphere absorbed us indifferently, a facade of what it must once have

been. Nonetheless, membership remained a prerequisite for status in Calcutta society.

Locating the secretary, a chubby, sarcastic fellow in a stained white
shirt whose tails hung over the shiny seat of his pants, Mansoor presented
the fax and the situation. The secretary scrutinized this crumpled document, shaking his head.

"We have rules," he announced. "No guests without members."

The hotel manager tried appealing to a better nature I could see this
man did not possess.

"No point in having rules if they aren't obeyed," I said, since he clearly
enjoyed sarcasm. I imagined how many Indians had been humiliated in
far worse ways when Sir Basil ffinch-Cholmondely, or some such, served
as secretary.

I assured Mansoor I didn't mind in the least. With his Indian reverence for hospitality, he was genuinely upset that I'd been treated so dis-
courteously. An elegant, sophisticated man in a shabby, crude city, he was
all the more determined to make what he did an exception to depressing rule—and he did a laudable job of it. We agreed to have breakfast at
the Tollygunge Club the next morning, a Sunday.

☙   ☙   ☙

The Tollygunge was another Calcutta landmark left over from the Raj.
Founded in 1895 by Sir William Cruikshank, it is less venerable than the
Bengal, but is in far, far better shape today—thanks to another Calcutta
institution: Bob Wright. Like Rajasthan's Colonel Tod, Bob Wright embodies what little was good about the British presence in India. Born in
Calcutta in 1924, he left in 1927, to return when his fellow Brits were
heading swiftly the other way—in 1947. He worked for one of the large
British corporations that was determined politics would not get in the way
of mutually advantageous business, and he eventually took on the task of
managing the Tollygunge, which, as he approaches his seventies, he continues to do with the same flair and efficiency as ever.

Mansoor and his friend, the head of public relations at the Taj, were
both members of his club, so at least I knew we could get in. Indeed, the
Taj Bengal had a standing arrangement that all its guests could use the
club's extensive sporting facilities.

Calcutta had just opened its first underground railroad in 1992, a
source of enormous civic pride, and the line ran as far as the Tollygunge,

so it was suggested I take this opportunity to see one of the city's few recent achievements. The thought of riding it *beneath* Calcutta, though, horrified me. Being aboveground was bad enough, but plunging through its bowels, even in the newest, cleanest train on earth, was something I could not contemplate. We drove.

After the crumbling, steamed, and frenzied misery of the city, the Tollygunge impressed me—a stately mansion, set in lush grounds, with outbuildings and guest rooms facing a golf course that could have been transplanted from Surrey. That morning there was to be an announcement of new members, an event attended by all those who had applied for membership, and offering the humiliating prospect of learning publicly whether or not you had been accepted. Indians have scrupulously preserved the elite nature of these clubs, the criteria for membership now being different, of course, but the process of applying for it the same. Most of the British in India would not have been considered eligible to join the great clubs; and now that they're owned by Indians, most Indians aren't eligible to join them, either.

Sitting with a beer, I watched this little-publicized other face of India with fascination. Tall, handsome Sikhs, with kerchiefs tied over their topknots instead of turbans, carried golf bags or sat discussing the new trade regulations. Dignified men with patrician noses came sweating from tennis courts, telling each other the latest Delhi jokes. Wives in sweatpants joined their husbands or sat with friends, exchanging salacious gossip in between debating whether IBM or Apple software systems would dominate the Indian computer market. Two young Western girls, wilting in the heat, wrote postcards at one table. Sporadically, the thwack of a golf club rang out, usually followed closely by cries of "Drive!" or "Bugger!" The country is not all poverty, chaos, and religion.

There was no mistaking Bob Wright. Even before I saw him, I knew that the voice saying, "Excellent stuff! We'll have you in the Derby next, Bunty," belonged to the legend himself.

As he's doubtless tired of hearing, he *does* resemble David Niven playing some field marshal on his way to the Burmese front. Relaxed, yet at the same time powerfully energetic, he was dressed in leisure gear, with open-toed sandals. I watched him shift effortlessly from a conversation with some industrial titan to a few words of encouragement for a groundsman, his movements almost choreographed, and the ubiquitous cigarette clenched like a pencil, its smoke billowing through the immaculate mustache it has been steadily dyeing yellow for many decades. Despite the clipped, decisive tones of someone educated to run an empire, you can't mistake the fact that he cares very deeply about what he does, and even more deeply about the country he calls home.

There are those who think every Westerner in India should be a missionary, but that overlooks the good to be done in countless other ways—not to mention painting the whole vast land as a charity case, rather than a richly varied, vibrant nation—and Bob Wright tends not to brag about the numerous other ways in which he does his adopted homeland good.

☙ ☙ ☙

In a long, spacious room above the main clubhouse, I sat at a well-laid breakfast table with Bob Wright and his wife, Ann. Every bit as handsome and vital as her husband, Ann Wright, though born in England, is now a passport-holding Indian citizen and has spent as much of her life in India as Bob, who was born there but has not become a citizen . . . yet. Surrounded by the exotic mementos of a lifetime in the subcontinent, they both talked of childhoods in India, while scrambled eggs, toast, and endless pots of fine Darjeeling tea were served.

I pictured the paradise of color, animals, and vibrant life a child would have remembered sorrowfully on returning to the gray skies of England, as the Wrights had. Both said that India, for a child, had been a wonderland. They both are trying to save this wonder for future generations to enjoy. Besides the club, Ann and Bob are involved with supporting orphanages and old peoples' homes, as well as various endeavors to save India's wildlife from extinction.

I asked Bob what it was about India that, often in spite of itself, retained a special place in the heart.

"Well, it's certainly not the mystique," he said. "It's the variation of people, surroundings. But it's the people, by and large."

"How hard is it to watch the gradual and steady deterioration of Calcutta?"

"Very, very sad. But it's happening elsewhere, as well. Look at London. Standards are deteriorating—which is worse than things falling down—standards of business, ethics. Of course, the decay of buildings is sad, but the decay of human beings is sadder."

"Is the simultaneous arrogance and lack of confidence you see in the postindependence generation a consequence of colonialism?"

"I don't think so. You can blame most things on the Raj, but not that one. The most serious thing in India now is the lack of job opportunities for the so-called educated—I say 'so-called' because a degree is of a pretty lowly standard. You have Calcutta University turning out twenty thousand graduates a year, and there are jobs for two or three thousand of them."

"Like Mother Teresa, you seem to do more work with the poor than most Indians. Why is there a lack of interest by Indians?"

"True, true, true. There are enormous charitable trusts here, but they're largely tax dodgers. The charity extends to trusts for temples and hospitals, of course, run by the families in question. But when it comes to helping people in need, these trusts are unable to help in any way. I think it doesn't hurt Indians to look at poverty the way it does us. When they see children living on the streets, who haven't got a place to kick a ball around, a place to *have* a childhood—it simply doesn't move them. Once they've been to their morning temple, said a prayer to the god, touched a cow before they've got to their office, they've achieved their goal for the day. The fact that they've made someone happier doesn't really interest them."

"As I felt with Mother Teresa, is this then more a religious business than a charitable one?"

"I think it is, yes. There's little actual interest in poverty per se."

"When the British shifted the capital to Delhi, they must have known they were sounding the death knell for Calcutta."

"The Bengali never forgave them. When the news came, it was taken very personally. But right up into the fifties, Calcutta was still the commercial and financial capital; and the Bengalis have only themselves to blame for the loss of that. The Naxalites in the late sixties made it impossible for business to remain here. Everything moved away. But, for example, the headquarters of Tata Steel is still in Calcutta. That's why they built the Taj Bengal hotel—it was a very kind gesture."

"Will Calcutta ever be restored like, say, Venice?"

"Imagine the *size* of the project. The Victoria Memorial alone cost the Tercentenary Commission an absolute fortune—with all the paintings inside—and the task hasn't been completed. There's no money at all. It's a very worthy project, but who could take it on? Millions are spent on slum development—putting in water, electricity, et cetera—but then there's no plan for the continued upkeep. It all deteriorates again in a mat-

ter of years. I can't imagine what it will be like even in a few years. The
population is staggering already. Refugees from Bangladesh are still coming across. No one supported Indira Gandhi's 'emergency,' or the reasons for installing it, but there were lots of good things achieved by it.
The country was more efficient, trees were planted, slums cleared, public works projects begun. I don't, however, support that dreadful forced
family planning. But you don't help people by just giving them money."

"Would you support another 'emergency'?"

"Calcutta *is* an emergency—but, no, I don't support that approach.
Something like it should be considered on a local level, however. The
Bengalis—those armchair Marxists—just want to *talk* about it, though,
or write poems about it. *Doing* something would require agreement, and
they can never *agree* on anything. To that extent, I blame them for the
conditions they have to live in."

The talk turned to the social ills currently besetting Britain. The home
of the Raj was decaying faster than the capital of its Indian empire.

He laughed. "We forget it's not just India that's in a mess! I never
thought I'd see the Western world in such a state. But there are still good
people everywhere. People who *try*—and *that's* what really counts, no?"

When breakfast was over, I wandered alone around the resonantly
empty Tollygunge clubhouse, staring up at and being stared back at by
portraits of past presidents. Shafts of dusty sunlight illuminated the dark
polished-wood surfaces. Club staff busied themselves with the morning's
tasks, most of them patently happy to exist in this oasis of order and calm.
They knew the alternative better than most.

Saying farewell to the Sinhas was hard. I had to admire the way they coped
with the collapse of their fortunes, though. In Calcutta, materialism
doesn't mean what it does elsewhere: It often means just having a roof
and food. It was not physical comforts they felt a lack of.

A few months after I left India, a cable arrived at my home from Lady
Sinha, saying Sanna had died. In her own way, Kali Ma had saved him.

11

"There's Far Too Much Muck to Rake Here!"

BOMBAY, 1992

❦ ❦ ❦

*Bombay was mind-boggling and I loved it. Which seems strange
now considering we arrived when the city is supposed to be at its
most unattractive: mid-monsoon. But the moment we stepped out
of the filthy train and on to the slushy platform at Bombay
Central, I knew I'd finally found 'my' city. Dirty, overcrowded,
impersonal and entirely wonderful. Everything fascinated me . . .*

—SHOBHA DÉ, *SOCIALITE EVENINGS*

*T*he monsoon had failed to arrive on time—it usually does—so Bombay on July 8, 1992, wasn't at its most unattractive yet. It was, however, at the end of its tether. Clouds like those above the Kuwaiti oilfields after the Gulf War billowed above the city, barely spitting the odd mouthful of their contents down on the steaming ants' nest jutting out into the Arabian Sea. The heat and humidity seemed to have driven nearly all the inhabitants to desperate measures. BOY'S HEALTHY LEG AMPUTATED, read a headline in the *Times of India.*

> BOMBAY, July 8: Owing to the negligence of the civic Rajawadi hospital doctors, a 12-year-old child lost his right leg while it was actually the left that had to be amputated!

Hospital staff had apparently threatened the boy's father "if he made their callousness public." But nothing in Bombay is ever simple.

Elsewhere in the paper, the heat had seemingly driven another individual to take out a personal ad.

I SANGEETA BALANI HAVE CHANGED
  my name to Priya Mahesh Karamchandani.
  Vide Gazette No: X-2584.

One wondered why. . . .

❧   ❧   ❧

WE KILL . . . FOR MONEY, read an ad in the same paper:

THE EXTERMINATORS pest control services
  Termite (White ant) Control (Pre/Post Construction) General
  Disinfestation (Cockroaches, bugs, silverfish, etc.), Rodent Con-
  trol, Carpet Moths, Powderpost Wood Beetles, Snails.
  ULTRASONIC RODENT REPELLENTS
  ELECTRIC FLYKILLERS
  coming soon: PIGEON CONTROL

But the big story was "octroi." What exactly *was* octroi? I wondered. And
why had it caused a trucker's strike?

BOMBAY, July 8.: "The most junior officer at an octroi post walks
away every evening with at least Rs 250 in his pocket," said a trader,
who has been subjected to what he describes as the worst instance
of corruption in India.
  . . . It begins at the lowest level, where illiterate truckers are made
to pay Rs 5 to an agent to get the octroi Form B. At much higher
levels, and going into thousands of rupees, are the deals made between agents, suppliers and the officers.
  . . . Another dealer described how he got away with paying Rs
1,000 to an agent in return for which he got a receipt saying that
his goods were rejected material and having no commercial value.
"The octroi value of my materials was actually Rs 2 lakhs," he
claimed.

It seemed unlikely that any dealer would admit this to the press. I deduced that octroi was a state tax imposed on goods coming in from other
states. The truckers were complaining about the corruption involved in
dealing with border officials, although "the worst instance of corruption
in India" seemed farfetched.

Pharmacists were threatening a strike the following day, too. So were cabdrivers and restauranteurs. I always got the feeling that I'd never be able to get out of Bombay, once in it. But the driver who propelled me at warp 10 away from a startlingly modern new terminal building had never heard of this strike.

"No, sir," he kept reassuring me. "Not striking, me. I working."

"Not now—tomorrow." I waved the newspaper at him.

"You want cab tomorrow? I come, yes? Vitch hotel?"

The bustees, the slums, were still there, just beyond the airport, but some had sprouted into concrete huts, or even low-rises. Now you could sell a shack in the slums for three times what it cost to erect a concrete home yourself, as long as the government supplied the land. The way the driver told it, the government didn't have much choice in the matter: Buildings went up overnight on empty lots, and it wouldn't be a popular move to bulldoze homes in a city where lack of housing was the main problem. I saw neatly dressed men carrying attaché cases coming out of the most squalid slums on their way to line up at bus stops.

"Office worker this mens," the driver explained. "Live here and save monies."

It was like an American post-office clerk economizing by raising his family in a packing case near some back-alley heating duct.

Even the potholed road I'd first encountered in 1974 was now a new two-lane highway. Things were improving—slightly. The initial effect of Bombay on a visitor was downright prosperous compared to what it once had been, the highway teeming with Marutis—the results of an Indo-Japanese coventure—among the Ambassadors and Premier Padminis.

"No one like it," the driver said dismissively of the Maruti. "Made with paper, not the metal."

The real reason drivers loathed the Maruti, I later learned, was that no one could repair it. The engine had to be dismantled before you could get at its heart. Anyone with a rock and a wrench could repair an Ambassador; and anyone anywhere could make you a spare part for one out of old motorbike engines and discarded pieces of steam train. Maruti parts had to be ordered from Maruti—a company that was, incidentally, the brainchild of Indira Gandhi's son, Sanjay. Its history probably *does* rank among the worst instances of Indian corruption.

FUTURE IS BLACK WHEN SUGAR IS BROWN, read a sign by the roadside. And later, DREAMS WILL DROWN WHEN SUGAR IS BROWN. The same poetry kept appearing. Was sugar being adulterated again? The city seemed to be overreacting if this was what the signs concerned. "Brown sugar" referred, as I should have guessed, to heroin. Such is "progress."

The Taj Mahal Hotel hadn't changed, fortunately; and the labor dock area, the Apollo Bunder, seemed rejuvenated. India's Gateway was no longer a shelter for the homeless. In fact, it served no function at all now.

Young girls and boys staffed the hotel, each wearing a nametag reading "Trainee." They acted with androidlike efficiency, which is not particularly efficient. Alas, the rooms in the old Taj had been renovated: They were larger and more Westernized in conveniences, but they weren't the old Taj rooms. An age had truly gone.

I phoned a friend. By some blunder of the phone company, her line had been connected to someone else's in the same building, so she had to run up four flights of stairs every time there was a call. It would probably take a year or so for this error to be corrected; but the neighbor— just as inconvenienced—seemed not to mind running *down* four flights every time my friend had a call.

I could hear a listlessness and a disinterest in any form of activity in the voices of everyone I phoned. The heat, the strikes, the failed monsoon . . . No one wanted to visit art galleries; no one wanted to visit. Only Rahul Singh was his usual ebullient self. Son of Khushwant, he's one of the most prominent and respected columnists in India, syndicated relentlessly. And he's a gracious and generous host, with time for everyone. He seems to know personally and intimately anyone you wish to meet in Bombay. Before long he was arranging parties, meetings, trips . . .

A glance through the Taj bookstore alone indicated changing standards. Any change in India occurs in Bombay first. The stars in the movie fanzines seemed far more Westernized in appearance, for a start, although the text surrounding them was still curried Hedda Hopper. Many new magazines catered to a less specific audience. One of these, *Gladrags,* exhibited a stunning Indian beauty. The banner on the cover promised Voyeuristic Glimpses of the Sexiest Women Around. Yet *Gladrags* seemed in reality more a fashion-cum-lifestyle-magazine, directed as much at women as men. The "voyeuristic glimpses" were certainly that, but there was no actual nudity. And among the many imported periodicals for sale, there was still not even a *Playboy* in sight—no matter that fifteen different profusely illustrated versions of the *Kama Sutra* were boldly displayed, some of them portraying in lavishly detailed color prints scenes of sexual congress that often defied belief.

But India's sexual equivocation—at least in print—would not last much longer, I soon learned.

I met Rahul Singh for a drink at the Gymkhana Club—a Raj-era sporting facility where dowagers now watched teenagers sweat on the cricket fields, and journalists huddled in the air-conditioned bar. He tossed me a magazine.

"Take a look at that," he said. "It's the first issue, and I promised I'd tell the editor what I thought of it. He'll probably be grateful for your opinion, too."

I wonder if he will, I thought, flipping the pages. It was the first genuine Indian equivalent of *Playboy*—or at least that was, according to Rahul, its intention. Bearing the title *Fantasy* in bold letters, and above that the label *The Awareness Magazine,* its cover featured one of those photographs distorted by computer into a cubist mosaic. Held at a distance, however, the image looked much like a naked girl bound in gaffer tape giving a hand job to a naked man holding something like a huge rat or groundhog to his chest. The bottom right-hand corner featured some eclectic content.

> Lee Iacocca
> Mulk Raj Anand
> Khushwant Singh
> David Davidar
> Rahul Singh
> SEX EDUCATION
> Autoeroticism

In an editorial titled "Of Dreams, Obsessions, Vision and Fantasy," Vicky Bhargava outlined his intentions.

> *Fantasy* attempts to break the taboos and misconceptions forced on the Indian sociocultural scenario in the latter half of After Death. With a mix of serious readings and bold visuals, our attempt shall be to bring sex out of the closet. What is considered sinful today, was a collective celebration of ethos for 700 years from the 3rd century to the late 10th century A.D. From the emergence of Tantra

to the temples of Khajuraho this sentiment has been proudly displayed in our art, literature, and religion.

Sex in the name of Hindu nationalism: It was a clever tactic—and historically true enough.

"What does he mean by 'latter half of After Death'?" Rahul scanned the page.

"A.D.," he replied, twirling hairs on his Captain Ahab beard. "After Death."

There were book reviews, articles on prostitution, abortion, masturbation, and a recycled election pitch from Chrysler's Lee Iacocca, written when he was still acting much like a contender for the I-put-the-company-back-on-its-feet-let-me-run-the-country presidential tactic. The piece concerned the stultifying effects of too much bureaucracy in America—although every word applied equally to India. There was an "open letter" by Mulk Raj Anand—a literary monument much given to writing rambling "open letters" instead of troubling himself with actual reviews or articles—to one of the best Western writers on India, BBC correspondent Mark Tully. I could not decipher exactly what Mulk's point was, though one could hardly miss its uncharitable tone.

Then, of course, there were pictorials. Or rather, there was a centerfold spread.

Name: Pinky Sahani
Age: 24
Occupation: Managing a Boutique
Other Interests: Painting

Rather pretty, with a large mole, Pinky exhibited a perfectly proportioned torso with huge, strapping thighs on legs that, despite black stilettos, seemed at least a foot too short. Photographed leaning or sitting on a high oval-backed wicker chair against a plain blue background, she quickly stripped from frilly white frock to white garter belt and stockings with a string of pearls around her neck, and then to nothing but the shoes. She looked very awkward, wooden, and uncomfortable. Of course, there was not even a hint of pubic hair. The spread was given the lofty title "Photo-Art-Story," and came with text headed "Summer of '92."

O Summer of '92! in white heat dear Lady Love burns—she burns with desire. The cool summer breeze doesn't help her. Sans clothes, sans inhibitions she waits with golden stars in her eyes . . . Do you know, she's still waiting!

Immediately following this centerfold, in a guilty balance, was a far more artfully photographed male nude spread, titled simply "Brute."

> Rahul Damle, 24,
> photographed by
> Raj Thakare
> in natural light on
> monochromatic film

So artfully was it photographed, indeed, that you never saw Rahul Damle's face in the burnished orange shadows. One shot, from glistening hairy chest down, had Rahul holding a grimly glass tumbler exactly where an erect penis would have been. The tumbler was empty. Compared to the stark clarity of Pinky's pictures—which would have enabled complete strangers to identify her in a crowd, Rahul's would not have helped forensic experts to track him down. It, too, was accompanied by a bodice-ripping text.

> He plunged into the sea of his being, and emerged with secret truths. In his strong embrace—wild and loving—she emptied the wine-glass of desire. When time was eternity, her silent rivers flowed through his land. With a languid look said he, "Where, O where is she?"

Although the pre-Muslim cultures in India had a healthily realistic attitude toward sex, they were far from the *Playboy* ethos. At Khajuraho the erotic stone carvings on temple exteriors serve a symbolic spiritual purpose, connected with overcoming desires. Of the danger, lust, and greed listed in the *Bhagavad Gita,* the most damaging of those desires the seeker of Truth must shed is lust. Devotees entering a Khajuraho temple face the whole panorama of lust—a way, perhaps, for an individual to measure the degree of his own desirelessness. Like screening hard-core porn movies in a convent or monastery.

A waiter informed us apologetically that the octroi truckers' strike had reduced our choice for lunch to rice and dal or dal and rice—sort of like being told in the West that your menu is limited to corn niblets and potatoes.

Vicky Bhargava, *Fantasy*'s editor-in-chief, arrived, nervous and out of breath. An intense, handsome, and affable man in his late twenties, he clearly respected Rahul deeply, and thus could hardly wait for the verdict.

"So, what do you think, Rahul?"

Rahul made some incisive and constructive comments about layout and content, introducing me in a manner that made me sound like a Nobel laureate. Vicky turned eagerly.

"It's not quite *Penthouse,* is it?" he said humbly. "Any suggestions?"

I thought of telling him he couldn't be the Hugh Hefner of India and go on calling himself Vicky—Vic, *maybe*—but instead confessed that I found it impressive for an inaugural issue. It certainly had more in the way of content than *Playboy* had these days.

"But the centerfold is," I began, "a little . . . er . . ."

"Stiff?" he suggested.

"Yes."

"She was very nervous. Needs to be more artistic, isn't it? More sensual, more . . ."

"Vaseline on the lens?"

"That sort of thing."

Before long, Vicky was inviting me to contribute. Months later I sent him a package with a short story and several outlined ideas for columns and other articles. I received no reply for five months. Then an unsigned card wishing me a happy New Year on behalf of Bhargava & Bhargava Printers (P) Ltd, Allahabad, arrived in the middle of February.

Fantasy was not the only sign of changing attitudes toward sex in India. Rahul Singh and his father, Khushwant, were also not the only contributors listed on the magazine's cover I knew personally. David Davidar, the young and brilliant publisher of Penguin Books in India, a writer of considerable talent himself, was also an acquaintance. Fast becoming something of a legend in Indian publishing, Davidar had heard a new voice in "Indlish"—Indian writing in English—and was busy discovering and promoting the best of it. Singlehandedly responsible for overseeing the publication of some hundred titles a year, he had managed to acquire the cream of India's literary talent as well as launch new authors by the score. The greatest compliment paid to Davidar's achievements on behalf of a nation's literature so far was when Vikram Seth took the unprecedented step of insisting that his epic novel, *A Suitable Boy,* be typeset, printed, and published first in India, by Penguin. This was a statement of faith as much as anything else. Seth wanted to show the world that India could produce books whose quality matched that of any other country. Davidar had proved that Indian books did not have to be poorly designed and bound, and did not have to contain *any* typographical errors, let alone a dozen per page.

But Davidar's major commercial coup had been publishing a first novel by a woman dealing with the lifestyles of Bombay's rich and famous—in graphic detail. Shobha Dé's *Socialite Evenings* received probably the first American-style promotion campaign in the history of Indian publishing. Advance propaganda hinted at the truth thinly veiled by the fiction; gossip columnists speculated about which jet-set fast-trackers would recognize themselves in the novel. And a frenzy of prurient interest was generated by rumors of the raw sex that this book, written by a *woman* (an *Indian* woman!) allegedly contained in superabundance.

Davidar had spent enough time in the West to know that sex sells— and sells *anything*—but it was a gamble all the same to invest mega-rupees in duplicating the process in India. Sex certainly sold Bombay movies, but would it sell books written in a language only a small percentage of Indians could *read?* The answer was a resounding *yes,* however. Perhaps *too* resounding, though. Amid the hullabaloo of the promotional blitz, the novel itself got somewhat lost. On a slow news week, presumably, a correspondent for *Time* magazine managed to sell his editor on the concept of an "Indian Jackie Collins," filing copy that soon made Shobha Dé, on the strength of one novel, an Indian writer known around the world—a rarity—but known for all the wrong reasons.

The furor surrounding *Socialite Evenings* blinded almost everyone to the fact that Davidar had published possibly the first truly modern Indian novel in English and by a woman, a novel that had far more of Erica Jong about it than it did Jackie Collins. The Indian hack pack makes Fleet Street's tabloid muckmeisters seem positively scholarly and altruistic. The scent of blood, not a sense of responsibility, let alone a literary sensibility, motivated most of India's literati as they jumped on *Time*'s band-wagon, pronouncing Ms. Dé's work Indo–Californian pulp: *Jackie Does Juhu.*

Socialite Evenings concerns the odyssey of a young Everywoman through the shallow, brittle world of Bombay's super rich. Ms. Dé's second novel, *Starry Nights,* tells the cautionary tale of a young girl's rise to fame and fortune as an actress in "Bollywood," the Bombay movie factories that churn out more celluloid than any film industry on earth. Neither book pulled many punches, but *Starry Nights* rained blows of prose so visceral and raw that it was swiftly branded pornography. Shobha Dé did not just write about sex, she wrote about *fucking.* There were stains on bedsheets, anal lubricants on fingers, toy boys, and sugar daddies. But most of all there was the shattering of two great Indian myths: Bollywood, which competes with the paradise of gods on an average Indian's wish list, was portrayed as a corrupt and seedy Nighttown of desperate prima donnas, ambitious sluts, and psychopathic billionaires enslaved by perversion and greed; and men, those little deities pampered from womb to tomb in traditional Indian society, were given the shocking news that the wives they had assumed adored them as unconditionally as their mothers did in fact despised them. This latter act of iconoclastic terrorism had male egos across the length and breadth of the subcontinent popping like great waterlogged balloons. For Ms. Dé told them in terms they understood that in bed they were leaden duds, not the heavenly studs they bragged about being to their friends. Their wives, she wrote, merely put on an act to protect frail egos and preserve harmony in the home. It was feminism Indian-style, and it thrilled as many women as it appalled—for *some* were ready for the truth that could set them free.

David Davidar was hardly surprised by Dé's subject matter. He had urged her to write the first novel because he sensed she could do it. She was well known before 1989, when *Socialite Evenings* was published, as founder and editor of *Stardust, Society,* and *Celebrity,* three fairly self-explanatory contributions to humankind's insatiable hunger for bitchy movie fanzines and prurient gossip about the rich and famous. Her poison pen and her well-placed sources had made her as feared and despised as she was courted slavishly and read avidly.

In the prose of Dé's columns, Davidar saw the "Indlish" he was after, the Indian writing in an English freed from its roots. Until recently, English writing in India had retained pretty much the same form and style as it had under the Raj. It had been learned in British-run schools, or even in Britain itself, and, from Tagore to R. K. Narayan, was generally twee and precious at best, or at worst bloated with floral oratory like Tennyson on evil drugs.

After Independence, however, Indian English said farewell to British English and began a life of its own. The British had shipped back a rich haul of linguistic booty over the years, too; many commonly used words—pajamas, jodhpurs, mogul, bazaar, and so on—were the offspring of what Khushwant Singh termed promiscuous couplings with Indian languages. Home alone, Indian English became even more flirtatious among so many exotic tongues, rapidly evolving into a form as distinct at times as, say, the Irish English of James Joyce, or the richly varied American English of Damon Runyon, or Thomas Pynchon, or Alice Walker.

In Shobha Dé we find an English virtually moving toward Creole. Her narrative is perfectly intelligible, but her dialogue is peppered with Hindi and portmanteau words, is faithful, in fact, to the language her characters would actually speak in real life. Only someone fairly familiar with the English of Bombay or Delhi would be able to understand it fully, but the problems posed to any average reader are no greater than, say, the Puerto Rican slang of a novel like Edwin Torres's *Carlito's Way*.

David Davidar had been circumspect about Shobha Dé's rocket-ship rise to superstardom during the summer of 1992, but that was probably because he had *A Suitable Boy* up his sleeve and took Vikram Seth more seriously than Ms. Dé—because Seth had made it in the West. Rahul Singh was more forthright: Dé was a victim of her past. He arranged a meeting with the "third most famous woman in India"—the competition was Mother Teresa and Sonia Gandhi, an Albanian nun and an Italian widow.

The thing about Shobha Dé, I realized—sprawled on her sofa in a room festooned with Indian artifacts and art, classical and modern, whose picture window overlooked the steaming gray Arabian Sea—was her beauty. Forty-five years old, with six children, she looked about twenty-five and acted like a wise teenager. Renaissance painters would have murdered one another to get her for a model.

She agreed with Rahul. Her years as "the wicked bitch from the East," casting a cold eye on the life in Bollywood, had made her few friends. But even she was surprised by the extremity of outrage her novels elicited, and *Time*'s "Indian Jackie Collins" label merely irritated her.

She was now the "Princess of Porn" or the "Sultana of Smut" to Indian hacks. It bothered her. Davidar's campaign had been a two-edged sword: The books sold in unprecedented numbers, but for the wrong reasons.

When I suggested she was a moralist and satirist at heart, she seemed pleased in a diffident way. Like F. Scott Fitzgerald, she was *in* the world she wrote about, but not *of* it. I could see quite clearly where her heroines came from: Ms. Dé was as uncontrived, as complex yet straightforward, as innocent and as experienced, as they were. And as confused about the raving new world built on the back of an introspective and ancient one as any of her peers were—*if* they admitted it. The old India had poverty, not wealth, as its underlying reality, and austerity, not decadence, among its chief traditional values.

In these new realities, Shobha Dé finds her subject matter, writing fast and intuitively because her grasp of the material and her sense of purpose are strong. She seemed bashful when I suggested her work would one day be viewed as the foundation of Indian feminist literature—which it will—and, like so many talented people, she was dismissive of her talent. She put one word after another: that was all. I left our chat believing that she genuinely did not realize how good a writer she was, deciding at the same time that that might be precisely why she *was* such a good writer. Many have agreed since then that Shobha Dé will probably get the recognition she deserves abroad before she does in India. Very far from the sentimental melodrama of *A Suitable Boy,* for example, Ms. Dé's novels provide a glimpse of an India few Westerners are even aware exists and hardly any will ever see. Out of all the authors Davidar has championed, none is more unique than Shobha Dé, and none is more suited to Western sensibilities, holding as she does the two cultures in which she lives in a perfect balance that acts as an instrument of vision rarely found in literature, and more useful than a shelf of textbooks in purveying that understanding of the "Other" we crave from the traders in words and ideas.

❦   ❦   ❦

That night Rahul Singh said he was throwing a party for me, inviting people I ought to meet. But first I had an appointment with a movie star.

We met in the Harbour Bar, where every head turned the moment we walked in, and waiters virtually ignored their other customers, replacing our peanuts, ashtrays, and drinks and lighting our cigarettes whenever these opportunities presented themselves. Four peanuts gone, and a new bowl came; a centimeter of ash required a fresh receptacle; we must have been served twenty drinks, while we actually drank less than two; and the slightest suggestion that either of us intended picking up his pack of smokes provoked a frenzy of action resulting in nine arms thrusting flames at us as if we were vampires.

"You must promise not to be using my name," said ＿＿＿＿.

"Otherwise I—" He mimed cutting his own throat, an action that brought nine flames to his side.

To be honest, I'd never heard of him before this trip to Bombay, and I'd certainly never seen one of his films, but I had been assured that he was "going to be the next megastar." As in Hollywood, megastars come and go all the time in Bollywood—some around for what seems mere months, others with more staying power. ＿＿＿＿ was presented to me as a cut above your average next megastar, a serious actor at heart, and using stardom as a way of doing what he really wanted to do, regarding which he was, however, somewhat vague—beyond invoking Brando, De Niro, Pacino, et cetera.

"Really turn people's heads around, you know?" he further explained.

There was also a project that sounded rather like *Raging Bull,* but set in fifteenth-century Delhi and about a professional gladiator whose uncle is the Moghul emperor. There was a lot of intrigue, and much fighting that would be filmed so realistically it sounded as if people might have to sacrifice actual limbs in the name of art. It ended in a Himalayan cave, with the gladiator now a guru, using his early years in the arena as a metaphor.

"Of what?" I dutifully inquired.

"The whole movie is really his philosophy," ＿＿＿＿ explained, plainly expecting me to howl with wonder.

I'd been told he despised the Bombay film world and was eager to expose its squalid secrets—as long as he wouldn't be exposed as the one exposing them. All he seemed eager to expose, however, was a vast ambition as formless as the universe itself and equally in danger of disappearing into itself for no apparent reason.

After an hour of recounting great American films he'd seen—but seen in terms of how much greater they would have been with him in front of the camera and behind it—he finally started answering the questions I'd been asking doggedly. After proving that his interpretation of Tony Montana in the *Scarface* remake would have humbled Al Pacino, with a

Cuban accent somewhere between Wales and Sweden, and how the film would have been greatly improved by adding song-and-dance numbers, particularly during the final bloodbath, he suddenly announced that moviemaking in Bombay had become very sinister over the past few years.

"Always now you are hearing stories of how some don's goons are paying visit to so-and-so after he is refusing movie role."

"Don's?"

"Big-shot gangster, like Brando as the Don Gollyonni," he explained. "Part One *Godfather.*"

I had to nip at the bud stage the asthmatic-Scot version of Don Corleone tap-dancing through a hail of bullets, asking if the Bombay studio system resembled Hollywood's in the good old days, when superstars got five hundred dollars per flick and had contracts enslaving them forever or for five minutes, whichever proved more profitable. I'd imagined it this way, although Shobha Dé's novel *Starry Nights* made it sound more like Capone's Chicago.

"There is no studio system," _____ informed me, amazed anyone could have thought there was one.

"Who makes the movies then?"

"Anyone who wants to be making them."

"Who makes the deals? Agents?"

He laughed. "Agents? We are having no agents here!"

"So who handles the stars, the directors, the—"

"Secretaries."

"Secretaries?"

It seemed that the major players—big directors, even bigger stars—all had "secretaries" in their employ. These "secretaries" were the real power brokers—like agents, except that they didn't sign up the stars, the stars hired them. Agents with one client, these "secretaries" were thus only as powerful as their employers.

"So how is it we hear of stars being worked to death, shooting three or four movies simultaneously?"

"No one is *making* them—they are just too greedy. Quite often you are finding the big star signing contract not for just three or four movies, but twenty movies at same time."

"How the hell can you make twenty movies at the same time? You'd have to memorize two thousand pages of script . . ."

"Script?"

Considering that most Indian movies were four hours long, I was about to up the count to four thousand pages—but apparently no one in Bollywood bothered with scripts. They improvised. Driving from set to set, changing from mythic king to high-tech assassin all day long, no one generally had much idea what any film was about, let alone where his or her character fitted into it. This certainly explained why the films looked as if they were made that way. It also explained why, although you read about famous actors, directors, and producers, you never seemed to hear any mention of famous writers. Even Hollywood has a couple of *those*. Here the actors, directors, or producers—whoever had more clout—usually claimed that credit, not that anyone cared. Where, I wondered, did the money come from?

"Sometimes the black money," _____ said in hushed tones. "Sometimes this big shot from place like Gulbarga—" I gathered this was a place of no consequence "—he come into town and rents big suite in suburban hotel. Then lets everyone know he wants to finance the movie."

It seemed an improbable explanation, but apparently it wasn't. The "big shot" picked a suburban hotel, because the movie community had fled to the suburbs—having first built these suburbs themselves. The "big shot" merely wanted to have his photograph taken with some stars, happily throwing away several million rupees for the privilege, then returned to his no-account village wielding a sheaf of photographs to show his serfs he was the kind of man they thought he was. Soon after these serfs would also witness the screening of a three-hundred-minute epic of fighting-dancing-singing-loving gibberish with their big-shot baron's name attached to it in the local flea pit, where it would probably continue to play thrice daily for the next decade.

"Black money," however, was a different kettle of sharks altogether. "Dons from the Gulf" were often behind this method of movie financing—and "dons from the Gulf" did not pay for movies in order to lose their money.

"Only *big* star guaranteeing that a movie become smash hit," _____ told me, nodding to emphasize this sad truth. "So these dons asking the big star to be in their film. But these stars are having too much ego often, isn't it? So they say, 'No. Fuck off, Don-from-Gulf.'" He shook his head, then made a gun from his hand and shot himself through the ear.

"So . . . it's like the offer you can't refuse?"

"Just like!" He brightened at the prospect of *The Godfather* as a Glaswe-

gian *Showboat* again; then his brows darkened. "Except you don't find the horse's head in your bed—you are finding your own head there, isn't it?"

This went on. It appeared that the fanzines had a somewhat overly optimistic view of show business.

"Everyone is paranoid," he confirmed. "Even Amitabh Bhajan—biggest star, *biggest*—he never has a party in his house, and he never invites anyone back there even. He will go to some party given for him, of course, but never, *never* is he letting even the friends come to his house."

"Why?"

"Fear, man, *fear*." He shuddered. "I tell you, this is a dark town now. Too much blood has been spilled. I am not lying. *Too* much blood. The gangsters run everything now, *everything . . .*"

He proceeded to tell me which female stars were which gangsters' molls—and in one case which *male* star was which gangster's moll. It did sound a bit worse than Los Angeles.

⚜   ⚜   ⚜

"Of course he's bloody right," said Vinod Sharma, a guest at Rahul Singh's party. "The film business is almost as bad as politics these days."

Vinod was some sort of businessman who wrote investigative journalism as a hobby, or maybe as a form of revenge—it wasn't clear. He specialized in investigating politicians.

"Muckraking?" I inquired.

"*Muck*raking?" He exploded into laughter. "If I were muckraking, I'd never have written a word—there's far too much muck to rake *here!* I have to be more selective: find the lead, follow it, dig up the documents, ferret out the witnesses, persuade the minions to spill the beans, then *nail the rascals!*"

Nail the rascals was a phrase that gave him much deep satisfaction, and he used it frequently. He had, Rahul informed me, nailed some pretty big rascals in his time, too. He was an irresitibly likable man, and his independence made him the kind of valuable nuisance every society needs. It did strike me, however, that if politics really was as bad or worse as the film business allegedly was, Vinod Sharma wouldn't have lived long enough to tell me about it.

I spent most of the evening talking to another of David Davidar's authors, Gurcharan Das. His first novel, *A Fine Family,* had been published by Penguin in 1990. I asked jokingly what dubious profession Davidar had dragged him out of before he'd become a novelist. He had been, I learned, and still was, the president and managing director of Procter & Gamble India Ltd.

Gurcharan Das was not the mystery I initially thought him to be, though. He had a Harvard degree in philosophy and politics, and had written three plays, which had won prizes and been performed in New York and several other major international cities. I wondered how all this got along with business. After all, you couldn't call being president of an entire international division of one of the biggest corporations on earth exactly "supporting your writing habit."

"One balances the other," he said simply. "Together they help keep me *me.*"

It was succinctly put, and he was a succinct man, formidably intelligent, eclectically well-informed, intense, sincere—but disconcertingly *balanced,* just as he'd said. He could shift the gears of a conversation like someone going through the Alps in a Ferrari, too, as comfortable discussing the current state of literary criticism around the globe as he was examining the repercussions of the latest changes in Indian foreign-investment policy.

He felt as positive about his country's future as I did, which was a change. Rahul, who'd recently returned from Indonesia, was depressed by India's lack of progress compared to what he'd seen of Indonesian leaps into the future. Both nations, he felt, had started out with the same handicaps. The fact that no one had ever cast a vote against the president of Indonesia, whose family owned virtually ninety percent of everything worth owning in it, didn't shake his gloom. India should have achieved more. It was the general feeling shared by those who, like Rahul, were capable of making a success of their lives anywhere in the world, but had chosen to stay in their homeland because they loved it. India is a harsh mistress: She seems to appreciate individual sacrifice so little. Yet she has never wanted for lovers . . .

Gurcharan Das was so much more upbeat, perhaps, because progress was definitely being made in at least half of his professional domain. After decades of operating in India with a 40-percent ownership of their company, Procter & Gamble had just been permitted by Narasimha Rao's government to boost that stake to a controlling 51 percent. This shift in policy had foreign companies long dubious about investing anything in India now virtually *fighting* to get into what was touted as the largest middle-class consumer market outside Europe. Rahul, of course, was a writer, and writers never see much change in business—until they find themselves shipped off to a gulag or chained naked in some cellar with their tongue on the floor.

Gurcharan Das, however, knew an awful lot about business—more even than he *needed* to know. At least this reassured me I wasn't just being romantic about believing India's economic future was going to surprise the world. At one point I asked him if he thought dropping the legislation protecting the Indian automobile industry—permitting the Japanese, for example, to establish plants there—would destroy it. Given the choice, it seemed unlikely that anyone but people who could afford to make symbolic gestures would ever buy an Indian car again.

I had a reason for asking. I recalled watching the windshield wipers on an Ambassador that had been purchased an hour before make fifteen feeble sweeps at a monsoon downpour before simply dropping straight off the hood in unison. Not ten miles on the clock, and a window in this same car, when wound up to keep out rain, flopped free of its doorframe, shattering somewhere back along the road. Within twenty-four hours, both of the little yellow flippers set between the doors on both sides as indicators dangled uselessly from mysterious threads of wire; the hand brake now rested beneath a seat; the left front wheel had nearly detached itself entirely from the axle, lacking bolts to secure it there; the speedometer needle, having been lodged at fifteen miles per hour for as long as anyone recalled, was next seen lying horizontally beneath zero; the battery, which proved to be ten years older than the car, died amid a toxic froth; and the fan belt melted just before the entire engine burst into flames.

No, buying an Ambassador *was* an act of faith. But when you'd fixed all the problems that it shouldn't have had in the first place, and found a mechanic who wouldn't replace your new parts with his old parts every time he serviced the thing, the Ambassador was actually a very durable and oddly charming car. It was tough as a tank, unscathed after collisions that would leave Padminis, and certainly Marutis—along with their occupants—crumpled irreparably.

Terming such measures "infant industries," Gurcharan Das was not in the least sentimental. "The infant has to grow up sooner or later. There's no respite. Either it can survive out there in the real world alone, or it can't. If it can't, it can't."

I was forced to admit that he might have a point. It could well take the threat of extinction to force Indians to build cars that actually work when you buy them *without* having to be repaired or overhauled before you ever drive them.

"You'll see," he predicted. "This country will start to work as soon as people realize they only have themselves to blame for it *not* working. Infantizing extends to the individual psyche, too, you know. So many centuries of foreign rule have the same effect as never letting a child leave home. The moment the child realizes it has to take care of itself, it *does*. There isn't any choice, is there? You see it in families: Mummy and Daddy do everything, so why should the child even try? Where thinking is unnecessary, or even discouraged, why think? But those days are over. It will be make or break—and I am sure we'll make it."

He was off soon, he said, for a sabbatical year at Harvard—to work on a new novel, do some research, think.

"You get sabbaticals in business?"

"Why not?" He sounded surprised.

I doubted that P & G executives back in the U.S. got sabbaticals, but then again, I don't think any of them write novels, either.

Much later that night, I curled up with Gurcharan Das's novel, *A Fine Family*. Utterly different from the headlong plunge into a damaged world that Shobha Dé had burned into her pages, here was still that new voice of Indian English.

An epic spanning the bloody birth of independent India and moving through a troubled childhood into a difficult and confused adolescence, ending in the hopeful period after Indira Gandhi's emergency, the novel followed a family that endured and survived the inner and outer torments it suffered because it was strong and because it had a firm foundation of belief to keep it going. Its generations were the generations of India, despair handing over the baton to hope, confident even in the depths that what had once been great would again be great—because it was possessed of a greatness hard-won and thus not so easily lost. It was a fine family, indeed, and a really fine novel. In every line I heard the quiet strength of the man I'd spoken to all evening.

> There was little hope from the rulers who were in power. So one
> had to rely on oneself. It required courage to reach out to the poor

and defenseless. But that was where hope lay. Hope lay in the private individual, who was liberal and educated, reaching out to the silent and the suffering, and showing through his example how the liberal institutions could work. 'Each one, teach one,' Mahatma Gandhi had said and he had reached out and identified with the weak with all his being—wearing their clothes, eating their food, living their life. We can't all be like Mahatma, thought Arjun. But each of us in his small world could reach out and help just a little bit to root the institutions in the people, so that they were just a little bit less like dream castles built out of middle class aspirations. Arjun had no use for the spiritual till human dignity was established through an unsentimental concern for others.

The following day, gazing out at a tormented sea and the looming edifice of the newly spruced-up Gateway of India, I wasn't certain whether or not my concern for others could be termed "unsentimental," but I knew for sure that my feelings about the grand old Taj Mahal Hotel were *definitely* sentimental. I'd stayed there so many times by now that it felt like a second home. But, I realized, I knew very little about the place that had played a unique role in Bombay's history for nearly a century.

Putting off the next stage of my journey, the stage I feared the most, I got permission to go through the hotel's archives, finding an embarrassment of riches, material that told an idiosyncratic tale of both the city and the country during this turbulent twentieth century.

Initially I assumed that the first place I ever slept in in India was left over from imperial days, like the triumphal Gateway it faced—Indian-owned now, of course, but essentially an inherited tradition, absorbed like the famous Calcutta clubs. I found out how very wrong I was.

Born in 1839, Jamsetji Nuserwanji Tata was arguably the first Indian to realize that the British would voluntarily leave his country, and, more significantly, the first Indian to carry on his business *as if they had already left.* From a wealthy family, he had established himself as the subcontinent's first industrialist, single-mindedly setting about the task of laying the infrastructure that India would need in order to flourish as an independent country one day.

In Tata's overall economic vision of India, hotels did not feature. The entrepreneur occupied himself with many, many different business ventures—but then something happened.

He had scheduled a meeting with several European investors at the Apollo Hotel, which faced the seafront near the harbor. Intent on potential business arrangements, he strode toward the entrance somewhat absentmindedly. There he was denied admission. This shocked him. The reason given was his skin color.

The episode stuck in his mind. Later he complained to a friend about it, and made a point of finding out how many first-class hotels in India permitted Indians entry. There was one. Tata's friend remarked to him that beyond this, not only were Indians not allowed into most hotels, but Bombay itself did not even *have* a first-class hotel.

The seed was planted, and it grew deep roots.

Tata set out to create a place where Indians and British could meet on neutral ground. He was, after all, a businessman, and he'd seen money overcome caste. In retrospect, this attitude seems all the more remarkable in an age when businessmen did not consider running hotels a profitable growth industry on the whole.

With absolute confidence in his vision, Tata scoured the capitals of Europe, purchasing the best of everything, including professional advice. The hotel he built would contain such state-of-the-art facilities as its own laundry, an aerated water-bottling plant, a crockery-washing plant, elevators, a Mora silver-burnishing machine, and even electroplating services for its silverware. Few establishments in Paris and London could boast such high-tech refinements at the time.

The Taj was a labor of love for him. Built on a site directly in front of the hotel that had refused him admittance in 1888, and commandeering the latter's view across the Arabian Sea, it impressed all who saw it with its classical sweep and grandeur. The Taj's exquisite symphony in stone eclipsed even the imperial architect Sir Edwin Landseer Lutyens's magnificent Secretariat. It was intended to fuse the best of East and West, of everything the world had to offer.

Few Indians had seen anything like it before, and Tata made very sure it would be the first sight any visiting dignitaries or viceroys would see on the subcontinent as they disembarked from their steamships in Bombay harbor and proceeded through the triumphal arch of the Gateway of India.

Ironically, the hotel also serves as a monument to the man who dreamed it into existence. Sadly, Jamsetji Tata did not live to preside over its opening ceremony in 1904.

This newest wonder of the East opened with great fanfare. It instantly gained many admirers—and fierce hostility from the Raj establishment. This hostility toward Tata's Taj manifested itself in a number of insidious ways. One rumor claimed the hotel had been meticulously designed by a French architect, but then built back to front, his imposing entranceway positioned on a narrow back street instead of facing the spectacular panorama of harbor and sea. (In fact, an Englishman named Chambers designed it, and the building was positioned according to plan, to give sea-facing rooms the view as well as a cool westerly breeze.) And newspapers reported any incident that could damage the hotel's reputation, no matter how trivial.

Nonetheless, the Taj became more and more accepted as a Bombay landmark, if only because anyone who *was* anyone visiting the city—including the Prince of Wales—now stayed there as a matter of course. It became a center of activity for the Bombay social circuit, the site of all manner of balls, recitals, and concerts, despite occasional outbursts of hostility from the British-controlled establishment.

As with all great hotels, the Taj reflects the fortunes and misfortunes of its city. During the Second World War, Bombay's port saw many British and Indian troopships on their way from and to the killing fields in Burma and the Middle East.

The Taj supported the war effort, converting rooms into dormitories for soldiers, and providing modified luxury for budget guests. Many significant meetings were held, covertly and overtly, in the Taj, and several major historical events were engineered or thrashed out in the hotel's restaurants, bars, and private rooms. Here, too, it is rumored, Nehru and Lady Mountbatten, wife of India's last viceroy, played out at least one scene from their love affair, according to a source inside the Gandhi family. Perhaps the affair's symbolism *is* a little too perfect.

But by 1948, the hotel was weary as its city, and indeed its country. Even back in 1940, the Taj's managing director, a Mr. Sabavala, wrote, "The present building is nearing its life's end."

But the Tata family were determined to modernize according to the needs of the twentieth-century tourist and traveler. They contemplated constructing a New Taj, but they were equally determined to preserve their ancestor's magnificent gift to an inchoate nation. So the old Taj still stands, alongside a new tower, the whole complex more elegant than ever.

From the outside, the hotel looks like an architectural anomaly—a modern high-rise grafted on to a nineteenth-century Indo-Bavarian castle—while its interior demonstrates the Tata passion for tradition blended with the advantages of modern technology. The building flows effortlessly across the lobby's Moghul inlaid white marble fountains from the old to the new, still offering a sense of how things were when the Chamber of Indian Princes used to hold their annual conference there. And in places like the Tanjore restaurant, the Taj still manages brilliantly to recreate the feeling of that vanished age, with antiques and an elegance extending from the service to what is served. Even the classical Indian dance and music performed upon the colonnaded central stage are reminiscent of those with which the Chamber of Princes would have been entertained while consuming a leisurely twenty-course meal—sampled by personal tasters for possible poison first, naturally.

Almost everyone I've ever *heard of* has stayed at the Taj: the Shah of Iran, Twiggy, Sean Connery, Norman Mailer, Farrah Fawcett, Sir Oswald Mosley, Edgar Bergen. . . . In terms of cultural and historic significance, perhaps the roster of postindependence politicians staying there reveals the most about the city's society at the time.

From the Third World came envoys, particularly from Indira Gandhi's so-called nonaligned nations, until their leaders died or were assassinated, one by one. And colonial ghosts continued to wave either bribes or olive branches from the U.S.A., Great Britain, and, for a long and uneasy period, in Western eyes, the Soviet Union.

In 1974, the rooms at the old Taj still looked much as they had back in the thirties: spacious, with ceiling fans, mosquito nets, and broad balconies overlooking the lugubrious Arabian Sea. They have been modernized now, to satisfy those tourists who cannot cope without the familiar environment of the five-star world. The old building itself, with its cavernous ten-story space, off which corridors stretch, leading to the rooms, differs little from the way it looked at its opening in 1904.

I asked an old bearer who had been working at the Taj for nearly sixty years if he noticed a change in the guests and the general atmosphere.

"Sahib," he replied, "the most big change is this: Europeans are coming to *my* country now. So I must try even more hard to give good impression of country. But, sahib, I am feeling that now people are coming here because they are liking the India, isn't it?" And he smiled proudly.

In 1989, Tata's heirs—as the Taj Group—bought the St. James Court hotel in London, going on to receive that city's prestigious award for excellence in renovating an historical building. Back in 1888, no Indian ever dreamed that the capital of the British Empire would need the help and money of his fellow countrymen to save it from crumbling into decay. It may be among the first of such karmic debts India will be entitled to claim.

❧   ❧   ❧

Ghosts and memories—the Taj teems with them. Many, I realized in 1992, were mine now, as well: ghosts of myself and others, memories of other selves . . .

Flying out of Bombay, as I had first flown out twenty years before, I felt truly haunted. That first time, I'd left to *find* something, indeed *had* to leave, because I'd never thought of staying there anyway. Now, however, it occurred to me that I was simply going because I *felt like* going, not because I *needed* to go. I knew full well that I could search for what it was I sought *wherever* I was. Now, I imagined I was just a tourist along for the ride. It seemed a liberating thought, and liberation was, after all, the name of the game. Liberation was something you could achieve anywhere, and any time you chose. Well, *wasn't it?* Who ultimately knows, though? Who *really* knows anything? Was it after all, ironically enough, I considered, perhaps an existential attitude toward liberation that I had arrived at over the past two decades?

An Indian Airlines jet during monsoon season, however, is not exactly the best place to dwell on such things. Plowing across a highway of clouds cobbled with what felt like vast boulders of sodden cotton wool, I suddenly had *no* desire to be liberated from the comforting security of matter and the chains of flesh—at least, to paraphrase Saint Augustine, not quite *yet* . . .

12

"No Like A-feesh?"

✤ ✤ ✤

Great teachers, whether the Buddha or the Christ, have
come, they have accepted faith, making themselves,
perhaps, free from confusion and sorrow. But they have
never prevented sorrow, they have never stopped
confusion. Confusion goes on, sorrow goes on. If you,
seeing this social and economic confusion, this chaos, this
misery, withdraw into what is called the religious life and
abandon the world, you may feel that you are joining these
great teachers, but the world goes on with its chaos, its
misery and destruction, the everlasting suffering of its rich
and poor. So our problem, yours and mine, is whether we
can step out of this misery instantaneously.

—J. KRISHNAMURTI, *THE FIRST AND LAST FREEDOM*

*N*ow I was back in Bangalore for the first time in fifteen years. The
place had changed utterly, turning into a bustling metropolis choking on diesel fumes, the center of the burgeoning Indian computer industry. There must have been five times the traffic there had been, and
the streets couldn't handle it. I was glad to escape the noxious gases and
noise, passing through the West End Hotel's gates into its opulent and
superbly maintained gardens. The hotel had changed, too: changed hands.
It was infinitely better than I recalled, with a huge, open-sided Indonesian-
style restaurant set in the middle of an artificial lake, reached by a narrow
bridge.

At night, a free-form chorus of frogs serenaded diners in the candlelit
restaurant, and the smells of bougainvillea, frangipani, and hibiscus wafted
in from the ingeniously lit gardens. The place was hopping, too. It was

Derby Week at the track across Race Course Road, and the West End teemed with owners and horse people, champagne corks popping at that day's winner's table. When I mentioned to someone in Delhi that it had been Derby Week, I was told I'd been mistaken: The Derby was run in February. It turned out that Bangalore had *two* Derbys per year, since the climate permitted two racing seasons. Indians still resented Bangalore its climate and its freedom from the urban problems other cities faced.

The climate was changing, though. Increased industry and population were raising the temperature. The city's tempo was rising, as well. Arriving at the new airport terminal, which would soon handle international flights, I could see that Bangalore wanted to make an instant impact on visitors. The place was a riot of artificial foliage; walls were festooned with framed and illuminated posters announcing high-tech business operations that welcomed you to their base of operations. But the city was still trading on its "Garden" reputation. A huge sign read:

INDO AMERICAN HYBRID SEEDS

WELCOMES

DIGNITORIES & DELEGATES

TO THE

NATIONAL SEMINAR ON FLORICULTURE

PRESENT & POTENTIAL

The place was still dark at night, too, except for new stores lit up like film sets. Chinese restaurants had sprung up everywhere, along with liquor stores—something you never saw in the seventies—and literally countless computer software outlets.

Brigade Road was no longer a seedy street of ill repute, but a lavish mall of proud new stores for the proud new Indian consumer. One out of three sold computer stuff. I wondered who was using all these diskettes and Accountech programs. Peanut and roast-corn vendors still hawked their wares on barrows by kerosene taper, though.

But an air of easy affluence hung over everything and everyone— except the beggars. Almost incredibly, I recognized the sweet-faced boy with the reef knot tied in his spine, still squatting in the dirt, wearing rags, holding up his mangled hands. He'd aged well, I found myself thinking uncharitably. I bought him a plate of gulab jamoons and handed over a hundred rupees. He didn't seem as grateful as I remembered him once seeming, taking the offering as if he expected it. He shoved the hundred-rupee note, which would have caused a riot twenty years before, quickly into a small bag he carried, and turned his attention back to the street.

There had been a commotion in the hotel lobby, a woman screaming, staff attempting to calm her down. Only later did I learn the cause: The woman's husband had arrived some days before, taking care of the business aspect of this trip before his wife came to join him. She'd telephoned the day before from somewhere like Kanchipuram, where they lived. The hotel had just installed a new phone system, with individual voice mail in each room. Put through to her husband's room, the wife had heard some woman answer the phone, claiming he wasn't in but she could leave a message. She'd hung up in a rage: He had a lover staying with him!

Blaming it on technology hadn't been easy, either. The staff tried to quiet her down sufficiently to show her the marvels of modern telecommunications. No one really felt she believed them even then. She was convinced that they were merely all in on the plot.

I'd made up my mind to spend just the day at Sathya Sai Baba's ashram, returning to Bangalore after evening prayers. I hadn't seen him in fourteen years, and he hadn't spoken to me privately since that interview more than seventeen years before. But hardly a week had passed throughout the preceding years when I hadn't thought of him. And occasionally I had dreams that bore the unmistakable stamp of his presence—love—and held relatively important messages, ones I had no trouble deciphering. When I least expected it, I'd feel that embracing glow of being loved, the sheer sweetness of Baba's enigma.

"Don't try to understand me, because you never will," he'd said.

This was true. I'd often decided it was all over, that he and I were through—I'd descend back into unalloyed matter, and he'd go . . . wherever it was he needed to go. But the bond never broke. As he'd promised, he was always there, hidden at times, but there, in the heart.

And as the years passed, I came to see the pendulum swing of my soul, from matter to spirit, darkness to light, the unreal to the real, back and forth—endlessly. I also came to understand that the momentum needed for leaps of faith was generated this way. I accepted more now, too, was kinder to myself, more forgiving, more *objective*. Slightly.

I never went to meetings of local Sathya Sai groups; but I did on occasion pray, in mosques, churches, synagogues, temples—whatever was handy. I realized that the image of God I'd chosen, besides his formless, nondualistic eternal oneness, was that of Sathya Sai Baba. He'd stood the test of time.

But the idea of seeing the reality, rather than the idea and the image, filled me with trepidation, even with dread. I knew I was drinking heavily—*too* heavily—and finding reasons not to go. But now I was on my way.

We drove from the West End Hotel at 3:30 A.M. I estimated that would get me there around eleven—generally in time for morning darshan—*if* things were still the same. The driver I'd chosen was someone I knew to be untalkative.

Memories of driving out with Abdul and Joy came back, but I just couldn't relate *this* me to *that* me. We were different people. I'd been a mere child then.

I wondered who I was kidding while I tried to snooze. This might be the most important day I would have for years, maybe *ever*. Because part of me wanted to exorcise Baba forever, or satisfy itself concerning his reality enough to make a serious commitment. Make or break: That was the attitude I took.

Hovering up above the parched plains of Andhra Pradesh, the bloody sun sat like a mothership bearing galactic emperors to an appointment at the end of the world. The sudden, awesome beauty of this spectacle felt like a punch to the heart. As we hurtled through the primeval landscape, I felt like the first man, or the last one. Slipping on headphones, I started listening to Ravi Shankar's *Shanti-Dhwani* where I'd left off after buying it the day before. Dedicated to Indira Gandhi—its sole shortcoming—it is a shimmering masterpiece, transcending musical definition. That dawn, however, I felt the hairs on my neck stand up as, instead of Ravi's orchestral sitar assembly, I heard the chanting of Sanskrit mantras, one of them the sole piece of Vedic wisdom I can still quote with the proper intonation: the *Gayathri*. It is the supreme and most profound plea to the Lord of this universe that humanity has ever uttered: Baba had once said that it was the only request worth making of God.

> *Om Asatomah sat gamayah*
> *Tamaso mah jyotir gamayah*
> *Mrityomam amrtam gamayah*
> *Om Shantih Shantih Shantih*

Eternal One
Lead me from the Unreal to the Real
From Darkness to Light
From Death to Immortality
To be with Eternity in everlasting peace

With around five hours to go, by my estimate, I was very surprised to see a sign reading PUTTAPARTHI 30 KM, assuming it was an error for 300 km. I mentioned it to the driver, who'd shot past the turn-off indicated by this sign, anyway, and he brought us to a slithering halt, backed up to the sign, nodded, and then turned off down the side road.

"Thirty kilometers?" I inquired, laughing sagely.

"Half hour more arriving," he replied.

"Arriving *where?*"

"Sai Baba place."

"It's only six o'clock!" I yodeled. "We've only been driving for two and a half hours. How can we bloody we all arrive there in *half an hour?*"

"Journey is three hours only."

"No it's not," I snapped. "It's at least *seven* hours."

"Three hours only."

First the *Gayathri,* and now—What? A warp in the space-time continuum?

"It took *seven* hours in 1974," I added, trying to sound less hysterical. "Why does it take three hours now? Hmm? Why?"

Because they'd built a new road was the answer. Instead of weaving north, then east, you could now go straight, on the new road. Humbled, I sank back, not wanting to be so near to Puttaparthi so soon.

Before long, we swerved around a corner I remembered well.

"Sai Ram, Sai Ram," rasped a familiar voice.

The old blind beggar Joy had condemned as a phony devotee and millionaire stood with his usherette's tray of framed Baba pictures, and his eye sockets like a dead dog's nose. I told the driver to stop, and gave the millionaire some more rupees to fatten his bank account, for auld lang syne.

In no time, I gasped slightly at the start of that breathtakingly elegant landscape that I'd never forgotten, with its giant outcrops of sculptured rock, its blackened mountaintops, its verdant paddies, its sense of timeless peace. I wasn't sure whether I'd change into Baba-devotee regulation white, but I'd brought the clothes along in case I felt like conforming. And I did.

Hopping around by the roadside, trying to find the hole in my pants for a foot, I looked up as a small bus hurtled into view. It was painted with Baba slogans and his emblem, and full of kids from one of his colleges. Most schoolkids, encountering a foreigner in the middle of nowhere with his big pale butt exposed to the elements, would have hooted lewd and humiliating remarks through the windows. These students merely looked away politely, and I could hear the singing of bhajans as they passed. The kids who attended Baba's educational establishments had been unnaturally well behaved every time I encountered them.

Vaguely recalling the lay of the land, I was surprised to find an ornate concrete arch spanning an otherwise empty stretch of road. WELCOME TO PRASANTHI NILAYAM, it read, ABODE OF BHAGAVAN SRI SATHYA SAI BABA. Since Puttaparthi was still a good few miles away, this seemed premature.

It wasn't premature, however. Around the next bend appeared a small, towerlike structure with a radar scanner on top of it—much like what you'd find in a minor airport. As we got closer, there was a sign proclaiming SRI SATHYA SAI AIRPORT. Beyond the tower was also, as one might expect, a runway large enough to land a medium-size jet on. *Jesus!* I thought. But beyond it I saw another unfamiliar structure. This one was massive: several wings, surrounded by many three-story officelike blocks, all in a compound recently planted with trees. Another sign: SRI SATHYA SAI INSTITUTE OF HIGHER MEDICAL SCIENCES.

"Holy shit!" I said out loud. "What's *that?*"

"Baba hospital."

"Oh."

There had always been a hospital in the ashram, but that one had been the size of a small family bungalow. This one was bigger than any in Toronto. Before I could be more amazed, we turned onto a shady, tree-lined boulevard that had been a stretch of country dirt road the last time I saw it. On either side were more colossal, immaculately maintained buildings. The Sri Sathya Sai University, the SSS Sports Arena, the SSS College of Arts and Sciences, and many others that seemed to be hostels and administrative buildings.

It gradually dawned on me that this *was* Puttaparthi. High on a hill to the left stood a seventy-foot-high painted concrete statue of Hanuman, the monkey god whose burning tail had scorched these mountains as he flew to Lanka and a showdown with the demon Ravana. Beyond this, just up from where "Nagamma's Hotel" had been, I saw what looked like a repro Hindu palace. *Oh dear,* I thought, *Baba's built himself a palace. That's it—he's sold out.* I was almost pleased. I asked the driver about it.

"Not *palace,*" he corrected. "That place museum of spirituality."

What would you exhibit there? I wondered, suddenly noticing dozens and dozens of buses parked everywhere in sight. Baba was certainly more popular than he'd been twenty years before, when the Puttaparthi bus terminal had handled one bus per day and had trouble coping with that.

"Today big festival," the driver explained.

"Which one?"

"Guru Poornima."

Guru Poornima: the festival held on the full moon night nearest to mid-July, according to the lunar calendar, and dedicated to your guru. It was the one festival I'd never attended at Prasanthi Nilayam. What a coincidence! Of all the days on which to come—a festival. There had never been much chance of contact with Baba during festivals—even twenty years before—because of the crowds. Indians love festivals, attending every one they can justify attending. A holy day, a holiday. I hated the crowds, mostly, and the chaos that disrupted my tranquil pastoral idyll. Baba seemed to place great importance on them, though, taking pains to ensure that the arrangements for the influx of people were adequate, and putting on a lavish display of Hindu pomp—Brahmins chanting the Vedas, elephants dressed up for parades, bands, free food, and always making a speech himself, then leading bhajans. Festivals were also where he performed some of the more extraordinary public materializations—but that was then. Now he apparently never materialized anything more than vibhuti in public.

I remembered watching him wave his hand inside a small jar, showering a three-foot-tall silver image of Shirdi Sai Baba with enough vibhuti to completely cover it—about three hundred times as much as the jar could have contained had it contained any at all before he put his hand inside.

Coming back to the present, I saw something I *did* recognize: the ashram wall. Over that wall, somewhere, was the person who had dominated half my life.

Then I recalled the time in 1974 when he'd said to us that Puttaparthi would be a city one day, and that the crowds around him would be so vast we would be lucky to catch a distant glimpse of him. I'd forgotten about it.

Now the memory made me tremble. Everything he'd said had come true. At the time it had seemed absurd, impossible. Yet here it was. I told the driver to pull over, jumped out, and went in the back gate to the ashram, as I'd always done, where the little shrine to Ganesh stood.

Prasanthi Nilayam was packed. Possibly a hundred thousand people milled around—Indians, Westerners, Chinese—all dressed neatly, all fairly orderly, too. The ashram had also grown, rows of dormitories stretching off farther than I even wanted to see. But the Mandir, the temple where Baba still lived, had not changed at all. The sand around it had been re-placed by concrete; but the three domes and the wedding-cake sculptures, and the atrocious pastel pink-blue-green color scheme, were exactly as I remembered.

Someone had once asked Baba what these colors signified.

Bad taste, I'd said to myself, but Baba had answered: "Blue is for the sky; green is for the earth; and pink . . . pink is for babies." I'd never been sure if this was a joke or some mighty profundity.

I was being jostled by a thousand bodies—all men; women were still on the "Ladies Side." It took some minutes before I realized that Baba was actually giving darshan as I stood there. Attempting to squeeze around the side, I found myself borne along by a human tide, eventually thrust toward a spot just outside the central compound. Craning my neck, I got some idea where Baba was by following the eyelines of other devotees. He was under the Mandir porch, where amplified lead singers sang bha-jans. Even without seeing him, I knew he was there.

Pressed by the mob behind me, claustrophobic and suddenly *very* hot and sweaty, I angrily jabbed back with my elbows. Somehow I found my-self shunted around until I ended up in the front row, right by the pas-sage formed by seated devotees that Baba used to walk down.

Unaccountably irritable by now, I told myself, *If he's really who he says he is, he'll come down that line and stand just there. Then he'll smile at me. That's all.*

I saw the familiar orange robe. He walked with that strange, majestic gliding step, as he'd always done during darshans, his hand poised in the lotus mudra, the index finger occasionally writing in the air—*altering the Akashic records of human destiny.* He'd scarcely aged at all. Nearly sixty-seven, he looked no more than forty-five, which was how he'd looked when he *was* forty-five.

He drew nearer, pausing to take notes or speak to someone here and there, nimbly stepping back if someone breached protocol and tried to touch his feet. I expected to feel something; instead, I felt nothing at all. This pleased me, too. Emotion wouldn't cloud my perception. He reached the end of the human aisle leading to where I stood, pausing motionless, as he'd always done, staring into worlds within worlds.

The denizens of all three Hindu *loka*s were said to seek the Avatar's darshan. I'd often thought how much more crowded the ashram must be than it already was. Half the population of the universe was out there— or *in* there. Then he walked closer, and I felt myself thinking, *No, I don't believe. Don't make me believe, either. But if you come and stand there and smile—I'll believe.* The reality confused me after years of living with the idea and the image. He drew closer. As I realized I knew what he was going to do, someone reached out to touch his feet. He skipped away with a reprimand. Then he stood, not twenty feet away, and looked straight into my eyes. Not a muscle on his face moved. Abruptly he turned and walked back down the aisle, heading across the compound.

That's that, I thought. *There's the answer: You feel nothing at all, and he doesn't even know who you are. . . .*

This seemed a perfect conclusion to the whole thing. I could probably get back to the West End in time for lunch, too, at this rate. Instead, I decided to walk where I'd once found unsurpassed serenity in the natural world.

First I offered a flower to Ganesh—good old Ganesh. Then I left the ashram, heading down the track that led to the Chitravati River. Or at least used to lead there. A hundred yards off the main drag, houses and minihotels for devotees ended and country began.

"Sai Ram, *appa,*" a crafty-looking, well-coiffed sadhu announced, holding out his kamandalam bowl.

"Fuck off," I told him with satisfaction. I'd never have said that back in 1974.

Turning the bend where I should have seen the river's edge, I found only a two-hundred-yard expanse of sand. The monsoon had failed here, too. All that was left was a twisting sand runway, with herds of goats being driven down it, and deep holes being dug to reach the shallow Chitravati underground. Baba had always warned people not to dig so many wells. It lowers the water table, he had explained. At the time, I had wondered what that had to do with us devotees, concluding it might be some sort of parable. Maybe it hadn't been.

I followed the dry bed. This aridity depressed me in a landscape that had once been so lush. After half a mile, I turned back, heading to the old part of Puttaparthi village—where Baba had been born. It looked exactly the same, charming and chaotic, full of fat water buffalo and happy children. Baba's house had been torn down, I was surprised to learn. He didn't want it to become a shrine. You can't stop Indians building shrines, though.

With a bicycle and a ledger, Baba's brother appeared. *He* looked older, but was as pleasant as he'd always been.

I remarked how the place had changed.

"It is amazing what he has done" was the reply.

Did he get to see his brother the god much these days?

"It is not possible now," he answered. "Swami is too busy with important matters. *Very* few see him now."

I asked if it was strange having such a . . . successful sibling.

"Swami is not my brother," he said patiently. "Long ago he ceased to be tied to these worldly bonds. He has come for everyone. I am no more important than . . . you."

Bad analogy, I thought. So he believed in Baba the way any other devotee did. The brother he'd grown up with was like someone who'd died— not someone who'd become too famous to speak to relatives who were no longer on his social level.

What an odd fate. I said good-bye to God's brother and walked back toward the main ashram gate. There, the little strip of lean-tos and stalls and mud-brick eateries had transformed itself into a thriving commercial street of concrete triplexes, covered bazaars, and air-conditioned coffee shops, bookstores, and even travel agents. There were banks, Kashmiri carpet vendors, and even a photographic-supply store that specialized in blowing up your favorite Baba snap to life-size posters or prints of any dimension.

I hated this ugly face of spiritualism. In the coffee shops and bookstores I heard Westerners engaged in the same conversations that had begun to sicken me by the time I finally left Puttaparthi, twenty years before:

"Did you see the expression on his face as he touched that old man?"

"Wow!"

"Remember how he took the jasmine mala and gave it to Raja Reddy?"

"He's *so* beautiful!"

"Sai Ram!"

"Sai *Ram, Sai Ram!*"

"What time is the discourse?"

"Eight. But we should get there by three to get a good seat."

"Or two?"

"Sai Ram!"

You can never go home. And I should never have come back to a place where I'd even willed my ashes to be scattered before July 14, 1992. It was just as well: You can't scatter ashes on a dried-up river. Unless you're a little too interested in symbolism.

The driver was disappointed to find we were leaving at 9:00 A.M., not 9:00 P.M. He was enjoying the holy day, had even found some friends to play with.

"Business meeting," I explained.

"Accha."

I took a last look at the city of Prasanthi Nilayam, feeling no regrets at all knowing I'd never see it again.

Before I even realized it, we were approaching the outskirts of Bangalore. I noticed a huge sign reading WINE SHOP and asked the driver to stop. A cocktail before lunch would be just the thing, no?

Knowing wine was probably the one alcoholic beverage the place *didn't* sell, I walked over, attracting much local attention on the way. Inside was a dingy room with a fenced-in counter, behind which were arranged many rows of bottles. Two yards away was a stone quarry: this dive evidently existed to part the quarry workers from their paychecks before they could get home. I realized why so many people supported Prohibition so keenly.

The rogues who ran this demons' den exhibited great joy at having foreign custom. It would hardly have amazed me to learn I was the first Westerner ever to step through their portals. I asked for a bottle of rum. This proved troublesome. They were not accustomed to such big spenders, and had only mickeys in stock. No problem—I asked for two half bottles, unfazed by having to pay three cents more for the same quantity of rum.

This freewheeling spirit moved them. One man set about laboriously wrapping the two mickeys in separate sheets of newspaper and enmeshing them in string. His colleagues disappeared through a door to the rear.

Wondering whether they had ever cleaned the place, I heard the man who'd disappeared out back going *Psst! Psst!* behind me.

"Afisth . . . afifeeth?" he asked me in covert tones.

"What?"

"Afeethsch . . . afhish?" He beckoned me to join him, to see for myself what it was he had.

He wants to sell me hashish, I realized, thinking these boys certainly covered their market well. I followed him into an even dingier back room that smelled like the Bangalore cabaret-brothel. I wondered how they smuggled their drugs—or *in what* they smuggled them.

"Ah!" the man said eagerly, indicating a mound wrapped in newspaper sitting on a wooden table so sodden with grease it was almost liquid itself.

He began to unwrap the mound. I was curious to see what sort of hashish one could find this far south of Swat. Instead of hashish, however, as a final sheet of virtually transparent newsprint was peeled away, I saw a small pile of very dead fish.

"Afhish," the man announced in triumph.

"A *fish!* Yes, yes—they're fish, all right. For eating?" I pointed at my mouth.

"Ah! Accha!" he said enthusiastically.

Very far from the sea, with no fishable rivers within five hundred miles—indeed, with no monsoon, no rivers at all to speak of—fish would have to travel some distance to arrive on the outskirts of Bangalore. Without the benefit of refrigeration, and *with* the benefit of humid 130-degree heat, these specimens smelled as if they were some weeks into their own putrefaction. I now remembered reading warnings in the press about illegal sales of poisonous fish, too.

"Very nice," I said, "but no thanks. I'm a vegetarian."

"Vesh darian, ha?" the man inquired, crestfallen.

I returned to collect my bottles.

"Vesh darian," the man explained to his partner.

"No like a-feesh?" he replied, astounded.

"Nor meat."

"But a-feesh goot, yes?"

"A-feesha ne," the other man reminded the partner.

This man tried again. "Goot a-feesh."

I walked back to the car, wondering who'd be having a fish dinner tonight near the quarry. Their last supper, probably.

In my hotel room, I went to unswaddle one of the rum bottles from its paper and string and accidentally dropped it. The container shattered on the thick wool pile of my carpet, its dark contents seeping out like blood.

The moment it happened, I remembered that the fish symbolized Christ and the soul. Wondering why this irrelevancy had occurred to me, I was suddenly overwhelmed by the sense of Baba's presence, of divine love. The fragrance of the incense that burned in Baba's temple distinctly permeated the room. It was a fragrance I hadn't smelled in decades. Staring at the rum stain, I knew. Beyond all doubt, Baba *was* omnipresent. Beyond *all* doubt. He who is one with the Father is no different from the Father. And the Father was very, very close right then—or really just more *accessible.*

The power of this incident engulfed me. Never before had I experienced such a feeling of God's proximity. It was and *is* undeniable.

Going for a swim later, I ran into Dick Workman, an IBM executive here to hook up his company to the Tata empire, forming Tata Business Machines—TBM. I liked Dick, and I didn't envy him his task. His job would be to train Indians in IBM work habits. A personable American from Georgia, he'd spent much of his life stationed in the East for his company, and he was married to a beautiful young Korean girl, Soo-Hyon— "Sue."

When he heard I'd once lived here, Dick was eager to pump me for useful information. Our conversations had been more on the secular side of profundity. I'd never mentioned Sai Baba before, and I told him only that I was going out of town for the day. But now I had the urge to mention Baba, wondering whether to give him the copy of Howard Murphet's *Sai Baba: Man of Miracles,* which I'd picked up again, for old times' sake, in Puttaparthi. The book provided a readable introduction, one that had attracted many people to Baba's ashram. As I decided Dick wasn't Baba material, and that I wanted to keep the hard-to-find book myself, anyway, an orange butterfly fluttered at my face. I whacked it away, reaching for my rum and fresh lime. Within seconds, the butterfly was back, swooping to batter itself against my lips. I brushed it off again. Seconds later, the thing flapped around my lips again, until I was spitting out wing dust. This happened several times more before Dick exclaimed, "That's the darnedest thing I *ever* seen!"

As he said it, the tidal sensation of Baba's love, the glow of *being loved,* washed over me. I could even smell that incense in the air again. It all clicked: orange butterfly; battering at my lips. And the whole time I'd been trying to decide whether to mention Baba. I excused myself, saying I had to fetch something I wanted Dick to read.

Back in the room, divinity was so tangible I started to weep from sheer joy. *I believe, I believe,* I told Baba, told myself. The room felt hallowed; I felt humbled and absurdly happy. I *hadn't* wasted my time. But, on the other hand, that bastard just wouldn't go away, would he?—and I'd have to take this into serious account before long. Time was running out, after all. It always is. Eighteen years had just trickled away without my noticing them.

I rejoined Dick and, now, Soo-Hyon, handing them *Sai Baba: Man of Miracles,* saying just that I thought they might like a glimpse of the local fauna.

"Soo-Hyon'll read it," Dick announced, pushing the book at her. "She likes that sort of thing, don't you, sweetheart?"

As he said that, and Soo-Hyon reached for the book, I knew it was intended for her, not him.

I was grateful. I promised I'd never let myself forget who Baba really was again. There was only one kingdom left in the empire of the soul that I needed to revisit now. Suddenly, I could see the end of the road.

Although God is omnipresent, there are places, as well as people, through which it is *easier* to look upon the Eternal.

13

"It Is Not My Fire That Burn You Here"

BENARES, 1992

❧ ❧ ❧

In the beginning the Divine Will arose.
This was the first seed from the Creator's mind.
Those who can see deeper by putting their mind and heart
together as one
Found the underlying essence of all existence was deep
beyond all that exists,
Found the non-existent existing in the existent.

—RIG VEDA 10.129.4

*H*ere you have the quintessence of classical Indian philosophy. Thinking with your heart; loving with your mind. All yoga and meditation aim to attain this one goal. Anything else is delusion, or worse. And when the heart sees, it sees the unknowable, nameless, formless, limitless, supreme God. He is called nonexistent because he is eternal, beyond existence. God manifest is the fabric of creation itself. They are one. The heart that learns to think realizes this truth and merges into the eternal oneness. As William Blake put it, "If the doors of perception were cleansed, everything would appear as it is, infinite."

This merging with the Eternal, this inner transformation, this direct experience of Truth—these are the goals of which the Vedic sages speak. They explain the nature of the universe, of life, while admitting that Creation itself is the one unknowable mystery.

As it did to the ancient Egyptians, to the priest-kings of the Vedic age, Creation indicated that point before which there was no Creator, the line between indefinable nothingness and something delineated by attributes and function, at least. Like the moment before the Big Bang. These concepts preoccupy high wisdom, the Truth far removed from mere religion.

Recent research and scholarship make it increasingly possible to believe that the Vedic era was the lost civilization whose legacy the Egyptians and the Indians inherited. There must have been one. There are too many similarities between hieroglyphic texts and Vedic ones, these in turn echoed in a somewhat diluted form and a confused fashion by the authors of Babylonian texts and the Old Testament.

> In the beginning there was darkness,
> Utter darkness, darkness upon darkness,
> The world then was merely its primordial essence, its formless
>   fabric.
> Thus what would become this world was first wrapped within
>   the all-pervading power of the Eternal One
> Before whom our material world is but a trifle brought into
>   existence
> By the omnipotent force of His will alone.
>
> —RIG VEDA 10.129.3

Yet the Vedas go further, being philosophy, or really spiritual science, rather than myth.

> Who truly knows, who can honestly say where
> this universe came from
> and where it will vanish to at the End?
> Those godlike wise men who claim they know were born long
>   after the birth of Creation.
> Who then *could* know where our universe really came from?
>
> And whoever knows or does not know where Creation came
>   from,
> Only one gazing at its vastness from the very roof of the final
>   heaven—
> Only such a one could possibly know.
> But does even He know?
>
> —RIG VEDA 10.129.7

The Bible begins with the Creation. Before the Creation, however, there was the Creator; but does even He know what was there before She existed? Long before such philosophical questions occurred to other historical peoples, Vedism posited the existence of something more ultimate than the one God: whatever must have created Him. *That* is presumably the absolute and basic reality. Or is it? This mystery of the connection between inaction and action is something the Vedas discuss endlessly—in each individual's life and as a universal principle.

This is mysticism that is simultaneously metalogic and the kind of thing those bardic sages living some twenty-five thousand years ago thought about a great deal, according to Hindu tradition. While the hymns of the Rig Veda are not the oldest *written* religious texts, they are, I believe, the oldest literary compositions. Indeed, they are the very first compositions mankind produced, dating back at least twenty thousand years. They are also the most sophisticated, most profoundly beautiful, and most complete presentations of what Aldous Huxley termed the "perennial philosophy" that is at the core of all religions. Many Hindu schools expound the Vedas as the original presentation of this universal Truth. This makes the Vedas, or "instruments of knowledge," a sort of user's manual for the universe, almost direct from the manufacturer.

Most orthodox historians and anthropologists strongly dispute such a view. They confuse writing with civilization and deny meaningful history to any peoples who did not leave a written record. A rich culture does not necessarily depend on writing, as the Celtic civilization proves.

Orthodox academics usually ascribe the composition of the major Vedic hymns to around 1500 B.C., although most will admit they were written down over a period that extended until at least the fifth century A.D.—two thousand years later. An oral tradition that long and that strong does not seem to make scholars consider the possibility of an oral tradition far preceding the first written records of the oral tradition's existence. The arbitrary 1500 B.C. happens to be the date when Vedic verses were probably first recorded by a culture that used writing.

In most of modern academia, of course, there is not supposed to be any "ancient wisdom."

※　※　※

I first went to Benares, the holiest place on earth for Hindus, in 1978, to study Sanskrit and Vedanta at the Sanskrit University there. Legend states that Siva himself still lives in the city. While I studied with Brahmin scholars whose lives and approach to Vedanta have scarcely changed in three thousand years, I became convinced that there was another version of what and when and where the Vedic age was. It's worth explaining briefly the argument behind this alternative version—if it prompts even one reader to take a look at the Vedic texts.

They hold within them enough information to rebuild human civilization from scratch, if necessary. I think someone did believe that might be necessary one day.

The Vedas still represent eternal truth in the purest form ever written. And they are what drew me to India in the first place, what kept me there, and what draws me back still.

First, it is essential to willingly suspend a belief in evolutionism in order to imagine the world I am going to describe—evolution as "progress," rather than change, I mean. Technology has certainly evolved at a rapid pace in the last century, when man began to gauge the quality of a civilization according to its level of technological advancement. However, Arnold Toynbee, the greatest historian of his age, maintained that the test for a major civilization was its fostering of a major religion.

The human race, in fact, reveals a marked deterioration in the quality of its advancement over the past five hundred years. It's made no *progress*. Yet Progress became a secular religion—even after Progress had advanced to the point of enabling mankind either to blast the planet into a radioactive wasteland or to poison it into uninhabitability. Better health care and global communications cannot be considered worth this kind of cost.

After Darwin, who was, to be fair, misunderstood, the concept undermined those sciences that developed around the same time as the theory of evolution—notably archaeology, Egyptology, and anthropology. Embraced by the academic orthodoxy, evolution-as-progress became intrinsic to the very thinking process of Western man, conditioned into him from early childhood on.

Above all, the notion of advanced civilizations, of "ancient wisdom" existing long before written history even began, was complete heresy in the Church of Progress. The great cultures of Old Kingdom Egypt and the Indus Valley were admired for the impressive remains they left, yet dismissed as ignorant and superstitious tyrannies dominated by megalomaniacal rulers obsessed with constructing monuments to their own egos and subjugating the masses with mumbo jumbo. There is not a shred of evidence to support such a view of, say, Old Kingdom Egypt.

The architectural achievements from such civilizations are feats of science and beauty that have never been equaled. Could evolution-as-progress be supported by a look at the Great Pyramid of Giza, the massive Temple of Amon at Karnac, the Qutub Minar, Chartres Cathedral, the Taj Mahal, compared to . . . what? The Empire State Building? Canary Wharf? The CN Tower? Marshall McLuhan once wisely observed that you could determine a society's major concerns by observing for what purpose its largest building was constructed.

Few scholars even bother to wonder whether philosophical and spiritual well-being were more advanced four thousand years ago at Memphis—and, more significantly, whether they were considered to be the only kind of advancement worth having.

Consider now a period still further back: the so-called missing-link period. Suddenly, mankind has all the organs and essentially the same appearance that he does today. This was not evolution, because no missing link exists to prove the theory; this is the apparent emergence of a new species. Neanderthal man is not our distant relative. He was incapable of growth—even survival—having a brain that lacked certain vital capabilities. While chimpanzees look vaguely human and can be taught certain basic skills, they can never develop further skills by themselves, cannot create a continuity, each generation building on the accomplishments of the previous one. Homo sapiens was not like this, and yet the species suddenly appeared.

Imagine. Man had no language, although he was fully equipped with vocal cords and organs of hearing. He had no vocabulary. He existed in an exquisite and pristine world, teeming with wildlife, lush with vegetation, the air so clear and clean he could see a hundred times more stars at night than we; he knew rivers sparkling with pure crystal water, gurgling streams and the songs of birds all the noise there was to compete with the drone of insects and wind in the leaves of mighty forests—besides the fearful, awe-inspiring crack of thunder. All these beauties and terrors—yet this man had no names for them? He moved, he sat, he ate, he drank, he slept—yet he had no terminology for such functions? Surrounded by color, a riot of it in an unrestrained, superabundant nature—white, red, green, azure, pink, yellow, black—but he had no terms for these obvious and dazzling differences?

It is at this moment, according to their own internal evidence, that the first hymns of the Rig Veda were composed and passed to this new species, our distant ancestors. Who composed them, however, is another question altogether. Whoever it was seems to have come from outside the society for which these hymns were composed. The level of understanding, knowledge, and wisdom contained in the Vedic hymns does not just spring out of nowhere. Nor does the language containing these, mankind's loftiest thoughts. Thoughts that also seem to have been mankind's first thoughts. This alone makes nonsense of "Progress."

The very first function of the earliest Vedic hymns is to assign names to objects in the natural world, and to assign these names in highly general terms. The great Rig Veda, in ten thousand verses, contains an astounding stock of some thirty-five thousand words, all of them imbued with great elasticity and enormous potentiality for the coining of new terms. This presents a strong argument for their representing the very start of language itself, the concept of human language. Through this means humans could communicate with fellow human being, and also establish a link with posterity for the first time. Without this desire to hand something on to the future, this instinct for stockpiling information, there would be no history, no culture, no science, no philosophy, no technology—no possibility of civilization—because there would be no continuity. Language, and language alone, made this possible. And it paved the way for Homo sapiens to become ruler of the earth.

The appearance of language is a miracle every bit as divine and ineffable as the Creation itself. For the Vedic sages, the three great Realities were Creator, Creation, and Language—all sacred, all interlinked. This was the knowledge passed on by men of staggering spiritual and temporal wisdom, preserved orally by the world's first priesthood—the Brahmanas, the original Brahmins—who impressed upon those to whom they in turn handed it on, apparently in a father-son chain, the crucial importance of not mispronouncing one single syllable. The link connecting the three great Realities should never be broken.

Above all, it is the harmony, the sheer orderliness of the universe that is stressed—and stressed so forcefully because it is humankind alone out of all creation that is capable of disrupting its serene and eternal harmony. For this, too, is the exact moment when humans acquire another extraordinary gift possessed by nothing else in all the universe: free will.

It is said in Hindu scriptures that the gods themselves envy human birth, because only within time is there free will and movement. Eternity in the Vedas is utter stillness; it exists entirely outside time, conceived of as that point where the future meets the past.

The present itself, then, is eternity, according to Vedanta, and only by stilling the mind through meditation can a person find the eternal present. Time is in the mind; one knows eternity, the very fabric of the universe, in the heart, the core where all things unite in complete harmony. Love, in the spiritual sense, recognizes our oneness with all creation and with what created it. The whole spiritual science that is Vedism concerns the overwhelming need to align human will with the will of the Eternal. This is conceived of as the purpose of human existence: that the many return to the One—*through their own volition*.

> Virtues and vices are linked forever
>   within the human body.
>
> When the Immortal Sculptor designed and
>   molded us, all manner of good and bad
> Came to dwell inside the mortal flesh,
>   came and made it their home.
>
> Greed, unkindness, hunger and thirst
> Live side by side there with generosity,
>   compassion, contentment, decency, and faith.
>
> Sorrow and joy, jealous hatred and love,
>   terrifying darkness, and dazzling brilliance,
> All are the warp and woof, the threads making up
>   that fabric named a human soul.
> The presence of these great opposites is
>   what makes a soul complete.
>
> Caged within the mortal frame of flesh,
>   this soul is called Brahman.
>
> —ATHARVA VEDA 11.8.30–32

It is generally claimed that the Aryan invaders brought the Vedic religion to India when they swarmed into the upper Indus basin some thirty-five hundred years ago. The nomadic Aryans lived around the area that is now northwestern Iran before their migration, and aspects of later Vedism resemble the religion of this region before the so-called reforms of Zoroaster, reforms that ultimately created a dualistic universe from the unity expounded in the Rig Veda. There is no stable principle of evil in Vedic philosophy. There is no infernal realm for sinners. Its nondualism is really beyond monotheism—which creates a fundamental duality of God and man. Evil is not envisaged as a quality opposed to good. It is the absence of good, just as darkness is the absence of light, not its opposite quality.

Because of these historical facts, some academics talk of an "Indo-Iranian" religion. But the Sanskrit of the Vedic verses also suggests a hypothetical Indo-European religion and language. Vedic Sanskrit may actually be that Indo-European language. The great nineteenth-century Sanskrit scholar Max Müller observed countless startling similarities between Sanskrit and languages like Greek, Latin, the Germanic, and the Slavic, many whole words being identical. If all languages shared a common source at an infinitely more remote period, this would be only natural.

If, however, we accept that the Vedas and language itself did not evolve within the hypothetical Indo-Aryan culture, but came from another source, fully formed from the very beginning, then it becomes easier to question whether the Aryans actually brought it to the Indus Valley, instead of finding it already there in some form. They might have simply merged the two forms into later Vedism and, eventually, Hinduism. The Aryans, whoever they were, might also have come from somewhere within the extreme northern part of the subcontinent itself. The point is that a spiritually oriented civilization indistinguishable from Vedism existed in northern India long before any Western invaders arrived.

Although research into this alternative theory is relatively recent, four discoveries are worth examination. In 1990, the *Journal of Indo-European Studies* carried an article entitled "Analysis of an Indo-European Vedic Aryan Head—Fourth Millennium B.C." The life-size head

> has a hairstyle that the Vedas describe as being unique to the family of Vasishtha, one of the great seers who composed parts of the *Rig-Veda*. The hair is oiled and coiled with a tuft on the right, and the ears are riveted. . . . Carbon-14 tests . . . indicate that it was cast around 3700 B.C., with an error in either direction of up to 800 years. . . . Stylistically the head is unique, with some parallels from the realistic torso that has survived from the Harappan era of the third millennium B.C. . . . Although identification of the head with

Vasishtha may yet be contested, it seems fairly certain that the head is Vedic.

Second, Professor Subhash Kak of Louisiana State University applied cryptological techniques in a computer analysis to prove a connection between Indus Valley scripts traced back to 7000 B.C. and the Brahmi script of India of about 500 B.C. "This suggests," he writes, "that the Indus language is likely to have been Sanskritic. . . . A well-known glyph that had been read as *sapta sindhu* based on some references in Sumerian literature is read identically when using my Indus-Brahmi theory. Another well-known inscription could be read as listing several Vedic gods."

Third, many texts of the late Vedic period, such as the Atharva Veda, Yajur Veda, several Brahamanas, the Upanishads, and the Mahabbarata epic—texts traditionally thought to date back to the first millennium B.C.—show a calendar that places the vernal equinox in Taurus (specifically the Pleiades). This corresponds to a date of around 2500 B.C. Georg Feuerstein and a few other scholars have also found references to the vernal equinox in Gemini and Cancer, suggesting 4000 to 6000 B.C.

Last, and most significant, is the more recent discovery that the majority of the ruins of Indus civilization are aligned not along the Indus River, but, as Georg Feuerstein writes,

> to the east on the now dry banks of a river that flowed roughly parallel to the Indus. The ancient river system on which this giant civilization was located has been called the Ghaggar, after the modern name of a small remnant of it, or the Sarasvati, after the traditional Hindu name for the river. . . . The Sarasvati is the most prominent river in the Vedas, where it is mentioned dozens of times and in greater detail than any other river. In fact, it is regarded as the very personification of the Divine Mother of the Veda herself. Subsequently, the Hindu Goddess of Wisdom and Inspiration was named Sarasvati. . . . The Sarasvati River was over five miles wide . . . If the Vedic people had not inhabited India while the Sarasvati was still a vital river, they could not possibly have referred to it with such intimacy in their scriptures. Thus, it follows that the people who gave us the *Rig-Veda* must have already been living in India many centuries, if not millennia, before the Sarasvati went dry around 1900 B.C. . . . The *Rig-Veda*, or at least portions of it, re-

flects a world that belongs not to 1500 B.C., as widely thought, but possibly to an age several thousand years earlier.

David Frawley of the American Institute of Vedic Studies sees in the Rig Veda the spiritual origin of humankind. His book *Gods, Sages and Kings* proposes a "spiritual model" of history, which posits that politicians or secular rulers did not found civilization; visionaries, sages, and mystics did. He also believes that the Sanskrit-speaking Aryans, the composers of the Rig Veda, hailed from the Himalayas and might have come down into the plains of northern India after the great flood all ancient mythologies record. This would suggest, he speculates, that the cradle of civilization might have been India rather than Sumer.

The Aryan-invasion theory, then—of blond, blue-eyed folk bringing great wisdom to dark-skinned people—looks suspiciously like a modern Progress-based myth. It may have more to do with racial theories popular around the turn of the century. These culminated in the Nazi Holocaust.

Certainly, the Aryans discovered no savage wasteland when they entered northern India. They emerged from the savanna of Central Asia with their religion and little else—if we accept conventional theory. As sophisticated as their philosophy indicates they were, the Aryans were nomadic and left very little evidence about their day-to-day existence. A little pottery, the odd burial mound: That's about it. They built from mud brick, wood, animal hides, and bamboo. What they found, though, was the Indus Valley civilization, a culture that had been thriving for some two thousand years when they "discovered" it, trading with the ancient Mesopotamian centers and building some one hundred cities along the river Indus, the major ones models of urban sophistication that rivaled those of Sumer or Middle Kingdom Egypt. Surrounded by high walls, laid out in grids, with advanced systems of water supply and drainage, centers like Harappa and Mohenjo-Daro were built to last. And, whatever the nomadic Aryans thought when they encountered this vast and sophisticated civilization, they could not have seen it as a primitive and ignorant land eagerly awaiting their culture. The Aryans were the ones who would benefit from the organized society they invaded. In any case, they seem to have absorbed what they found, and blended into it, quickly enough.

If the script found on thousands of terra-cotta seals in the excavations of the two major Indus-basin cities could be translated properly, we would know a little more about this civilization. The sites being worked are the largest archaeological excavations ever attempted, and progress is painfully slow, expensive, and plagued by bureaucratic and political problems. Yet, among the items already unearthed is a carved relief from the third millennium B.C. that clearly depicts a man sitting in the classic yogic lotus position, the position used solely for meditation. This discovery provided the first hard evidence that Vedic spiritual science, and particularly the meditation techniques that offered direct experience of Truth rather than faith, were certainly far from unknown in the Indus Valley.

The orthodox view, of course, is that the Indus-basin peoples had some kind of basic and animistic fertility cult going that easily succumbed to the obvious superiority of the Aryan religion. The evidence for this gratuitous insult is pitifully flimsy: several images of a fat female figure, ergo fertility cult. Orthodox anthropologists suggest that the Aryan religion was appealingly macho, and therefore easily overwhelmed the intrinsically feminine Mother Goddess cult—as if the whole of Vedic culture were a metaphor for rape. Hinduism began to develop out of Vedism around this time, however, the One fragmenting into many, as the Rig Veda warned it would if abandoned.

It was also time for a change. Not for the Aryans, but for all of humankind. The preceding millennia had seen dynamic leaps in humankind's understanding of and ability to work with the natural world. Cattle had been domesticated; lentils, rice, and barley had been cultivated; the foundations had been laid for the earliest physical and life sciences, particularly mathematics and astronomy. Even material progress was as dynamic during this period as it has been in the twentieth century.

Language made all of this possible. Man was firmly established as another, superior order of being—not an animal—and his relation to the natural world was changing. He could control that world, could create his own world. Or, to put it into Vedic terms, spirit was sinking farther into matter.

The astrological age of Aries the Ram was beginning, moving out of the age of Taurus the Bull. The image of the bull in cults all over the ancient world—Mithras, Montu—was disappearing. The rams of Amon emerged in Egypt; Moses brought the Decalogue down from Mount Sinai to find his people still worshiping a golden calf, the old bull god. Ever since Abraham sacrificed a ram instead of his son Isaac, the ram has been an important symbol in the Torah, and to this day the ram's horn is blown in synagogues on the holiest days of the Jewish year.

During the same period of upheaval, as one age blended into another, the Indus peoples set the stage for the emergence of the world's busiest religion. The move from Vedism's formless One God to Hinduism's estimated thirty-six million deities was no mean feat. It corresponds to the drying up of the Sarasvati River and the movement of Indian civilization east, to the wetter Ganges-Yamuna region, which is precisely where Hindu scriptures composed after the Vedas, such as the Puranas, place it. The Vedas show the geography of the ancient India of the Indus and the pre-Indus eras, but not of the later period commonly associated with the so-called Aryan invasion.

What was happening all over the ancient world around 1500 B.C. transformed religion. It was moving out of the hands of an elite priesthood or hierarchy of initiates and adopting forms that ordinary people could understand. From gods and sages emerged the age of kings and heroes. Few can relate to a formless and unknowable entity. Thus the disputatious Children of Israel received the Law written on stone tablets, and the warring, fun-loving tribes of India got a mythology as colorful and heterogeneous as they were themselves. Such was the age of Aries, with no major changes in religion until the Piscean era introduced the further reforms of Pythagoras, the Buddha, Mahavir, Confucius, Jesus, and others.

In the Vedic scheme of vast universal cycles, which move above the astrological ages, moved still greater ones many thousands of years long, the *yugas*. In this system, the whole of known history has been in Kali yuga—the age of heavy metal, of gross materialism. The cyclical concept was still expounded by Renaissance philosophers like Giambattista Vico in his *Scienza Nuova:* an age of gods, an age of heroes, an age of men, and then a *ricorso,* or return to the beginning. W. B. Yeats's concept of "gyres" contains similar ideas. Early Vedism ushered in the age of gods; Hinduism and Judeo-Christianity and, later, Buddhism and Islam are very much products of an age of heroes. We are now quite clearly in an age of men, and signs of the ricorso are appearing everywhere, although Kali yuga has several millennia yet to run. . . .

> He is without any form, yet dwells inside and outside all things
>   with form and shape,
> Yet He is entirely free of error, faultless and pure.

He is far beyond anything a human body can comprehend,
And being the Divine Poet, He is inspiration itself.
He maintains peace and harmony because He is both peace and
   harmony made manifest.
Thus He sustains His Creation in its perfect order.

—YAJUR VEDA 10.8

He is present in all places and rules everywhere.
His power controls utterly all the three regions:
Earth, the Middle-Air, and the highest heavens.
One foot is rooted in things we understand;
But the other rests in a realm of deep, dark mystery,
A place far beyond the knowledge of mankind.

—ATHARVA VEDA 7.26.4

He pervades all things, He is changeless and supreme,
More pure than even the purest,
Yet he dwells inside the hearts of those who seek Him;
He is the inspiration behind all holy words uttered by priests at
   the altars.
Yet he is treasured, like a dear guest in our home.

He is the substance of every great eternal law,
And He can be perceived in the universal forces of life.
His presence is there in the vast seas,
   across the teeming earth,
   and in the soaring mountain peaks.

—RIG VEDA 4.40.5

Hardly polytheism. Long before the burgeoning Hindu pantheon; long before Siva, Vishnu, Rama, Ganesh, Parvati, Saraswati, Laxmi, and the 35,999,993 others, this is the God of the Vedas, and religion in its most pristine form.

As "spiritual science," Vedism and other ancient forms of high wisdom relate *knowledge* to God. Knowledge of God's creation cannot be achieved without the Creator. Whether physics or metaphysics, both refer ultimately to the source of Creation. This world is thus a sourcebook for study.

The Sanskrit language is especially revealing: *Para vidya* is mundane knowledge; *apara* vidya is the knowledge of ultimate reality. One leads to the other. Within the body are dimensions beyond scientific understanding: How do the sensory organs and brain function, for example, in the case of music? The outer world is viewed as a reflection of the inner or absolute world. "As above, so below" was the way Hermes Trismegistus put it.

In the para vidya, the lower stages, the disciplines of knowledge are distinct and separate. But what biology is not also physics? What hearing is not also seeing? What knowing is not also feeling? And the micro leads to the macro: In apara vidya, all disciplines merge into one. The Vedas see this ultimate Truth behind all ephemeral truths. The Creation leads us to the Creator, to the highest knowledge, which is integrated into one.

Some Vedic hymns paint the exquisite glories of the natural world: the preternatural beauty of predawn light, its rosy fingers holding the iridescent steel-blue sky; some celebrate the welcome cool of evening, the scented breezes of a calm and refreshing night, its basalt dome studded with shimmering pearls and diamonds. Beauty permeates them, a reflection of Truth.

Other hymns concentrate on different aspects of nature's wonder, very specific in their knowledge of the great cycles that sustain life. Vedic writings detail a scientific knowledge of the rain cycle that startles with its accuracy.

The Vedic term for rain clouds is *vrittra,* and they are described with a dozen or more names: demons, serpents, boars. Similarly, the sun has many names. These verses delight in describing the endless conflict between Indra, the sun, and the dark forces of the "shrouder," the clouds that conceal light and warmth. Indra, of course, is ultimately the victor, but the story is endlessly repeated, the poet of the Vedas never tiring of it. The quintessential Indian climate, and the way it absolutely dominates human life, are strong arguments indeed regarding *where* the Vedas were composed. Just as early Christian interior architecture was designed to resemble the forest glades of the pagan faith that the new religion supplanted—for example, British churches were often built upon the same sites and with the same rock used in pagan stone circles—so Vedism tried to speak in terms that the people it was converting could understand.

The outer conflict of sun and clouds was a parable for the constant battle between our own higher nature and our lower one. The great Ga-yathri mantra, most sacred of all the Vedic chants, can be translated simply as

> Lead me from darkness to light.
> Lead me from ignorance to knowledge.
> Lead me from death to immortality.

All religions perform an inner, or spiritual, function and an outer, or societal, purpose. The laws of the Torah lay the foundation for a just and harmonious society, and they also indicate a way of aligning the inner being to great eternal laws, the perfect harmony of the Universal, of God. Jesus' teaching of love adds to Moses' Decalogue, a commandment to love that really summarizes the Law, yet also enables its followers to attain oneness with the eternal. Pythagoras' number mysticism describes the mathematical harmony of the universe, and shows how the structure of music relates to the great order of the heavens. Confucius defined a just and harmonious society as one that obeys natural laws. The Buddha said the path to enlightenment begins with recognizing natural truths and merging the individual self with them, aligning it to universal law in order to achieve oneness with reality. The Vedas go much further in outlining the nature of reality than any other religious texts still in use.

Like the Creator, human beings create, but humankind's creations are separate from humans themselves. The Vedic God is an architect whose structures all exist *within* him. Nothing can exist outside the Supreme Reality, and it in turn is *within* all:

> It is always moving, yet it never moves.
> It is infinitely far away, yet it is so close,
> It is within all of this creation,
> And yet it is beyond everything.
>
> —YAJUR VEDA 22.5

Vedic terminology for "creation" implies that it is the steady process transforming *asat,* the unmanifest, into *sat,* the manifest. In this sense, the entire space-time continuum, all the vastness and infinite variety of creation, exists *within* the existence of the Eternal One—as if it were a concept in his mind. God is also called *hiranyagarbha,* the "Womb of Light."

The Womb of Light existed before there was any other thing. It gave birth to all. It is the sole ruler of all existence, maintaining and upholding everything between earth and heaven. To this Lord alone, and to no others, we should offer all our love and respect.

—RIG VEDA 10.121.1; ATHARVA VEDA 4.2.7

This Supreme Reality is not a mere abstract concept of philosophy, either. It is a reality in the Vedas, whose invocation and evocation are essential for the whole process of spiritual growth and the fulfillment of life. God is a dynamic reality that should concern an individual every moment of his life. We forget this, or ignore it, but many hymns remind us that God never neglects us.

God is always near, He never leaves. But near as He always is, no one and no thing ever sees Him. Such is the great Art of the Lord—Poetry that is deathless, Songs that will never seem old.

—ATHARVA VEDA 10.8.32

Vedic invocations, which are deemed animistic and crudely pagan by many scholars, merely invoke God through his attributes and functions. He is the Force behind all of nature's mighty forces, the Light behind light; the Terror behind terror; the Delight behind delights; the Ultimate Activity behind all activities. These forces and qualities are praised and admired in the hymns, but as a way of drawing closer to the One behind and within them.

Similarly, God's various names in the Vedas are the one God viewed in terms of his attributes, functions, and nature. There is no real suggestion of anything besides the One.

The Yajur Veda (60.17) states that, removed from the context of its creation and its relationship as the ruler of souls, the Ultimate Reality would have only one name: Om, which is written in Sanskrit and pronounced more like *Aum,* and represents the utterly comprehensive syllable, embracing within it the scope of the complete phonetic alphabet containing the potential to create, sustain, and bring about dissolution. When it is uttered correctly, the mouth proceeds from being fully open through all stages toward being tightly closed, lips pursed, the final *mmm* almost inhaled, vibrating low back in the throat—the opposite of the initial exhaled *aaa* sound.

> In the beginning was the Word, and the Word was with God, and
> the Word was God. All things were made by him; and without him
> was not any thing made that was made. In him was life; and the
> life was the light of men. And the light shineth in darkness; and the
> darkness comprehended it not.
>
> —THE GOSPEL ACCORDING TO SAINT JOHN 1:1–5

Saint John's account of the Creation begins at an earlier moment than
the Genesis account, and its similarity to Vedic writings is startling. The
gospel is the most mystical of the four included in the standard New Testament, although others excluded by the early Vatican councils, like that
of Saint Thomas, also contain philosophically deeper material. The author seems to be familiar with more abstruse concepts of spiritual science,
even if his translators are not. The original version of Saint John uses the
Greek term *logos,* which Latin translators rendered as *verbum*—hence
"Word." But logos is a mystical term quite common in the writings of
Plotinus and the Neoplatonists, where it is used to designate something
closer to the Vedic Om. The word is usually left untranslated by those
English writers who deal with Greek mysticism—to indicate the impos-
sibility of rendering it accurately.

Occasionally, logos is also applied to Jesus, thus becoming part of the
Trinity, associating this concept even more closely with the three Vedic
Realities. A common Indian legend has Jesus studying in India before returning to the Holy Land and starting his ministry. The Wise Men from
the East are also often popularly identified as Indian rishis, the term implying both seer and king, and Jesus is said to have returned to India after
the crucifixion, a punishment which rarely killed people, and lived there
until his natural death many years later. Indeed, I was once even shown
what was alleged to be his tomb, in Kashmir. Reality is less important
than myth.

But the comparison between a great deal of Jesus' actual teachings, as
recorded in the Gospels, and Vedic spiritual science continues to fascinate scholars. Considering controversies caused by material in the Dead
Sea Scrolls, as well as other texts suppressed or even quite clearly falsified,
it seems foolish to dismiss any speculation.

The Torah opens with an account similar to Saint John's, though more
prosaic. At times it seems confused, and it is clearly not the basis of Saint
John. In Genesis, God creates light twice—on the first day and, as if for-

getting he's done it, again on the fourth day. One cannot blame the translators here so much as the author, who seems to be adapting something
from a cultural tradition that his own language does not yet have the terminology for.

As the kabalists of Jewish mysticism point out, the first "light" is a different kind of light from the light of the sun, moon, and stars created on
the fourth day. In the Kabala, God is a limitless light, unknowable, beyond all, yet gradually manifest through a series of descents into more material realms—the process of Creation.

Much of Jewish mysticism, which is the real heart of the religion, all
but scorned since the so-called Enlightenment, closely resembles the spiritual science of both ancient Egypt and the Vedas. All three demonstrate
a reverence for language, the belief that words have power, and that some
combinations of words should be hidden from the uninitiated. All three
describe God through various attributes rather than by name. It is thus
curious that Judaism—in which it is forbidden to speak or write God's
name in full—consistently uses the same attributes and is thought of as
monotheistic because of this, whereas Vedism, which gives different
names to different functions or attributes, is thought of as polytheistic.
Actually, Judaism *could* employ one name because it was essentially dualistic—God is very separate from man—and Vedism, which was nondualistic, not even monotheistic, is considered polytheistic because of the
very practice that characterizes its nondualism: seeing God in everything.
Comparisons with the ancient Egyptian texts, the spiritual context out of
which Judaism emerged, are worth noting:

> I am the Eternal Spirit,
> I am sunrise over the Primeval Ocean.
> My soul is called God, I created the Word.
> I abhor evil, and thus I do not see it.
> I created the perfect harmony in which I dwell,
> I am the deathless Word,
> Which lives forever in my name of "Soul."
>
> —BOOK OF THE DEAD, COFFIN TEXTS, SPELL 307
> (ELEVENTH DYNASTY, c. 2,000 b.c.)

Just as language is divine, itself constituting a parable of creation, so society reflects the nature of creation in its structure; and the human body

contains a version of the eternal, its parts and proportions the measure of all things temporal, just as the universe is the body of the Timeless. In the Vedas, the human body is an entire world of its own, ruled by the soul, with sense organs as lieutenants, and so on.

A yagna was any organized attempt to improve the human condition. It was a selfless act, technically a sacrifice and therefore considered sacred. Too many evolutionist scholars, however, want to believe the yagnas were merely primitive, superstitious, and barbaric events involving ritual slaughter of animals, or worse. They even insist that fire was worshipped rather than employed as a symbol. Such events, to the evolutionist's eye, after all, were a well-known feature of many primitive cultures.

Fire was a great mystery to those who could not control or harness it. Accordingly, the Vedic hymns speak in terms the less developed people receiving them would have instantly understood. The Vedic seers seem to have taught the process by which fire could be created at will, tamed, and used. The yagnas appear to be part of this teaching process, ensuring that the art is passed down to posterity. I watched a traditional yagna at the Dasara festival in Puttaparthi that began with the symbolic creation of the sacred fire by Brahmin pundits, who, in the ancient manner, twirled a stick with a bow in wood shavings until they ignited.

There were minor yagnas and major ones. The earliest Vedic writings, the Samhitas, refer to a "Cosmic yagna," the ritual of nature's cycles: sunshine, clouds, rain, the growth and death of vegetation, and so on. The yagna obviously related to far more than ritual sacrifice and sacred fires. In fact, the entire eighteenth chapter of the Yajur Veda explains yagnas as any selfless action that contributed to society's general good. A large number of verses end with the same refrain—*yagnena kalpatam*—concerning each person's duty to continue exploring new ways to use nature's limitless resources for the common good.

Out of this came a frenzy of exploration and discovery perhaps equalled only by that seen over the past century or so, but with very different consequences. Flora and fauna were studied intensively, their multifarious uses—medicine, pigment, food, textile, labor—carefully documented. Organic and inorganic resources were surveyed. What were essentially the foundations for a welfare state were even laid. The science and craft of agriculture were developed; animals were domesticated; countless natural resources were adapted for use as food, clothing, tools, housing. The list is endless. And all of this dynamic activity stemmed from the *yagna-*

*shala*s, the ritual centers that served as open-air laboratories, observatories, and academies. There, anything and everything that might advance and enlighten society was studied.

To subjugate and destroy a culture, of course, which is a major facet of every imperial adventure, you *have* to regard it as worthless, savage, and primitive. You can then avoid the guilt that could otherwise spoil everything. Not coincidentally in this context, the age of Darwin was also the great age of the British Raj in India.

Subjugated, certainly, the Vedic spiritual science was never totally destroyed. Aspects of it survived at the core of many later religions. The original pure form itself, after so many millennia, is practiced by isolated groups and expounded by holy men like Sathya Sai Baba and Ramana Maharshi. Even some of the chants and hymns—in a language related to, but more ancient than, Sanskrit—are recited during ritual ceremonies. Vedic pundits in different parts of the country—some of whom are unable to read the original texts for themselves—can still recite from memory ten thousand or more Vedic verses with only a handful of minor variations. These feats of memorization were common in the ancient world. To us, they prove that the original intonations were preserved, passed down over the long centuries in that highly precise oral tradition established when language itself first began.

Only a tiny part of the Vedic corpus was ever written down. So very sacred were the words considered that to write them down would have destroyed their power and violated the sacred trust. Only part of these writings has survived. Yet the texts that do exist are copious, enormously long, and bewilderingly varied in content. Scarcely an aspect of life is not dealt with somewhere.

A person in the Vedic age is not considered an individual, but rather a social organism, with responsibilities to both fellow beings and the whole natural world. It is a vision of a coordinated life. A man or woman lives, works, and dies for society. All things are integral to the Creator, who made them and moves within them. Great importance is placed on dynamic activity, the striving to improve society's lot, to enjoy a happy present, and work for an even happier future. Between inaction and action is choice, free will. The Vedas seek to guide and influence this free will in order to ensure good rather than harm from the gift, for the individual and for society.

To us, such ideas seem Utopian. Traces of the Vedic age can be found

today deeply embedded in the Indian psyche: the admiration for selflessness, for austerity, for piety—particularly in the nation's leaders. Even the
reverence for language can be detected, albeit in a grossly debased form,
in that incorrigible predilection for public speaking found in even the
humblest official. Few Westerners can stand up before a crowd and speak
without notes for an hour or more with ease, even if the effect is frequently rambling, repetitive, and excruciatingly boring. Yet this kind of
oratory has its genesis in the mnemonic devices taught in the yagnasha-
las, where recitation and discourse seem to have been highly valued—as
they were to the ancient Greeks and the medieval grammarians.

Big yagnas are rare now, but Vedic rituals, with chanted hymns and
mantras, are still performed at those functions that once symbolized man's
integration into society, especially marriage. Now they are largely empty
gestures, excuses for a party. But if society in general has degenerated,
many members of Indian society continue to cherish Vedic ideals. Om
is still chanted; and Brahman, a neutral-gender noun, remains a name for
God. Language, our making, also contains the seeds of our downfall, fragmenting the One Reality. The Vedic seers seemed to know this, too,
which is why their hymns constantly urge man never to lose sight of the
unity in creation. In a dualistic world, language is merely a tool by which
one can eventually understand the underlying unity of reality.

A postal clerk you meet in a third-class Indian train carriage will expound such matters if you let him. Swathed in the motley bandages of
Hinduism, the invisible man of Vedism is present yet on Indian streets—
and probably will be until the golden age returns and the Womb of Light
swallows all her children.

The last *mahayagna,* the last truly major Vedic sacrifice, was held in
1946, as the world reeled drunkenly out of an orgy of bloodshed, geno-
cide, and unprecedented destruction culminating in Hiroshima and the
prospect that the next bender the planet went on might be its last. India,
too, was on the brink of civil war and chaos then, Hindu fighting Muslim, blood literally flowing in the streets, and the British nobly deciding
that, since there wasn't much left to steal anyway, after a two-hundred-
year looting spree, this was a good time to leave the colony to sort out
its own problems.

A great female Bengali saint, Ananda Mayi Ma, supervised the mahayagna. It was performed on the banks of the Ganges at Benares, and
lasted without interruption for *three years,* from January 14, 1946, until

January 14, 1949. It included ten million sacred offerings and ten million chantings of Gayathri, the supreme Vedic mantra, the plea to be led from the unreal to the Real. In keeping with the ideals of the ancient yagna-shalas, the purpose of this unimaginably complex undertaking was to "promote the welfare of the entire world." Only in India could such a project be realized in the twentieth century.

To be in Benares while becoming steeped in Vedism was, for me, to come as close to the soul of India as I imagine is possible for a Westerner.

Today Benares (also called Kashi, Varanasi, or Banaras, and briefly re-named Muhammadabad by the Moghul emperor Aurangzeb, for obvi-ous reasons) may be the oldest city on earth. Even if it is not, it *is* unquestionably the holiest place on earth for a Hindu. Every Hindu yearns to visit that one place of pilgrimage, and hopes to die there, too. For those who do die here are said not to go straight to heaven (as a Chris-tian might wish), but to finally escape the wheel of birth and death for-ever. No one seems to know who said this or where it is written, yet all believe it. The Hindu views heaven as a place where the good are pun-ished before they return once more to this great stage of fools.

If one city can ever represent anything so vast and so sensationally het-erogeneous as Hindu India, Benares—called Kashi in the legends—is that city. It is where the very first king built the very first city in a forest dense with sacred kusha grass, a "City of Light," a "City of Knowledge." It is Siva's city, entirely dedicated to him, and he is believed to live here still, watching over all the two-thousand-odd temples dedicated to him. And Kashi still feels as if Siva lives there: It is fierce; full of death; austere yet grandly beautiful; sinister, if not dangerous; and singularly attractive.

During my first night there, walking the maze of pitch-dark or blaz-ingly overlit alleys and bazaars weaving down toward the ghats, the tiers of long stone steps leading to the Ganges, I felt as if I had entered a zone linked invisibly but tangibly to another world, a realm more subtle and more powerful than ours.

Figures wearing long, grotesque white hoods—a sort of Ku Klux Klan minidress—thrust oarlike poles into the blazing funeral pyres on the burning ghats, the riverside cremation grounds, shifting a sizzling human thigh to where the flames were more intense. Skulls popping. Bodies wrapped in shrouds, like mummies, awaiting their turn. The shrouds white—except the red ones, which identify women who have died be-fore their husbands. The fires burning night and day; the supply of corpses endless. Shielded from the heat, the final fire, these stokers in their hoods seem nonchalant about their job. Huddled groups of friends and relatives watching husbands, wives, fathers, mothers, even children—sorrowful, stunted little bundles—go forever, purified by flame into ash, the ash then pouring into the soul of Ganga Mata, Mother Ganges. The goddess flows out from the sacred Himalayas, realm of gods and saints, to sanctify the land on her 1,250-mile journey to the eternal ocean.

Only children under five and saints are not burned. Instead, they are "buried" in the Ganges. But a pyre requires up to eight hundred pounds of sandalwood logs—sold just behind the main burning ghat—and ghee, clarified butter, is the traditional fuel. Many cannot afford the cost of cremation. Not only babies and saints end their days consumed by the element of water rather than fire. In my experience, wild pariah dogs perform a fair bit of water's job now.

A curious calm hung over these burning grounds. Despite the smoke, the crackling of several pyres, the sparks shooting up to join the vast skein of stars above us, the *aghoris*—naked ascetics who sit in meditation near the cremation grounds—and despite ghostly hooded stokers, there was a resigned inevitability about it all. There is no real sadness about death in Hinduism, especially death in Benares. It is part of an endless cycle. The Vedic idea that life implies death—is life's only absolute certainty—also implies that there is no cause for grief. For death also implies life.

The eldest son performs the most important task in this final ritual. He lights the pyre and, when the body has burned, tosses a container full of Ganges water over his shoulder into the embers, walking away without ever looking back. For the next month he performs further rituals, eating only food he has prepared himself. This final ceremony alone is one reason the Hindu places such importance on having a son. Those involved with cremation, the process of destroying all traces of an individual life, are also subject to dangers.

Aghoris, sadhus clad only in ashes from the funeral pyres, are feared as much as they are revered. Their waist-length hair matted into coils with cow dung, they make no attempt to seem part of our species. Some Hindus suspect them of diabolical rituals involving corpses and the souls of the dead. They have no Western equivalent.

Other people involved in these last rites on the banks of the Ganges are also essential to the rituals' purity, yet are condemned by the caste system for their involvement in it. The doms are Untouchables who manage the burning ghats and provide the fire that lights the pyre. Scripture assigns them the vital task of ensuring that cremation leads to the deceased's salvation. Yet their task is considered unclean: Dead matter is ritually impure, and those who provide the fire that burns it take on the karma of the deceased. This, yet again, is a typical Indian paradox. Here in Benares, you find the greatest anomaly in the caste system, and its only obvious traditional advantage. The doms are supervised by the *dom raja,* the "king of the Untouchables," perhaps Benares's most infamous citizen, and also reputedly one of the wealthiest men in India. What is the price for taking on someone's karma? In 1992, I asked the man himself.

☙ ☙ ☙

Back in the seventies I'd lived in a converted palace on the banks of the Ganges. It was owned by Mataji, a wealthy California woman of White Russian descent. She'd spent thirty years studying yoga and meditation with various gurus in India, and then brought the crumbling maharaja's palace and turned it into an ashram of sorts—really more a hostel—for Westerners on the road seeking something in the subcontinent, the way she once had.

All along the west bank of this great curve in the Ganges, which has been likened to the shape of the new moon that Siva wears as a crown, are palaces, most still belonging to the great princely families of India. They seem forlorn, decayed, abandoned now. But they are not. Like the tides in the lagoon at Venice, the waters of the Ganges are capricious, rising thirty feet or more during the monsoon flood. Thus, ground-floor rooms exist through expediency only—as do the many steps leading down to the Ganges. At flood tide the river reaches or exceeds the upper steps. In late July 1992, the monsoon had so far failed, and the great steps, the ghats, descended some fifty feet before reaching water level.

Layer on layer, side by side, the palaces and temples jockey for position above the ghats along nearly two miles of the west bank. Across the Ganges, which is nearly a third of a mile wide here, the east shore is empty. Only Ramnagar Fort, the maharaja of Benares's palace, is visible on that side, far to the south. Some will tell you this is because only the king of the holiest city was allowed to build on the eastern shore. In fact, nothing *could* be built there. When the Ganges floods, the entire area north of Ramnagar is a swamp. Yet the effect is odd, haunting: This swarming city of some million and half souls confined to one side of the river, daily watching the sun rise over the deserted eastern bank.

Mataji was an ethereal presence. She said little, and expected the same from her guests. I had a Spartan room: charpoy, table, chair. There was no charge, and food was my business. I ate out, or, if invited, ate with other guests. An atmosphere of stillness, of inner concentration, reigned. People came and went. We all accepted that what we were doing was only our concern. If it wasn't, we should question why we were doing it. It was as close to a truly monastic life as I have ever come. Much like the Brahmachari Vedic schools where I spent my days studying: an austere yet loving existence. I feel fortunate to have known such days from another age and to have been able to study Vedic philosophy and Sanskrit under such conditions. I cannot imagine studying such knowledge under any other.

By 1992, however, I had changed. I felt truly submerged in matter as I checked in at the Taj Ganges Hotel, not Mataji's. It was nowhere near the Ganges, as it turned out, which disappointed me until I realized why: the floods, the ceaseless noise. For this Indian city, more than any other, can shock the fragile sensibilities of the Westernized traveler. It's not poverty you find here—it's the absolute core of a living faith so alien to Westernized minds that it can seem terrifying.

To outsiders, pagan evil flourishes in all its vileness and wanton perversity in India: worship of the phallus, of animals, of sensuous goods, of a goddess who devours human skulls, of gods who destroy; and the propitiation of demonic forces, fertility figures, entities with power over natural elements. Downtown Benares makes Hieronymous Bosch look like Norman Rockwell. And it's real—not an ethnic spectacle laid on for tourists used to visiting dead cultures and having them revived for their entertainment.

Demonic is an expression I have often heard employed to describe Hinduism. The first Christian missionaries used it when they encountered outlandish customs and ceremonies that reminded them of those abominations Jehovah wiped from the face of the earth in the Bible. Idolatry. Strange gods. Golden calves. Yet the first Commandment does not say there *are* no other gods—merely that "thou shalt have no other gods before me." Nietzsche once said that the old gods laughed themselves to death when a god proclaimed there was only one God.

Conversion has largely failed in India because Christianity offers noth-

ing that is not already available somewhere in the many forms of Hinduism—Hinduism never rejected the teachings of Jesus. Those who have
converted either agreed with a gun pressed to their skulls, as in Goa, or
because it provided an escape from caste tyranny, as well as guaranteed
professional advancement. Legend has it that Saint Thomas was martyred
in Madras after failing to win a debate on theology with local Brahmin
pundits. He agreed to accept death if he lost the debate. *Vanitas vanita-
tum.*

Through its Vedic legacy, Hinduism respects all faiths. It clearly states
that God is one, but has many forms. The Christian message must sound
preposterous: that God is indeed one, but has only one recognized form,
his son.

The "savages" of India were sophisticated—so sophisticated that the
imperialist mixture of church and state in Europe could not grasp such
sophistication. The British were more cunning at the game than the Portuguese, careful to show respect for Indian religions. Yet they sneered at
the pagans behind their backs, educated the Indian elite in British-run
schools, or at Eton and Cambridge—which, if it did not guarantee conversion to Christianity, resulted in lapsed Hinduism, agnosticism, or an
intellectual humanism. They had not banked on Marxism as another option. Nehru leaned that way, but in the manner of a Cambridge idealist.

In India, Anglo indoctrination produced a generation of "brown
sahibs" who looked down on the religion of the masses, the opium of
the people. Rajiv Gandhi's downfall can be attributed to a milder form
of this same conditioned insensitivity. So can his mother's murder.

Twenty years ago, all talk of modernization in New Delhi constantly referred to educating the masses, a euphemism for destroying the excesses
of Hinduism.

In 1992 it was a different story. Narasimha Rao was in his second term
as prime minister. Few had thought he would win one, but he had. No
fundamentalist Hindu fanatic, he was, however, as I knew firsthand, a
deeply religious man. To clear up Rajiv's mess, he needed to be—and
with the wisdom of Solomon. The mess Rajiv had generously added to
had been piling up for centuries.

It was Mahatma Gandhi who scared the British, not Jawaharlal Nehru.
The sheer power of Hinduism terrified the Christian soldiers, and Gandhi

embodied that, embraced it, used it. He was, or his public image was, Vedic Hinduism incarnate. Fortunately for the British, he was genuinely spiritual, and his principles were unshakable. One could argue that Partition was pushed so hard because, beyond a farewell divide-and-rule, it would also guarantee that Mahatma Gandhi would not pull the strings of India's first independent government.

Opposed to the division of India, convinced that Hindu and Muslim could live side by side, as they had done, Gandhi chose to face chaos rather than partition. Finally he lost even Nehru's support over the issue. Thus Britain got the man it had nurtured for the role, Nehru, in power, his umbilical cord to Gandhi severed. And the imperialists left their man to cope with insoluble problems, problems that could not fail to lead to war with Pakistan. Gandhi realized this.

Those naive days of exhilaration following independence after so very long, freedom's euphoria, have evaporated now. It was a long party, but India is sober once more, finally learning to take control. Such are the effects of colonialization that a whole generation must pass before the paralyzing spell wears off.

❧ ❧ ❧

Everything in India has subtext upon subtext—a palimpsest. And Benares, along with all else, is an architectural palimpsest. Buildings built upon buildings, palaces on palaces, temples upon temples, the place is a layer cake of history. But it's unlikely any archaeologist will ever get permission to excavate it: Every inch is holy ground.

Rishikesh, Allahabad, Hardwar: The great Mother Ganges sanctifies many cities as she flows from the sacred Himalayan peaks, twisting and turning south through the parched lowlands. Like so many rivers in myth and imagination, the meanderings of Mother Ganges represent the inexorable wanderings of life itself. The image, of course, is in the Vedas, part of that great cycle: sun, cloud, rain, river, ocean, sun, cloud.

The Ganges is not always a gentle mother. Sometimes she overflows her banks, washing away homes, temples, palaces. Sometimes she withholds her life-giving waters, running so low that the fields shrivel and die, the *dhobis* wash clothes in mud, corpses get lodged on rocks and tree stumps, vultures circle above, the air stinks of waste and death.

Kashi has been flooded countless times. Even now, parts are still sinking gradually from sight. Near Harischandra Ghat, the main burning

ground, an entire monolithic temple the size of a small house lies half submerged, at an angle in the waters, a leaning temple of Kashi. I pointed it
out to my companion, the dom raja's son.

"Not sinking," he assured me. "Temple is offering itself to goddess
Ganga."

How many other temples had offered themselves to Ganga Mata over
the millennia? Is the oldest city on earth down there?

It was certainly thriving as a religious and commercial center long before Babylon, long before Solomon built his temple. Buddhist scriptures
describe Kashi as a great center of civilization 2,500 years ago. They should
know: The Buddha preached his first sermon in the deer park at Sarnath,
five miles northwest of the city.

Capricious as Ganga Mata can be, she is never angry for long. She fa-
vors Kashi above all cities, for here Ganga reaches her southernmost
point, embracing the home of Siva in her broad cool arm before returning north toward the home of the gods. Eventually she bursts into a fountain of rivulets before falling into the arms of that awesome Father waiting
eternally in the Bay of Bengal. . . .

❧   ❧   ❧

How out of touch with India I'd become. I asked the hotel to deliver a
letter to the dom raja requesting an interview. I wasn't surprised later
when the messenger said he couldn't locate the dom raja's palace. This
was like a New York courier claiming he couldn't find Rockefeller Center. Why was I trying to do things this way?

Benares scared me, was why. Those long months I'd spent studying
the Vedas at the Sanskrit University nearly two decades before scared me.
The 150,000 manuscripts to which my Brahmin pundit had then allowed
me free access scared me. I had been allowed to transcribe texts no one
had opened in hundreds of years, let alone translated—just to practice my
Sanskrit. In Benares, scholars simply assumed that I studied as they did,
as those who *lived,* as well as studied, their subject, in search of *real* knowledge.

I had never really doubted the wisdom I'd come to find and had found
here. I had no questions about the big issues. Even death no longer really scared me. And I was even finally at peace with Sathya Sai Baba.

I looked hard for exactly what *did* scare me. And I found it: *I scared
myself.* Why had the wisdom my mind had absorbed so long before not

moved into my heart, my body, my life? Reading a memo does not stop you starving.

I was back in Benares, where some generous fate, and Baba's inspiration, had given me exactly what I'd asked for long ago. But what I had *asked* for was clearly not what I *needed*. Perversely, I now wanted to meet the dom raja, the "shrouder"—not any Sanskrit pundit, no holy man, no sadhu, saint, or astrologer. I wanted to meet the untouchable king of death, the man said to have amassed a fortune in the tens of billions by taking upon himself the karma, the sins, the unknown crimes of the uncountable men and women he burned with the flame from his sacred fire.

Somehow I felt this hanged god, this inverted Christ who had voluntarily assumed the sins of the world—*for a price*—had something to say directly to me now. It seemed as if we might have a great deal in common.

I met Amar, one of the dom raja's sons, at Dashashvamedha Ghat, where the whole city seems to pour through a funnel into the river. An overcast sunset grazed through teasing clouds, and bells were ringing in hundreds of temples. The monsoon had not yet come here, either. The Ganga Arati, the evening hymn to Mother Ganges, blared out of a hundred rattling tin speakers.

An unpleasantly soft and perfumed man in a silk kurta had approached me, saying, "Massage, sahib? Two rupee?" I had refused, but he then had taken my hands and started firmly massaging the fingers and wrists. It felt quite pleasant.

I said I was looking for the dom raja.

"You take massage, sahib. I send boy with message for Dom Raja's man. *Mass*age finish, *mess*age arrive—*he* come. Yes?"

All along the main ghats are circular straw umbrellas like huge, old, dry, thin mushrooms from Wonderland. Beneath them squat pundits, astrologers, and, oddly enough, masseurs. No other professions squat there, shaded from the sun—even at night. We walked over to this man's spot. I lay on the warm stone, and a bunched rag was placed beneath my head. Suddenly I felt four men seize a limb each and begin massaging with strong, practiced fingers.

"Maharaja massage," the soft, perfumed man explained as I looked up in surprise.

If you've never been massaged by four people at once, try it. There was something perversely enjoyable about the helplessness and the surrender required of me. My whole body was kneaded, pummeled, squeezed, tossed around like a doll. Few tourists—fearing for their wallets, their lives—ever take up these riverside massage offers. They should. Where else can you get four expert masseurs to extract twenty years of tension in twenty minutes for ten cents?

By the end I felt as if I'd been filleted, reduced to a great happy blob of tender meat. I glowed. I hummed. I wondered if this meant I might be gay after all. . . . And standing over me was Amar.

In his early twenties, gaunt, and wonderfully laconic, he gazed at me with the dreamy, liquid eyes of the opium addict. Only his silks and his mud-stained Reebok sneakers betrayed wealth. Wealth in India betrays itself differently from the ways it does in the West—although it's usually wealthier.

"First we take *bhang lassi,*" Amar suggested, after I'd paid the masseurs and strolled off with him along the hectic ghat. "Dom Raja is having some business. You like the bhang?"

Near the top steps was a stall bearing a large, buckled, rusted tin sign hanging at a 20-degree angle. It read GOVT. SHOP OF BHANG in English and Hindi, and bore two images—one a Siva lingam decorated with the Om symbol, the other what appeared to be an empty sardine can.

Bhang is a mild blend of hashish—like beer compared to whiskey—and, although the drug is illegal in India, the government in Benares obviously felt a need to control its sale. Many chillum-toting "skyclad" sadhus smoke it as a sacrament, an ancient rite connected to Siva, and no Indian government wanted to get into the kind of legal hassles entailed in banning the religious rites of these spiritual Hell's Angels. Besides, how do you fine renunciants? There have been enough problems over banning sati, the burning of widows. The Govt. Shop of Bhang also sold opium and milk candies. Tax it, cash in on the sweet-tooth munchies the drug incites, while you're at it—no doubt Western governments will shortly be eschewing "principles" for such revenue, too.

But it was not to the government's dope emporium that Amar took me. Instead, we weaved through various twisting alleys pungent with spices, arriving at what looked like a café. High on his counter, a skinny old Brahmin in loincloth and sacred thread sat cross-legged by a vast cash register, his well-stocked naked belly like a basketball, selling drinks to passersby, eagerly pouncing on the till's keys, which were almost smacked aside each time its drawer's maw pinged open and he fed it more rupees.

Inside, past an extremely rudimentary kitchen, was a small back room with wooden benches lined against its four walls. The place was packed beyond capacity with both men and women.

Amar and I squeezed in beside a fat, jolly fellow sparkling with sweat.

"South Indian peoples," Amar explained, indicating the other customers. "They like too much the bhang—even the woman, she like it. Good for sex, you understand?" He clenched the fingers on his right hand, shaking it in a universal gesture that seems to have everything and nothing to do with sex.

All the tourist-pilgrims here were dressed in their best silks and satins. Dark, small, restrained in this alien environment, the women scarcely spoke or looked up; and the men continued a seamless conversation, really a barrage of simultaneous monologues in those massively polysyllabic Tamil words that sound like Italian played backward. Everyone held a large glass of milky ocher liquid.

"I ask for extra strong," Amar announced. "You like the strong?"

Eventually, we were handed bucket-size tumblers of the same wizards' brew the south Indians were swilling. It *was* lassi—thin yogurt—but with a powerful, gritty, and somewhat bitter herbal flavor. It tasted the way you'd expect a handful of pot, a dash of sand, and a pint of watery curds to taste after a minute in the blender. All the same, thirst, along with the humid, airless room, made me down mine in seconds. If a south Indian woman could handle a glass, I thought, then how strong could the stuff be?

"You like more?" asked Amar.

"No. Let's go."

He shrugged and drained his glass. Well-fueled junkies tend to be pliant. The bill was nearly fifty cents—steep by Indian standards. Twenty cents was probably an illegal-activity surcharge, and another twenty most likely Amar's finder's fee. Western custom was prized, worth twenty times local business, and those bringing it were always rewarded. Everyone in Benares seemed to double as commissioned sales agents for countless enterprises.

Fully expecting to be discussing metaphysics soon with cactus deities and mushroom gods, I followed the loping inferno-fortune heir back into the swarming Indian night. By kerosene tapers, *paan wallah*s, squatting chin to knee on stall counters like huge birds, sprinkled their arcane concoctions of betel nut, lime paste, herbs, and spices into damp green leaves, then folded and pinned them together with cloves to form them into triangles. These bulging wads were meant to dissolve slowly, tucked between teeth and cheek, and functioned as part digestive, part mouthwash. One could last more than two hours. Some rare paans, rumored to contain powdered rhino horn, crushed gemstones, dried goat testicles, and such, allegedly possessed aphrodisiac and narcotic properties and could cost many thousands of rupees.

Next to the paan stalls, pakora wallahs ladled deep-fried lentil-paste balls from bubbling vats of blackened oil; farther along, curds were poured into sweating earthenware pots, beyond that, milk sweets wrapped in edible silver foil were set out carefully, like chessmen, upon polished trays of brass. The Indian dinner-hour trade was in full swing.

Finally, we were back on the ghats, walking north a few yards from the river, through pockets of deep, fetid mud. No wonder Amar's Reeboks were in such a state. Not far from the main ghat, as I well knew, stood the dom raja's palace. Huge, square, a medieval-keeplike structure, this edifice rose up windowless and almost featureless to a walled neo-Moghul balcony, behind which rose several more extravagantly zany structures some fifty feet above water level. The only evidence of its owner's lofty status was two life-size tigers with sparkling glass eyes. Sculpted from concrete and gaily painted in high-gloss, they were perched as if on guard at either end of this hectically creative balcony. To the building's right side, at ghat level, a steep, narrow flight of stone steps led vertically up to the only visible door. An unusually hard-bodied, muscled youth, wearing only obscenely skimpy bathing trunks, was running up these steps as we arrived. Instead of proceeding through the stout door when he reached the top level, he began running back down.

"My brother," Amar said, languidly waving an arm at the burly, sweating figure bouncing powerfully toward us.

"Exercise?" I inquired.

Amar shrugged as if he did not care.

I nodded to the brother as he drew near.

"Sorry," he gasped as Amar and I edged against the frail wall to let him pass.

"In training?"

"Olympics," he spluttered, reaching ground level and springing around there energetically before starting back up the steps behind us.

"Which Olympics?" I inquired, as he bounded past again.

"Olympic G-G-Games."

"Oh."

"It is some . . . this thing," Amar explained helpfully. "Atheletical sportings, you know?" He didn't sound as if *he* knew.

His brother had already ascended and descended the seventy-degree staircase three times when we paused two-thirds of the way up for Amar to get some oxygen back into his viscous blood. This was no place for a junkie to live. There was something about vigorous exercise and the climate that didn't mix. Walking horizontally was difficult enough in July. Even sitting down was strenuous.

"How old is your father, Amar?"

"He is . . . very old man." The answer evidently satisfied him deeply.

"You should put in an elevator." I smiled to myself, knowing he couldn't tell an elevator from a joke.

Amar looked at me as intently as his opiated eyes would allow, formulating a mighty thought. "It is," he finally said, "custom to make some offering . . . for the poor peoples. You see, Dom Raja gives his service free to the many poors. Some gift—two, three thousand rupees—very little . . . It is the custom." He nodded humbly.

It is the con, I thought, but I said, "I'm here working. I can't tell my publishers they donated their advance money to charity . . . can I?"

He weighed this answer carefully. What did he know about expense accounts, author advances, or even publishers?

"Well," I added, "let's discuss it after my interview, hmmm?"

The Olympic brother huffed past again, spraying spicy sweat in his wake, and we plodded up to the portentous, waiting doorway. It crossed my mind that the bhang lassi might be stronger than a small beer after all.

The thick, sturdy door—after Amar smacked it once with his open palm—was opened in slow motion by an owlish fellow with magisterial acne. He showed us in and onto a broad open veranda with an enviable view of the Ganges's dark curve, the city's twinkling crescent—in the middle of which we stood. Between the sculptured tigers, in the center of the veranda's wall, stood a little temple: a hutlike concrete shrine, covered in white ceramic tiles like a public washroom, and lit inside by flickering oil lamps, wisps of incense lazily emerging from its tiny open entrance to sketch fragrant messages in the sultry air outside. Perched imposingly upon the temple roof, illuminated by an overarching electric lamp large enough to light up a thousand yards of freeway, rose a life-size concrete statue of Siva as Mahayogi, the great yogi, lord of sadhus, complete with a ten-foot-long trident.

Three small children beating gongs played near the shrine's entrance— as if it were their toy house. They giggled shyly at me, tiny hands covering big, toothy mouths. Facing the mahayogi's temple, across the empty concrete space, were numerous peeling double doors, all but one of them closed.

"Come, my friend," Amar said, walking through the open one.

Within was a small, bare room containing two charpoys. Another doorway led to a walled-in open area surrounded by small rooms, their entrances variously open or closed. Many people, mainly women, came and went, glancing briefly at the room in which I stood.

On one charpoy, the dom raja, a slender little old man with a profuse, startlingly white beard, was emerging from a nap. I was offered the charpoy opposite, watching as the regal old fellow demanded a silk kurta to slip on over his undershirt. This shimmering, creamy kurta had diamond studs instead of buttons.

In Hindi, Amar explained that I was an American writer who wished to interview him.

"British-Canadian," I added, but this did not seem to make either of them aware that I understood enough Hindi to make furtive conversation unwise.

The king of death turned his unnervingly piercing black eyes to his son. What did this visitor want to know? he wondered. What was his actual name, for a start? I asked. This resulted in much discussion; "Kalu" seemed to be the answer. How had his family come to be dom rajas? At least six assorted men had drifted into the room by now, perched on the dom raja's charpoy, squatting on the floor, or leaning against each other. They all babbled loudly at once, repeating each question in every possible way it lent itself to being interpreted. The group decided that I was interested in the history behind the title. I soon wondered if any of them actually knew it. Numerous books give various accounts, but what follows is what the man himself believed to be his family history, at least on July 21, 1992.

A long time ago, there was a great king in Benares: Harischandra.

What was a long time ago?

Amar suggested six hundred years; another man disagreed vehemently, insisting six thousand years was more accurate. The dom raja looked wearily from one to the other, then shrugged at me. Anyway, Harischandra was renowned as a generous and godly man, always giving to the poor, always devout. Naturally, such a man aroused the interest of the gods. Indra decided to test how genuine he was.

Give me all you have, demanded Indra. Harischandra immediately, happily, handed over everything he owned. *It's not enough,* said Indra. *I need more.* So Harischandra sold his wife, then his son, handing over the money to Indra. *Uh-uh,* said Indra. *You can do better than that—I still need more.*

By this time ruined, destitute, his kingdom in tatters, reviled by his subjects, Harischandra set out to get himself a job. Whether he was overqualified or underqualified, we don't know, but no one would give Harischandra a job. Except Kalu Chaudri, the Untouchable in charge of the cremation grounds. The pay was probably as much of an insult as the job: You earned nothing, and the whole of society spat on you to boot.

This must have been the nadir of humiliation, because Indra was finally satisfied that Harischandra really was a decent guy, according to the dom raja, and he made him a god.

It also occurred to Indra that Kalu, the cremator, wasn't a bad sort himself, having given the king a break. Everyone smiled at what was obviously their favorite bit.

Godhood wasn't for Kalu, of course, but Indra did give him a runner-up's token: a sacred fire. *Anyone cremated with a flame from this fire,* the god announced, *will achieve eternal salvation.* The original Kalu Chaudri kept that fire burning, and so did his descendants.

"How long has the fire been burning now?"

"Since Harischandra's time," Amar replied.

"When was that?"

Up to me, seemed to be the final answer. Since Harischandra belongs more to myth than history, the answer was definitely a long time. All present assured me of this.

Why did the doms originally perform this task?

Because the Brahmins could not, the dom raja answered matter-of-factly.

Why?

The Brahmins could perform cremation rituals, chant mantras, and so on. But they couldn't provide the actual fire.

Why?

Because burning a body was a sin, like murder. The karma of the deceased could be passed on. No one wanted *that* responsibility. So the job, like every else that was unpalatable to caste Hindus, was given over to the Untouchables, the doms. They would bear the consequences. But, unlike cleaning out septic tanks, this task, being cosmically indispensable, carried with it a certain amount of kudos.

I asked him why he personally would take on such an awesome and hazardous job.

"Because he has no other way of earning a living," Amar answered quickly, a tone of desperation creeping into his voice.

His father nodded.

If he burned a murderer, I inquired, would that mean he might have to suffer those consequences, endure the punishments for that man's crime?

The dom raja nodded thoughtfully, as if this idea had never before crossed his mind.

Amar explained that even the son who actually lit the pyre with the dom raja's flame was considered impure for days after.

"Even a man dying of thirst," he emphasized, "would not accept water from this son during that time."

How much did the king of death charge for his flames?

There was all-around shrugging and more debate. The reply, ultimately, was that, like much else in India, this depended on how much a customer could afford.

"If poor man has no money," Amar told me expansively, not wishing to give the impression that his family were greedy, "then he can give some land."

"Land?"

"Some little . . . a few acres . . ."

I'd heard that the dom raja was reputed to be one of the largest landowners in India. A field here, a paddy there, a thousand miles separating them—it must have been hell to manage. My guidebook claimed that his fees ranged from 11 to 501 rupees, for some reason. Neither sum would buy you even a "few acres" of swamp land in India.

"All you have to do is keep a fire going," I elaborated. "A license to print money."

The dom raja looked worried, as if I were now accusing him of forging currency.

"Responsibility is very great for him," Amar explained.

I asked the Untouchable king if he really believed he was taking on the karma of those his fire burned.

His eyes met mine for the first time. They were truly scary eyes. Fierce, dangerous—and there was an aimlessness to the ferocity and danger burning behind them.

I'd expected to feel the answer was *Of course not.* Yet I did not feel this. What I felt was that he knew no man can suffer for another man's sins, and that no man should pretend he could, either—let alone profit from the pretense. He was well aware of the price he would have to pay for what he did—but he also knew that fraud was not murder. And he knew I knew it. I swear he did, because he suddenly became more of a presence.

"What do you do?" he asked, telling Amar, who was about to answer, to shut up.

I told him I wrote—fiction and nonfiction.

He asked what the difference was. I told him, saying I preferred fiction.

"Lies," he stated more than asked. "You earn money from telling lies?"

"Not really. It's entertainment—I hope. . . ."

He laughed. "You give people pleasure, yes?"

"I try . . . Well, I try to try . . ."

He stood up abruptly, saying, "You know all you need to know about me, I think. Because I know all I need to know about you. You understand what it is I say?"

I looked at those eyes. I nodded. He placed an arm around my shoulder, lowering his voice conspiratorially. "There is room for all of us between earth and heaven, no? You make your living—I make mine. We all need to live, I think. Yes? Few of us are saints, few are sinners, really. The rest—we live. No? I have nine children, five grandchildren. They, too, must live. Also . . ." He paused. "I also have a brother," he finally said, leading me out onto the broad veranda, adding no more to this bizarrely weighted statement.

So what? I felt like saying. I've got a brother, too. But he'd made his point all the same. We both lived by peddling lies that pleased, softened the pain of the living. And the dead. The boredom, the pain—that was our business. We were colleagues.

I suddenly respected the man. You do not have to be holy to be wise. To know yourself and accept what you see is enough—often more than enough. He knew that I had not come to hear him repeat some old myth.

"You see those lions," he said, pointing to the two gigantic tigers.

"Yeah . . . I did sort of notice them. Aren't they tigers, though?"

"Only a king can have lions outside his home. It is special for the king only."

The difference between lions and tigers was obviously as inconsequential as the difference between centuries and millennia.

"Really?"

Again I got those baleful eyes. "So," he said, very slowly, "you see— I *am* a king."

Those vulgar tigers represented a lot. In terms of caste, he was the lowest of the low. Yet the system, perversely, allowed him to be a king in more than just name. The dom raja had challenged the system itself, and won. He knew how corrupt the whole structure of caste Hinduism now was if it could make an outcast king—just because he had something no one else had and *everyone* needed.

"You think that because you die in Kashi and burn in the fire of Indra you will not pay for your sins?" the dom raja asked.

"Definitely not."

He smiled. "Why?"

"It would make the entire order of the universe nonsense. . . ."

"I do hope you will not write stupid things about me," he added incongruously. "Everyone does."

"Like what?" I asked.

"I think you understand what is a stupid thing. . . . Come!" He grabbed me by the shoulder and, flinging a huge pink scarf around his throat, wheeled me toward the exit. "I will take you for a boat ride."

Amar traipsed behind us, looking pissed off. Despite his years, the dom raja fairly skipped down the precipitous steps, calling out to a toothless old man in a rowboat. The man tried to stand, and promptly sat again.

"You remember you promise?" Amar said as soon as his father was out of earshot. "For the poor peoples? Some small gift . . ."

"Sure, sure."

Soon four or five of us seated ourselves in a long boat, rowed by the man, who was probably older than all of us combined. We headed north at an indescribably sluggish pace. The dom raja leaned back in kingly fashion, lit a beedie, and inhaled hard, deeply satisfied with the result—until his lungs started to violently and noisily object. He looked quizzically at the beedie. Illumined by the shore lights, he cut an extraordinary figure. Tourists braving the darkened ghats stared; neo-hippies, stoned, gazed reverently. In fact, he looked like Central Casting's version of the "Indian Guru": the eyes full of cosmic secrets; the immaculate whiteness of the lavish but tamed beard; the suavely sumptuous but traditional clothes. I think he knew this.

"Look!" He waved the crackling beedie ahead, toward where the smoke and fires of Harischandra, Jalasai, and Manikarnika Ghats, his kingdom of death, reached upward, all the more visible beneath the prodigiously dark, throbbing night. "Siva's wife—Sati—committed suicide, you know?"

I didn't.

"Yes. Her father gave some insult to Siva, and she killed herself, because the pain was too much." His lungs reprimanded him for several seconds. "So the god, the Siva, he carried his wife's body over his shoulder, mad with grief. And he passed by this very place, you see? As he passed, Sati's earring fell off into the well just over there." He pointed without even looking. "But the priests, the Brahmins, they managed to find the earring . . ." He thought, his broiling gaze narrowing, directed at the sky now. "No," he continued, correcting himself sharply. "They found just the jewel in the earring, those priests. And they returned it to Siva, you see? It was called *manikarnika,* this jewel. And the god, the Siva, he was so happy to get it back that he blessed this place forever. You do understand? He made this place sacred above all places."

I nodded. It was hard to tell if he'd just made this tale up, or told it so frequently that he tended to skip vital details. Sati's toe had fallen in Calcutta.

"And this is my place now," he added portentously.

"Yours?"

"I will show you. . . ." He burst into laughter, glancing up at the swirling charcoal vapors, and then over at me, laughing until his lungs started barking back, demanding silence. "These are old stories," he added, minutes later.

The vintage oarsman, practically dead with fatigue, was rowing us to a dock where I knew from experience tourists were forbidden to land. They were forbidden even to photograph anything as they passed by. No one seemed to mind allowing this ancient man to do all the work.

Amar had his feet up and was puffing idly on an explosive beedie of his own.

"Should I leave my camera?" I asked.

"Why?" the dom raja asked. "You are my guest here. You do what you please."

It was like putting ashore at the end of the river in *Apocalypse Now*. Huge fires flared and crackled on every side, temple spires quivering and alive in the hellish glare, the air acrid with smoke, yet fragrant with sandalwood, and—oh, yes—the nauseatingly sweet aroma of burning human meat. Hooded figures abruptly left their personal infernos, rushing to greet their king. Small boys—apprentice cremators, perhaps—bent to touch his feet. The dom raja studiously ignored them all.

Through the swirling smoke, parties of mourners stood, uncertain what was required of them, yet absurdly relaxed, some chatting and even laughing. Pundits intoned Vedic chants that sounded jaded, profoundly bored. Bells clanged discordantly. Drums thumped and thundered, keeping no discernible beat. On a ledge, some dozen corpses lay—two shrouded in red, the rest in soiled white. Wilted flowers were scattered randomly, like garbage, over them. A woman wailed piercingly. Straight ahead of us, one stoker hoisted an entire sizzling head and spinal column high on his oar, flipping it deeper into the blazing soul of fire. The woman wailed even louder.

The dom raja started to explain everything to me like the CEO of some plastic-extrusion plant giving his investors a tour of their investment. I mentioned that business was certainly booming.

"Yes," he agreed. "Too much of work; also little space."

Siva obviously hadn't considered the population explosion. The sacred spot was extremely small. The essential space required between blazing funeral pyres is quite well defined: It's the space a man needs to stoke without cremating himself. The dom raja proudly drew my attention to a high-tech worker's safety feature: the hoods. Though not asbestos, they were, he claimed, nonetheless fireproof. They didn't look it—a couple were definitely smoldering.

Unable to bear the suspense any longer, I asked where the Founding Fire was. Accordingly I was shown up some slimy steps to a sort of open stone porch in a crumbling temple above the infernos. Inside, on a narrow ledge, fumed a rather pathetic little fire.

"This is the fire that Indra lit, then, is it?"

The dom raja nodded with enormous disinterest. This surprised me. I'd imagined he would at least fake some reverence for the oldest and most important fire in the world—or certainly in *his* life.

Nearby was a vat of Ganges water, presumably stored for ritual uses. A valuable commodity across the length and breadth of Hindu India, Ganges water was not quite so valuable on the banks of the sacred river itself. Indra's fire—burning now for some thousand years, perhaps—the life-giving blood of Mother Ganges . . . I suddenly had an irresistible urge to douse the sacred fire with the sacred water. I had to physically restrain myself, folding my arms and looking away.

It did occur to me that so lucrative a business as the dom raja's surely could not depend on this little puffing pile of dull embers and blackened wood.

"What would happen if someone accidentally put the fire out?" I asked.

The king of death looked at me as if he'd expected better.

"There are many fires," he replied scornfully. "All lit from the god's original flame. Flame has never died, you see?"

I saw. His eyes felt like twigs stabbing at my nervous system. I had to agree with him. All the fires were sacred. The business *was* a license to print money. . . .

Another gruesome perk, I learned, was gold—the gold from dental fillings that are raked out when a pyre has burned to cool ash, but before the cool ash is surrendered to Mother Ganges. Amar speculated that, retrieval being an imprecise business, there were probably several tons of gold fillings deep below the riverbed. The doms can't survey a corpse's mouth before burning it, since the bodies arrive shrouded.

Suddenly, appalling screams came from below. Two old women were thrashing with their fists at an aghori sadhu, a massive figure at least six foot six, entirely naked but for the ash that gave his body an eerie incandescence in the firelight. He held a giant metal trident in one hand, and had the other raised high above his head, his fingers forming an odd forked mudra. His hair was coiled up on the crown of his head in a tangled turret that made him seem even taller; and on his forehead, painted in bloodred, was the crescent moon clutching a star between its pincers: a Saivite symbol that I have very rarely seen, identical to the emblem of Islam.

Unperturbed, the dom raja walked down with a stately gait to this disturbing scene. The women were hysterical, cursing the sadhu, smashing at his chest with their little fists. He stood immobile, a man preoccupied with weightier matters. His eyes looked somewhere else, seeing into another world, perhaps. A yard or so from flames that scorched bystanders ten feet away, he seemed to feel nothing, although his hair *was* steaming. And behind the pyre's glaring eruptions and its spitting tongues, I noticed, he also had some friends. Ten or so more aghoris steadily advanced as if materializing from the smoke. None of them was as menacing as this titan, though.

"What's the fuss about?" I asked the king of death.

"Little problem."

He spoke sharply to the women in what sounded like Bengali.

They merely screamed on incoherently and kept whacking and pushing at the giant sadhu, who might as well have been made of granite.

"Siva!" he uttered abruptly, the word—as it usually is—more like rumbling thunder than language.

His friends were closing in now, nude Rasta ghosts with attitude. Everything seemed to be closing in. I started to take some photographs, wondering if they'd ever be developed.

"No!" the dom raja snapped. "No camera now!"

One of the women hurled a rock at the sadhu's head. It landed hard on his left cheekbone, splitting the skin, which instantly poured blood. The man scarcely flinched, blinking slightly on its impact. Then he opened his broad, dark, glistening mouth as if to howl in pain. Instead, he intoned a lengthy Sanskrit chant, presumably an invocation of heavy gods. Blood trickled through the crisp, dry ash covering his skin, crimson rivulets weaving down his chest, circling his formidable gut, snaking down the vortex of his groin, to collect in his pubic hair, then roll out over his crumpled penis.

The dom raja shouted firm commands in various directions. Many people ran from the shadows. The old women were seized, as respectfully as possible, and dragged away, protesting at full volume, to a huddle of very nervous and embarrassed relatives. The king of death briefly mumbled something to the sadhu, who nodded condescendingly—as if admitting the night wasn't going as planned—and turned to stalk back with a robot's steps through the smoke to where his colleagues lurked. All of them muttered and nodded. They turned to retreat some fifteen yards, where they squatted cross-legged as one, starting up a droning chant.

༈ ༈ ༈

Back in the boat, where the aged oarsman had either passed out or died from fatigue, I asked the dom raja what had happened. It was all an occupational hazard, the way he explained it. Amar and the other henchmen nodded grimly. The widow and her sister thought the sadhus were stealing her husband's soul. They wanted the aghoris to leave the soul where it was and go away.

"They do not understand how aghori must be treated," said the lord of the burning ghats sympathetically.

"How should they be treated?"

"A little gift . . . something."

Amar rudely shook the venerable oarsman awake, ordering him to head for home. The old man groaned, coughed, wheezed, hefted oars twice as wide as his legs, and pushed off, this time straining against the current.

"What exactly *do* they do, anyway, those sadhus?"

"Ah . . ." the dom raja sighed, glaring up again at what could have been clouds or smoke, as if annoyed. "They do their job. Like you, like me."

"What is their job?"

We collided with the rotting hulk of a houseboat emblazoned across one side with a legend PEPSI—THE CHOICE OF A NEW GENERATION. All of us lurched, grabbing for support. The oarsman cursed and spat and considered whether rowing with his back to the direction he was heading might not be such a good idea.

"To be *there* is their job." The dom raja laughed. "To be who they *are*. If this were not so, they would not *be* there, would they?"

"So what?"

He reminded me of John Cleese playing a Vedic sage: You knew he *could* be serious, but you weren't sure when. It was a kind of hell: to be surrounded by wisdom but see it all as a joke. *Lead me from the Unreal to the Real. . . .*

"There is a small creature—a worm, isn't it?" the dom raja continued, as if to confirm my terrors. "Why is it there? Who would miss it? But if it was not there—" he sighed mightily again"—then perhaps we *would* miss it, no?"

"Do they steal souls, those sadhus?"

He laughed so loudly that the noise bounced back from crumbling palace walls, bounced back from damp tiers of rotting steps rising indefinitely into the smoke or cloud, then bounced away and dissolved over the dark, lugubrious expanse of the Ganges.

"Who would want to steal a soul?" he managed between epileptic fits of mirth. "Would *you?*" His lungs barked what sounded like an angry *Huh?*

I shrugged. "If I didn't have one, I might . . ."

"You understand much, and yet nothing at all," he then said, clear as a temple bell.

"Yeah?"

"But you do not want as much as most, do you?"

"What?"

"Come back at dawn and I will show you something," he said.

"Tomorrow?"

"Unless, of course, the sun does not rise tomorrow morning." He hissed like a boiling kettle. "But it tends to be, ah, *reliable. . . .*"

The ancient oarsman slumped back, arms spread over the bows, a noise similar to the distant squeal of car brakes emerging through his toothless mouth.

"Poor bastard," I remarked.

"Too much lazy, these peoples," Amar commented.

I felt like hitting him.

I should have. Instead, I let him lead me through the mud—which probably wasn't even mud, since wild dogs showed too great an interest in its contents—back to the carnival lights and the seething human river of the main ghat. I knew what this totally unnecessary guided trip was really about.

"Boatman need *baksheesh,*" he now added, right on cue, to my mounting tab. "And you promise to give for the poors . . ." He paused. "You not forget?"

"I told your father I'd send him some photographs, and my book," I replied, which was true. "He seemed happy enough—not that he ever asked for anything, anyway."

"He does not want book or photograph," Amar scoffed. "He is big whiskey drinker—he care only for whiskey. And for the money," he said hastily.

"Really?"

"I would not lie to you, my friend."

"Well, he *seemed* to want the picture and the book—and *there's* a few thousand rupees already, Amar. Book, photo enlargement, postage, insurance . . . Is he really your father, by the way?"

He stumbled slightly, propping himself against a silversmith's stall and almost knocking it over. "I think your eyes say yes but your heart says no," he told me, clumsily rearranging the bracelets he'd scattered from the table there. The angry and very fat silversmith frowned at both of us.

"Translate that, can you? Please."

"You will not send book or picture. I know. Too much America peoples promise but never send. You will never send. So give for poor peoples, yes? This is better."

"Be honest, Amar. . . ."

"Of course—I am always honest. . . ."

"How much opium do you use in an average day?"

He staggered with staged shock, affecting the drunkard's exaggerated simulation of sobriety, careful to steady himself against a wall this time.

"Only the bhang," he replied defensively, sweat seeping from his brow. "That is all . . . *all*. I promise you, my good friend."

"Fuck you, Amar." I wanted to say this more than I had any reason to say it.

"You are not understanding our custom. All the time for being guide I have give for you . . . I have many good America friend . . . Many . . ."

"Then you should understand that it is our custom to tell a cheap little zonked-out con artist like you to shove it where the sun don't shine. . . ."

"My *friend* . . ." he pleaded. "I *never* take the ofium . . ."

I hailed a rickshaw. Amar tried to clamber in beside me, anguish pickling his face. I pushed him back into the dust and debris of the main street.

"Someone should put you in a book, Amar," I said, looking down at a face quilted in its futile attempt to produce a better line in con. "Or maybe in the airport, on a huge cautionary poster . . ."

He brightened at this suggestion.

"I am good guide for America people, yes?"

"No, Amar. You're everything that people hate about this country rolled up into one miserable sack of doped meat. You must cost the tourist business millions. Jesus! If I'd met you twenty years ago, I'd have crossed the whole fucking country off my itinerary. And you don't even need the money. You're going to inherit the family sinecure! One day they'll be *your* fires! Isn't that a big enough con?"

"You are wrong," he wailed. "I inherit nothing, my friend. We are poor people, and you come to spit on us. . . ." He looked all but speechless with hurt.

"It would be a good idea, Amar, if I had any saliva left."

I told the driver to hit the pedals.

The inside of my mouth indeed felt as if some small furry creature had died in it, continuing to use the place as its crypt. What the hell was *in* bhang lassi anyway?

"I meet you tomorrow, yes?" Amar shouted, shuffling along in the hooting, swirling hubbub far behind me. "We take boat . . . yes? *Best* boat . . ."

"No doubt we will, Amar, no doubt." The rickshaw picked up pedal power, plowing through the turbulent slough of raw, unpackaged humanity.

"You my good friend, Mr. Paul . . . my good American friend . . ." were the last words I could make out.

The strategies for survival in downtown Benares boggled the mind. A spacious closet sold only weights for primitive scales. Another seemed to sell almost anything as long as it was red: children's tricycles, fire extinguishers, cashboxes, tripods. Set into the wooden sides of a stall that would have appeared unremarkable in medieval Cairo were three television sets wired into some kind of video game. A noisy scrum of children crouched, full of wonderment, in the cathode glare, watching or playing. This entrepreneur—who also sold one brand of candy and a thousand varieties of padlock—was on to something: No one had more business than video night in Kashi.

Beyond were egg wallahs, with buckets full of water so that customers could test the eggs for freshness (they should sink, not float). Bicycle repair specialists glued more rubber patches on inner tubes already half made of rubber patches. And still further on shoe stalls—always lit, for mysterious reasons, to virtual incandescence; a row of muffler vendors (though I never noticed anyone who owned one out on the streets); motor scooter repairers, kept busy by Benares's 200,000 Indian-made scooters and their 200,000 built-in faults; the string wallah—Indians being unusually fond of string and insisting on several hundred different kinds for the many functions string performs; fruits and vegetables for vegetarians stacked exquisitely like art—eggplants, gourds, cucumbers, mangoes, tomatoes, papaya, breadfruit, potatoes, onions, chilies in reds and greens and yellows and oranges—in tiny, small, medium, large, enormous, short, fat, long, thin; more fan belts; screws; nuts and bolts; deep-fried chilies; seven men with sewing machines, furiously pumping the pedals on the sidewalk, feeding through new cholis, kurtas, smart Western shirts—thirty cents a job; near them, the sari stalls ablaze with shimmering rainbows of color; then the lungi wallah, his walls sober, white on white, the khadi cloth dhoti—symbol of rebellion against British rule, and now symbol of political power—prominent by its coarse dullness . . .

Every need the citizens of Benares had was catered to somewhere, and catered to by the small businessman, the one-man op, the Ma-and-Pa shop. This is life before industrial capitalism. Poverty or slavery is the choice. And thrown in for those who make the right choice: that ubiquitous smell of corn roasting on open charcoal braziers, basted with lime juice and spices. Two for three cents.

I soon learned what the dom raja had meant by that brother he'd mentioned so enigmatically yet so pointedly: After a recent fraternal squabble, the family had divided in two, sharing equally the fire and the burning—and the loot. Amar, son or not, probably did stand to inherit nothing. The position was passed to the son deemed most suitable, not the eldest. I was forced to admit Amar's future was not something to dwell on. I hardly blamed him for weaving a narcotic cocoon in which to snooze away the hours, a refuge where no past or present, let alone future, could intrude upon his personal Eternal Emptiness. I felt ashamed for what I'd said to him.

Determining what time dawn was sparked great debate. I asked the clerk; and he asked the travel manager; and he asked the general manager; and he phoned a friend, who was out, then consulted some Kashmiri merchants who ran the hotel's only store. These last looked terminally depressed. They tried to sell me a twelve-thousand-dollar rug.

Kashmir was in chaos, sealed off and under military rule. They'd had no word from relatives in months, and, far worse, no shipments of handicrafts. Kashmiris were interested in business, not politics—except when they were militant fundamentalist Muslims, who felt Allah would rather see the state razed and bankrupt than still joined to a nation of infidels. With handicrafts in short supply, these boys were obliged to go for a 10,000-percent profit on everything they had to keep the cash flow at flood tide. I bought a postcard for a staggering twenty rupees to help them out and then retreated to my room.

The Star TV Network was broadcasting Bill Clinton's presidential campaign minibio. It made me despair for America and Americans.

While watching this confection of lies and saccharine, I sat writing a letter. Hearing the good citizens of Arkansas claim they once were lost but now were found through the amazing grace of Governor Clinton, I killed the audio.

Finally I completed the letter I'd been scrawling and read it through. Its morbid tone alarmed me so much that I tore it up. What time *was* dawn? A meal, a drink, I suggested to myself. That usually works.

A German tour guide I ran into assured me that dawn here would arrive *punctually* at 6:00 A.M.

"Ofer tirty trip I make here," he assured me. "Alvays ve leafink vor der ghat at fife-sirty vor der dawn boatinks."

"You must like India very much to come back so often," I remarked, to be polite.

"Like!" he yodeled. "I am *hatink* der country zince I virst zee it, und iss vorse effery drip."

"Really?" I wondered if we had a language problem.

"Diss mein bizniss, *jah?* I cannot tell der tourizers vere dey goink, am I? Zey vant der Indra, zey gid der Indra, *jah?* Or I am makink grade bick ole in der bank, *nein?* I zay go Dailund—zere you vind preety liddle girlz vor der tree mark, oo zuck-you-vuck-you ole day und nide, *jah?"* He cackled. "You haff been? You haff der Dai girlz?"

"No. Not yet."

"You go now, iss mein advise, *jah!* Leaf diss sheiss pitz und ged der neggs plane vor der Bank-gock." He slapped me on the shoulder. *"Jah,* you ged vuck-you-zuck-you ole veek, not der belly off Delhi."

"Thanks for the tip."

After dinner, I sped back to my room. Dawn was still about seven hours away.

✣   ✣   ✣

At 5:00 A.M. I was in a rickshaw, heading down to the ghats. Dawn must have come ten minutes earlier. So much for the Teutonic tour guide and his thirty trips. No one would have noticed this dawn, anyway, with low charcoal clouds swooping across the middle air like the flapping cloaks of warring sky gods. Always a busy time of day in India, dawn in Benares was a frenetic peak period for every business remotely connected to religion, which was nearly every business in town.

The flower sellers were out in force; this hour comprised almost their entire business day. The flowers had mostly been threaded into malas, garlands to place in the god's hands, around his or her neck, or, particularly here, over the shaft of a gleaming black Sivalingam. Frequently, malas and other oblations were simply tossed at the base of an idol. Few could afford enough flowers to garland a circumference like the mighty lingam in Kashi's Vishvanatha Temple daily. The statue was set in pure silver and was bathed by devotees with more than five gallons of milk each morning.

The juglike base of most lingams is called a yoni: The male force is considered passive, inactive, without the presence of shakti, the feminine force. The classical lingam is egg-shaped; it is said to derive from the shape formed when two circles bisect—an image of the spiritual world merging with the realm of matter. This was the object I had watched Sai Baba give oral birth to.

"Today *very* holy day, sahib," the rickshaw wallah informed me, mopping his brow as we creaked to a halt near two thousand other early risers already thronging around the main ghat.

"Really? Why?"

"Varanasi city of Siva-god," he explained. "Today special day sacred to this Siva. All peoples taking the holy bath in Ganga this day . . . Does sahib understand Siva-god?"

I nodded and thanked him. The street teemed with stick figures like my driver: calf muscles like Popeye's forearms, brows prematurely furrowed, and faces hollow from pedaling giant tricycles with sofas mounted on the carts behind their saddles all day long. Most often pedaled through half the night, as well, yet they were unfailingly cheerful and very often seemed to have the egoless humility of saints.

From dawn to dusk the Indian laborers broke their backs in fields and waterlogged paddies, knee-deep in the mud of building sites or on the blistering hardtop of roads blurred with dust and tar fumes. At twenty-five they were old men, used up, drained, consumed like spent matches, their wrecked backs goosenecked, the light gone from their pained and wondering eyes. By thirty they were dead, many having worked for twenty-five of those thirty brief years. Yet they were proud men and women; the work that devoured their bodies fed other bodies, older or younger. They kept life going on, without questioning why. Few would stoop to begging if there was an ounce of strength in them left for honest work.

In return for offering me his waning strength and any small facts at his disposal that he felt might interest me, this rickshaw wallah expected only an extra rupee or two. He would have been content if I merely gave him the fare he requested. "Horrified" by Indian poverty, Westerners show their deep humanitarian concern all too often by haggling with paupers over ten cents.

"Why is this day special?" I asked him.

He concertinaed his brow, big, eager bloodshot eyes rolling up as if he were literally attempting to read his own mind.

"The Siva-god," he began uncertainly, "he love too much the moon—you know moon?"

I nodded.

"Ah! So the god have moon when she shape like beautiful silver bangle in his hair—he love moon *too* much. Yes? And this day is day for big moon. . . ."

"Full moon—*poornachandra?*"

"Hah. Yes, complete big moon this one, sahib."

Then he told me shyly the fare was usually five rupees. Eight cents.

I gave him far more than that.

Out of Vedism's nondualism emerged the Hindu Trinity: Brahma—the Formless, the Unknowable; Vishnu—the Creator and Sustainer of Life; and Siva—the Destroyer, who paves the way for new creation. This corresponds to the three great Vedic Realities—Creator, Creation, Language—if, that is, Siva represents Language, since he is the Destroyer of Worlds. Fragmentation of the whole into separate names for the parts unleashes chaos. That chaos must be resolved, and drawn back to Oneness— *through* language. The original unity is not lost in the concept, which merely uses attributes and functions anthropomorphically, as gods and goddesses. In most processes of life, Siva—Destruction, Language, Chaos—is more active than Vishnu. The former's activity is more Jehovah-like than the Christ-like work of Vishnu, who incarnates to assist mankind through a series of avatars, such as Krishna.

The Siva force is less comprehensible to the Christianized Western mind, which invented a devil to perform those functions of Unity it disapproved of and which it did not really understand. Among the many "works of the devil," remember, were anything that had a tendency to reconcile opposites: science, for example, or sex.

Saraswati is the goddess of music, as well as wisdom and inspiration. Kali is the implacable goddess of death, whose thirst a river of blood will never quench. They are one and the same—consorts, Shakti forces activating two gods, who in turn are attributes of an ultimate Truth.

One plus one is always three, not two, the process of one becoming two implying a third presence: the force of becoming itself. Pythagoras explained it—as did the ancient Egyptians he'd learned it from. Such ineluctable features of the universe, say the Vedas, are the inexplicable unity, something susceptible only to direct experience, the merging of subject and object—but they can be portrayed through the mystery and through the physical forms of number: music composed according to the laws of harmonics, and architecture based on the understanding of proportion and harmony that comes from studying natural laws just as clearly evident out in the galaxies as they are deep within atomic structures or Mandelbroth's fourth-dimensional sets.

If you drop a chunk of burning camphor down into the deep darkness of a well in Kashi Karavat, a shrine near the golden temple of Vishvanatha, you can glimpse the image of its god; and beside this dim and awesome form you may also see, in that pulsing, variegated, endless night, the coldly glinting metal of a huge and sinister sword. This was the tool provided for devotees to sacrifice themselves, when the moment arrived, in a final all-consuming passion to please the fierce Lord. No one is permitted to descend into that well anymore, a Brahmin priest told me.

Rivers of blood; rivers of life: Benares is where you are supposed to learn to resolve mighty opposites.

❧   ❧   ❧

On the banks of Mother Ganges, the sadhus sit motionless for days, meditating on the funeral pyres that continuously burn alongside them the great life-giving waters into whose eternal current the ashes of death are thrown, carried from swerve of shore to bend of bay and lastly into the unimaginable vastness of the seas. From there they are born again, just as the waves reach up with invisible hands to the heavens and fashion clouds from black pearls of gleaming spume, from diamonds of sparkling mist. Jewels soon to be showered once more upon the parched wastelands, hung from the ears of Himalayan peaks, twined around the necks of graceful hills, slid in silver belts over the broad hips of fertile plains . . . to be born again.

The sadhus suddenly reminded me of those people you say *Well, think about it* to: They *were* thinking about it, all right, by merging ever closer to the sole object of their thoughts, intending to lose themselves within it. The dom raja had said that they were there because that was where they were.

When I discovered Vedism, with all its glorious celebrations of the universe, its Creator, Language, Man, I discovered it contrasted with the pointless and barren academic ways I had known as thinking about the universe. Immediately I found certainty of tone; I found logical purity; these answers felt true.

The seekers of Truth I met in India were, above all else, happy—albeit in strange ways sometimes. The seekers at Oxford, or Harvard, or indeed any branch of the Church of Progress, tended to be bitter, depressed, self-obsessed, and terminally pessimistic. Their minds seemed composed of heavy metals, whereas the Vedic authors dance across their timeless pages with thoughts as nimble as their hearts seem light—and a light heart lives long.

They were there because they were there, the dom raja had said. And I suddenly felt it was enough. Aware of how brittle I'd grown inside in twenty years, I now felt a weight lifting. Something *had* been resolved. I no longer needed to "understand" Sathya Sai Baba: Knowing beyond doubt that he understood me, and knowing he loved me, was more than enough.

Parked next to where I stood was a large truck, a sign over its cabin bearing the legend FRIGHT CARRIER. That was what I was, all right, shouldering the burden of my fears when I could just unload the ten-ton backpack and skip away, yodeling Ommm . . . The reason so many wise and wonderful men and women have never ceased speaking Truth into deaf ears, I thought that dawn, is that Truth exists to bear the burden, carry the fright. It's not our problem. *There's nothing either good or bad but thinking makes it so. . . .* Not a bad thought.

I had wandered for an hour through the narrow lanes, in and out of small-looking temples that, once you'd passed through a closet-size entrance, expanded into a maze of pungent stone passageways, burning camphor within incense, jasmine petals within rosewater, shrines within shrines, halls within halls. Bells clanged; another brand of incense made the very air sexy, beguiling. Priests intoned the morning hymns while devotees humbly brought their little tokens of esteem to the gods. I had no intention of seeing the king of death again. I corrected myself: I wanted to avoid Amar, not the tricky old merchant of terminal fire—because it was Amar who had dredged up what I had thought had gone forever into my deeps, what I'd thought I'd become. It was Amar who had pushed that inner pendulum, whose movement from heaven to hell never ceases.

The fires of Siva serve a purpose, whether they burn within you or around you. It's like smelting metals: Heat them to liquid and the scum rises to the surface, where you can see it, and from where you can remove it.

> Every fool's got a reason to feel sorry for himself,
> And turn his heart to stone.
> This fool's halfway to heaven and a mile out of hell,
> Yet I feel I'm coming home.

Nearer hell than heaven still, I had the profoundly moving feeling that I *was* finally coming home. My heart was so high, so suddenly light that it seemed to scatter across the heavens like stars or falling leaves—leaves the color of a renunciant's ocher robe, falling from the tree of this world. I'd had the feeling an age before, in Tiruvannamalai. I looked up, said *Thank you,* and turned a corner to find Mother Ganges a vast road of dull silver flecked with orange where she caught fragments of the teasing sun and swept them off like autumn leaves.

Then, as if tipped from a truck, tumbled a hundred or so men and women, all swathed in stridently new orange cloth, spilling down the ghats, chanting joyfully, then plunging into the eternal waters.

Is this what I should do? I thought. *Take that sacred bath millions traveled days or weeks to perform at least once in their lives—even if it was the only trip they could ever afford?* Faith enables millions to leap into some of the most polluted water on the planet without a second thought, and without many ill effects. Half the population of Benares did it daily, and they seemed fine. It wasn't just a bath, either; it was a mouthwash, an offering, and probably a latrine, too. You needed faith to take a sacred bath—but then, why else would you take one?

As I began to strip off my shirt, I noticed a sadhu standing on one leg, like a flamingo, holding his left arm above his head. This arm had a withered, atrophied look, its hand poised like a desk lamp above his mangled head of hair. I made a few quick inquiries. This sadhu was doing *tapas* penance. He'd held his arm above his head now for twenty-three years. He'd also stood on one leg for twenty-three years, though not always the same leg. Once a month he changed legs, the event apparently by now something of a festival in itself. People came from miles to witness the Changing of the Leg.

I walked toward him. He was not young; nor was he clean. His hair looked like something that had been swept out of a yak's cage and dumped on his head. Sheer dirt coated him, not ash, dulling his skin to elephanthide gray. He did, however, make one concession to modesty in his nakedness: Dangling from a bristly, filth-encrusted piece of string over his groin was what looked like a fragment from the Shroud of Turin. The fingernails on his left hand were a treat, too. They had actually grown right through the flesh of his palm, some protruding on the other side if they hadn't encountered bone after their slow journey. His eyes were not quite closed, they were just not there, the balls rolled up until only the jaundiced yellows of his "whites" showed behind lids like the halves of walnut shells.

I wanted to ask him why the hell he was doing this to himself.

He slept standing on one leg, too, this sadhu—although at the moment he was leaning against a wall. He ate only warm milk in which Kit-Kat bars had been soaked. Or so I was told. I wonder which mystic treatise advised this diet as ideal for someone in his position. How long did he propose to keep this penance up, anyway?

"He will finish in just seven year," my best informant, a paan wallah, said authoritatively, handing me a three-inch triangular wad of leaf. On first bite I thought I recognized the taste of industrial disinfectant mixed with birdseed soaked in eau de cologne, then very sweet string, Wite-

Out, gravel of various flavors, battery innards that made my teeth feel as if I were chewing on live electric wire, and a good deal of the kind of stuff you scrape off lawn-mower blades.

It was not the best choice for breakfast, and I was still encountering remnants of it hiding in crevices and folds of my mouth twelve hours later.

"Seven year?" I tried to say through the mess in my mouth. "Woth ee goan oo enn?"

That was anyone's guess. Sadhus don't seem to retire, and the public would certainly miss the Changing of the Leg.

"He is great saint," the paan wallah announced, as if he were lauding the talent of someone who builds model ships in bottles. "The saints they do what the god he want them to doing." He nodded to himself. "He has no, er . . . this thing . . ." He tapped his head.

"Ears?" I tried.

"Hah! No mind . . . yes. This saint he is not having mind of own like you and me. Such man they are having too much the fate . . ."

"Fate?"

"Yeees . . . Fate in the god, isn't it? They are not even noticing you and me people."

"Oh." I finally got it. "Faith—you mean faith?"

He nodded sagely, repeating, "Fate in the god—like the god his childrens, no?"

"Ah . . ."

"You have wife?"

I confessed that I did.

"Any shoes?"

"What?"

"Shoes," he said again.

"Well, *yes!* I have shoes. . . . Back home, you mean?"

"How many shoes?"

"Jeez, I don't know." I thought, trying to picture my closet.

"You are not knowing how many shoes you are having?" He found this hard to believe.

"Oh . . . twenty, thirty, maybe."

The paan wallah looked thunderstruck. He dropped the wad he had been busily folding, then stood up to get a better look at me.

"Twenty! Thirties!" He seemed somewhat overexcited.

"Yeah," I replied, defensively. "Something like that."

"How is it you are not being sure?" he asked. "I myself am having just two—one boy and one girl."

"Boy and girl?" I inquired stupidly.

"Woh, yes! Two childrens only for me." He said this with some pride.

I asked what we were talking about—shoes or children.

"Issues!" he squeaked. "You say you are having too much the *issues*, isn't it?"

Issues! The issues of your loins!

The old sadhu coughed, and we both turned, as if interrupted by some major cosmic event. But he made no more signs.

Faith, I thought to myself once more. *That* is faith. Holding your arm up there while standing on one leg for a few decades: *faith*. If someone ever asked what faith was, I'd now know how to answer. The Tibetan sage Milarepa's spiritual discipline—his faith—consisted of building houses and then demolishing them. This was the price of experience—according to Milarepa's guru. *This* was faith.

I rebuttoned my shirt. If that was faith, I didn't have it, I knew beyond any doubt. And I didn't want it. I most certainly didn't want to take a bath in Mother Ganges and risk ruining a beautiful metaphor by catching some pretty ugly microbial parasites intent on nesting in my vital organs. I'd been told only faith prevented this happening. It was a relief finally to understand I no longer had to pretend I was a Hindu. Because I *did* have faith in reality, once more—just not someone else's reality.

Somehow I'd come to the end of a long and convoluted road, only to find I'd returned to the place where the journey started. But for the first time I *understood* it. Across the span of twenty years, my two selves felt reconciled—so much so that I no longer saw any contradiction between them. Even the smoke from the funeral pyres smelled fragrant, beguiling.

༶   ༶   ༶

I set off, intending to walk back to the main ghat. I knew I would hear his voice the millisecond I heard it.

"The sun was reliable, no? In his way . . ."

The dom raja sat alone on a neat pile of sandalwood logs, cleaning his long fingernails with a splint. He had that freshly-washed-wearing-clean-clothes look all wealthy Indians revel in at daybreak. The Indian summer will soil, wilt, and crumple it long before noon.

"I'm sorry," I said.

"Why?" He looked genuinely unsure.

"I said I'd come at dawn. . . ."

"Did you?" He stared with professional interest at the construction of a fresh pyre nearby.

"You told me you'd show me something. . . ."

"Show, is it?"

"Yes. In the boat—that's what you said."

"Today I am too much busy."

He continued to work on his nails.

"That's okay. I'm a little rushed, too. . . ."

"Dashashvamedha, probably."

"What?"

"This ghat—" he pointed toward the main one "—where all the pilgrim peoples go. But you have seen many thing here now, is this correct?"

I said I had.

"Are you knowing what name mean?"

"Name?"

"Dashashvamedha."

"I forget . . ."

He proceeded to tell me the story in the bored and disinterested tone of a parent with a naughty child.

Long, long ago, there had been no rain for as long as anyone could recall. Nature was out of control; something had gone desperately wrong, and the planet was dying. Even Brahma, the Lord of Creation himself, was helpless. There was just one man who could make a change. It was a king named Divodasa. He was so wise that he had given up his throne, given up all worldly things, and come to Benares to spend his days in silent meditation by the waters of Mother Ganges. Brahma begged him to renounce renunciation and come back to accept the position of planetary ruler. For only he, Brahma insisted, could bring back the harmony, the order that had fled the world, leaving it in chaos.

After some thought, Divodasa agreed, but on one condition: Brahma must order all the gods to leave Kashi. Divodasa believed the other gods would only hinder things, get in the way of returning to the traditional order. Brahma agreed to Divodasa's demand. Even Siva, to whom Kashi was dearer than all places on earth, had to leave with the rest.

Siva's not the sort of god who takes kindly to such treatment. Thus, he pondered darkly in his exile, hatching schemes to compel Brahma to permit his fellow deities the right to return to their favorite spot. He decided that Divodasa had to be discredited as king. So he challenged Brahma to prove that Divodasa was fit to be king and—more important—knew the rituals only a king could perform.

Nobody refused Siva. So Brahma, disguised as a priest, visited the court of Divodasa, now the king of all the world. He begged the king to preside over one of the most powerful and involved Vedic rituals of all: the simultaneous sacrifice of ten *(dashan)* horses *(ashvamedha)*. Siva was convinced that Divodasa was bound to make a fatal mistake at some point during such a complex rite. As patron of the ritual, the king had to furnish every single one of the components required and also make certain that everything ran precisely according to plan.

Siva misjudged his man. The king of the world conducted the super-ritual faultlessly—even conscripting Brahma himself to perform the role of chief priest. Ten horses were sacrificed at precisely the same moment—on the spot now known as Dashashvamedha Ghat, "Place of the Ten Horse Sacrifice." Siva was furious. But Divodasa did manage to restore order; and when the rains finally came, he asked Brahma if he could now return to his peaceful spot by the once-more-churning waters of the Ganges.

"So," the dom raja concluded, "a man he bathe in this place—it is *same* as performing big sacrifice itself. Why else would so many people come here?"

"But it's still Siva's city," I complained.

"Kashi?" The old man had been distracted by some nuisance involving the pyres.

"Yes. Today is even a very holy day for Siva here."

"Is it?" He looked surprised.

"That's what I was told."

"Every day sacred for Siva here. He is our god. He is always being with us here."

"What about the story?"

"Agh!" He spat an oyster of phlegm over his shoulder. "These are old stories, isn't it? We are never knowing what is the truth."

I told him I imagined he'd seen more truth than most men, running the burning ghats as he did.

"In Kashi there is *only* the truth," he replied. "What use is this truth if not being true?"

"Yeah."

I told him to explain that I was very sorry for being rude when he next saw Amar. I'd been very tired, that was all.

"Amar?"

I explained that I meant his son, the one who had brought me to him the night before.

He laughed without warning, his lungs even joining in, until he sounded like an entire audience all by himself.

"That boy, he is not *son!* Very bad boy, this Amar—too much taking the ofium, isn't it? Always he ask for money—is it not so?"

I nodded.

"Last night I tell him not to be coming my house. Because always he is bringing too much of troubles, this Amar."

"So who is he?"

"Hmm?" He looked up, then fixed me with his old and weary stare. "He is one boy like there are so many boys in our city. They are not having the job, yes? They are living like the wild beast. They eat the tourist people, I think—isn't it?"

"Yeah . . . that's what it's like. But say sorry anyway, would you?"

"Sorry?" He looked deeply insulted. "I am not man who say the sorry to such boys. Why must I be sorry for *them?* It is *they* who are being sorry to *me.*" He paused, then stood up, facing me. "No people dying here without the dom fire, hmm? I say *give fire, not give fire.* If I *not* give fire . . ." He spat, punctuating his next point: "Peoples dying so full of the fears. I never am having to say sorry, you see? No one ever harm dom raja. The god, he give them life, isn't it? Dom raja, he give the death. Which one more important, hmmm?"

"Life?"

He smiled, turned away, and strolled toward a freshly lit pyre. As he walked, he was saying, "You will see the thing different, my writer friend. Then you come back here, I think. If not—" he coughed stupendously"—you burn one day, also. In your native place, or here—what difference?"

"Exactly!" I shouted after him.

"Difference is," he said, pausing, yet not looking back, "in your place it perhaps easy to forget the true things. So when you walk from fire into arms of Siva you start to die again, all over again . . ."

"What?"

"Because you will not see him—though *he* see *you.* Only blind man he know what the eyes were for . . ." Twenty yards off, he turned. "In Kashi *no one* forget what the eyes are for, isn't it? It is like this boy Amar . . ."

"What is?"

"He wish to be blind, but the god keep him with eyes. You see, my friend, it is not *my* fire that burn you here. No . . ." He chuckled. "For stupid man the fire is too much cold. Another man, he feel just the dawn wind to be like fire. This is how *you* feel."

He pressed his palms together briefly, nodded his blinding white nimbus of hair, and then walked away.

Epilogue
The Father of the World

I am what is, I am what is not.
—THE *BHAGAVAD GITA*

"You're so intractable, you people!" screamed the American girl at the airport, in tears.

She'd paid her airport tax back at the hotel, but the airport officials denied this was possible, insisting she pay again. She couldn't find her receipt, and she had no more Indian money. The officials wouldn't take U.S. dollars—she'd have to change them at the bank. But the bank did not seem to be open, and her plane was leaving soon. Without the airport tax chit, she couldn't check in or even put her bags on the plane. Someone offered to change the money for her, but the officials demanded an official bank receipt.

She was hysterical, mascara streaming, panic setting in. She thought she'd never be able to leave the damn country. I recalled the feeling.

"Let me apologize for my ridiculous nation," said a tall, handsome, elderly Indian gentleman.

He calmed the officials, bought the airport tax chit from them himself, and presented it to the girl. She offered him dollars, but he smiled, waving the money away and walking off. Now *she* felt bad—foolish and rude. I could see everything that she'd ever loved about India flooding back into her heart.

"It's been a *strange* trip," a young man with expensive clothes and hair said to me as we sat with coffee in the Maharaja Lounge at Delhi's ex-

travagant new airport. With Bauhaus-style recliners, the place was furnished better than most Indian palaces.

"Yes," I replied. "It's *always* a strange trip, though."

I'd assumed he was American, and he turned out to be a Sikh from
San Francisco. This had been his first visit to the land of his forefathers.
He'd come to scatter his mother's ashes on the Beas River, near Amritsar, and then he'd traveled around for two weeks. He'd never come again,
he assured me, *never,* adding, "I did better than my father—*he* left after
four days."

"But your *mother* must have loved the country?"

"Yes . . . she loved it very much."

When she was dying of cancer, his mother's last wish had been to
arrange marriages for him and his brother to Indian girls who'd never even
been to the U.S. before.

"How did *that* work out?"

"I wasn't sure at first," he confessed. "I'd been involved with a couple of American girls. . . . I didn't know if I could relate to an Indian, understand? But it's *great!* She treats me like a king. Hey—" he leaned over
"—she even massages my feet when I get home from work."

"Didn't the American girls do that?"

He laughed. Born in the U.S.A., he wasn't as American as he thought.
But he was still American enough. Discovering that Air India boarded its
first-class passengers last, he complained to the official: "In America we
board them *first,* man. . . ."

"We like them to feel comfortable, sir," he was told.

"You have to be patient here. You must have noticed that," I said.

"Jeez!" He shook his head. "What a place! The drive in from the airport took twenty minutes; coming out this morning—with no traffic—
it took *ninety!"*

"Didn't you find *something* you liked?"

"You know," he replied, after we'd spoken for nearly half an hour,
"it's funny, you, a Westerner, telling me, an Indian, why I should love
my own country, no? Don't you think that's funny?"

As the plane left the ground, rising up over the central plains of India,
heading out over Rajasthan, I gazed down at the fast-disappearing features of the land. The thousands of tiny villages; the mountains; the
rivers; the jungles; the deserts; the temples; the great holy cities; and all
those people—I was leaving them *all* yet again. On the headphones an

Urdu *ghazal* singer was wailing out that Oriental version of country
music: Whatever he sang about, it *had* to involve broken hearts, broken
dreams. I felt the bittersweet ache of love inside, too; felt my heart
swelling up—as if wanting to embrace the whole world. India: I couldn't
live with her, and I couldn't live without her.

> And I have presumed, from love and casual regard,
>   called you Krishna, Yadava, and friend,
>   thinking you a friend, forgetting who you are.
> I have lowered you in laughter, in resting, eating,
>   and walking, alone and in company.
> Forgive me, Krishna.

> For you are the Father of the World . . .
>   —THE *BHAGAVAD GITA*

PWR
Bangalore–Bombay–Delhi–London–Toronto, 1974–96

Index